Social Thought in
Tsarist Russia

Alexander
Vucinich

Social Thought
in Tsarist
Russia

*The Quest for a
General Science
of Society, 1861-1917*

The University of Chicago Press
Chicago and London

ALEXANDER VUCINICH is professor of history
at the University of Texas at Austin. He is
the author of a three-volume series on science
in Russian culture and a number of scholarly
articles.

The University of Chicago Press, Chicago 60637
The University of Chicago Press, Ltd., London

Library of Congress Cataloging in Publication Data
Vucinich, Alexander S   1914–
  Social thought in Tsarist Russia.

  Bibliography: p.
  Includes index.
  1. Sociology—History—Russia.   I. Title.
HM22.R9V8   301'.0947   75-12229
ISBN 0-226-86624-6

Contents

Acknowledgments

I am most grateful to professors Martin A. Miller, Laurence H. Miller, Reginald E. Zelnik, Terence Emmons, and Robert M. Crunden, who read parts of the manuscript and gave me valuable criticisms and suggestions of a substantive, logical, and philosophical nature.

To the American Philosophical Society I am thankful for a summer grant which made it possible for me to work in the libraries of the University of Illinois at Urbana-Champaign, the University of California in Berkeley, Stanford University, and the Hoover Institution. I am also thankful to the John Simon Guggenheim Memorial Foundation and the University Research Institute of the University of Texas at Austin for financial grants which gave me the necessary time to bring this study to completion.

I wish to express my deep appreciation to Professor Ralph T. Fisher and the Russian and East European Center at the University of Illinois for generous and consistent support of my research. To my wife, Dorothy, I am indebted for encouragement and valuable help during every phase of the work on the manuscript.

Introduction

The idea of progress, the central theme of nineteenth-century social theory, found unusually fertile ground in Russia during the turbulent period from 1861 to 1917. A noted historian observed at the end of the nineteenth century that every Russian high school student of his generation was exposed to multitudes of schemes depicting the inexorable progress of human society. It was not unusual to encounter natural scientists—such as the chemist Dmitrii Mendeleev, the embryologist Il'ia Mechnikov and the mineralogist Vladimir Vernadskii—with clearly articulated philosophies of history spelling out the "regularities" in the processes of history and promising a more tolerable and gratifying social existence. If the Russian intelligentsia—that unwieldy and elusive sociological category—had a common denominator, it was the passionate belief in social progress and a preoccupation with designs for the improved quality of human life.

In tsarist Russia, as in the West, all general theories of the structure and dynamics of human society fell into two major groups.

One group included the metaphysical theories guided by the grand assumption that human society was too complex to be treated adequately by the tools of science. A typical representative of this orientation argued that human societies are workshops for divine designs independent of the whims of history and regularities of nature, and that they operate outside the laws of science. He contended that a general science of society can reach only the most elementary links between social phenomena and that metaphysics alone can unravel the deeper meanings of social relations and social action. Arguing that metaphysics is an elaboration of religious thought, he asserted that positive science cannot reveal the fate of mankind, for it operates within the bounds of "total uncertainty."[1]

The second group included the wide range of theories professing a primary commitment to the scientific study of the nature and evolution of human society. While readily admitting that no existing theory of society was firmly established as a scientific discipline, the representatives of this orientation agreed that since the time of Auguste Comte sociology had made substantial progress and was well on the way to becoming a complete science.[2] There were many reasons for the relatively slow development of a general science of society. The theorists found the task of establishing an empirical base for their theoretical constructions particularly arduous. Most of them erred in trying to answer the questions outside the legitimate domain of science and in assuming that a general science of society must be built on natural science models. Despite strong differences in their theoretical and methodological views, the representatives of the second group agreed that only the scientific study of society could produce trustworthy knowledge of the inner workings of human society.

Behind the two groups of theories were distinct views on the origin and nature of human society: while the first group concentrated on the eternity of sacred values that make the spirit and the inner order of human society impervious to the ravages of time, the second group placed heavy emphasis on the idea of historical relativity in value systems and on the increasing secularization of social institutions. While the first group based its explanations on otherworldly causation, the second group stayed firmly within the bounds of terrestrial causation.

This book deals with the most accomplished and influential representatives of the second group. The theorists selected for discussion differ in their explanations of the nature of science, the rules of scientific methodology and conceptualization, and the interdependence of scientific and nonscientific modes of inquiry. However, all are united by a professed belief in the power of science as the basic source of objective information on the workings of human society. To all, science is both the most reliable method of dissecting the intricacies of human society and the major cultural activity contributing to social progress. All place major emphasis on the study of the social attributes of science. Each theory incorporates both a scientific approach to sociology and a sociological approach to science.

As unique systems of thought, the general theories of society are related to four distinct dimensions of social inquiry.

First, each theory is, or purports to be, scientific: each represents a specific effort to formulate the scientific framework for a general study of society. Each is a product of a unique search for a logically integrated system of scientific principles explaining the universal aspects of human society. The basic function of a general theory of society is to conceptualize the dynamics of social integration, the pivotal elements of social structure, the interaction of social institutions and social systems, the place of the individual in social structure, and the relationship of the state to society.

Second, each theory is philosophical: each elaborates a distinct philosophical view on the nature of scientific inquiry and knowledge, the strengths and limitations of the scientific method, and the ontological, epistemological, logical, and methodological differences between the natural sciences and the social sciences. All theories are also important as instruments in the diffusion and enrichment of modern philosophies of science. In nineteenth-century and early twentieth-century Russia, for example, the leading social theories were the primary and most influential agents in the diffusion and elaboration of the philosophical ideas of various neopositivist and neo-Kantian schools. In addition to a philosophical interpretation of the nature of science, each social theory presents a philosophical view of society, and each treats the intricate problems of the convergence and divergence of philosophical and scientific approaches to social reality.

Third, each theory is ideological. The ideological element finds its primary expression either in the criticism of the existing values and social arrangements, or in the articulation of the structural principles of "the great society" of the future. In some social theories, ideology mixes freely with science; in others, it is presented with more subtlety and circumspection. In Marxist and anarchist theories ideology is inseparable from science.

Fourth, each theory is an integral part of history: each places concrete historical material into abstract sociological forms. Although their primary interest is in the universal aspects of society, social theorists rely on their own societies as sources of empirical information and suggestive models of social action and behavior. They supply broad interpretations of the vicissitudes and social attributes of the Russian rural commune (*obshchina*), Russian law, the Russian state, Russian science, and all other major components of Russian society and culture. In a way, they look at humanity through a Russian prism. In pre-1917 Russia, the general theories of society provided rich commentaries on the problems of a society caught in a bitter and unrelenting conflict between the forces of irreversible modernization and the powerful institutional vestiges of feudalism.

1. The Beginning of Sociology in Russia

THE GREAT REFORMS AND THE SEARCH FOR A SCIENCE OF SOCIETY

The Crimean debacle in 1854–55 helped accelerate the political, social, and intellectual processes that led to the downfall of the feudal order and the emergence of modern Russia. It gave rise to forces antithetical to the values and institutions of a social system based on "autocracy, aristocracy and orthodoxy." N. V. Shelgunov observed that the emergence of "the intellectual movement of the 1860s" was "as inevitable and as organic as the emergence of a new forest on a sun-drenched glade." He added that the Sevastopol catastrophe influenced all "intelligent Russians," regardless of their position on the social ladder, to concentrate their thoughts on freedom and on "the creation of better living conditions for all."[1] During the Crimean War, according to the Slavophile Iurii Samarin, public opinion was less concerned with the fortunes of the Russian military forces than with the internal chaos. He said: "We surrendered not under the blows inflicted by the military forces of the Western Alliance, but under the pressure of our internal powerlessness."[2] Ivan Turgenev wrote in 1855 that the fall of Sevastopol should serve the same purpose for Russia that the fall of Jena served for the Prussians: that it should be the main catalyst of a new era of national emancipation from both "the shackles of political oppression and the debilitating burden of the lingering vestiges of the feudal system."[3] "Feudalism," wrote Saltykov-Shchedrin, "was not limited to the relations between landlords, aristocrats, and the enserfed masses ... but was deeply embedded in our entire social life: it drew estates—privileged and nonprivileged— into a morass of degrading lawlessness, unmitigated craftiness, and fear of imminent destruction."[4]

The unrelenting clamor for a critical national "self-examination" went hand in hand with the search for new principles, cultural values, and intellectual standards. The most concrete and monumental products of the collective search for a way out of the fetters of feudalism and stagnation were the Great Reforms which emancipated the serfs, liberalized the judicial system and university administration, and inaugurated the *zemstvos* as territorial units granted an unusual degree of independent initiative in civic affairs of local importance. According to Boris Chicherin, the 1860s marked the first appearance of public opinion in Russia. Herzen noted that the 1860s marked a turning point in Russian literary history: while the heroes of the earlier literary works were "superfluous men," the time had now come for a literary portrayal of the "men of action."[5] Still another writer saw in the 1860s an accelerated process of the secularization of wisdom; this was the time, he said, of a search for "a substitution of anthropology for religion, inductive method for deductive method, materialistic monism for idealistic dualism, empirical aesthetics for abstract aesthetics, and the theory of rational egotism for morality based on supersensory principles."[6]

A modern writer compared the intellectual and social fermentation of the 1860s with the philosophical and ideological excitement produced by the French Enlightenment and the publication of the *Encyclopédie*. In both periods, the massive reevaluation of the entire cultural tradition and dominant institutional norms was an unceasing, fiery process. In Russia, the role of the *philosophes* was assumed by the *raznochintsy*—a class born in the crevices of the growing urban community and epitomizing the inexorable decay of Russia's estate system anchored in the institutions of autocracy and feudalism. The clamor for "the destruction of all authority" (even in aesthetics) and "the ridiculing of all *res sacrae*" best expressed the raznochintsy movement.[7] As in the age of the French Enlightenment, a group of academic men and contributors to journals of critical thought undertook to produce the first Russian encyclopedia of grand proportions—an effort too ambitious to be successfully completed (the project stopped after the publication of the sixth volume, covering the sixth letter of the alphabet). Although an unsuccessful venture, the encyclopedia gathered a group of men who echoed the philosophes' conviction that the scientific study of man, realism in art, humanitarian goals in legislation, and unalloyed faith in the perfectibility of institutions and social relations are the main sources of social progress.

Nikolai Chernyshevskii, the editor of the *Contemporary*, was the most influential spokesman for the ideals of the Reform epoch. The first Russian encyclopedist in the true meaning of the term, he played the major role in making the social and philosophical thought of contemporary Western Europe part of the mainstream of modern Russian thought. He contributed more than any other person to making the intelligentsia of the 1860s aware of "the decisive importance of rationalist preeminence and reasonable conviction."[8] He dealt with all the great ideas that troubled contemporary Western and Russian social and political theorists: the concept of social progress, the role of personality in history, the importance of the economic factor in social evolution, the dominant forms of political systems, the differences between utopian socialism and scientific socialism, the relative roles of the peasants and industrial workers in socialist movements, the debt of Russian intellectuals to the people, and the role of the family in giving Russia a new breed of socially conscious and intellectually alert men.[9] Chernyshevskii was the first consistent advocate in Russia of a scientific study of society—of a social science based on the model of natural science. He rejected the phenomenalistic bent of Auguste Comte's positivist philosophy, but he accepted the Comtian view of sociology as an extension of the natural sciences. According to him, the laws of causality, motion, and transformation apply to the "moral" order as much as they do to the "physical" order. His was a powerful and influential plea for a scientific study of society, for an understanding of the "physiology" of society; he entertained the idea that the function of the human body holds the key for the understanding of human society—that both are equally perfectible and open to continuous progress. In his advocacy of a scientific study of the "moral" order, he spoke not as a competent scientist but as an ideologist, a man determined to provide a philosophical justification for the rapidly growing demands for radical changes in the structure of Russian society.

Science, according to Chernyshevskii, is not only the most reliable method for the study of society, it is also the most reliable index of social and cultural progress. The exaltation of science is the most distinctive feature of the Reform period: during the 1860s, idealistic metaphysics, allied with the mysticism and spiritualism of Russian Orthodoxy, reached its lowest ebb of the century. P. D. Iurkevich, the chief representative of idealistic thought, was largely ignored by his generation, which looked to materialistic philosophy and science for guides for practical action.

Nihilism, the movement which fought for rationalism with a fervor that bordered on irrationality and which grew out of the legacy of Chernyshevskii and Dobroliubov, was the mainstream of Russian philosophical thought during the 1860s.[10] The main architect of Nihilist philosophy was D. I. Pisarev, a graduate of St. Petersburg University and an editor of the journal *Russian Word*. He saw in Bazarov, the hero of Turgenev's *Fathers and Sons*, the paragon of the Nihilist movement, the embodiment of its guiding values and views. Bazarov was a medical student; he was familiar with the chemistry of life and the method of science; and he wholeheartedly accepted Francis Bacon's aphorism that "human knowledge and human power meet in one; for where the cause is not known the effect cannot be produced."

The philosophy of Nihilism—Bazarov's philosophy—dealt primarily with the values that encouraged a sweeping secularization of wisdom and an increasing dependence on science as a source of models for moral life and of instruments for practical existence. Untempered individualism was the backbone of Nihilist philosophy. While Dobroliubov and Chernyshevskii looked for new types of social relations that would emancipate the individual from enslavement to anachronistic customs and routines, Pisarev argued that the individual must effect his own emancipation through his own actions—through relentless and continuous criticism of every authority. According to a literary critic: "The basis of Pisarev's moral ideal is the individual, self-liberated and freely given to his own passions and lusts for the purpose of exacting from life as many rational enjoyments as human nature can absorb. It is this very ideal that Pisarev detects in Turgenev's Bazarov and lauds him for it."[11] Another critic noted that Pisarev's social philosophy rested on the idea that "everything emanates from the individual, and everything returns to it" and that the individual "needs no protection or guidance—he needs only science and knowledge."[12] Underlying Pisarev's emphasis on unmitigated individualism and Nihilist values was a belief that Russian society could find its way out of feudal darkness, sustained by oppressive law and petrified custom, only by a total and unrelenting attack on every existing institution, myth, and practice. To enter the stage of democracy and advanced civilization, Russia, according to Pisarev, must first of all produce individuals free of internal and external constraints.

The "emancipation of the individual," however, was not the only path to a higher stage of social development. Equally important was the intellectual development in the spirit of realism by means of acquiring knowledge free of superstitious belief in supernatural interference. Rationality—the cultivation of and reliance on man's rational faculties—was viewed as the only fountain of free thought, or "critical realism." A. P. Shchapov echoed the true sentiment of the intelligentsia when he said that "rationality," most realistically expressed in the laws of natural science, was the only realistic source of designs for a new society unencumbered by internal conflict. The world view embedded in rationality and sustained by natural science provided the most reliable prospects for the emancipation of Russia from the gnawing effects of feudal institutions.[13] Only "reason," engaged in the pursuit of science, can enrich "intellectual and material culture."[14] Although Herzen exalted the social power and intellectual dignity of science to a degree not emulated either by Chernyshevskii or the Nihilists, Nihilist raznochintsy firmly refuted his inclination "to blend positivism with Russian mysticism"; to them science stood for the categorical rejection of every kind of anti-rationalism.[15]

The emphasis on the utility of knowledge was the third pillar of the Nihilist value system.[16] Expressing a strong Nihilist attitude, N. D. Nozhin attacked the notion of "science for science's sake" and was particularly categorical in his claim that "the worth of science is measured by its practical utility and its contributions to the solution of social needs."[17] Utilitarianism placed emphasis not only on the search for socially applicable knowledge but also on the professionalization of techniques and manpower involved in the processes of the acquisition of knowledge. It was also the point of departure in the search for the elevation of work in general—and of scholarly work in particular—to the level of a fundamental social value. In Nihilist philosophy, work both creates and emancipates the individual; it is the nerve center of the processes involved in the formation of personality.[18] Pisarev and the

Nihilists gave prominence to Dobroliubov's dictum that "societies with a great respect for work occupy higher levels on the ladder of cultural achievement." Or, the more civilized a society is, the more precise and adequate are its skills for judging the true value of knowledge. It was by combining the criteria of utility in the appraisal of knowledge and rationality in the acquisition of knowledge that the Nihilists elevated scientific knowledge to the level of a prime mover of modern civilization. Nihilist philosophy was the philosophy of scientism: to the Nihilists science was a panacea for all social ills and the only sure path to a better society. The three cardinal values which they emphasized were actually values which created the intellectual and social atmosphere indispensable for the growth of modern science. The Nihilists did not create these values; they merely brought them into sharper focus and codified them. They showed that the libertarian movement of the Reform epoch had produced, among other effects, an intellectual climate favoring an intensive national concern with the development of science; the values which sparked the Russian intelligentsia in their search for a society of democratic institutions were the same values which created indispensable conditions for a versatile and accelerated development of scientific thought.

Pisarev and the Nihilists subordinated moral and aesthetic values to science. They followed Comte's dictum that in the future the conflict between "the intellectual" and "the moral" would completely disappear by a full dissolution of morality in scientific thought. Again, like Comte, they believed in a gradual subordination of the aesthetic quality of "the sentiment of ideal perfection" to the scientific quality of "the idea of real existence." Small wonder then that Pisarev gave priority to the popularization of science over all other literary forms and that he advised Saltykov-Shchedrin to stop writing satires and dedicate himself to the dissemination of knowledge. He said that the "highest, most beautiful, and most human duty of the arts is to blend themselves with science and thus give science a practical power, which it could not achieve by relying on its own resources."[19]

Following Chernyshevskii and Dobroliubov—who in turn followed Comte and the materialist philosophers Moleschott, Büchner, and Vogt—Pisarev emphasized the unity of the sciences: he viewed the "moral" sciences as a mere extension of the natural sciences; he did not speak about sociology as a distinct science but about the application of the methods of natural science in the study of human history and social life. The natural sciences bring man into direct contact with nature and help him rise above the obscurantism of various moralistic theories and unfathomable metaphysical systems. He had respect only for the philosophical thought that was grounded in science. He was convinced that to understand the structure and the function of cells meant to understand the life of an organism; and to understand the life of the human organism meant, in essence, to understand the historical life of mankind. Pisarev, like Chernyshevskii and Dobroliubov, believed that physiology held the key to the understanding of human society. They accepted Saint-Simon's view that a full understanding of the intricate functioning of the brain would provide the best insight into the complexities of social relations. N. D. Nozhin, a biologist turned journalist, made his position perfectly clear: "I direct the attention of the reader to the fact that the main goal of my anatomic and embryological studies is to discover the laws of the physiology of society."[20] He spoke for his generation when he extolled natural science as the only infallible guide to a healthier future. Preaching a "fantastic belief in science" as the true force of reason, he declared that "all scientific knowledge in the hands of honest servants stands in direct opposition to the existing order" and that "in the world there is only one evil—ignorance—and only one way of salvation—science."[21] Pisarev saw in science not only a dynamic system of positive knowledge but also a school of critical thought, a realistic attitude toward society and culture, and an optimistic view of the future.

Thoroughly imbued with the spirit of science, Pisarev raised his voice against the romantic studies of the Russian national character which dwelled in the world of "optical illusions" and diverted attention from the critical problems of social existence.[22] He was particularly critical of so-called philanthropists who rejected all unflattering descriptions of Russian culture and who nurtured the quixotic ideal of "the coming dominance of Russia in the intellectual life of Europe."[23] He argued that, in their efforts to establish an objective study of Russian society, the members of the intelligentsia must reject the world view of the masses as "fully incompatible with all the basic truths of physics and geography." The function of science, according to Pisarev, is to dislodge both the despotism of the government and the ignorance of the masses. He was the spiritual leader of a generation of young Russians who chose science as their vocation. The famous neurophysiologist Ivan Pavlov, who entered St. Petersburg University in 1870 after having graduated from a theological school, stated many years later that it was the magic of Pisarev's influence that inspired many young men to dedicate themselves to scientific research.[24]

Although Pisarev did not formulate a system of sociological thought, he helped generate an interest in the scientific study of society. His work was more important as a codification of the problems, aspirations, and dilemmas of the intelligentsia of the 1860s than as a contribution to the conceptual tools and logical designs of sociology. According to a contemporary writer, Pisarev wrote at the time when the avant garde of the Russian intelligentsia was convinced that "moral truths could no longer be accepted in their orthodox form," that a scientific world view should fully replace "the supernatural and mythical world view," and that the full rejuvenation of society depended on the triumph of "reason, science, and freedom."[25] Like many of his contemporaries, Pisarev adhered closely to positivism, which provided powerful arguments against all current efforts to consolidate idealistic philosophy as an ideological weapon of the autocratic system.[26]

According to Pisarev, every search for an integrated social science must bypass history because historians are partial interpreters of the national past; they search through the maze of documentary material to select and embellish events that illustrate their ideological biases. Statistics—the systematic collection and scrutiny of numerical data bearing on every aspect of social life—was, in his opinion, the science with the most promise of evolving into a systematic and thorough analysis of social existence.[27] However, his main argument was that the growth of the natural sciences is in itself the safest path to objective and comprehensive knowledge of society—knowledge of its present-day structure and its future evolution. The natural sciences do not handle social problems directly; they provide models for an objective analysis of social problems by an educated citizenry; they elucidate the place of man in nature; and they are the indices of social progress.

Pisarev, the most effective pioneer of scientific social thought in Russia, combined a positivistic and a voluntaristic approach to social reality; social theory, according to him, should concentrate on the discovery not only of the inexorable natural laws of social development but also of the techniques for the most rational mobilization of human effort to help bring about predetermined social progress. Unlike the leading Western sociologists of his day, Pisarev did not view social progress as a rectilinear and irreversible process. He preferred Saint-Simon's somewhat outdated idea of alternating "organic" and "critical" periods, the former characterized by the vitality and systematization of cultural material, the latter by the destruction of established cultural systems.[28] Implicit in Saint-Simon's argumentation is the idea that each successive organic period represents a higher point on the scale of social evolution.

There were other intellectual developments during the 1860s which helped inaugurate the age of science in general and of sociology in particular. One of these was the reopening of Russia to Western influences of massive proportions. The revolutionary tides that swept Western Europe in 1848 led Nicholas I to isolate Russia from intellectual contact with the West. Russian professors and students were forbidden to visit Western European universities, and a rigid censorship imposed drastic limitations on the importing of Western books. Only the underground activities of isolated circles in Moscow and St. Petersburg, constantly dodging police surveillance, helped maintain a semblance of contact with the newest developments in Western science and philosophy. After the Crimean defeat, the situation changed rapidly. Russian professors and students went in droves to Western institutions of higher education and to scientific laboratories. Influential journals carried long articles discussing current philosophical themes and new developments in science. Translation activity assumed unprecedented proportions. Leo Tolstoy noted that university students received most of their education not from formal lectures by individual professors but from the informal activities of mushrooming circles, activities which consisted mainly of reading "old articles" by Belinskii, "new articles" by Chernyshevskii, Antonovich, and Pisarev, translations of such currently popular Western European writers as G. H. Lewes and H. T. Buckle, and the banned books written by Feuerbach, Büchner, Herzen, and Ogarev.[29] Russians could now read in their own language Sir Charles Lyell's *Principles of Geology* and *The Antiquity of Man*, Darwin's *The Origin of Species*, and Claude Bernard's *Introduction to the Experimental Study of Medicine* and not only widen their scientific horizons but also reinforce the newly discovered idea of social progress. In an effort to free their thinking of the decadent elements of the past, the young intellectuals of the Reform era "sought the guidelines of the future in the social doctrines of the West and studied them assiduously for principles and values they could embrace."[30]

Henry T. Buckle's *History of Civilization in England*, translated into Russian in 1863, was one of the most discussed books of the generation and the "unchallengeable authority" for the young people.[31] It was particularly well received by numerous worshippers of "positivism, materialism, and skepticism" who considered the method of science the only trustworthy approach to natural and social reality. Buckle's claim that the real function of the historian is to reduce a maximum of historical events and observations to a minimum of general and immutable laws appealed to an unusually wide spectrum of the Russian intelligentsia.[32] His approach to history as a uniform and continuous process—rather than as an aggregate of discrete events—and his identification of cultural and social progress with the growing quality of knowledge found many supporters among the Nihilist intelligentsia particularly involved in the search for a science of society. Buckle's lengthy discussion of the democratic spirit of the scientific fermentation that paved the way for the French Revolution helped reinforce the Nihilist belief in science as the basic source of progress.

A. P. Shchapov, an eminent social historian who taught at Kazan University before he was exiled to Siberia on charges of extensive links with the student revolutionary movement, was the first Russian scholar to be attracted to Buckle's social theory and to apply it to the study of Russian history.[33] Known as the "Russian Buckle," he undertook to substitute a "natural history" of Russia for the prevalent "political history"—to replace the mode of historical narration, dominated by the historiographic tradition of N. M. Karamzin and S. M. Solov'ev, by a "scientific" search for regularities and empirical laws of historical change. His writing after 1863 belonged to the category of historical sociology. He built his theory on

Buckle's idea that sociocultural progress is measured most accurately by the growth of secular wisdom and the advancement and expansion of the scientific method. The essence of national history must be sought in intellectual growth, or rather in the evolution of the prevalent modes of cognition.

The Russian mind, according to Shchapov, is strictly sensualistic; it does not stray from immediate and accumulated experience and is adverse to abstract and theoretical thinking. He viewed sensualism not as an innate Russian characteristic but as a product of the conditions which molded the history of Russian society. In his voluminous treatment of the intellectual evolution of the Russian people, Shchapov was concerned primarily with the conditions which worked against the emergence of abstract thought and rationalist tradition. The low density of population, the wide spatial distribution of settlements, and the general geographical isolation prevented the primeval East Slavic tribes from establishing intensive and intellectually productive ties with the classical civilizations of Greece and Rome. Russia did not pass through the "classical phase" of sociocultural development, the phase during which the foundations were laid for theoretical science and systematic philosophy. When contact with European civilization was finally established, it was dominated by the activities of Byzantine science, which showed little interest in abstract thought. Under a pronounced Byzantine influence, the Russian intellectual tradition provided no room for skepticism, critical attitude toward authority, individual interpretation of experience, and confidence in man's rational faculties as the ultimate source of socially useful knowledge. Shchapov made it clear that the conditions which worked against abstract scientific thought were also the conditions favoring autocracy and feudal institutions. He gave credit to Peter the Great for having recognized that abstract thought, and a preoccupation with intellectual rather than with moral questions, could be made part of Russian culture not by a spontaneous internal development but by massive borrowing from the West enforced by the state. Although Peter brought science to Russia, he did not solve the problem of the essential incompatibility of autocratic values with the ethos of science. Post-Petrine Russia was deeply involved in an acute conflict between the "archeological" orientation, supported by the government and official ideology, which emphasized classical philology and legal history, and the "rationalist" orientation, dedicated to the advancement of modern natural science.

Shchapov's rigid categorization of the Russian mind and Russian culture was challenged by many contemporary writers. However, even the most severe critics admitted that he was successful in opening wide new areas of national history to scholarly scrutiny, that he was a true pioneer in correlating the intellectual and social evolution in Russia, and that he was the first major Russian scholar to combine a critical examination of historical events with an analysis of social structure. He was more successful in showing the enormous potentialities of an integrated and generalized approach to the complex realities of social change than in formulating a consistent and precise sociological theory.

Interest in science during the 1860s was sufficiently acute to justify the publication of a Russian translation of William Whewell's monumental *History of the Inductive Sciences* in 1867. Whewell's work provided the Russians with the first systematic survey of modern scientific thought from astronomy to historical geology. While Whewell provided enthusiastic support for the idea of progress based on accumulative, even though not continuous, growth of scientific knowledge, he made no effort to deal with the "moral" sciences, either as special branches of knowledge or as extensions of the natural sciences. M. A. Antonovich, in his Introduction to the Russian translation of the *History*, lamented Whewell's failure to examine the contributions of the natural sciences to a gradual eradication of deep-seated prejudices which stood in the way of the affirmation of true humanity.[34] The function of science, according to Antonovich, is not only to create goods of practical utility but also to liberate the human mind from the biases of the past and to create a world view based on critical thought and continuous inquiry. Antonovich resented Whewell's failure to extend the logical models of natural science inquiry to the study of social life.

Whewell's omission was counterbalanced by the publication of a Russian translation of Adolphe Quetelet's *A Treatise on Man and the Development of His Faculties, or Social Physics*, in 1865. This book represented the boldest effort made in the nineteenth century to create a "moral science" within the Newtonian mechanistic paradigm. It inaugurated a systematic search for the mathematicization of the social sciences and particularly for an adaptation of the probability theory to the study of structural continuities in seemingly discontinuous types of social behavior. Quetelet's book marked a complete denial of free will as a source of sociologically relevant action and a full identification of "social physics" or "moral statistics" with physics and astronomy. Quetelet—like Chernyshevskii, Dobroliubov, and Pisarev—saw in the gradual advancement of knowledge the most reliable index of social progress. While Whewell supplied the Russian readers with extensive surveys of the growth of individual natural sciences, Quetelet provided strong arguments in favor of extending the theoretical models and methodological instrumentalities of these sciences to the study of the world of social relations. Together they helped reinforce the scientific bias of the Nihilist world view. The influence of Quetelet on the sociological "realism" of the 1860s was limited. Quetelet's treatment of society as an integral part of nature—and of the unity of the natural and social sciences—appealed to the Nihilists and other social critics. However, Quetelet's interest in stability as the only social attribute of scientific significance was diametrically opposite to the Nihilist belief in the possibility of a rapid and complete transformation of the existing Russian society.

The Russian translation and joint publication of *Auguste Comte and Positivism* by John Stuart Mill and *Comte's Philosophy of the Sciences* by G. H. Lewes, in 1867, gave the reading public the first systematic and detailed surveys of the principal ideas of "the father of sociology." Both Mill and Lewes emphasized the two pivotal arguments of Comte's philosophy of history and sociology: the law of the three stages of universal history—the theological or fictitious stage, the metaphysical or abstract stage, and the scientific or positive stage—and the classification of the sciences in terms of increasing complexity and diminishing generality. These laws contained two general ideas incorporated in Nihilist philosophy. The first law underscored the gradual secularization of wisdom—best expressed in the growth of science as a system of knowledge, a mode of inquiry, and a world view—as the most tangible indicator of cultural progress. The second law recognized sociology as an abstract science of society and as an integral component of the ontological continuum of the basic sciences. According to Comte, sociology has two kinds of laws: the laws carried over from the previously developed sciences—astronomy, physics, chemistry, and biology—and the laws not shared with other disciplines. While the carry-overs make sociology a legitimate component of general, unified science, the unique laws make sociology a distinct discipline, subject to its own development. Mill and Lewes also emphasized Comte's statement that sociology had not yet emerged as a science par excellence—that current sociology was related to a future scientific, or positive, sociology in the same manner as alchemy was related to chemistry.

Although Mill and Lewes tried to give an authentic presentation of the pivotal ideas of the voluminous written legacy of Comte, their analyses were not free of personal views, emphases, and criticisms. Lewes, for example, was very eager to convince his readers that, despite Comte's primary concern with the progressive development of man's rational faculties and the expanding scientific foundations of society, he did not underestimate the social role of man's affective faculties and of the moral code. He said: "The moralist, the metaphysician, and the man of letters may be assured that if Comte's system has one capital distinction more remarkable than another, it is the absolute predominance of the moral point of view—the rigorous subordination of the intellect to the heart."[35] Mill selected Comte's phenomenalistic epistemology for special emphasis; he made it abundantly clear that Comte viewed scientific knowledge not as an automatic reflection of the outside world but as a subjective construction of the human mind. Mill's inclination to attribute a vital social and historical role to the individual was definitely not in tune with Comtian sociology. Both Mill and Lewes gave due prominence to Comtian ontology, which considered ideas the prime movers of history.

Thus a combination of free reinterpretation and true recounting of Comte's philosophical thought planted the seeds of a world view partially opposed to the Nihilist philosophy. The arrival in Russia of systematic studies of Comtian philosophy coincided with the beginning of the rapid downfall of Nihilist scientism, materialism, and epistemological objectivism. It also marked the beginning of the Russian subjective school in sociology inaugurated by the publication of P. L. Lavrov's *Hisorical Letters* in 1868 and N. K. Mikhailovskii's "What is Progress?" in 1869.

The Nihilist social philosophy must be credited with bringing to Russia an awareness of the urgent need for a scientific study of society, of the pivotal role of the individual in the complex fabric of social relations, and of the imperative necessity for recognizing "society" as a much broader sociological category than the "state." The Nihilist dictum that a scientific study of society was part of a critical reexamination of the sacred culture of the autocratic polity was not seriously challenged by any of the leading Russian sociological schools during the last three decades of the nineteenth century.

A healthy stimulus for the emergence of sociological thought during the 1860s also came from the unusually intensive and versatile development of the natural sciences in Russia. Within a decade, Russia produced a galaxy of scientists whose contributions were duly noted in the West and helped open new vistas of scientific research. Ivan Sechenov is rightly considered a pioneer of modern neurophysiology, while A. O. Kovalevskii and I. I. Mechnikov were among the founders of modern comparative embryology and V. O. Kovalevskii of evolutionary paleontology. K. A. Timiriazev conducted his initial research in photosynthesis during this time, and A. M. Butlerov helped found structural chemistry. P. L. Chebyshev, who began his scientific career in the era of Nicholas I, became the founder of the most influential modern school in the theory of probability, and D. I. Mendeleev formulated the periodic law of elements, one of the greatest feats of nineteenth-century chemistry. Many other scientists were leaders in their fields or noteworthy builders of the empirical base of the scientific edifice. The prevalent attribute of the "men of the sixties" engaged in scientific work was a rising consciousness of the social role of science and of the need for an uninterrupted flow of scientific knowledge to agriculture and industry. The leading scientists did not hesitate to enter public debates on topics related to the current problems and future prospects of Russian society. Although many professors of economics and law were deeply involved in sociologically oriented research, sociology was not recognized as a distinct part of the university curriculum during the entire tsarist era.

The scientists of the 1860s looked upon Turgenev's Bazarov as a paragon of a new realism built upon science. Kliment Timiriazev likened Bazarov to Peter I: the two, according to him, combined an ascetic dedication to work as a source of happiness and dignity with a profound respect for scientific inquiry, and both were ready to use the most drastic measures to uproot stagnant institutions and outdated ideologies.[36] Reminiscing about the 1860s and the ideas expressed through Bazarov and by the Nihilists, the mathematician Sof'ia Kovalevskaia noted: "We were so exalted by all these new ideas, so convinced that the present state of society could not last long, and that a glorious time of liberty and general knowledge was quite certain."[37]

Sociology: A General Science of Society

Neither a well-known social philosopher nor a natural scientist, but an obscure young revolutionary, associated with the subterranean *Zemlia i Volia* (founded in 1861) and educated in the spirit of Chernyshevskii's philosophy, gave the first precise outline of sociology as a distinct science. Born to an aristocratic family and educated in the Tsarskosel'skii Lycée, N. A. Serno-Solov'evich made several trips to Western Europe where he met A. I. Herzen, N. P. Ogarev, and several other critics of the Russian political system. He wrote primarily about the vital questions related to Russia's groping for "economic, political, and cultural" progress. In 1865, at the age of thirty-one, he was exiled to Siberia and died a year later. His ideas on the urgent need for the creation of sociology and on the subject matter of the proposed discipline were presented in a brief article entitled "Does the Present State of Knowledge Need a New Science?"[38]

Accumulated and accumulating scientific knowledge is, according to Serno-Solov'evich, the primary wheel of history, but knowledge by itself is not sufficient. Only scientific knowledge related to social reality should be tolerated; the function of science is both to add new knowledge and to discard those "archaeological relics" which have proven totally useless from the standpoint of social progress. In his search for knowledge, the scientist must be ready to create new disciplines when sufficient empirical information is accumulated and when there is a social need for them. In his age, Serno-Solov'evich argued, there was a realistic need for a survey, examination, and integration of all knowledge related to social life: for a social science which he identified as sociology. In their quest for a new social science, scholars must look to the natural sciences for models and general ideas. The natural sciences, despite their promising future, cannot satisfy all the needs of modern man. They must cooperate closely with the social sciences, otherwise they face the risk of falling into the abyss of metaphysical futility. While an important task of the natural sciences is to provide the social sciences with superior methods of inquiry, the task of the social sciences is to give the natural sciences a social orientation.

Serno-Solov'evich argued cogently that no existing social science was a science in the first place. Statistics, "the most exact of the social sciences," fell far short of meeting the most urgent "politico-economic and financial needs" and was still in an "embryonic stage." The greatest successes in "social economy" resulted from conjectures put forth by great men rather than from scientifically rigorous inquiry; "the logic of the truly great thinkers who have created various schools in economics, cannot span the abyss created by the insufficiency of reliable data."[39] Criminology was still struggling with philosophy and conservative government authorities. History had failed to become a comprehensive science because it was too involved in the study of individual societies to face and understand the universal problems of social existence. To raise themselves above the narrow limits of their research interests, the social scientists were required to meet two conditions: to master the methodological tools advanced by the natural sciences for gathering factual information of scientific import and to formulate the general principles of scientific explanation. Only by meeting these conditions could the social scientists expect to lead their own disciplines to higher levels of scientific abstraction and to enrich the natural sciences by supplying them with a social orientation.

To achieve these goals, the social sciences must be guided by sociology as a "central and supreme science." The basic function of sociology, in Serno-Solov'evich's view, is to study the principles of social integration and differentiation and to assign to each social science a precisely defined area of operation. The aim of sociology is not to achieve a mechanical summation of the contributions of various social sciences and history but to provide a comprehensive theory for a study of societies as organic units. Sociology is an antithesis to atomistic studies of society: it searches for general patterns underlying and integrating social phenomena. In order to achieve this integration, sociology must not depend only on the information supplied by various social sciences but must bring new areas of social life under its own scientific scrutiny. Serno-Solov'evich particularly emphasized the need for a systematic study of the social attributes of urban and rural communities, industrialization, political-administrative centralization, education, and the taxation system. The future of sociology, according to him, depended on the unqualified rejection of "a-prioristic and hypothetical methods" and on the development of precise techniques of observation and comparison.

The search for a conceptually integrated study of society during the 1860s, particularly from 1861 to 1868, did not produce a system of sociological thought. However it did provide a basis upon which most Russian sociology was built during the following decades. The main thrust of its legacy was in the emphasis on the idea of progress as a law of social change, the alliance of sociology and ideologies dedicated to comprehensive political and social reforms, the search for reciprocity in the interaction of society and the individual, and the treatment of sociology as an integral part of the general development of abstract science.

2. The Subjective Sociology
of Russian Populism:
P. L. Lavrov and
N. K. Mikhailovskii

Nihilism had a meteoric career. It blossomed during the first half of the 1860s but by the middle of the decade had begun to wane and in a few years disappeared from the historical scene, transmitting the scattered residues of its legacy to new ideological movements. The most influential of these movements was Populism which, in comparison with Nihilism, was more deeply rooted in the Russian tradition and was more moderate in its interpretation of science as an instrument of social change and a beacon of intellectual progress. By a general consensus of contemporaries, P. L. Lavrov and N. K. Mikhailovskii were the ideological and philosophical architects of the Populist movement.

Lavrov and Mikhailovskii had similar backgrounds. Both hailed from aristocratic families of modest means and both learned French and German before they entered public schools. Both were trained in mathematics and the natural sciences: Lavrov in the Artillery School and Mikhailovskii in the Institute of Mining Engineers. Both were engaged in literary work: Mikhailovskii published an unheralded novel and Lavrov wrote poetry distinguished "neither by the richness of expression, nor by a special beauty of form."[1] One of Lavrov's early poems was dedicated to a reconciliation of religion and science.[2] Both were early exposed to influences of socialist theories: Lavrov identified himself with the Young Hegelians, particularly Feuerbach, and Mikhailovskii went through a phase of admiration for the social thought of Proudhon. However, both quickly rose above these initial influences and developed elaborate systems of original philosophical and sociological thought.

Lavrov graduated from the Artillery School at St. Petersburg in 1842 and two years later was appointed instructor of mathematics at the same school, a job which he held until 1866. As a lecturer, he impressed his students by frequent excursions into the philosophical foundations of mathematics and into the history and social attributes of science.[3] The police were alerted to Lavrov's penchant for injecting "liberal ideas" into explanations of scientific topics. His forte was the history of mathematics and related sciences; he not only lectured in this field but also contributed articles to the *Artillery Journal* and the *Naval Symposium*.[4] These lectures and publications may be considered the beginning of Lavrov's deep involvement in the study of the history of thought as a key to the understanding of the history of human society. But teaching and writing in the history of science, and in science in general, were overshadowed by Lavrov's growing interest in the fundamental problems of modern philosophy, particularly the theory of knowledge.

Nineteen years older than Mikhailovskii, Lavrov became widely known in 1860–61 when he published several philosophical essays dealing with Hegelianism, the "anthropological view" in philosophy, and the epistemological foundations of scientific knowledge. He rejected both philosophical idealism and philosophical materialism as metaphysical orientations built upon one-sided abstractions without empirical foundations. He became the advocate of a "practical philosophy," a philosophy built upon scientific knowledge and dedicated to answering the essential questions of human history and social existence. Lavrov's philosophy was a unique amalgam of the Hegelian philosophy of history, Kantian phenomenalistic epistemology, and Baconian inductionist philosophy of nature. Although Chernyshevskii placed the label of "eclecticism" on Lavrov's early philosophical work, he acknowledged felicitiously its innovative qualities and called Lavrov a "progressive thinker ... imbued with a sincere desire to help the society to which he belongs to acquire those moral and social benefits which we still lack owing to our ignorance."[5] Chernyshevskii's praise helped ruin Lavrov's chances for an appointment as professor of philosophy at St. Petersburg University, for which he was considered by an academic committee. Anticipating the "Back To Kant" movement and the rise of various neo-Kantian schools, he claimed that science is not concerned with the essence of nature (the noumena, in Kantian terminology) but with "phenomena" (nature as perceived by man).[6] The task of epistemology, according to him, is to recognize the human meaning of all knowledge.[7]

In a critical essay on "the mechanical theory of the world," Lavrov argued in favor of a clear differentiation between three kinds of "science": natural science, the "phenomenology of spirit," and history. In the mechanistic model he saw the best guaranty for the elevation of natural science to the state of perfection; the study of motion is the basic mechanism for a scientific inquiry into all natural phenomena, from celestial bodies to the cerebral cortex. The "phenomenology of spirit," another expression for the theory of knowledge (or epistemology), concentrates on the processes of cognition and on the systematization of cognitive material. History is the science of society. Its primary duty is to show how individuals progressively widen their knowledge of both the internal and external worlds and how they embody human aspirations for justice and beauty in "the transitional forms of civil institutions, religious beliefs, philosophical systems, and political and artistic forms." Each of these three huge areas of intellectual endeavor has its own independent mode of inquiry and laws. The future will show whether these laws are "analogous" and whether they could be subsumed under even more general laws. If this ever happens, then "science and belief will become identical, and there will be no need for metaphysics."[8]

The same article expressed the four ideas which dominated much of Lavrov's subsequent philosophical and sociological writings: the growth of knowledge is the most reliable indicator of social progress; materialism and idealism are equally one-sided and misleading; metaphysics is built upon the flaws, rather than upon the positive achievements, of the natural sciences; and, social theory cannot rise to the level of scientific rigor if it is treated as a mere extension of natural science.[9] Implicit in Lavrov's compounded argumentation was the idea that the essential differences between the natural sciences and the social sciences are epistemological rather than ontological. Science, according to Lavrov, is not a mere acquisition and systematization of socially useful positive knowledge; it is the very essence of the modern world outlook. He was convinced that "in the struggle against all world views based on phantasy, the reading of textbooks on geometry, excellent memoirs on physics and chemistry, solid studies in critical history, and Mill's *Logic* is much more productive than the reading of [such studies in popular science as] Büchner's *Kraft und Stoff*."[10]

In 1866, Lavrov was arrested and sent to an isolated area in the Vologda province where he lived under daily police surveillance.[11] During the next two years he published two of his most remarkable works: *Positivism and Its Problems* and *Historical Letters*, first in journal installments and then as separate volumes. The volume on positivism—actually an oversized review of the Russian translation and joint publication of John Stuart Mill's and George Lewes's monographs on Comte—was the first Russian study dealing with the Comtian philosophy of history and the philosophy of science in significant detail. Although he was critical of many aspects of Comtian philosophy, he saw in it a laudable effort to integrate the knowledge advanced by individual sciences, to introduce clear criteria distinguishing scientific from nonscientific knowledge, and to link the "objective phenomena of nature" to "the process of the historical development of humanity."[12] He recognized positivism as an integrated approach to the major concerns of modern thought: the external world, the process of cognition, the evolution of civilizations, and the practical problems of rational education.[13] Lavrov was inclined to think that "in all probability" Comte's thought would provide the foundations for a reigning philosophy of the future. Only the philosophy whose assertions are grounded in "the achievements of science" and in "the critical procedures of the scientific method" could hope to meet the needs of the future. The German "phenomenology of spirit" and French positivism had one thing in common: both thought that the understanding of the inner logic in the development of man's cognitive powers was the key to the understanding of social and cultural evolution. However, French positivism, in Lavrov's estimation, was superior to German idealism because it considered the scientific mode of thought an advancement over religious dogmatism and metaphysical speculation.[14] Comte's philosophy of history was correct inasmuch as it anticipated the coming of the age of science.

Historical Letters, written in the gloomy tranquility and isolation of Russian provincial existence, is Lavrov's most celebrated work. As a work of scholarship, it contains the essence of Lavrov's sociology. As a philosophical treatise, it marks a carefully specified retreat from the excesses of Nihilist scientism and an elaborate examination of science as a mode of inquiry, a world view, and an instrument of social and cultural change. As an ideological manifesto, it became the bible of Populism: it marshalled arguments in favor of the Going to the People movement and it spelled out the role of the intelligentsia as a guiding force of social change. Its trenchant analysis of the paramount historical role of the individual appealed to the growing ranks of the intelligentsia engaged in a determined battle for the elimination of the last vestiges of feudalism and for the affirmation of the idea of citizenship, embodied in personal and political freedom.[15] To the young generation, it was a philosophical synthesis of the noblest aspirations and efforts of the age. It was the philosophy of "a new faith in the future," pointing out "the path of progress," awakening "critical thought," giving birth to a new world view, and depicting the main attributes of the ideal personality of the reform era and of the "progress of critically thinking individuals."[16]

In 1870, helped by a clandestine revolutionary circle, Lavrov fled Russia, never to return. He arrived in Paris in March 1870, several days after the death of Herzen, and promptly became engaged in the activities of the Paris Commune and the First International.[17] During a visit to London he met Marx and Engels, with whom he remained lifelong friends. Marx respected the versatility of his knowledge, the astuteness of his intellect, and the fervor of his dedication to socialism but was critical of his philosophical "eclecticism" and moderate views on political activism. In *Dialectics of Nature*, Engels made a footnote reference to his ambitious but uncompleted *Essay on the History of Thought*. It was in a letter to Lavrov that Engels formulated the most generally accepted Marxist interpretation of the sociological attributes of Darwin's theory. For his part, Lavrov refrained from direct criticism of Marxist social theory; in Marxism he saw an essential component, but not an all-inclusive theory, of modern socialism.[18]

Despite a long residence abroad, Lavrov remained a Russian in habit, political interest, philosophical bent, and historical perspective. He wrote all his important works in Russian and addressed himself to Russian readers. As the editor first of *Vpered!* (*Forward!*), a journal dedicated to the articulation and diffusion of socialist ideas, and then of the *Vestnik Narodnoi Voli* (*Messenger of People's Will*), published by a faction of revolutionary Populism, he kept in touch with his native country, particularly the Populist intelligentsia. A Populist group was named after him; the Lavrovists were known primarily for their conviction that, since every revolutionary action in Russia was foredoomed to be quickly and totally crushed by the authorities, the first and foremost duty of socialists should be to concentrate on the political education of the masses and the training of dedicated leaders. Lavrov was in direct opposition to the views of Mikhail Bakunin, who advocated local disorders as a means of weakening the power of the police and of paving the way for a general revolution.[19] He expressed skepticism toward the efforts of Russian Social Democrats to organize an active political group; again, he saw in "the existing conditions of absolutism" an enemy of unchallengeable and awesome power ready to pulverize any overt revolutionary action. In 1882, together with the young G. V. Plekhanov, he founded the Russian Social-Revolutionary Library, an enterprise concentrating on the publication of contemporary socialist literature in Russian translation. One of the first publications was a new translation of the *Communist Manifesto*, with a special introduction by Marx and Engels.[20]

In addition to extensive writing on themes of a political-programmatic nature, Lavrov wrote a great deal on subjects outside politics. He contributed to the *Revue de l'Anthropologie*, a journal of the Paris Anthropological Society, and published several anthropological articles in Russian journals. In the field of literary criticism, he spanned a wide range from Lessing and Longfellow to Hugo and Zola. In intellectual history, he found it worthwhile and challenging to write about scientific thought during the Renaissance and Reformation and on the universal history of thought as a means for reconstructing the evolution of human society. He wrote about the Paris Commune, the Populist "propagandists" during the 1870s, the "political types" in the eighteenth century, and many other historical topics. During the 1890s he published *Problems of Understanding History*, a work in which he brought together his thoughts on the philosophy of history and social evolution. The philosophical and sociological ideas presented in this work were essentially the same as those propounded in *Historical Letters* some thirty years earlier; in words of Sh. M. Levin, "Lavrov never abandoned his adherence to the principles of Populism."[21] He was not only one of the leading theorists of the Populist movement but also one of the most sagacious chroniclers of its historical fortunes.

N. K. Mikhailovskii started his writing career in 1860 with a piece on literary criticism which went virtually unnoticed. During the next nine years he wrote book reviews and translated fragments from Proudhon's works. Particularly fruitful was his association with the journal *Book Messenger* where he worked with the young biologist N. D. Nozhin, who helped him develop a strong interest in the scientific foundations of sociology and the relations of sociology to biology. Nozhin was a professional embryologist who did graduate work under H. G. Bronn, the translator of Darwin's *The Origin of Species* into German. Nozhin himself produced a Russian translation of Fritz Müller's classic *Für Darwin*, a pioneering study in evolutionary embryology.[22] As a comparative embryologist, he worked within the evolutionary scheme unfolded by Darwin's theory of biological evolution; as a revolutionary, he rejected the Darwinian struggle for existence as a sociological conception, for it justified class warfare and ruled out the possibility of a socialist society based on cooperation. He argued that the increasing division of labor in society leads to growing economic contradictions and deepening social conflict. According to him, the struggle for existence within individual species is not a law of nature but a pathological aberration.[23]

From 1869 to 1884, Mikhailovskii was the chief editor of the reputable *Fatherland Notes*, a journal that he quickly transformed into a mouthpiece for the intelligentsia dedicated to democratic ideals and identified with Populism. His articles made him the indisputable intellectual leader of the Populist movement; even the revolutionaries affiliated with such fringe groups as Land and Liberty and The People's Will considered him one of themselves. In 1873, Lavrov asked him to emigrate in order to take an open part in revolutionary propaganda. In rejecting Lavrov's invitation, he stated that Russia had not yet produced a "radical social opposition" strong enough to press for extensive social reforms and that he did not consider himself a revolutionary in the first place. He said that a "socialist opposition" could prepare the country for radical social changes by a realistic study of national needs and a clear understanding of positive and negative influences coming from the West, rather than by parroting Moleschott's materialistic clichés and playing with toy obshchinas.[24]

In 1878, moved by the court trial of Vera Zasulich, a revolutionary who tried to assassinate General F. F. Trepov, the military governor of St. Petersburg, Mikhailovskii published the famous "Leaflet" in which he demanded the convocation of a national congress of zemstvo leaders for the purpose of establishing a constitutional regime.[25] In *Narodnaia Volia* (*People's Will*), the organ of a new revolutionary organization, he published (under a pseudonym) several articles entitled collectively "The Letters of a Socialist" in which he advocated an opposition to the government in form of activities calculated not to set off a revolution but to coerce the authorities into carrying out liberal social policies. He also advocated a common front of revolutionaries and various factions of liberals.[26] In a comment on Dostoevskii's *The Demons*, he declared that political reforms, regardless of how extensive they were, would be essentially useless if they were not accompanied by basic social reforms.[27]

In 1884, *Fatherland Notes* was closed by a government order, leaving Mikhailovskii without employment. After trying his luck with several journals, including the popular *Russian Thought*, he accepted the position of the chief editor of *Russian Wealth* in 1892, a job which he held until 1904, the year of his death. *Russian Wealth* immediately became a mouthpiece of

Populism which, at this time, directed its most powerful guns against Marxist political economy and sociology.

The theoretical foundations of Mikhailovskii's sociology were laid during the first years of his association with *Fatherland Notes*; however, he did not return to sociological themes until the very end of his long writing career. To his contemporaries, he was primarily a sociologist, even though most of his writing was in literary criticism, politics, and sociocultural history. These contemporaries disagreed on only one point: while some contended that his sociological theory was a complete system, characterized by an elaborate logical structure and theoretical consistency, others thought that his studies supplied all the vital ingredients for a sociological system of large magnitude but that he had failed to bring even the major ideas into a tightly knit and logically consistent system. N. S. Rusanov's interpretation seems to be most accurate. It is true, he said, that the reader is bewildered by the frequency with which Mikhailovskii leaped from one subject to another, failed to carry his discussion to a conclusion, and overelaborated episodes that were interesting to him even though they were not germane to the topic under discussion. But despite all this, "the more thoroughly one is acquainted with the works of Mikhailovskii, the more he is impressed with the internal unity and definiteness of his world view"—a world view from which he did not deviate during the four decades of his literary activity.[28]

The evolution of Mikhailovskii's social theory fell into two distinct stages. During the first stage, he concentrated on formulating the guiding principles of a general theory of society. From 1869 to 1871 he wrote most of his major sociological papers, including "What is Progress?" "Darwin's Theory and Social Science," "The Analogical Method in Social Science," and "Louis Blanc's Philosophy of History." These essays, some of book length, presented the theoretical core of his sociology; his subsequent sociological work, despite its enormous scope and thematic diversity, expanded and clarified the ideas presented in the early papers. In articulating his sociological theory, Mikhailovskii relied heavily on a minute criticism of two dominant currents in Western sociological thought: Comtian positivism and Spencerian evolutionism. He fully accepted Comte's interpretation of social progress in terms of the evolution of thought and secularization of wisdom, but he rejected Comte's unfavorable attitude toward the individualism of the eighteenth-century philosophes. He endorsed Spencer's interpretation of universal evolution as a process leading to the increased diversification of nature and society, but he rejected the English philosopher's organismic model of society.[29]

The second phase, which began in the early 1890s, was dominated by Mikhailovskii's effort to help derail the onrushing forces of the Russian Marxist movement which threatened to replace Populism as the guiding force of opposition to the established authority. The Marxists looked at the development of Russian society through the prism of universal social evolution; Mikhailovskii looked at universal social evolution through the prism of Russian ideals and realities. The Marxists operated under the cloak of scientific objectivism; Mikhailovskii championed a "subjective sociology." The Marxists addressed themselves to the growing ranks of the urban proletariat; Mikhailovskii treated the peasantry as the body and soul of Russia.* Mikhailovskii also found time to clarify and retrench his theoretical position vis-à-vis the new Western orientations in sociology. Particularly noted were his essays refuting Emile Durkheim's broadly conceived efforts to build sociology upon a conception of society as a reality independent of and "exterior" to the subjective attributes of personality.

SOCIOLOGY AS A SCIENCE

While rejecting all arguments in favor of the ontological unity of the sciences, Lavrov and Mikhailovskii accepted the epistemological view that all the sciences are united by the fact that they do not deal with the unknowable "essence of things" but with the knowable "interrelations of phenomena."[30] Endorsing phenomenalistic epistemology, they acknowledged the futility of both materialism and idealism as philosophical orientations. All knowledge, according to them, is subjective in origin. They argued, however, that the difference between the subjective knowledge dealt with by the natural sciences and the subjective knowledge dealt with by the social sciences is a difference of kind rather than of degree. Thus they rejected the Nihilist notion, defended most categorically by Pisarev, that the social sciences are epistemological, logical, and methodological extensions of the natural sciences. Mikhailovskii criticized "the unscientific and crude habit" of transferring "simple truths of the natural sciences to the complex phenomena of culture and social life," a habit which was popular among the intelligentsia of the 1860s. He was largely responsibile for a noticeable decline in Russia of the popularity of Spencer's "organic theory," which invited a treatment of human society as an organism and of various institutions as specific organs, and which made sociology a mere extension of biology. Lavrov was consistent in his deep respect for the natural sciences, but he too was adamant in stressing the inadequacy of natural science models and methods in the analysis of the facts of social history.

Sociology, in the Populist view, depends on an interlacing of "objective" and "subjective" methods of inquiry and interpretations that is absent in the natural sciences. Sociology, unlike the natural sciences, blends the "objectively" established facts with the unique contributions of "internal materials" representing the "subjective-psychological world," expressed in human desires, motives, and goals. Only in the science of society, in which the

*Mikhailovskii's views on Marxist theory will be discussed in more detail in chapter 7.

investigating subject is simultaneously the object of inquiry, is there an imperative need for a harmonious blending of objective facts and subjective (psychological) interpretations.[31] Lavrov and Mikhailovskii do not deny the existence of an objective base of the social sciences, but they consistently emphasize that the unique feature of these disciplines, particularly sociology, is that they are made up of subjective interpretations of objective data.

To Lavrov and Mikhailovskii a sound sociological interpretation considers both social causation and social teleology.[32] Anticipating the subsequent trend in German sociology, it combines the methods of *Erklärung* and *Verstehen*. The principle of the complementarity of "causality" and "purposiveness" was sharply criticized by numerous representatives of various Russian sociological schools. The Marxists rejected "purposiveness" as totally incompatible with the very essence of the scientific mode of inquiry.[33] The neo-Kantian B. A. Kistiakovskii accepted the notion of "purposiveness" but criticized Lavrov's and Mikhailovskii's failure to explore more fully the methodological potentialities of "causality."[34] During the mystical phase of his philosophical odyssey, N. A. Berdiaev thought that "causality" should be completely ruled out of social studies; he also thought that all contemporary efforts to raise sociology to a scientific level were exercises in futility.[35] While Berdiaev and other representatives of revived idealism talked about transcendental purposiveness, about the goals of human action originating outside both nature and society, Lavrov and Mikhailovskii accepted only immanent purposiveness, the goals defined and interpreted by man. Their teleological view of society was part of a thoroughly antimetaphysical orientation.

The Populists also argued that sociological analysis, unlike physical or biological analysis, must recognize a complex interrelationship of theoretical and practical aspects of knowledge. In the natural sciences the differences between theoretical and practical branches can be easily recognized; in sociology the differences are not clear because human needs in specific social and historical situations are both the facts of theoretical inquiry and criteria for selecting theoretical truths to be applied in practical fields. In the social sciences, it is virtually impossible to draw a line between pure theory, guided by the inner logic of scientific development, and applied science, guided by the needs of society.

Moral appraisal occupied a preeminent position in Populist sociology. Mikhailovskii rejected Spencer's notion that sociology must be confined to the study of the laws of social change regardless whether this change meant progress or regress from the viewpoint of the investigator. Spencer wanted sociology to rise above all ethical questions and to treat social phenomena in the same way a scientist treats physical and chemical phenomena. Mikhailovskii, on his part, wanted sociology to concentrate on the developments which contributed to the material and spiritual betterment of human collectivities, and the method of natural science alone could not do this.[36] The subject-matter of sociology, according to Mikhailovskii, is covered by the double meaning of the Russian word *pravda*: "truth" and "justice." "Truth" denotes the objective aspect and "justice" the subjective aspect of the subject matter of sociology. While the natural sciences are concerned exclusively with "truth," sociology and the other social sciences deal also with "justice," that is, the moral side of social existence. Purposiveness of social action and value judgments are integral parts of subjective sociology.[37] According to Lavrov, sociology must be concerned with what is necessary, what is possible, and what is desirable for human society.[38] Mikhailovskii and Lavrov saw in subjective sociology a scientific weapon concerned not only with understanding the social world in which they lived but also with changing it.

The interpretation of present-day social relations from the vantage point of the ideals of a future society is the method of subjective sociology. "Whether we like it or not," wrote Lavrov, "the study of history requires a subjective evaluation; the historian must adopt an ideal corresponding to the level of his moral development and helping him place all facts in historical perspective."[39] Mikhailovskii stated: "Theory of progress must place the motley mass of historical facts in a historical perspective produced by ideals expressing what is desirable from the standpoint of the investigator."[40] All this gives subjective sociology an ingredient of "objectivity": it demands from all students of society as a historical category to state clearly and unequivocally their ideological biases.[41] Mikhailovskii argued that, although objective knowledge is indispensable, it must be constantly reexamined from a subjective point of view for the purpose of arriving at socially beneficial recommendations. When interpreted objectively, the law of the struggle for existence, he reasoned, may be found to be valid not only for natural evolution but also for social development. But only when interpreted subjectively and modified in the light of desirable goals, can it become a source of socially valuable guides.[42]

Lavrov and Mikhailovskii were "subjectivists," first, not because they denied the role of objective determinants but because their main concerns were the subjective dimensions of human social existence, and, second, because they believed that man has more power to modify the laws of society than he has to modify the laws of nature. Mikhailovskii defended this position by relying on the Comtian dictum that the more complex reality is, the more conducive it is to human control—and that society is infinitely more complex than nature. He readily admitted that man has always lived under the control of the laws of nature, which regulate "every hair that falls from his head" and "every stride that he takes in his daily life."[43] But he acknowledged that man has always acted as if he planned his own life and as if he pursued self-conceived goals, ideas, and ideals. He made it clear that in sociological inquiry the objective nature of "historical necessity" is less paramount than the subjective nature of the "illusion" of free choice in taste, aspiration, and interpretation of experience. "It is true," said Mikhailovskii, "that society, in its development, is subject to certain laws; but man's consciousness of his full choice of activity is equally true."[44]

Mikhailovskii thought that the history of modern social thought has oscillated between two approaches to social reality: at certain periods the objective, causal approach is dominant, while at other periods the primary emphasis is on a subjective, teleological, and moralistic view. Alluding to the survivals of Nihilist philosophy, burgeoning Marxism, and the scientistic bent of a strong wing of the intelligentsia, he claimed that contemporary Russia was overcommitted to a world view anchored in natural science. Eager to modify and combine the two views, he claimed that the sociologist is doing only a part of his job if he limits his study to the laws of causality and ignores purposiveness and extensive, though not limitless, reliance on the freedom of choice from among the alternatives provided by the society in which he lives. Lavrov summed it all up when he said as early as 1866: "The objective element in the domain of ethics, political science, and sociology, is confined to the activities of individuals, social forms, and historical events. These are open to objective description and classification. But in order to understand them it is imperative to examine the *goals* embodied in social forms as well as the *goals* elicited by historical events. What is the goal? It can best be described as something that is desirable, pleasant, obligatory. All these attributes are purely subjective."[45]

Subjective sociology, Mikhailovskii reasoned, had no real counterpart, for there was no truly objective sociology in the first place. He argued that scholars who tried to create an objective sociology depended on subjective judgments in the selection of natural science models for their theories. For example, the "objectivists" who turned to the Darwinian theory for help relied on subjective preferences in choosing from among many current interpretations of the scientific legacy of the great English naturalist. They inevitably absorbed many biological propositions of a purely hypothetical nature. They were victims of the fact that the Darwinian theory had raised a multitude of questions to which the community of biologists had responded with a multitude of answers, often of a "totally unexpected variety." He advised his readers to steer away from "simple explanations" of natural and social phenomena and to remember that only a few isolated scientific "doctrines" were true in every detail.[46]

Lavrov and Mikhailovskii knew that they had not succeeded in their efforts to make sociology a full-fledged science, but their faith in the possibility of a scientific study of society was unwavering. During the revolutionary phase of his career, Lavrov envisaged sociology as the queen of all sciences. Addressing himself to the "socialist revolutionaries," he stated in 1875: "A social revolution will bring about an alliance of science and society, because its goal is to transform society in accordance with the natural and immutable laws of sociology, to merge the vital personal aspirations with the conditions of social progress, to interpret everything essential from the vantage point of this progress, and to make sociology, as a part of social existence, the supreme science for which all other sciences perform auxiliary functions."[47] However, a quarter of a century later, Lavrov was ready to admit that sociology was still looking for sound scientific foundations and that, in order to become a science, it must work out the necessary logical and methodological procedures to distill the specific laws of social development from diffuse ethnographic data.[48] Since sociology was still an infant science, it could not offer much help to historians interested in unraveling the universal laws of social evolution.[49]

In his assessment of the future development of sociology, Mikhailovskii relied on a combination of the Comtian notion of the universal evolution of science and his own subjectivist views. He wrote in 1888:

> Psychology and particularly sociology are still far from having been fully formed. The lower sciences, that is, the sciences with subject-matters that are simpler than psychic and social life, are in command of an entire series of laws expressing constancies of causally linked combinations of phenomena. Psychology and sociology are extremely poor in this type of combination. These sciences have accumulated many facts but the mutual ties between these facts are too tenuous—and too controversial—to serve as a basis upon which the laws of coexistence and sequence could be constructed. Despite this, direct observation and the general evolution of science and the scientific world view convince us that here too causes and effects follow each other with the same inexorable consistency as in astronomy and chemistry. We do not know the laws of coexistence and sequence in psychic and social phenomena, but we know that such laws exist—that here too no external force can interfere with the predictability of the effects of known causes. This general idea, perhaps the most valuable of all the achievements of the human intellect, has spread with remarkable consistency ... beginning with the most general and simple phenomena of mathematical nature, where quite early so-called axioms were formulated, and ending with the most complex—psychological and sociological—phenomena, where even today we too often wander in the realm of uncertainty. The causes of the delayed development of psychology and sociology are, first, the extreme complexity of phenomena with which these sciences deal, and, second, the peculiar nature of these sciences in which the investigating subject is at the same time an object of inquiry and which, therefore, cannot disregard love and hatred, hope and despair, and human passions in general. However, it is beyond any doubt that in the future the conditions which have delayed the rise of higher sciences to a truly scientific level will be overcome in principle.[50]

The distinctive feature of sociology, according to Populist sociologists, is not merely that it is a science but that, as a science, it is an arm of socialist ideology. Sociology, science, and socialist ideology are parts of a general view of social action. This is stated with particular forcefulness in the writings of Lavrov, who, by virtue of his foreign residence, evaded the Russian censors. He wrote in his *From the History of Social Doctrines*:

> Real sociology is socialism. The theoretical study of social questions shows invariably the need for activities aimed at the transformation of society. It is impossible to understand the facts of social life without trying to give the course of that life a particular direction. He who limits himself to a mere understanding of facts shows by that very fact that he does not understand them. Social facts are in essence a sum total of individual contributions to the transformation of the structure of a society from what it is to what it ought to be.[51]

If the function of sociology is to bring about socialism, then the function of socialism is "to embrace all thought directed toward the enhancement of solidarity and cooperation among men and toward the elimination of exploitation of man by man."[52] Socialism strengthens social well-being by expanding the bonds of social unity. In its scientific form, it accomplishes its goals by rising above the routines of custom and "fantastic methods" of religion, by guaranteeing "a harmonious satisfaction" of all the "normal needs" of man, and by eradicating monopolistic institutions in the economy.

THE BASIC CONCEPTS OF SUBJECTIVE SOCIOLOGY

"The struggle for individuality" is the key concept of Populist sociology, particularly as seen by Mikhailovskii. Following Haeckel's notion of the six-rung ladder of individualities in the organic world—from the individualities of "cells" as the simplest forms of organic life to the individualities of "colonies" as the most complex forms of social life—he recognized a parallel ladder of individualities in social forms, from the personality, at the bottom, to the state, at the top. According to the law of organic evolution, the individualities of lower forms are limited by higher forms of which they are component parts. The organic theory of social evolution claims gradual engulfment of the individuality of lower forms of social groupings by higher forms; it disregards personality as a sociologically significant datum. Mikhailovskii's sociological theory is based on the notion of social evolution as a gradual strengthening, rather than weakening, of the element of individuality in persons and groups. According to Mikhailovskii: "I do not know what is the essence of the historical process ... but I know that I can capture the central thread which runs through, and helps explain, a large number of historical phenomena; this central thread is what I call the struggle for individuality."[53] His attention is focused on one type of individuality, that of the person. To him, the individual or the personality is neither a functional "organ" nor a structural "cell" of society; it is the essence of society, its moving force. The individual is not a mechanical product of society but a result of a harmonization of subjective individualities and objective social conditions. The origin of both the individual and society is in the human need for "spiritual communication" and in the selection of a number of individual and subjective "perceptions" as a common normative system.[54]

The term "individuality," as used by Mikhailovskii, has a cosmic and a sociological meaning. In the cosmic sense, it stands for every totality distinguished by the unity of its component parts and their subordination to the "whole." Universal evolution can best be understood as a continuous struggle between higher individualities and lower individualities; the former, according to Karl von Baer's law, are characterized by higher complexity in the makeup and interaction of component parts. Darwinian struggle for existence is but a ramification of the struggle for individuality. In the sociological sense, the "struggle for individuality" must not be equated with the struggle for diversity of individual types but with specific unities of values internalized by individuals at different stages of social evolution. Individuality means a challenge to anachronistic values: not a whimsical challenge by random persons but a systematic and concerted challenge by persons guided by the ideals of the future. Thus the struggle for individuality is the propelling force of social progress. The key of progress is provided by the notion of cooperation: every ascending stage of social evolution is characterized by a substitution of more advanced forms of cooperation for less advanced forms.[55]

As the common denominator of the basic forms of the division of labor in society, cooperation is the central conceptual tool of sociological theory. In "Darwin's Theory and Social Science," Mikhailovskii noted: "Our basic task is to determine, from the point of view of Darwin's theory, the interrelationship of the physiological division of labor, that is, the division of labor among the organs within the limits of an indivisible organism, and the economic division of labor, that is, the division of labor among the complete indivisible organisms within the limits of species, races, peoples, and societies. From our point of view, this task is the same as the search for the basic laws of cooperation, that is, the fundamental principles of social science."[56] To the question "What is Progress?" Mikhailovskii answered: "Progress is a gradual realization of the wholeness of indivisible organisms, of the ultimate maximum division of labor among organs and the ultimate minimum division of labor among men. Immoral, unjust, harmful, and irrational is everything that stands in the way of this development. Moral, just, rational, and useful is only that which reduces the heterogeneity of society and, at the same time, strengthens the diversity of its individual members."[57] This is the guiding idea of Mikhailovskii's sociology.

The emphasis on personality in sociology is only a special reflection of the more general emphasis on the individual in political ideologies that equated the conception of citizenship with democratic rights. Looking at this development from the vantage point of the twentieth century, Viktor Chernov noted: "In Russia, where the individual was fully engulfed by the family, the obshchina, and the state, the revolutionary *raznochinets* was driven to dream intensely about the rebirth and advancement of human individuality in all its ramifications. He was particularly obliged to dream about the destruction of all kinds of large and small obstacles in the form of social functions that suppress the individual and elevate themselves above him as self-fulfilling goals."[58] Pisarev, with his notion of "critical realists," and Lavrov, with his idea of "critically thinking individuals," were the first writers who tried to give a sociological formulation to the newly discovered ideals of individualism. Nozhin carried the same idea a little further by introducing the category of "total personality," the personality with a harmonious unity of internally generated goals and social ideals.[59]

According to Mikhailovskii, there are two major kinds of cooperation: simple cooperation which emphasizes social equality, common goals, and versatile development of individuals, and complex cooperation, which emphasizes social inequality, differential goals of various social segments (castes, estates, classes, professions, and related groups), and a strict technical specialization. While complex cooperation is based on "the division of labor in society," simple cooperation is based on "the division of labor among various organs" of the individual but not on the division of labor among the "whole" individuals as members of society. Complex cooperation does not recognize the physiological division of labor as the main law of the organization of labor in society. The organism progresses as a result of the increasing specialization of individual organs; society can progress only by an increasing realization of the "wholeness" (or nonspecialization) of the individual. Mikhailovskii agreed with Spencer's definition of progress as "the process of individualization," but he rejected the English scholar's definition of "the process of individualization" as a growing inter-dependence of individuals and groups, a product of increasing specialization in social labor. Through differential social valuation of labor and fragmenta-tion of social goals, complex cooperation leads to hierarchically organized societies, social strife, and asymmetrical development of personality; through equalitarian social evaluation of labor and unity of social goals, simple cooperation leads to democratically organized societies, social peace, and symmetrical development of personality. However, the Populist sociologists did not answer the question of the harmonization of the reality of accelerated technical development in modern society and the ideal of simple cooperation. Even their most dedicated followers admitted that their writing was more successful in unraveling the dehumanizing effects of modern technology than in presenting concrete plans for a society dominated by unfragmented humanity.[60] As a realist, Mikhailovskii was ready to concede that such a result of complex cooperation as the formation of "castes, classes, and parties," all expressing a fragmentation of solidarity within individual societies, was not likely to disappear in the foreseeable future. As a dreamer, however, he clung tenaciously to the traditional village commune, or obshchina, based on simple cooperation, as a social mechanism that, despite numerous anachronistic features, could alone lead Russia to a path bypassing capitalism, the most pathological form of complex cooperation.[61]

It was Mikhailovskii's personal background and social identification that led him to idealize simple cooperation as embodied in the versatility of the individual. A typical member of the intelligentsia, he was interested much more in the breadth than in the depth of knowledge. Indeed, he was a classic victim of the superficial education and nonprofessional orientation of the Russian intelligentsia. Instead of facing squarely the growing processes of the professionalization and specialization of skills in modern society, he retreated into the imaginary world of pristine simplicity. As a popularizer of modern ideas and as a champion of a critical approach to every authority, he contributed to the triumphs of the scientific world view in Russia; as a lay writer on themes that required high technical competence, he worked against a more rapid professionalization of scientific research in Russia.

In elaborating his notion of social progress, Mikhailovskii found it necessary to draw a line between the *type* of progress and the *degree* of progress. The type indicates the progress of a society on the scale of values that governs social relations and expresses the ideals of humanity. The degree denotes the level of techniques and institutional mechanisms available to a society in its struggle for existence. The type and the degree of progress do not necessarily go hand in hand: there are societies (typified by capitalism) in which a high degree of progress is matched by a low type of progress, and there are societies (represented by the obshchina-dominated part of Russian rural community) in which a high type of progress is matched by a low degree of progress. Since the type indicates the value orientation of a society, it is the true indicator of progress. In Mikhailovskii's logic of history, the societies based on the principles of obshchina communalism are closer to the ideal community of the future than are the capitalist societies of today. He was realistic enough, however, to admit that the values clustered around obshchina could assure a progressive development of society only if they did not stand in the way of modern technology. He appeared a romantic to his critics merely because he chose to write more about the values of obshchina than about the techniques of modern industrial societies. In his reasoning, the socialist polity of the future would be achieved in the West by a *revolutionary* destruction of dominant values; in Russia it would be achieved by *evolutionary* advances in the technological base of society. To avoid a materialistic bias, Mikhailovskii argued consistently that the type of progress was not dependent on the degree of progress, just as the latter is not dependent on the former.

Mikhailovskii's concept of cooperation was essentially indistinguishable from Lavrov's concept of solidarity. Social progress, according to Lavrov, is synonymous with the evolution of various forms of "solidarity of socially conscious individuals" as the key social force.[62] He defined the essential role of progress in history-writing:

> Without a formula of progress it is impossible to undertake a rational reconstruction of history. What should be made part of a historical study, and what should be ignored? What should stand on the first plane, and what on the second? What is the meaning of particular events and what is the historical importance of particular men? All these questions could be answered only on the basis of the historian's view of progress. If a historian has clearly understood the need for the idea of progress and has truly understood the meaning of progress then his work will make sense. . . . If he does not construct a conception of progress, he will rely on ephemeral views . . . [and] his work will have no scientific value.[63]

Every formula of progress must contain three elements: an expression of the intertwining of objective and subjective interpretations of social phenomena; a recognition of social ideals which show the possibility of progress; and an indication of the applicability of the idea of progress to all phases of history and to the general development of civilization.[64]

The formula of progress must point out the growth of solidarity as the most significant indicator of evolving humanity. Lavrov devoted much attention to the nature and dynamics of solidarity.[65] He considered solidarity a cosmic phenomenon that antedated the emergence of the human species, and he made extensive excursions into geography, cosmography, and biology to prove his point. Particularly interesting is his discussion of the instinctive solidarity that welds together the societies of ants and bees. In developing his arguments, he combined the claims of various deterministic schools in sociology, including the geographical, biological, and economic schools. By taking the assumptions of other schools as partial explanations of the origin and evolution of solidarity, he achieved a synthesis of current orientations which concentrated on the search for key causes of social change.

Lavrov's discussion of the evolution of solidarity is neither systematic nor lucid. It is clear, however, that he differentiated between three types of solidarity, each dominant in a special type of social formation. "Unconscious solidarity," or "solidarity based on custom," provides the principle of integration for the earliest forms of human society. "Affective solidarity" is characteristic for intermediate social formations. "Historical," or "conscious," solidarity is the basic attribute of modern societies.[66] In other words, the first form of solidarity is based on the sharing of habits, the second on the affinity of sentiments, and the third on the unity of convictions. The first is instinctive, the second affective, and the third intellectual. Intellectual, or conscious, solidarity, according to Lavrov, is the most potent tool of social progress. The motive force of conscious solidarity is critical thought—"the unity of convictions brought forth by the imperative needs of social development." The intellectual and moral progress of mankind "depends exclusively on critically thinking individuals."[67] Only the societies which are integrated along the lines of conscious solidarity and are guided by critically thinking persons—by the intelligentsia—deserve to be categorized as historical societies. Again, only the communities which have produced an intelligentsia, as the true carrier of critical thought, are historical societies. The intelligentsia becomes the prime mover of the "historical process" for it is responsible for the adaptations of old and the formation of new forms of social life. The study of the evolution of thought and of the emergence and vicissitudes of "critically thinking individuals" is the foundation of Lavrov's sociological edifice.

Behind social progress, the Populists saw a balanced interaction of "culture" and "critical thought," the former consolidating the established values and the latter giving birth to new values. Lavrov made the dichotomy clear and explicit:

> Everywhere and always, the *culture* of a society represents the medium in which the critical thought of the individual develops but which, left to itself, manifests a natural inclination toward stagnation, toward a solidification of habits and traditions .... In opposition to this inclination, the *thoughts* of the individual bring forth new ideals, expressed at first in beliefs and artistic creations and then in scientific criticism and full awareness of justice as the basis of morality. A study of the history of mankind is rational only inasmuch as it examines the role of thought in the process of cultural transformation. Great thoughts mark the great epochs in the life of mankind. A suppression of thought by cultural habits and traditions impedes the development of society and causes a stagnation, or even a decline, of civilization. A study of the *history of civilization*, in its rational essence, must show the formation of cultures under the influence of social laws, historical conditions, and the thoughts of individuals; it must show the critical thought as both a product of each new culture and the motive force of cultural transformation.[68]

The term "intelligentsia," for "critically thinking individuals," has a distinct Russian meaning. Mikhailovskii showed no sympathy for the Russian writers who argued that this term was unacceptable for the simple reason that it had no equivalent in the West. He resented the fact that among these writers there were many who in all other respects were staunch defenders of the idea of Russia's cultural uniqueness. In any case, Mikhailovskii contended, "in the very existence of this term, which does not sound very sonorous to the Russian ear, there is something partly comforting, partly lamentable, and, in any case, peculiar to the character of Russian history."[69] He made it clear that he "did not have anything in common with the members of the intelligentsia, who, out of misunderstanding, serve pure science and pure art, and who preach abstract wealth and abstract justice."[70] He also noted that he had nothing in common with "the representatives of science, art, journalism, and practical activities," who, without any misunderstanding, serve "the hazy image of the emerging Russian bourgeoisie." In the West, he said, there was no need for the term "intelligentsia" for there the intellectuals were at first inextricably woven into the bourgeoisie which gave them what they needed most: the universal freedom of thought and expression.[71] Subsequently, large segments of alienated intellectuals identified themselves with the "fourth estate" rather than with the bourgeoisie, but they did not fit the term "intelligentsia" because they were bourgeois in origin and habit. The Russian intellectuals, Mikhailovskii contended, have learned from history that the bourgeoisie and the intellectuals work at cross purposes and that the earlier freedoms given to the intellectuals by the Western bourgeoisie were "accidental" rather than "substantive." The Russian intelligentsia, as defined by Mikhailovskii, included the men of knowledge who wanted no alliance with the burgeoning bourgeoisie. The intelligentsia was neither a social class nor an estate engaged in a war with other classes and estates; it was a special group crossing the boundaries of individual classes and creating multiple bonds of solidarity. In the context of Populist ideology, the intelligentsia was the avant garde of a new society free of class antagonism and blending individualism and collectivism, democracy and socialism. It was the bastion and the source of "critically thinking individuals," the true architects of social progress.

Populist sociology is built upon the notion of social solidarity or cooperation as the primary factor of social stability and cohesion and upon the notion of the progressive affirmation of individuality as the primary factor of social change. "Solidarity" and "individuality," as they work in social life, are interdependent: the gradually expanding solidarity or cooperation leads to a more versatile expression of individuality, and the growing individuality opens new avenues of solidarity and cooperation. Personality is a product of society, but the social progress is directly contingent on the degree to which a society allows the individual to introduce subjective modifications into the objective rules of behavior. Lavrov is particularly clear on the interaction of society and the individual:

Society apart from individuals has no real content. The interests of the individual, clearly understood, demand that he strive to fulfill the common interests; social goals can be achieved exclusively in individuals. Thus a true social theory requires not the subordination of the social element to the individual and not the absorption of the individual by society but the *fusion* of social and particular interests. The individual must cultivate an understanding of *social* interests, which are also *his* interests. He must direct his activity toward bringing truth and justice into social institutions, because this is not some kind of abstract aspiration but is *his* most intimate personal interest. At this level individualism becomes the realization of the general welfare through individual strivings—but the general welfare simply cannot be realized in any other way. Sociality becomes the realization of individual goals within social life—but they simply cannot be realized in any other context.[72]

The notions of "the unity of individualism and socialism" and of the intelligentsia as the chief architect of this unity occupy a prominent position in the sociological theories of Lavrov and Mikhailovskii.[73] However, most followers of the Lavrov-Mikhailovskii sociological legacy belonged either to the group that placed the primary emphasis on "individualism" or to the group preoccupied with "socialism."[74]

Despite their consistent emphasis on cooperation as the moving force of social development, the Populist sociologists recognized the vital historical role of conflict between society and the individual. According to Mikhailovskii, modern society, with its increasing specialization, tends to atrophy the humanistic base of personality; the individual, in turn, resists specialization and seeks to widen the humanistic base of society. Certain structural principles of a social system work in favor of the individual, others against him. The English political system works in favor of the individual; the English economic system works against the individual.[75] A society may declare war on persons with high moral standards and intellectual resourcefulness when they do not fit the pattern of social expectations. In the ideological "nonconformity" of critical individuals Mikhailovskii saw the main source of social progress. In Lavrov's words: "As a critically thinking person, man becomes an enemy of social stagnation, an organ of social reforms and upheavals, a worker for the cause of progress, and a factor of history."[76] Societies are involved in the continuous struggle for survival in which "artificial selection,'" rather than natural selection, is of primary significance.[77] The trademark of artificial selection is that it favors the feeble conformist over the strong nonconformist. Progress is possible only because no society can prevent the emergence of nonconformists, who, in challenging the values of the social system under which they live, are guided by a dedication to the higher ideals of humanity.

The constant presence of nonconformists makes it impossible for human society to become an organism, working through the full union of its intertwined parts. Social progress is possible because of the presence of social forces standing in the way of a full internalization of dominant values by individual members of society. Nonconformists responsible for progress are not individuals guided by idiosyncratic personality traits resisting every influence of institutionalized rules of behavior; they are individuals guided by common values embodied in an ideal society of the future. "Individuality," in Mikhailovskii's theory, denotes a special type of conformity: a conformity to the values which represent social progress. It is a new and higher expression of social adaptation. To Mikhailovskii, the key to "individuality" must be sought not in unique (unshared) but in general (shared) personality traits. To emphasize "individuality" means to emphasize the sanctioned values of a future society, occupying a higher position on the scale of evolution. This was one of the basic reasons why Berdiaev accused Mikhailovskii of having limited his conception of personality to purely biological, that is, most general attributes.[78]

Lavrov noted that history is replete with examples of antagonism between the established forms of social solidarity and the emerging critical attitudes and nonconformist motivations of individuals. Progress, therefore, is not continuous: a society progresses only during the historical periods of essential harmony of established social forms and the cognitive and affective needs of individuals. A society ceases to progress either when the established social order drastically limits the development of personality, or when the emerging ranks of "critically thinking individuals" undermine the very basis of social solidarity. Although Lavrov and Mikhailovskii viewed progress as evolutionary, they did not rule out revolutions as instruments of socioeconomic advance. Lavrov stated explicitly that, despite the enormous suffering they engender, revolutions are the only—even though regrettable—instruments of progress in societies in which the established order imposes strangulating limitations on the intellectual and moral development of individuals.[79]

Mikhailovskii made several excursions into "mass psychology" in search of the types of behavior resulting from social conditions inimical to the development of individuality.[80] He examined hypnotism, somnabulism, "natural magnetism," "psychic epidemics," and many other forms of "psycho-pathological" phenomena which show that a heavy concentration of human attention on a relatively small number of activities, and the accompanying monotony of repetitive impressions, render a person partially or totally incapable of governing his actions and an easy prey to control by other persons or things.[81] In these situations the individual becomes an "automaton" depending exclusively on imitation as a result of a full loss of capacity for independent, individual creativeness. What is true of pathological cases, he said, may be even more true of healthy individuals whose life and work require concentration on a narrow scope of activities producing limited experience; the inescapable results of these limitations are a loss of self-initiative and a total subordination to external controls. The pathological attributes of hypnotism and somnabulism are thus viewed as prototypes of behavior engendered by specialization, which is the trademark of capitalist economy. Although Lavrov wrote little about psychology, he was ready to acknowledge the growing importance of this discipline in the family of social sciences. He noted that a study of "psychological questions constitutes one of the scientific needs of our age" and that psychology, when fully established, stands to become one of the basic branches of knowledge, built upon the natural sciences. The time will come, he said, when psychology will provide the foundations for jurisprudence, sociology, and history.[82] Mikhailovskii was among the pioneers in the sociology of alienation in modern society. The academic community, represented brilliantly by Ivan Sechenov and Ivan Pavlov, concentrated on the study of the neurophysiological (biological) basis of personality; the Populist intelligentsia, represented by Lavrov and Mikhailovskii, concentrated on the sociocultural basis of personality.

There were many differences—some basic but mostly minor—between the sociological theories of Lavrov and Mikhailovskii. Mikhailovskii was a political realist: his writings were critical assessments of current political events and developments. Even his most general essays were directly related to the practical problems of social existence. Lavrov, on the other hand, was an abstract thinker: his most noted studies were logical deductions from general principles that assumed the power of mathematical axioms.[83] Mikhailovskii's idea of progress, with its emphasis on simple cooperation, could be interpreted as a call for a return to an earlier stage of social evolution and for the elimination of entire branches of science and technology not accessible to *all* persons. Lavrov, on the other hand, envisaged progress as constant additions to knowledge through the inventive power of gifted individuals and the diffusion of new ideas among the increasing numbers of people. Mikhailovskii treated the growing specialization and the development of harmonious personality as mutually exclusive processes; Lavrov considered them as complementary. Every society, according to Lavrov, is an arena of two processes: one leading to the development of values and cultural attributes of humanity as a whole, and the second leading to the cultivation of socially useful specialties congruent but not identical with the common denominators of humanity.[84]

These differences between the social theories, world outlooks, and temperaments of Lavrov and Mikhailovskii would make a challenging and enormously profitable topic of a special study of the most intricate and subtle variations in the thinking of the Populist intelligentsia during the 1870s and 1880s. However, these differences are not as sharp as they may appear at a first reading of Lavrov's and Mikhailovskii's sociological studies. Mikhailovskii was not really an advocate of the return to a golden age of the past: he envisaged a new society as a higher synthesis of the communalism of the past and the individualism induced by professional specialization of the present era. He did not reject the technical division of labor in which various participants in the process of production performed specific functions; what he rejected categorically was the social division of labor, or "complex cooperation," in which various social groups occupied unequal positions.[85] Mikhailovskii and Lavrov were in full agreement in their scrupulous efforts to unravel the organic ties between sociology and psychology—not the psychology grounded in the neurophysiological basis of human behavior but the psychology concerned with the interaction of society and personality. They shared almost identical views on the scientific nature of sociology as a discipline unfettered by natural science models. Lavrov was correct when he asserted that he and Mikhailovskii often used different words to express identical ideas. He said that his view on "the development of critical thought and science" as the primary source of progress in modern society was fully contained in Mikhailovskii's definition of progress as "the maximum physiological division of labor among various organs"—as the evolving versatility of the individual.[86] Their definitions of sociology are identical. The primary goal of sociology, according to Lavrov, is to help inaugurate "a new social system that would satisfy the natural and other vital needs of a people."[87] Operating within the same Fourierian framework, Mikhailovskii stated that "the basic task of sociology is to point out the social conditions satisfying the needs of human nature." Their general theoretical orientations are no less similar. R. V. Ivanov-Razumnik noted in his *History of Russian Social Thought*: "Lavrov was the first leader of our old Populism to approach the problem of individualism from a theoretical-sociological point of view, and in this respect he was the most direct predecessor of Mikhailovskii. In their views on the problems of individualism, Lavrov and Mikhailovskii did not always see eye to eye, and on occasion took opposite sides; however, they espoused a view which united supreme individualism and unconditional sociality—the most typical attributes of the Populism of the 1870s."[88] N. S. Rusanov noted that, although Lavrov came to social theory from ethics and Mikhailovskii from biology (under the influence of Nozhin), they were firmly united by their views on the individual as the basic concept of sociology and the essential component of the world outlook of the Populist intelligentsia.[89]

Having lived in Russia, under constant police surveillance, Mikhailovskii found it advisable and practical to give a minimum exposure to his adherence to socialist ideals; having lived among the Russian exiles in Western Europe, imbued with a revolutionary spirit, Lavrov found it necessary not only to give a prominent display to his socialist ideals but also to place them in a revolutionary cast. But, in reaiity, the two men were moderate socialists supporting their ideological views by almost identical social theories. Both were much more socialist than revolutionary.

Lavrov and Mikhailovskii were also united in their efforts to anchor sociology in the phenomenology of Kant's *Critique of Pure Reason* and in the ethicism of Kant's *Critique of Practical Reason*; but both were also firmly convinced that a synthesis of two Kantian traditions should be effected within the framework of science and a union of epistemological and historical relativism. They were among the most distinguished forerunners of both the Marburg and Baden schools of neo-Kantian philosophy. They were impeccable fighters in the bitter battle to emancipate sociology from metaphysical dogmatism and improvisation. Although both recognized the work of multiple causation in social change, they were strongly inclined to regard the growth of secular wisdom as the prime mover of progress. Both dreamed of a future society in which the elite positions would be occupied not by a predatory class of economic exploiters but by the enlightened intelligentsia who are at once the guiding force of social evolution and the true representatives of the aspirations and moral ideals of total society. The social theories of both men bear unmistakeable imprints of utopianism. However, utopianism was not a unique feature of their sociology: their theory of social change was neither more nor less utopian than that of Comte, Spencer, and Marx, the stalwarts of nineteenth-century sociological thought.

When examined from a modern vantage point, many theoretical ideas of Lavrov and Mikhailovskii appear rather naive, and many of their expectations and fervent hopes have been refuted by modern history. R. V. Ivanov-Razumnik's judgment that Mikhailovskii was as weak in the analysis of the *depth* of personality as he was strong in the analysis of the *scope* of personality applied equally to Lavrov. Yet many of their ideas have retained innovative vigor and challenging relevance. Their idea that social evolution and social progress are not identical is still very much alive, as is their claim that sociology will be off the mark as long as it apes the concepts and methods of physics and biology and does not develop research techniques and conceptual tools to handle the external conditions of social existence as well as the inner motivations, drives, and goals of the individual.

Modern developments have validated Mikhailovskii's and Lavrov's sociology of alienation—their fear of the growing disharmony between technological specialization and the higher values of humanity. Their view that society and personality each follows its own inner logic of development and that only societies which bring these two developments into harmony are assured of progress is the central topic of several modern currents in philosophy, social psychology, cultural anthropology, and the theory of art. The identification of sociology and ideology, which they accepted without the least reservation, is still the major dilemma of sociological theory.

The Populist arguments against the notion of capitalism as a universal stage of social development provide important insights into the acute dilemmas of underdeveloped countries caught in the process of accelerated technological and political modernization, often in conflict with traditional institutions and cultural values. Walicki noted correctly that there was nothing surprising in the fact that "it was the Russian Populists who were the first to postulate the non-capitalist industrialization of the backward countries—after all, Russia had embarked on industrialization much later and was more backward than other of the Great European countries and, thus, had to carry it out in conditions strikingly different from the classical pattern."[90] Populist theory allows for the existence not only of noncapitalist economies in modern society but also of unique economic systems as blends of capitalist institutions and national traditions in economic relations.

THE SOCIOLOGY OF SCIENCE

Populist sociologists recognized science as the most formidable tool in modern man's inexorable drive to conquer nature and to eradicate ignorance. They rejected both the Slavophile view of science as a Western phenomenon that is essentially alien to the spirit of Russian culture and the Nihilist view of it as the mainspring of social dynamics.

Mikhailovskii argued that the Nihilists and their Western European teachers erred in making science the primary source of social progress and in identifying the evolution of science with the evolution of political and social democracy. He criticized H. T. Buckle's assertion, fully accepted by the Nihilists, that moral precepts are stationary and that therefore "the role of the moral element in the gradual development of civilization is negligible."[91] No doubt, Mikhailovskii did not forget Pisarev's bold assertion that modern education should ignore moral indoctrination, for morality is steeped in the petrified past, and instead should strongly emphasize science, which alone opens fresh vistas for continuous and irreversible progress. Mikhailovskii found it expedient to present his readers with a Russian translation of a passage critical of Buckle's position from Friedrich Lange's *History of Materialism:*

If it is shown that certain elementary principles of morality have not essentially changed from the days when the Indian Vedas were composed until now, we may simply point to the elementary principles of logic, which have likewise remained unchanged. We might indeed maintain that the fundamental laws of knowledge have remained the same from time immemorial, and that the fuller application of them in modern times is to be ascribed to essentially *moral* grounds. It was, in fact, *moral* qualities which led the ancients to think freely and independently, but to content themselves with a certain amount of knowledge, and to lay more stress on the perfection of individuality than on one-sided advancement of knowledge. It was the *moral* characteristic of the Middle Ages to form authorities, to obey authorities, and to limit free inquiry by traditional formulas. The self-abnegation and determination with which, at the beginning of the modern epoch, Copernicus, Gilbert, and Harvey, Kepler and Vesalius pursued their aims, were moral in their nature.... In truth, neither is intellectual progress essentially a result of moral progress, nor the converse; but both spring from the same root, absorption in the object, the loving comprehension of the whole phenomenal world of the natural inclination to shape it harmoniously.[92]

By translating Lange's arguments into his own sociological terminology, Mikhailovskii asserted that Buckle was guilty of separating the objective *pravda*-truth from the subjective *pravda*-justice and of negating the basic conditions for the harmonious development of the individual and society. Specifically, Buckle had failed to recognize that the work of the scientist is deeply embedded in a complex system of moral relations, a phenomenon which is particularly obvious in the work of the social scientist. The scientist qua scientist must meet certain moral standards called for by the ethos of science, the rules of the, game tacitly agreed upon by the scientific community. Mikhailovskii calls these rules personal morality, morality engendered by the scientific community. In addition, however, the scientist assumes moral obligations imposed upon him by the world outside science. Mikhailovskii terms these obligations social morality or political morality, which he views as an embodiment of social ideals. He rejects the theory that, by the very nature of their work, the scientists conform automatically to the rules of social morality: scientists who violate the ethical code of their society do so consciously or unconsciously. Scientists who violate social morality consciously are also the violators of personal morality; scientists who violate social morality unconsciously are not necessarily violators of personal morality. Marx, in Mikhailovskii's opinion, met the high standards of personal morality even though he unconsciously violated social morality. Mikhailovskii thought that Marx was a man of intensive and exemplary dedication to scholarship; but he considered Marx's theory of class struggle an unconscious deviation from the higher values of humanity. It is irrelevant here whether Mikhailovskii's appraisal of Marx was justified or not; what is relevant is his firm conviction that science and morality are tightly interlaced and that the evolution of one cannot be clearly separated from the evolution of the other. Mikhailovskii and Lavrov made it clear that, in order to enrich his discipline, a scientist must combine intellectual resourcefulness and accomplishment with high standards of morality.

A major criticism which Mikhailovskii directed at Buckle and his followers among Russian Nihilists dealt with the relationship of science to democracy. Buckle had noted the great interest in science in France on the eve of the French Revolution and had assumed that the two were causally related—that scientific thought had stimulated the growth of revolutionary forces committed to democratic ideals. "The lectures of chemists, of geologists, of mineralogists, and of physiologists, were attended by those who came to wonder, as well as by those who came to learn. In Paris, the scientific assemblages were crowded to overflowing. The halls and amphitheaters in which the great truths of nature were expounded, were no longer able to hold their audience, and in several instances it was found necessary to enlarge them. . . . The highest and most durable of all pleasures, the pleasure caused by the reception of fresh truths, was now a great link, which banded together those social elements that were formerly wrapped up in the pride of their own isolation."[93] By bringing all classes together, "the hall of science" became "the temple of democracy." "Those who come to learn confess their own ignorance, abrogate in some degree their own superiority, and begin to perceive that the greatness of men has no connection with the splendor of their titles . . . but that it depends on the largeness of their minds, the powers of their intellect, and the fullness of their knowledge."[94]

Mikhailovskii acknowledged an important kernel of truth in Buckle's assertion that the intensified interest in natural science in France had stimulated the growth of democratic revolutionary forces. First, by undermining the authority of the church, the sciences had undermined feudal institutions and thus indirectly helped the cause of liberty and equality. Second, the natural sciences had shown that social inequality had no basis in nature but was a historical phenomenon that could be changed by concerted human action. Third, by modernizing technology, science had brought about the rise of an industrial class, which fought for liberty and equality in order to abolish the social superiority of the landed aristocracy.[95]

Mikhailovskii remarked that the lectures of German idealistic philosophers, religious preachers, and scholastic thinkers had also attracted people from all social strata, eager to satisfy their intellectual curiosity and to widen their intellectual horizons. He wondered how Buckle would have explained the connection between these lectures and democratic ideals. Or, how Buckle would have handled Professor N. A. Liubimov, who taught physics at Moscow University (and thus allegedly helped the cause of democracy) and at the same time published reactionary articles in the *Russian Messenger* and *Moscow News*.[96] Or, how he would have interpreted the widespread contemporary efforts to give natural science support to the theories of the biological and psychological inferiority of women and black people.[97] His view was that whether the scientific discoveries and investigations could contribute to the strengthening of democratic principles depended on the structure of individual societies.[98] In other words, natural science was likely to help the democratic process only in countries that already had strong democratic elements or were receptive to democratic values. Mikhailovskii did not deny that democracy creates favorable conditions for the growth of science; however, he was not at all sure that science by itself would make a society democratic. This did not prevent him from viewing science, in contrast to metaphysics, as a mode of inquiry and an organization of human thought governed by democratic principles.

Mikhailovskii also warned that a scientific idea may strengthen democratic principles in some respects and weaken them in others. Darwinism, for example, was democratic in that it strengthened the arguments against feudalism, and antidemocratic in that it justified class struggle. Technology leads to man's increased control over nature, but it may also lead to chronic and discriminatory unemployment. The benefits that the common man receives from science may be offset by the ruthless techniques of economic exploitation by the bourgeoisie.[99] Mikhailovskii was also convinced that on occasion natural science may translate an undemocratic social view into a law of nature: Darwinism, to give a concrete example, is a "biological doctrine" but its origin is mainly in "the moral and political conditions of contemporary Europe." When these conditions improve, and Mikhailovskii seemed optimistic that they would improve, the struggle for existence would be thrown out of both biology and sociology and relegated to the archives.[100] Darwin's notion of the struggle for existence is a sociological categorization of capitalist social values translated into a universal law of organic evolution. Mikhailovskii may have selected the wrong illustration, but his view that, in their choice of topics and interpretations, the sciences are not immune to ideological influences cannot be ignored.

In his discussion of the reciprocal relations between democracy and science, Mikhailovskii was fully aware of the fact that the attitude toward science marked one of the basic differences between Russian liberals and conservatives. "The program of the people labeled 'conservatives' includes, among other things, a hatred for democratic ideals and a fear of the harmful influences of science." On the other hand, "the program of people labeled 'liberals' includes an admiration for both the natural sciences and democratic ideals."[101] Most contemporaries would have agreed with Mikhailovskii.

Most contemporaries would have agreed also with Lavrov's contention that, in order to comprehend the real sociological meaning of science, it is imperative to recognize that science is much more than an acquisition and accumulation of verifiable knowledge—that, above everything else, it is a world view. In addition to bettering the material welfare of society, it emancipates the human mind from superstition and mystical belief, it encourages critical thought and a rational use of intellectual energy, it constantly challenges authority in the domains of both sacred and secular wisdom, and it clarifies the prospects and perspectives of social progress. Lavrov criticized the Nihilist popularizers of science who were content merely with the writing of long essays on specialized scientific topics in vogue and who overlooked the deeper meaning of science as a force for social and moral integration. He was also critical of the Nihilist claim that natural science alone is the source of social progress and that the social sciences are intellectually sound and socially beneficial only inasmuch as they are mere extensions of the natural sciences. The Nihilists had committed a philosophical and a sociological error. Philosophically, they had failed to recognize the unique features of social reality: while the natural sciences deal with the forces which are transformable but are not accumulative, sociology deals with the forces which are both transformable and accumulative.[102] Sociologically, the dogmatic treatment of sociology as a natural science misdirects the scientific study of society, cripples sociology as a source of wisdom on the nature of social reality, and, in general, introduces all sorts of unrealistic notions into the assessment of social evolution. In Mikhailovskii's terminology, it opens the doors for a misleading identification of "social idols" and "social ideals." In brief, "the facts supplied by the natural sciences cannot serve as the exclusive guides to persons consciously engaged in social activity."[103] As a source of social wisdom and social activity, the much-heralded "realism" of the Nihilist writers was doomed to failure, for it was blinded by a strong natural science bias that ignored the moral dimension of social reality. The naive scientism of Pisarev and the arrogant antiscientific crusade of M. N. Katkov, the spokesman for archconservatism, were jointly responsible for the fact that in the epoch of the Great Reforms science did not play a social role commensurate with its intellectual resources and the demands of modern culture.

Lavrov had reasoned that professional scientists had failed to contribute to a firmer and broader interaction of science and society. Concentrating on constantly narrowing specialties, the scientists—even the greatest ones—had withdrawn into the isolation of their ivory towers, failing to grasp not only the intellectual but also the social power of science. Lavrov noted the caste-like attributes of modern scientists as a new aristocracy with a cultivated unconcern for the acute problems of social existence. Most scientists are prisoners of their narrowly conceived roles that isolate them from the corporate body of science as a cultural subsystem and from the society at large. Excessive specialization, reinforced by the dedication to "pure science," frustrates all efforts to rally scientists to a higher responsibility for human values and ideals. Science is a rigorous method of measurement and inquiry but it is also a historical process of vital social importance. Without the full understanding of the latter, the scientist is a technician without the social consciousness indispensable for making science a true instrument of humanity. In Mikhailovskii's terminology, excessive scientific specialization prevents the realization of the "internal unity" of the scientist's personality: the scientist as a specialist "is not a man but an organ, a part of man."[104] Despite this warning, Mikhailovskii's view of the future of science was generally optimistic. He was encouraged by the fact that the great men of modern science, typified by Darwin, von Helmholtz, Virchow, and Berthelot, were not strict specialists but versatile and daring scholars combining intellects of the highest order with deep social consciousness.[105] The thesis that the greatest discoveries in modern science were made by men of broad interdisciplinary competence has received empirical verification in the work of Robert K. Merton.

Despite their extensive criticism of the scientific community, Lavrov and Mikhailovskii were only too eager to emphasize the growing social consciousness of modern science. They reasoned that in order to render a maximum service to his community, the scientist must, above everything else, adhere not only to the established standards of scientific inquiry but also to the higher ideals of humanity. The scientist must never forget that in addition to a scientific view of morality there is also a moral view of science—and that the two must be fully integrated. The scientist must work for both the *pravda*-truth and the *pravda*-justice.[106]

THE INFLUENCE OF POPULIST SOCIOLOGY

One of the basic contributions of subjective sociologists was in providing the first systematic and critical survey of modern Western sociology in the Russian language. Lavrov and Mikhailovskii brought to Russia both the Western European pioneering ideas on the scientific foundations of sociology and a logically integrated and philosophically erudite criticism of these ideas. Lavrov was the first Russian to undertake a detailed examination of the sociological legacy of Auguste Comte; Mikhailovskii made the name of Herbert Spencer a household word in the Russian intellectual community, and he was among the first serious reviewers and interpreters of the Russian translation of Marx's *Capital*. In particular, the work of Mikhailovskii was a measured and meticulously executed criticism of four major sociological orientations of the time: the Spencerian theory, which treated human society as an organism and which viewed the evolution of human society as an extension of biological evolution; the Darwinian theory—as applied by Benjamin Kidd and the Social Darwinists—according to which the struggle for survival is the vehicle of social progress; the Marxist theory, which had little use for the individual as the nucleus of society and which saw in class struggle the propelling force of human history; and the Durkheimian theory, which treated the grand evolution of human society as a gradual transformation of "mechanical solidarity" into "organic solidarity," based on the growing heterogeneity in the division of labor in society.

However, the contributions of Mikhailovskii and Lavrov go far beyond the dissemination and critical appraisal of modern sociological thought. They made sociology part of an essentially democratic ideology which opposed both the stationary view of society as built into tsarist ideology and the revolutionary view of society that was the essential component of Nihilist and Marxian ideological commitments and that emphasized not the divisive attributes of social classes and estates but the integrative functions of "the people." Again, it was their primary ideological and sociological interest in "the people" that led them to consider the peasant—who made up 85 percent of the Russian population—the basic topic of both political and scientific debate. According to Lavrov, sociology must study the progressive evolution of individual cognition and the corresponding advancement in social solidarity; social solidarity, in turn, must be studied as both an existing historical reality and a blueprint for the great society of the future.

The view of the peasantry as both the base of society and the quintessence of the polity led Mikhailovskii to a frontal attack on capitalism in Russia. His interpretation of capitalism was simple and straightforward: technological specialization, the motive force of capitalism, leads to social differentiation; social differentiation leads to class stratification; class stratification leads to class warfare; and class warfare leads to the perpetuation and consolidation of excessively powerful political authority and controls. His fight for the "wholeness" of personality was the most essential part of his relentless war against incipient capitalism in Russia.

Mikhailovskii saw only one solution for Russian society: the reorganization of social life on the model of the traditional rural community (obshchina) uncorrupted, so he assumed, by the division of labor and unmolested by "external" controls over the life and work of individuals. He failed to explain how he would have stopped the wheels of industrialization in Russia or how he would have revived the moribund obshchina. The communal senti-mentality of the ideologists of Populism was one of the basic reasons for the rapid decline of the classical Populist subjective sociology during the last decade of the nineteenth century—the decade, by the way, of the first serious industrial conflict in Russia.

The influence of Populist sociology on the Russian intelligentsia was of gigantic proportions. According to Viktor Chernov, Populist sociology satisfied the basic intellectual needs of Russia for a this-worldly philosophy which was simultaneously a philosophy of reality and a philosophy of action. He added:

> The sociological doctrine, which in the minds of all Russians is indis-solubly linked with the names of P. Mirtov [P. L. Lavrov] and N. K. Mikhailovskii, reigned supreme over the minds and hearts of several generations of the most active Russian intelligentsia ... because it appeared as an integrated and complete system satisfying both the theoretical and practical needs of its adherents. It was an edifice chiseled out of a single piece of granite. This determined the attitude of the reading public toward it. It was either completely accepted or completely rejected. The blending of the real and the ideal, the objective and the subjective, and the theoretical and the practical—this was the bond that held together the entire architecture of this system from the most general and abstract propositions to the simplest and most concrete statements.[107]

No Russian sociological orientation was more popular during the 1870s and 1880s than Populist sociology; it is equally true that during the 1890s and the first two decades of the twentieth century no Russian social theory was attacked more widely and with more bitterness than Populist sociology. The Russian pioneers of Marxist theory considered the attack on the Mikhailovskii legacy the order of the day. They did not like the Populist emphasis on the individual as both the product and the creator of society and history, and they left no stone unturned in their crusade against the communal romanticism built into the Populist social thought. N. A. Berdiaev, at the midpoint of his journey from Marxism to mysticism, called Mikhailovskii's sociology a misguided concoction of naive metaphysics and undigested epistemology; he attributed some historical value to sociological subjectivism but was glad that it was dead.[108] Petr Struve, after he had completed his journey through Marxist waters, found a common denominator for subjective sociology and Marxism in the form of "relativistic positivism," a "philosophical world view" whose basis is belief in "the relativism of both truth and ethical percepts."[109] When Berdiaev entered the world of mystical metaphysics, the last province of his intellectual odyssey, he saw in Mikhailovskii's brand of Populism a degenerate social philosophy characterized by "provincialism," "paganism," "anarchism," and "pseudo-*sobornost*'" and by a worship of the Russian people as a "quantity" rather than as a "mystical unity" forged during a millennium.[110] He was disturbed by Mikhailovskii's dedication to democracy, which prefers the voice of the majority to the wisdom of the chosen minority. P. I. Novgorodtsev, a modern exponent of natural law who was more enamored with Kant's *Critique of Practical Reason* than with his *Critique of Pure Reason*, thought that Mikhailovskii blundered in trying to combine the ethical and scientific inquiries in the first place.[111] The "ethical element," he argued, could be treated by moral philosophy, not by science, whether it be "objective" or "subjective" sociology. The neo-Kantian sociologist B. A. Kistiakovskii, in his contribution to the *Problems of Idealism* (1902), criticized the Russian sociological school as a pseudo-scientific endeavor guilty of sacrificing the causal "necessity" of the social process to the romantic dreams of purposive "desirability" as expressed in the ideals of a political ideology. In a perceptive review of Lavrov's *Problems of Understanding History*, M. Filippov pointed out that subjective sociology suffered from a strong aristocratic bias which divided mankind into two entities: an extremely small group of active participants in history and a huge conglomeration of individuals and "entire tribes" unable to rise above a passive adaptation to the environment.[112] Filippov also noted that while Mikhailovskii and Kareev were inclined to identify "subjectivism" with "individualism," Lavrov—in his later work—widened the concept of subjectivism so much that it ceased to be essentially "individualistic."[113]

During the 1890s a swift diffusion in Russia of the ideas of the French sociologist Emile Durkheim encouraged a critical reexamination of the basic postulates of Populist sociology. Durkheim's sociology, at this time, was dominated by three general ideas. In the first place, it was based on the concept of society as a reality sui generis, that is, on the idea of the irreducibility of "collective representations" (or group behavior) to "individual representations" (or individual behavior). In Durkheim's sociology, personality is not an essential factor of sociological inquiry. In the second place, Durkheim contended that "moral reality" could be approached from two different points of view: one concentrating on the "understanding" and the other on the "evaluating" of moral norms. If sociology was to become a science, it must limit its study to "understanding" morality—to a systematic search for a full explanation of moral rules, and must leave evaluation to moral philosophers. Sociology must be free of value judgments. In the third place, Durkheim identified social evolution as a gradual substitution of "organic solidarity," based on a constantly growing differentiation of labor in society, for "mechanical solidarity," based on a minimum division of labor in society. Translated into Mikhailovskii's terminology, Durkheim viewed social evolution as a gradual but universal transition from "simple cooperation" to "complex cooperation."

Mikhailovskii endorsed Durkheim's view that social research would be total waste if it stayed within the limits of "speculation" without any regard for practical usefulness. He also liked Durkheim's claim that all that is "inevitable" is not necessarily "moral." He gave credit to Durkheim for his willingness to treat moral reality both objectively, as "causally related phenomena," and subjectively, as action guides related to certain basic social and political principles.[114] He appreciated Durkheim's admission that the growing division of labor posed a moral dilemma of large magnitude. Durkheim asked the same question that troubled Mikhailovskii: "Is the division of labor, at the same time that it is a law of nature, also a moral rule of human conduct and, if it has this latter character, why and in what degree?" However, his answer was diametrically opposite to Mikhailovskii's views. "It is not necessary," he said, "to show the gravity of this practical problem; for whatever opinion one has about the division of labor, everyone knows that it exists, and is more and more becoming one of the fundamental bases of social order."[115]

In the process of developing his sociological analysis, Durkheim came to the conclusion that the growing division of labor in society was both inevitable and desirable, that it was the keystone of social solidarity, and that it should occupy the central position in all moral and political theories. He dedicated *The Division of Labor in Society* to these propositions. However, as Mikhailovskii was quick to point out, Durkheim readily admitted that the division of labor in society was not totally free of "antisocial," or "immoral," elements; this division, for example, stood in the way of a harmonious development of personality for it tended to transform the individual from a

"whole being" to "an organ of an organism." Mikhailovskii cited
Durkheim's concern over the growing specialization in scientific research as
a possible threat to the very survival of science.[116] In a critical review of the
Durkheimian conceptualization of the division of labor in society, Mikhailovskii, in addition to pointing out several inconsistencies in the
arguments presented by the great French sociologist, restated his view of the
incompatibility of the growing specialization with the "wholeness" and
"internal harmony" of the individual. He wrote:

> Every society is a kind of individuality, striving toward increased com-
> plexity by means of a *social* division of labor (as shown by Durkheim in his
> chapter on the causes of the division of labor). A person, as a separate
> category, is also an individuality, but of a different order; it strives
> toward increased complexity by means of a *physiological* division of labor.
> These two processes are essentially opposite: while, among other things,
> the first emphasizes the differences between persons, the second empha-
> sizes similarities.[117]

However, Mikhailovskii was now willing to admit that the two processes
could enter into "multiple combinations." At the bottom of his arguments is
the unchallengeable idea that modern societies could gratify the basic
humanity of the individual by planning comprehensive steps to counteract
the dehumanizing prospects of overspecialization and to check the threat of
alienation. He categorically rejected Durkheim's professed aim to treat the
evolution of solidarity (and the division of labor in society) independently of
the idea of progress.

It is noteworthy that most critics aimed their fire at Mikhailovskii and not
at Lavrov. In the case of the Marxists this can be easily explained: Lavrov was
not too keen about the advisability and feasibility of the revival of the
obshchina; he was a friend of Marx and Engels; he had said that "socialism
is the best sociology"; he had written favorably about the Paris Commune;
and, despite his unceasing devotion to subjective sociology, he thought that a
general theory of society could not ignore the contributions of Marxism. The
search for a satisfaction of economic needs, he said, is at the root of all social
activity. His long absence from Russia and from direct participation in
domestic political affairs also helped him avoid a concerted attack from
Marxist quarters. In comparison with Mikhailovskii, he was less categorical in
his sociological pronouncements and enjoyed the reputation as the mildest
and most learned Russian socialist of his generation. However, he did not go
unscathed. In 1893 Plekhanov called him an "eclectic"—the term used
earlier by Chernyshevskii and Marx for the same purpose—who did not
advance beyond the pre-Marxian social and revolutionary theories. Plekhanov noted that despite his association with the socialist movement,
maintained chiefly through his editing of *Vpered!*, Lavrov never abandoned
his subjectivist social philosophy laid down in *Historical Letters.*[118]

Plekhanov was correct in stating that Lavrov was an unwavering articulator and defender of subjective sociology. In *Problems of Understanding History*, published in 1898, Lavrov lamented the rapid decline of classical positivism, which had given birth to sociology and had helped it in its modern search for a scientific status. Behind the elaborate front of Lavrov's sociological subjectivism was a quiet dedication to positivism—to the belief that, in the final analysis, it is the gradual advancement of "critical cognition" that holds the keys to social progress. In a pure Comtian tradition, he divided the history of socialism into theological, metaphysical, and scientific (positive) stages and devoted an entire study to it.[119] However, by identifying the evolution of socialist ideas with a progressive search for a science of society he transgressed the legitimate limits of Comte's philosophical thought. Lavrov was critical not only of the debilitating effects of the revival of metaphysics but also of the internal splintering which had led to the formation of two feuding factions among modern positivists: one refusing to attach any philosophical relevance to ethical theories and the second preoccupied with a search for a new "religion" and thus engaged in undermining the very foundations of the Comtian legacy. Although in his earlier writings he was an astute defender of a Kantian type of phenomenalistic theory, he was now ready to condemn the "agnosticism" of the neo-Kantian schools as a serious hindrance to the growth and consolidation of a scientific study of society.[120]

While badly outnumbered, the admirers and followers of subjective sociology worked busily on several fronts. Some tried to provide historical documentation for the lofty peaks occupied by the leaders of subjective sociology in the annals of Russian intellectual history. M. Nevedomskii noted that, both as a sociologist and as a spokesman for the intelligentsia, Mikhailovskii was the most articulate and influential modern representative of Russian thought built on the legacy of Herzen, Chernyshevskii, Dobroliubov, and Pisarev. Viktor Chernov noted that "Mikhailovskii opened a new philosophical and sociological era in Russia" and that, more than all the academic philosophers and other scholars, he helped philosophy descend from the clouds to the earth and enter the age of a rapid secular growth of values.[121] Maksim Kovalevskii, the dean of Russian sociologists, wrote in 1913 that Mikhailovskii was the indisputable teacher of the generation of Russian intellectuals who made sociology an inextricable part of Russian thought and who created a distinctive Russian sociology.[122] He credited Mikhailovskii with bringing to Russia not only sociological theory but also social psychology. While Kovalevskii considered Mikhailovskii a giant of Russian thought, S. N. Iuzhakov considered him a giant of European stature whose powerful intellect found a middle ground between the two leading currents in modern social theory: the sociology which looked for models in Darwin's theory, which viewed the scarcity of natural resources and the struggle for existence as the motive force of social evolution, and the economic theory of Adam Smith, Ricardo, and Marx, which saw in growing wealth and cooperation the guarantees of social progress.[123]

Two men were particularly important contributors to the preservation and elaboration of subjective sociology: N. I. Kareev, who gave himself the task of constructing a logically integrated and philosophically coherent system of sociology based on Populist social thought; and Viktor Chernov, who was particularly noted for his interest in the aspects of subjective sociology which anticipated, and received extensive support from, several modern sociological theories, particularly those of neo-Kantian and neopositivist vintage.

ACADEMIC POPULISM: N. I. KAREEV

Kareev was an academic man—a rare phenomenon among Russian sociologists. An authority on French social history, he taught first at Warsaw University and then at St. Petersburg University; in 1899, he was dismissed from the staff of St. Petersburg University for alleged involvement in student unrest and was not reinstated until 1906. His major historical work, *The Peasant in France During the Last Quarter of the Eighteenth Century* (published in 1879, and in a French translation in 1899), was the first comprehensive study of the role of the peasantry in the French Revolution. It was also the first large-scale study of the French Revolution to be undertaken by a Russian historian. Subsequently, Kareev wrote about the activities of Paris revolutionary factions during 1790-95; he also published *The Historians of the French Revolution*, in three volumes (1923-25).

In 1879, Kareev read a paper before the Juridical Society in Moscow on the Russian subjective school in sociology, an event which marked the beginning of his extensive writing in sociology and philosophy of history. *The Fundamental Questions in the Philosophy of History* (1883-90) and *An Introduction to the Study of Sociology* (1896) are products of the first efforts in Russia to present the philosophy of history and sociology as complete and distinct systems of theoretical thought. They helped make the social theories of Populism a dignified component of academic debate and scholarly writing. Both provided sublime and powerful arguments against metaphysical approaches to social and historical realities which, in one way or another, sought to contribute to a perpetuation of the autocratic system.

Sociology, as viewed by Kareev, is the science of the universal laws of social organization and social change. Its function is to provide a "scientific basis" for forecasting the main lines in the future development of human society and for widening the scope of man's "conscious" role in social change.[124] As the most abstract social science, it is not a synthesis of the general conclusions, or empirical generalizations, of particular social sciences; on the contrary, the latter are amplifications and special applications of general sociological laws. Kareev fully embraced Giddings's dictum that experts in specialized social sciences who ignore the fundamental principles of sociology are similar to the students of astronomy and thermodynamics who bypass the Newtonian laws of motion. The universal laws of sociology are not logical distillations from empirical generalizations supplied by specialized social sciences: their origin is in the intuitive insights of the great men of science, and at first they are mere hypotheses. Without empirical verification, however, no hypothesis can be transformed into a scientific law of social life.

A good Populist, Kareev traced the origin of sociology to A. Schlözer, the eighteenth-century historian who introduced the first conceptually clear differentiation between society as the total web of social relations and the state as a specific agency of society. The social thinkers from Plato to Rousseau had erred in treating society and the state as synonyms. Comte deserves the title of the father of sociology for he was the first to refute the claims of the juridical school in sociology that law contained all the structural elements of social integration and to introduce the concept of society as a "natural system," subject to universal laws of internal organization and development. In Kareev's opinion, sociology combines the Comtian view with the traditional juridical orientation; it deals with the most *general* principles of social organization (as a natural system) which regulate "the relations among individuals and unite them into systems of cooperation," and with *specific* legal structures which protect societies from disintegrative forces. In carrying out this dual assignment, sociology must operate as an abstract science, concerned exclusively with scientific laws.

Kareev's sociology is a detailed elaboration of the Populist thesis that man's social life is reducible to multiple patterns of behavior of interacting individuals and groups.[125] The individual is the core of all social life; law, society, and polity are webs of relations among individuals.[126] Without a psychological base, human society could develop only in accordance with biological formulas; psychology alone constitutes the true basis of sociology. As a scientific base of sociology, psychology must meet three requirements: it must concentrate on group behavior rather than on individual behavior; it must consider not only the intellectual but also the volitional and affective aspects of collective psychology; and it must examine the unconscious, not less than the conscious, phenomena of social life.[127] In full agreement with the theory of Mikhailovskii and Lavrov, he defined society as "a living product of experience," as a harmonious union of personalities who, while involved in multiple social relations, preserve their distinct individualities. Relying on Spencer's terminology, he identified social evolution as a "superorganic development" leading to the ultimate attainment of the highest expression of "the human spirit," embodied in "social forms."[128] Sociology, according to Kareev, is essentially a science of social ideals, not as a priori categories of "pure reason," but as a posteriori categories validated by empirical studies of social behavior. Social ideals, as shared values, are "social facts" of the first magnitude: they alone can reveal human motivations behind social actions of historical significance. He reasoned that "the social ideals must express higher ethical, juridical, economic, and political goals; but they must also be psychologically and socially realizable."[129] The "ideals," as "noble desires," must come from human hearts, but they must be founded on the knowledge of laws of social relations—primarily the laws of social evolution—which, in turn, must be validated by empirical knowledge.

True to the basic postulates of Populist sociology, Kareev argued that in addition to a scientific or objective method there is also an ethical or subjective method.[130] In his thinking, "scientific objectivism" and "ethical subjectivism" are complementary processes in the study of social reality: the former concentrates on the external conditions and forms of social existence, while the latter deals with the inner life of personality—personality as a pure carrier of moral duties and social ideals.[131] While the scientific method *establishes* objective facts and draws theoretical conclusions from them, the ethical method *evaluates* "objectively established facts" and draws moral conclusions from them. However, the ethical method goes a step further: it also examines the norms of moral behavior which elude objective or scientific scrutiny. Kareev admitted that it would be futile to try to reduce every moral norm to a scientific explanation. Perhaps, he was ready to concede that Mikhailovskii's notion of social development as a gradual realization of "simple cooperation" is morally defensible even though it is beyond the reach of scientific corroboration.

Kareev argued that the Russian "subjective sociology" and Durkheim's "objective sociology" are not mutually exclusive. Both are united in their opposition to Spencer's insistence on keeping value judgments outside the realm of sociology. Durkheim's "objective method" and Mikhailovskii's "subjective method" provided equally stringent safeguards for keeping sociology unencumbered by metaphysical speculation. Durkheim was in general agreement with subjective sociology when he noted that the "objective" approach to morality should not make the sociologist "an indifferent and obedient student of reality" and that to be "scientifically objective" does not mean to be "ethically neutral."[132] Both Mikhailovskii and Durkheim, each following his own scientific path, considered the "wholeness" of the individual the essential yardstick of social progress. According to Kareev, by asking the same basic theoretical questions and by recognizing the moral duties of persons engaged in the pursuit of science, they helped create the intellectual atmosphere favoring the development of complementary relations between methodologically different sociological approaches. While Mikhailovskii criticized the general ideas presented in Durkheim's *Division of Labor in Society*, for the purpose of defending and consolidating his own theoretical views, Kareev was satisfied with presenting the Russian reader with a dispassionate account of Durkheim's arguments in favor of the thesis that the increasing division of labor in society leads to an expanding affirmation of *la personalité individuelle*—to the development of personality as an "autonomous source of activity."[133]

While making the individual the key concept of the theory of social structure, Kareev made evolution the pivotal concept of the theory of social change. Social evolution, as he defined it, has several distinctive characteristics. First, it is universal and unilinear, for its basis is the law of the psychological unity of mankind. Second, it is not automatic; Kareev rejects Comte's notion of *l'évolution spontanée* and Spencer's laissez-faire philosophy. Man is an active agent in social evolution. The Populist notion of "critically thinking individuals" as the motive force of social change finds full expression and passionate endorsement in Kareev's writings. Third, social evolution is not a mere repetition, or extension, of natural evolution: while natural evolution generates conflict and is conducive to causal explanation, social evolution brings forth an expansion of solidarity and requires both causal and teleological explanation. These characteristics, more than any other, show that even though sociology is an abstract science concerned with universal laws, it is qualitatively different from the natural sciences.

The purposiveness of social evolution is the bridge which, in Kareev's view, connects sociology and the philosophy of history. In the philosophy of history, "social evolution" becomes "social progress." "Social progress" is "social evolution" translated into values. It does not embrace the totality of history or evolution; it is only a specific vantage point from which history is viewed and future developments are predicted.[134] It contains an ethical judgment, but it has no room for supernatural interference. It provides an ethical evaluation of historical facts produced by science. Kareev admits that the philosophy of nature and the philosophy of history are separate branches of philosophy: while the former deals exclusively with the world of natural causation, the latter is preoccupied with the world of social purposiveness. While the former searches for an integrated picture of the universe in its full independence of man, the latter searches for an integrated picture of social history as a progressive realization of man's search for an ideal society. One of the basic functions of the philosophy of history is to adduce logical and substantive arguments in favor of a synthesis of "causal necessity" and "ethical purposiveness" as the scientific base of sociology.

Kareev's philosophy of history is the philosophy of Populist utopianism: it ignores the social heterogeneity of modern industrial society and idolizes the social homogeneity of the obshchina. It reduces the class configuration of modern society to a level of nonstructural significance; instead, it elevates the intelligentsia, as a social formation without social-class attributes, to the level of a prime mover in social evolution. It generalizes on the basis of Populist interpretations of the obshchina and the intelligentsia; and it echoes the Populist rejection of the notion of capitalism as a universal stage in the development of industrial societies.

THE SOCIOLOGY OF NEO-POPULISM: V. M. CHERNOV

The philosophy and sociology of neo-Populism, a logical and historical offshoot of the theoretical ideas of Lavrov and Mikhailovskii, is an elaboration and codification of the ideology of the Russian Socialist Revolutionary party. The leading theorists of neo-Populism criticized their Populist ancestors for their overconcern with the lingering residues of feudal relations in agriculture that led them to minimize the problems brought about by the emergence of the proletariat, a child of sprawling capitalism.[135] Unlike their ideological forebears, the neo-Populists recognized the class struggle in modern society as a disunifying force of historical consequence. However, this did not lead them to refute Mikhailovskii's legacy that stressed the common class-interests of the workers and the peasants as "the totality of toiling people." V. M. Chernov, for example, directed his main arguments against Karl Kautsky, who emphasized the class differences between the workers and the peasants and who thought that the peasants should be excluded from positions of leadership in the forthcoming socialist revolution.[136] In a critique of Lenin's theory that, by implication, placed the peasantry into the general category of "bourgeoisie," Chernov relied on Marx's statement that the "exploitation" of peasants differed from the "exploitation" of workers only in form, for both the peasants and the workers had the same exploiter—capital.[137] By harmonizing the class interests of the workers and the peasants, Chernov returned to the Populist conception of *narod* (people) as the basic sociological category in the study of the structure of Russian society. At any rate, in analyzing class struggle, he and other neo-Populists "so diminished its significance and so diluted its content as to change it beyond recognition."[138]

R. V. Ivanov-Razumnik added even more to the dilution of the idea of class struggle as a mechanism of social change by emphasizing the division of Russian society into two "diametrically opposite" groups—the intelligentsia and the *meshchanstvo*—neither of which was a social class or a social caste but a conglomeration of individuals representing the entire social-status spectrum. The distinguishing features of each group were not in shared economic attributes but in common values. The intelligentsia, according to Ivanov-Razumnik, was dedicated to changing the inner structure and cultural values of Russian society in such a way as to assure "a physical and intellectual emancipation of the individual."[139] The intelligentsia, in his view, was guided by the philosophy of "individualism," which recognized "the individual as the fundamental and leading social value" and which viewed the well-being of the individual as the true criterion of "social and cultural progress." As a world view, individualism rested on the principle that society was "not a limitation but a fulfillment of human personality."[140] The meshchanstvo, on the other hand, consisted of persons whose world view had no room for "individuality" and was dominated by "narrow-mindedness" and "superficiality." It embraced most of the educated people, including a vast majority of university professors safely cloistered in their ivory towers. The meshchanstvo, in a phrase Herzen borrowed from John Stuart Mill, was "conglomerated mediocrity," dominated by crowd behavior rather than by critical thought.[141] The basic conflict in modern Russia was the conflict between the intelligentsia as the champions of political and social modernization, and the meshchanstvo, as the defenders of the social status quo. The future of Russian society, according to Ivanov-Razumnik and most other neo-Populist social theorists, was not in the peaceful outcome of a class war but in lifting the meshchanstvo out of intellectual lethargy, political conservatism, and deeply rooted anti-individualism.

Although generally critical of Marxist ideology, the neo-Populists took a conciliatory attitude toward many components of Marxist social theory. They were particularly well disposed toward the Marxist economic theory of capitalism and the sociological theory of alienation. N. S. Rusanov thought that the Populist leaders made a grave error in not giving Marxist sociology serious consideration. He said that Mikhailovskii's notion of "cooperation" as a general form of the organization of work had much in common with the Marxist view of "social technology" as an organization of the productive forces in society.[142] N. Sukhanov, writing in 1912, stated that Populism and Marxism were moving toward each other and that the time had come for thinking about their merger into a single socialist party.[143] He admitted, however, that the two movements were still far apart on such questions as "the role of the individual in history," the nature of social classes and class struggle, the place of the peasantry in the socialist movement, the obshchina, and the social functions of the intelligentsia. Chernov asserted that "Marx is our great common teacher in the realm of economics, but we do not feel constrained to make of him an idol."[144] He claimed that Mikhailovskii came much closer to a true interpretation of Marx's views on the "form" and "substance" of capitalism than the Russian Marxists, represented by Tugan-Baranovskii.[145] Instead of rejecting Marx's theory completely, Chernov tried, it seemed, to "save" it from modern Marxists. He gave Marx credit for having transformed socialism from a fragmented "humanitarian-philanthropic" orientation supported by ideas borrowed from capitalist economic theories into an original and fully integrated system of thought.[146] He credited historical materialism with having shown the growing impact of economic relations on the structure of society. He claimed, however, that

Marxist theory is steeped in "metaphysical fetishism": it gives the economic component of social structure the causal primacy over all other components; it formulates a mechanistic model of society which has no room for the individual as a maker of history; and it treats social evolution as a self-propelled process, explicable solely in terms of an "internal logic."[147] Moreover, Chernov argued that socialism cannot be built on scientific theory alone: it must also draw support from a system of ethical precepts, a problem left unattended by the fathers of "scientific socialism." According to Chernov, the Russian experience during the revolution of 1905 and the events leading to it provided many examples of the rapid deterioration of socialism when it sought the support of science but not of ethics. Without deep ethical foundations, socialism degenerates "from a revolutionary movement to a tyranny of rebels, from an organized struggle to partisan escapades, and from political activity to brigandage."[148]

V. M. Chernov, the most important link between Populism and neo-Populism, began his political and journalistic career during the 1890s, contributing articles to *Russian Wealth* at the time when Mikhailovskii was its chief editor. He considered Mikhailovskii his teacher and was particularly attracted to his "exciting, powerful, and versatile intellect."[149] In Mikhailovskii's sociology he saw an admirable combination of "science and conscience." While Mikhailovskii concentrated on the huge area of disagreement which separated Populism from Marxism, Chernov showed considerable interest in current sociological and philosophical developments in the West which reinforced Populist theory. However, at the end of the 1890s he began to write about Marxism, mainly in search of specific theoretical guides and practical models for a revolutionary movement. He was perceptive enough to note the futility of the current efforts of a number of ex-Marxists to build a social philosophy on the common ground of Kant's moral philosophy and Marx's socioeconomic theory. In 1898–99, he helped organize a revolutionary peasant group in Tambov, a model for similar organizations in other communities. In 1905, he prepared the program for the organizational congress of the Socialist Revolutionary party held in Imana, Finland. The program advocated a socialist revolution preceded by a democratic revolution. It stood for a complete socialization of land and the development of a democratic and modernized obshchina as the primary community of rural Russia.

In 1917, after many years in exile in Western Europe, Chernov returned to Russia to preside over the rapidly swelling organization of the Socialist Revolutionary party. As the minister of agriculture from May 5 to September 1, 1917, he was disappointed that his plan for the socialization of the land was not carried out. The October Revolution made him a bitter foe of Bolshevism. He presided over the ill-fated Constituent Assembly that went out of existence one day after its first convocation in January 1918. Having left the Soviet Union in 1920, he spent the early years of emigration in elaborating the basic principles of a "constructive socialism"—a new synthesis of "utopian socialism" and "scientific socialism" and a "concrete" plan for a socialist transformation of modern society.[150] A gradualist, he placed the major emphasis on education imbued with the ideals of socialism. The socialization of land, he now thought, should be the final goal rather than the initial step in a planned transformation of society, and it should preclude both a nationalization of natural resources and a centralization of political authority. Behind his dream of socialism loomed the deep shadows of obshchina romanticism: he never abandoned the old Populist dream of the obshchina as a "natural phenomenon" capable of further growth and structural transformation and as a healthy start in building a society on the foundations of rural socialism.[151] However, his view of the historical role of obshchina was not a simple endorsement of the sentimental attachment of the old Populists to rural communalism. In the words of Oliver H. Radkey: "He divested the village community [obshchina] of the mystical halo with which the elder generation of Populists had so fatuously surrounded it, and instead of active emanations in the direction of socialism ascribed to it merely an important equalizing tendency and the negative significance of having served as a block to the development of a property consciousness."[152] He died in 1952 in New York City.

In the *Great Russian Revolution* Chernov described himself as "a theorist, a man of speech, literature, the writing desk and lecture platform rather than a professional politician."[153] Radkey observed that "Chernov had a splendid mind," that "his powers of social analysis lifted him out of the category of sectarian prophets," and that "in his thinking there was a strain of pessimism and a sense of limitation which lessened his effectiveness as a revolutionary leader but increased his philosophical stature."[154] A contemporary observed that Chernov devoted most of his attention to effecting an epistemological synthesis of Populism and empiriocriticism (a popular neopositivist orientation) and to a philosophical analysis of modern politics and its ethical foundations. He also gave a theoretical formulation of "Populist *praxis*," conceptualized the ideals of Populism, and "illuminated the psychology and logic of the historical development of Populism and its reflection in literary and artistic works."[155]

As a sociologist, Chernov distinguished himself less by originality of ideas than by command of vast, up-to-date theoretical knowledge and by skillful blending of subjective theory with modern Western epistemological and sociological thought. Indeed, he undertook to show that subjective sociology anticipated, and was subsequently confirmed, by some of the most influential developments in modern thought. He, for example, took a close look at Wilhelm Dilthey's classic *Introduction to the Cultural Sciences*, published in 1883, and saw no essential differences between the German philosopher's notion of *Geisteswissenschaften*—the sciences concerned with the cultural foundations of human society—and Lavrov's and Mikhailov-skii's conception of subjective sociology formulated during the late 1860s. He also showed that Heinrich Rickert's views on the dichotomy of "nature" and "culture," and on the qualitative differences between the natural and social sciences, were essentially similar to Mikhailovskii's and Lavrov's views on the unique features of value-oriented (subjective) and value-free (objective) realities and on the specific methodological features of the natural and social sciences.[156] Rickert's statement that a historian, or a social scientist, should not ask whether a value is *real* but whether it is *valid* describes the very essence of Populist sociological theory.[157] Both the German neo-Kantians and the Russian Populists viewed nature as "external" to the inquiring mind and "society" as part of this mind's "inner" life. The sociologist, according to these writers, must create special tools of inquiry that would enable him to take into account the fact that he, as a person, is both a student and a creator of social reality, and that he is both the investigating subject and the investigated object.

There is, however, a fundamental difference between neo-Kantian and neo-Populist sociology: while the neo-Kantians were concerned with a sociological study of values, the neo-Populists (not less than the Populists) were satisfied with a sociology immersed in and guided by values. Loyal to the legacy of Populist sociology, Chernov criticized Pitirim Sorokin's effort to develop sociology as an "objective" science operating totally outside the realm of value judgments. He rejected Sorokin's claim that sociology, as science, should be above good and evil and that it should deal with "what is" and not with "what ought to be."[158] In a critique of P. B. Struve's sociological views, Chernov made his position clear: "Mr. Struve thinks that science and ethics are alien to each other; he cites Sombart's statement that in Marxism, to which he subscribes, 'there is not a single grain of ethics.' I assume that this elevates neither science nor ethics but denigrates both. I prefer Lassalle's fervent exclamation: 'What is science if it does not give an ethical direction to the intellect? And what else can morality be but a result of true knowledge?' "[159] Unlike the neo-Kantians of the Marburg school, who contended that the social scientist must approach values as expressions of universal principles of ethical life—the quintessence of humanity—Chernov, like Lavrov and Mikhailovskii before him, concentrated on values as specific and concrete guides to irreversible social progress as defined not by objective laws but by human ideals. The neo-Kantians were interested in absolute values transcending the historical limits of individual societies; Chernov, on the other hand, concentrated on "historical" values built into ideologies. He criticized the "rationalism in ethics" as formulated in Kant's moral philosophy because it constructed a logical system of absolute values transcending both the limits of history and the power of inductive science. In

Kant's moral code he saw an ahistorical phenomenon in which "logical universality" is the only substance and in which there is no room for "logical contradictions" as agents of change.[160]

Populist sociologists made knowledge the prime mover of social change and the most significant indicator of social progress. Their social theory concentrated on the *results* of cognition—on the substance of knowledge. Lavrov, for example, undertook to write an extensive history of knowledge, as embodied in science, which he identified as a general record of social progress. Neo-Populist sociologists, on the other hand, were attracted mainly to the *processes* of cognition—the socialization of knowledge. Viewing "truth" exclusively as a social conception, Chernov elaborated the theme that "the entire logic of mankind, the main processes of thought, all norms of cognition and language (as the essential tool of knowledge) are products of intellectual communication, social relations, and cooperation."[161] "Truth," he said, "is consensus." Truth is both "subjective" and "objective": it is subjective in origin and objective in practical verification. It represents a specific form of dynamic equilibrium in relations of persons and groups to the social and natural environment.[162]

Chernov looked for an answer to the most basic of all questions of subjective sociology: how does the private and subjective experience of the individual provide the real ingredients for the formation of social thought, norms of behavior, and common culture? He elaborated on Simmel's contention that "the being of truth" is only a "relational concept," expressing an agreement in "the content of consciousness" which is shared by a majority of interacting and interstimulating individuals. The statement that "the truth is a bias of the group while the untruth is a bias of the individual" sums up the Simmelian relativistic epistemology which found an echo in Chernov's explanation of the psychological origins of human society and culture. In Simmel's statement that the objective world is a generalized version of subjective experience Chernov found a true formulation of the axiomatic basis of Mikhailovskii's subjective sociology.

In his systematic search for modern philosophical support for subjective sociology, Chernov allied himself with the "scientific philosophy" as generally formulated by Alois Riehl, Carl Göring, Joseph Petzoldt, Ernst Mach, and Richard Avenarius. In selected epistemological statements of these philosophers he found strong support for the basic principles of subjective sociology. He was a neopositivist inasmuch as he accepted the epistemological unity of scientific knowledge and inasmuch as he made a concerted effort to present the sociology of knowledge—concerned with the processes of the objectification of experience—as the essential study of human society. However, unlike neopositivist philosophers, he did not accept the idea of the logical and methodological unity of the sciences.

Chernov calls his social theory philosophical monism, based on the notion of the epistemological unity of knowledge. All objective knowledge—the knowledge shared by men—originates in subjective knowledge or personal experience. The process of the socialization of knowledge is the same as the process of the objectification of knowledge. The essence of philosophical monism is that, in reality, there is no such thing as "subjective" knowledge or "objective" knowledge as distinct categories but various transitional phases between the two extremes. In Chernov's words: "Modern philosophy has shown that the most 'objective' theoretical truths are the most broadly generalized 'subjective' experiences and that there is nothing in subjective experience that does not show a potential generalizing tendency." The socialization of knowledge is the essence of social evolution: it manifests the progressive growth of the objective component of knowledge at the expense of the subjective component. The growth of "theoretical truths"—the purest expressions of objective truths—is the best measure of social progress for it is the same as "the process of a progressive *adaptation* of the individual spirit to the social conditions of human existence."[163] "Theoretical truths" are closely related to "practical values," without which there could be no "socialization of spiritual life"—no culture. "Theoretical truths" and "practical values" are two sides of the same coin. There are no "theoretical truths" without the social standards established by "practical values," and there are no "practical values" aside from cognition and logic.

Chernov accepted the idea that the knowledge of both physics and sociology is subjective in origin, but he also argued that, as a science of "the indivisible person," sociology is doubly subjective, inasmuch as the sociologists are both architects and investigators of social reality. However, this double subjectivism did not prevent him from making a special concession to the "objective" element in sociology. He reasoned that although sociology dealt with subjective reality, it employed an objective approach inasmuch as it relied on a rigorous scrutiny of the relationship of social ideals to the concrete content and conditions of social life. Social ideals are distilled from subjective experience and personal aspirations, but they become sociologically significant only when they are related to the objective needs of man and to the concrete means for the satisfaction of these needs.[164] Although it is thoroughly infused with social ideals, sociology must reject all "abstractions" that are not reducible to "empirical generalizations."

The base of Chernov's social theory was not only in "philosophical monism"; it was also in "social monism." As he defined it, social monism stood for viewing society as "a higher unity," irreducible to a mechanical summation of its constituent elements. Sociology, as a science of social integration, must concentrate on the search for laws which govern "the simultaneous motion" of "intertwined and interdependent" social components, rather than on individual areas of social action.[165] In addition to avoiding an atomistic or mechanical approach to social reality, social monism has no room for approaches which divide institutional complexes and processes into primary and derivative. It rejects Marxist sociology as a theory which concentrates on analyzing society into its elements as a prelude to attributing to these elements either infrastructural or superstructural qualities. In Marxist sociology, the source of social integration is in the genetic or causal primacy of the economic base; in Chernov's sociology, the source of social integration is in the interdependence, or reciprocity, of simultaneously acting elements. Marxist sociologists considered the moral code a derivation from the "economic base"; Chernov considered "economic materialism" and "ethical idealism" complementary, yet not all-inclusive, components of a total pattern of sociological inquiry. He said: "There are no separate intellectual, economic, and legal processes—there is only a social process which, in order to be fully comprehended, must be looked at from intellectual, economic, and legal vantage points."

In sum, Chernov detected three major flaws in Marxist sociology. First, Marxist sociology does not look at Hegelian contradictions or Kantian antinomies as expressions of larger unities of thought and social action; for example, it treats "economic materialism" and "historical idealism," the two prevalent currents in modern social thought, as mutually exclusive philosophies rather than as complementary descriptions of two sides of the same cultural system. In the second place, its genetic orientation prevents it from bringing the causal-mechanical and purposive-historical explanations into a logically integrated system. In the third place, by viewing it as a reality sui generis, it isolates society from the rest of the universe and from a philosophical basis for a search for general laws of social development.

Chernov's sociology is a theoretical codification of a unique notion of revolution—a revolution that is moral and economic, national and universal, and purposive and necessary, all at the same time. It is a defense of a revolution that would make the individual a creative member of society, unfettered by political restrictions, economic inequality, and intellectual authority. The core of Chernov's sociology stresses the individuality of both personality and social and national entities. In order to be successful and to have a moral base, a revolution, in his opinion, must build on national resources in democratic processes, not on the prescriptions of so-called objective laws of science. In a way, his sociology recognizes the objective conditions of social life but not the objective laws of social development.

SUMMARY AND CONCLUSIONS

Subjective sociology was the product of a unique combination of science and ideology. As a "science" its origins were in a widely held view that human society can be fully understood only when its workings are subjected to scientific scrutiny. As an "ideology," it was part of a philosophical articulation of the Populist view that the individual held the keys to history. The idea of the primary historical role of the individual found many converts in Russia, particularly since the time of V. Belinskii. Together with the belief in the inevitability of social change and the secular nature of political institutions, it formed the basic creed of the intelligentsia.

Although their attention was centered on such universal sociological problems as the interaction of the individual and society, the nature of cooperation and solidarity as mechanisms of social integration, and the relationship of "social evolution" to "social revolution," Populist sociologists were essentially Russian sociologists, with their eyes and ears close to Russian social realities. Their social theory was to a large extent an elaboration, and a critical synthesis, of two strong ideological orientations of the 1860s: Chernyshevskii's socialist philosophy, which saw the future of Russia in social arrangements steeped in the democratic values of rural communalism and dedicated to social and economic equality, and Pisarev's radical individualism, which advocated relentless criticism of officially sanctioned values as the best method of achieving a full emancipation of the individual. Populist philosophy, as a philosophy of "the critically thinking individual," treated the individual as a social link and an autonomous unit. According to Lavrov and Mikhailovskii, personality internalizes the values of society but it also forces society to discard or modify anachronistic values. Subjective sociology as the ideological weapon of Populism demanded that the intelligentsia go to the people in order not only to guide but also to learn; in other words, the social function of the intelligentsia was to prepare the ground for basic social changes by both fighting against the institutional relics of the feudal era and grasping the democratic core of national life upon which modern institutions could be built.

The Populist interpretation of the social and historical attributes of personality was a blend of the anti-individualism of "repentant nobility" (the leaders of the Going to the People movement and the champions of narod) and the ultraindividualism of the raznochintsy (the worshippers of the uncompromising war of the individual on the existing institutions).[166] Both the "repentant nobility" and the raznochintsy were engaged in a war against the pivotal institutions of autocracy. The raznochintsy, as represented by the Nihilists, did not think that the conflict between the individual and the autocratic state could be resolved favorably by building a buffer between them; the "repentant nobility," on the other hand, considered the people, united by firm bonds of solidarity, the most effective buffer protecting the individual from the encroachments of the autocratic state. While the Nihilists emphasized the individual as the destroyer of the established social system, the Populists were interested in the individual as the builder of a new society, free of the fetters of authoritarianism.

The Populists (Mikhailovskii much more than Lavrov) contended that the obshchina could serve as an institutional nucleus and a model of a future Russian society. By making the obshchina an integral part of their social theory, they achieved a unique synthesis of Slavophile sociology and utopian socialism that found in Russia many spokesmen and many programmatic expressions.[167] The Populists were concerned not only with the elimination of the debilitating survivals of feudalism in Russia but also with working out concrete designs for helping their country bypass capitalism as a stage of social evolution. They recognized that the obshchina was too deeply scarred by a long association with the feudal system; they merely sought in the primeval, or prefeudal, obshchina a source of models for simple cooperation to be used in tempering the threats of specialized technology, complex cooperation, and general alienation. They acted as utopian socialists, rather than empirical sociologists, when they thought of escaping capitalism by blending the complexity of industrial technology with the simplicity of obshchina cooperation. Their fear of capitalism came from an intimate familiarity with Marx's works in political economy rather than from a firsthand study of burgeoning capitalism in Russia.

Populist sociology stood squarely between two unofficial attitudes toward social change: Leo Tolstoy's view of passive resistance to, or noninterference with, the evil-producing social forces as the basis of virtuous life and the views of small groups of radicals who saw in revolution the only way out of the backwardness and stagnation of Russian society. Although they did not rule out the role of revolutions in social change, Mikhailovskii and Lavrov saw the future of Russia in evolutionary changes affecting the very structure of society and carried out under the pressure of the masses imbued with a revolutionary spirit. In Russia, they thought, without a revolutionary mass psychology there could be no evolutionary social change marked by a progressive affirmation of the basic principles of democracy. Mikhailovskii was firmly convinced that the gradual democratization of political processes and institutions, rather than structural changes in the national economy, should provide the most solid basis for the emergence of a modern Russian society. The need for political freedom was, according to him, the most fundamental need of modern Russia.[168]

The leading Populists made it abundantly clear that their sociology was thoroughly antimetaphysical and that it was dedicated to laying the groundwork for a scientific approach to society. They noted that contemporary sociology, like the natural sciences of a century ago, lacked internal unity; it consisted of empirical facts not reduced to generalizations and of abstractions not grounded in concrete data. The Populists operated on two fronts. On the one hand, they played a major role in encouraging and helping to organize a systematic gathering of empirical facts of sociological relevance. "Populist ethnographers of the 1860s, Populist belletristic writers of the 1870s, and Populist statisticians of the 1880s played a direct role in organizing inductive sociological research on the economy, law, and culture of the Russian peasantry.''[169] Empirical sociological research evolved from a total reliance on casual and amateurish observations to an extensive dependence on original and complex statistical methods. The zemstvo statistics, which owed much to Populist support, made the Russian village one of the most thoroughly investigated communities in Europe. On the other hand, Populists made an effort to construct a general theory of society reducible to a broad empirical substratum. In doing this, they articulated a consistent and comprehensive antimetaphysical orientation and relied on the more common safeguards developed by the natural sciences.

All this does not mean that Populist leaders were successful in their search for a general theory of society that would meet the rigorous standards of modern science. Despite a devotion to careful empirical research and to general theory, Populist sociologists were steeped in ideology that brought disunity to their total scientific endeavor: while their empirical research dealt with the stark reality of the existing society, their general theory elaborated designs for a grand polity of the future. In their thinking, ideology was an inextricable part of sociological theory. Ideology provided the key for the construction and understanding of social theory and for the evaluation of empirical evidence. In a way, Populist sociologists placed the main accent not on an objective study of social change but on a subjective analysis of the idea of progress. Their ideology gave them the necessary weapons to criticize the existing reality and to set up the broad framework of a future society. The essence of their commitment to science was not so much in the methodological rigor of their scholarship as in the consistency of their adherence to an ideology that considered the scientific method the only legitimate approach to both social reality and nature.

Populist sociologists evaluated the existing society in the light of the ideals of a future society. Their criticism was not a dispassionate academic exercise; it was a call to action. Social criticism and political activism were two sides of the Populist sociological equation. Subjective sociology was not a theoretical platform upon which the Populist political program was constructed; on the contrary, it was an intricate and erudite derivation from Populist ideals. It was a unique effort to place both the intellectual power of science and the lofty ideals of humanity behind the Populist dreams of a democratic society. Essentially it was a grand scheme of theoretical insights and guides for practical politics, many of which remained insufficiently explored. Summing up the status of subjective sociology during the first decade of the twentieth century, a sympathetic interpreter stated that, by not having produced a philosophy of history, a general scheme of the historical process, and an adequate explanation of the derivation of "the subjective point of view" from the objective social reality, Populist sociology did not resolve the problems that were of primary significance to it.[170]

Although in empirical substance, philosophical bent, and ideological idiom Populist sociology was more Russian than any other major sociological orientation, it owed a notable intellectual debt to Western thought. The social philosophies of Proudhon and Comte played a particularly important role in helping to forge the major axioms upon which the leading Populists constructed their general theory of society. Proudhon, whom Herzen named the Hegel of socialism in recognition of his contribution to transforming "the dialectics of ideas" into "the dialectics of concrete phenomena," provided the initial intellectual and social models for a theoretical elaboration of Populist ideals.[171] Influenced by Proudhon, Mikhailovskii tied "justice," as the pillar of the moral unity of human society, to "truth," embodied in scientific knowledge and in the laws of social progress.[172] The Populists found in Proudhon's writings a powerful defense of the key role of the individual in social progress and a suggestive analysis of parallel developments in man's intellectual power and economic skills, both contributing to growing individuality and versatility in social relations. The Populists, very much like Proudhon, developed a general theory of social change that was a "philosophy of reforms" rather than a doctrine of revolution. The Populist theorists, like Proudhon, expressed an unwavering belief in social progress as a product of the combined work of the objective laws of history and purposive social action. In equating historical determinism with objective limits within which man has ample room for free action and choice, the Populists were under the spell of Proudhon's philosophy.

The influence of Auguste Comte's positive philosophy and sociological theory on Populist thought was far-reaching and of profound consequence. Both Lavrov and Mikhailovskii echoed Comte's view of the evolution of scientific wisdom as the key to social progress: Mikhailovskii's interpretation of the evolution of cooperation and Lavrov's views on the evolution of solidarity as the basic elements of progress were actually phrased in terms of the Comtian notion of the evolution of "human mind." The Populists made an extensive sociological use of Comte's dictum that the sciences deal not with *what* nature and society are but with *how* they work; the shift of emphasis enabled them to make a clear differentiation between science and metaphysics and to transfer the emphasis from ontological to logical questions of scientific knowledge. Comte's epistemological argument that the sciences deal with nature as perceived by man rather than as it exists independently of man helped the Populist sociologists to blunt, but not to erase completely, the differences between the natural sciences and the social sciences.[173] They were obviously impressed by G. H. Lewes's claim that, despite his extensive concern with the evolution of scientific knowledge, Comte treated intellectual and moral developments as independent, yet interacting, variables. It was under the influence of Comte that the Populist sociologists rejected Buckle's view of morality as a by-product of intellectual development. They accepted and elaborated Comte's idea that, despite its reliance on biological models, sociology must design its own research methods to account for the unique features of its subject-matter.

3. The Social Theory
of Anarchism

MIKHAIL BAKUNIN: THE ARCHITECT OF REVOLUTIONARY ANARCHISM

Born in 1814 to a family of landed gentry with historical roots in medieval aristocracy, Mikhail Bakunin traveled a long and tortuous road from a lowly army position in an isolated military garrison in the Minsk *guberniia* to the exalted position of a major builder—and destroyer—of the First International; and from an amateurish defender of Hegelian idealistic metaphysics to a rebellious spokesman for anarchism, a social philosophy based on materialism and a complete rejection of metaphysics.[1] A graduate of the Artillery School in St. Petersburg, where he learned "all the dark, filthy, nasty side of life," he boasted of scholastic achievements that were "undistinguished," even though he acquired "some knowledge of higher mathematics and a capacity for vivid and vigorous writing."[2] His contemporaries recognized him as an extraordinary person, combining a keen but unruly mind with overflowing energy, a fiery temperament, and a religious dedication to an irreligious philosophy. Herzen said that Bakunin was born not under an ordinary star but under a comet. Richard Wagner noted: "I was impressed by the unusual, imposing appearance of this man. Everything in him was of colossal proportions, everything had a breadth of pristine freshness."[3] Karl Marx called him "a Mohamet without a Koran," a spiritual leader without established principles.[4]

A bridge connecting the classical anarchism of Godwin and Proudhon with the modern anarchism of Petr Kropotkin, Bakunin was more a man of action than of theory: all his writings are incomplete beginnings of books and "impetuous" and "muddled" responses to the burning political questions of the day. All are stronger in pathos than in argumentation, in enthusiasm than in logic.[5] Despite the fragmentary nature of his theoretical legacy, Bakunin gave the most comprehensive explanation of anarchist principles during the period of the transformation of anarchism into a socialist movement of revolutionary orientation. This, however, does not justify the claim of one of his biographers that he was the first to bring the scattered strands of contemporary socialist thought into a "complete system."[6]

Bakunin transformed anarchism from a speculative theory of society to a program and a strategy of political action. Bert Hoselitz's observation is to the point: "Bakunin is not satisfied to outline the evils of the existing system, and to describe the general framework of a libertarian society, he preaches revolution, he participates in revolutionary activity, he conspires, harangues, propagandizes, forms political action groups, and supports every social upheaval, large and small, promising or doomed to failure, from the very beginning."[7] Although his sociological ideas are not organic parts of a carefully thought out system of theoretical principles, they show that he had a keen philosophic mind and an astute interest in both the scientific foundations of sociology and the sociological foundations of science. If his scientific and sociological ideas are not part of a comprehensive system of thought, they are vital ingredients of a complex world view and of an ideology that stood for revolution as the only way of unburdening mankind of the growing inhumanity of modern society. "A passion for destruction is at the same time a passion for building," was the guiding idea of his political philosophy and strategy. Herzen saw him as a combination of agitator, advocate, preacher, and fighter. Kropotkin observed that Bakunin's place in the modern revolutionary movement should be judged not on the basis of his writings but on the basis of his ideas and actions. According to Venturi, Bakunin distinguished himself more by helping create a revolutionary mentality than by organizing a revolutionary movement.[8]

In the evolution of Bakunin's social theory, the influences of Proudhon and Marx were particularly important. Proudhon provided him with a set of general principles describing anarchism as a sociological category. Under the influence of Proudhon, he condemned property as "theft," looked at the state as the worst enemy of personal freedom and social equality, attacked religion as a tool used by the wealthy classes to safeguard the social status quo, and despised universal suffrage as hypocritical camouflage for the growing class conflict. Bakunin's theory incorporated Proudhon's notions of political federalism, or uniting small communities into larger cooperative units, and of economic mutualism, based on an elaborate system of interest-free credits issued by "people's banks." In his philosophical reasoning, Bakunin showed a strong influence by Hegelian thought; however, like Proudhon, he relied much more on the language than on the dialectic of Hegel.

Bakunin's attitude toward Marx was less favorable than toward Proudhon. Indeed, it was Marx's attack on Proudhon, in *La misère de la philosophie*, that contributed to both an intensification of Bakunin's aversion to Marx's mode of operation in the labor movement and the instability of the First International.[9] Bakunin valued Marx's scholarship and revolutionary zeal, but he resented Marx's impatience, high-handed tactics, and heavy reliance on sarcasm in dealing with real and imaginary foes. He gave Marx credit for having played a major role in the development of scientific socialism, but he resented his "pan-Germanism" and his commitment to the principles of an "authoritarian" or "state" socialism—in contrast to Proudhon's position favoring stateless or egalitarian socialism. Bakunin readily admitted his debt to Marx. He accepted Marx's notion of revolution as the only path to socialism, and of the proletariat as the vanguard of the revolutionary forces. He wrote: "As a thinker, Marx is on the right track. He established the principle that in history all political, religious and juridical developments are not causes but consequences of economic evolution."[10] Marx's major contribution, according to Bakunin, was to combine the best from classical English economics with Hegelian dialectics and a communist orientation.

Although it was under the influence of Marx that Bakunin became a materialist and a socialist, the differences between the two were much more basic than the similarities. Marx was a "scientific" socialist who grounded his social theory in extensive and sophisticated knowledge in political economy; Bakunin, by his own admission, was an "instinctive" socialist, moved much more by sentiment than by knowledge. Marx put his faith in the coming of a revolution, a qualitative leap in the history of human society, as a combination of the work of objective laws of "nature" and premeditated and organized social action; Bakunin was an advocate of *buntarstvo*, the ceaseless and spontaneous unrest accelerating the natural attrition of the state system. Nor did Bakunin fully endorse Marx's conceptualization of historical materialism. He argued that specific components of the superstructure—for example, law—could gradually assume the role of primary social determinants. He also noted that the role of "necessity" in social evolution is acceptable only inasmuch as it does not contradict the ultimate goal of history—the full triumph of anarchy. By combining "causality" and "purposiveness" in the explanation of social evolution, Bakunin was one of the pioneers of "subjective sociology."

H. E. Kaminski's comparison of Marx and Bakunin is relevant and essentially correct. For Marx, he noted, theory is the beginning of action, while for Bakunin action precedes theory. Marx was inductive, Bakunin was deductive. Marx relied on reflection, Bakunin on inspiration. Marx thought that the organization of capitalist production was too anarchical to have a strong survival potential; Bakunin thought that capitalist production was not anarchical enough to be a true expression of humanity. Marx was concerned with order, Bakunin with liberty. For Marx, socialism was a science, and revolution was a methodical process; for Bakunin, socialism (or anarchism) was an ideal, and revolution was a spontaneous eruption. Marx's dream was to rely on a grand party as a rallying point of revolutionary proletariat; Bakunin preferred to rely on secret societies. The purpose of Marx's grand party was to take over the state apparatus and transform it into a tool of socialist construction; the purpose of Bakunin's secret societies was to destroy the state and to create a world unencumbered by constraints imposed by the state. Marx was essentially an authoritarian, Bakunin was an egalitarian.[11]

The philosophical roots of Bakunin's social theory are in materialism and positivism. It is true, he said, that the universe is made of "matter" and "ideals," but it is equally true that ideals are derivations from matter: the entire universe from man's most sublime feelings to "the natural gravitation of bodies" is reducible to matter. He noted categorically: "All intellectual and moral acts ... have their sole source in the purely material ... constitution of man, without any spiritual and extra-material influence. Briefly, they are nothing else but products of various combinations of the purely physiological functions of the brain."[12] In this respect, the difference between Hegel and Comte, as seen by Bakunin, is particularly important. Hegel, as a metaphysician, spiritualized matter and nature, deducing them from the logic of the universal spirit; Comte, as a champion of a philosophy grounded in science, materialized the spirit by making it conform to the objective laws of nature.[13] If ideals are derivations from matter, then human society is but a special ramification of nature. However, under the influence of Marx, Bakunin avoided the slippery path of biological reductionism; he noted that the evolution of human society brought forth a decreasing dependence of man on his biological endowments.

The source of human ideals and moral values, which together are the cornerstone of humanity, must be sought not in human nature as a biological phenomenon but in human society as a cultural phenomenon. Since the denial of nature in human society is in a way a dialectical continuation of the working of nature, the laws of society are as objective, absolute, and universal as are the laws of nature. Sociology, as a science searching for the universal laws of society, is guided by the idea that "just as we cannot dominate nature and transform it in accordance with our progressive needs unless we rely on our accumulated knowledge of its laws, so we cannot achieve freedom and prosperity in a society unless we know the laws which govern it."[14] Bakunin fully accepted the Hegelian dictum that the freedom of an individual is directly proportional to his knowledge of the universal laws of the development of nature and society. Thus, materialism begins by "denying free will" and ends in "the establishment of liberty."

As a champion of positivism, Bakunin interpreted social progress in terms of a gradual secularization of wisdom—a long intellectual odyssey, from the supremacy of animistic thought woven into mystical supernaturalism to the triumphs of science. Science brings both the consciousness of freedom through acquisition of positive knowledge and the realization of freedom through an effective organization of labor. Bakunin fully endorsed Comte's classification of sciences and treatment of sociology as the newest, and the last possible, addition to the small family of fundamental sciences. He accepted Comte's notion of positive philosophy—which he labeled "rational science"—as a universal science, based on the principles of the logical continuity and epistemological unity of scientific knowledge.[15] The Comtian arrangement of the sciences shows "a single existence, a single knowledge, and, in essence, a single method," which becomes increasingly more complicated as the facts grow in complexity.[16] All this did not prevent him from attacking Comte's notion of "positive polity"—the positivist dream of the state of the future—as sheer nonsense.

As a "materialist" and a "positivist," Bakunin recognized science as the basis upon which all sound philosophy rests and as the chief force propelling human society to higher points on the evolutionary scale. However, his enthusiasm for science as a mode of inquiry and a growing body of secular knowledge was matched by a distrust in science as a social institution. Obviously responding to the Nihilist exaltation of science as the panacea for all social ills, Bakunin wrote in *The People's Cause* in 1898—when he presented the final formulation of his theory of anarchism—that "the path leading to the liberation of the people by means of science is closed to us; only one path remains open to us—the path of revolution."[17] While recognizing "the absolute authority of science," he rejected "the infallibility and universality of the savant." Bakunin went so far as to advocate the abolition of universities, along with the abolition of churches and state structures. His arguments against institutionalized science run in many directions. Social revolution, he thought, was imminent, so imminent that it could not depend on the gradual development of science and on the long process of the diffusion of scientific knowledge. All science, as cultivated at universities, is "government science" or "official science" working against rather than in favor of revolution. Much scientific knowledge belongs to the realm of the social sciences, which do not have a basis in the natural sciences (and, therefore, have no sound foundations) and are inseparable from theology and metaphysics. University science is a class science, a tool in the hands of the bourgeoisie, and this is particularly true for the social sciences. University savants are notorious for their deliberate efforts to isolate themselves from social and political fermentation, to deal with impractical problems, and to cocoon themselves in the world of caste exclusiveness. Noting the "stupendous progress" of modern science, Bakunin argued that the more rapidly science grows, the more it becomes "the cause of intellectual and consequently of material slavery, the cause of poverty and mental backwardness of the people; for it constantly deepens the gulf separating the intellectual level of the privileged classes from that of the great masses of the people."[18]

In all this criticism, Bakunin made it clear that he recognized science as one of man's "most precious treasures" and "greatest prides." Urging the proletariat to keep up with the advances of science, he also issued a warning that science could not by itself ignite a revolution and carry it to completion and that only a spontaneous social revolution could make science a property of all. Even the internal makeup of science prevents it from becoming a revolutionary force: while science is dominated by abstractions and laws, revolution needs concrete facts and practical action. Bakunin's claim that "scientific abstractions" could not be made the tools of social revolution could be interpreted as a criticism of Karl Marx's revolutionary activity, which combined practical politics with a deep involvement in building the theoretical foundations of a new political economy and sociology. It should also be noted that, like Lavrov and Mikhailovskii, Bakunin was irritated by the claims of Pisarev and his immediate disciples that every true revolutionary should devote most of his time and energy to the diffusion of natural science knowledge. Nor should it be overlooked that he reproached Herzen for thinking that literary work was much more important than practical engagement in politics.[19] Bakunin argued that bourgeois science was essentially undemocratic, for its knowledge, condensed into abstruse categories and abstractions, was beyond the reach of the masses.[20]

Bakunin stood firmly against the scientistic philosophy that dominated the social thought of Russian Nihilists. Nihilist scientism not only made science the prime mover of social and cultural progress, but it also categorized nonscientific modes of inquiry as of little or no social usefulness. Bakunin accepted the Nihilist denunciations of theology and metaphysics as unreliable modes of inquiry, but he firmly rejected Pisarev's contention that art should be a tool of science, that its basic function should be to facilitate the diffusion of scientific knowledge. As a unique approach to nature art, in Bakunin's view, is in one important respect superior to science, for artistic representations are much closer to the realities of life than scientific abstractions: while science translates life into abstractions, art brings abstractions back to life. While science illumines the path of progress, art contributes to making progress a concrete reality. But both science and art are parts of a rationalist world view that has no room for transcendental intervention in the work of nature and society, and that makes the interaction of reason and society the source of wisdom beneficial to mankind.

Foreign residence that placed him beyond the reach of Russian censors, a personal inclination to wrestle with "big issues," and an unalloyed dedication to rationalism combined to make Bakunin an outspoken champion of atheism and a relentless critic of religion as a world outlook, an institution, and an approach to the fundamental problems of human existence. In his sustained criticism of religion, Bakunin expressed the Emancipation spirit which pervaded the thinking of the members of the intelligentsia during the 1860s and which guided them to a severe "abomination of Christianity."[21] In his critcism of religion, Bakunin also recalled the 1840s, the epoch of the "critical critique," when the struggle against political and social evils flew under the flag of religious criticism.[22] A bitter fight against Mazzini's *Dio e popolo* movement gave Bakunin an excellent opportunity to sharpen his criticism of religion while laying the theoretical and ideological foundations of anarchism.[23]

Whatever his motivations, the fact remains that no Russian revolutionary writer surpassed Bakunin's criticism of religion. Religion, he admitted readily, was the first awakening of human reason and the first manifestation of morality. The emergence of religion marked the transition of man from the state of a savage existence regulated by instinct, to the state of "human" existence guided by reason. But from the very beginning of its existence, religion was a cultural force inimical to progress. Although it awakened reason, it quickly turned to "unreason," to fetishism nourished on fear and impeding the processes leading to a gradual rationalization of human existence. And although it awakened morality, it subordinated it to the whims of supernatural forces, enslaving rather than liberating man. "With the help of religion, man-animal, emerging from the world of bestiality, takes the first strides toward humanity; but as long as he continues to be religious he cannot achieve his goal because every religion condemns him to the world of the absurd and, by confusing him, compels him to search for divine instead of human guidance. Thanks to religion, the peoples, as soon as they are liberated from slavery to nature . . . are enslaved by powerful men and by castes privileged by divine choice."[24] The power of religion is essentially in the fact that it permeates every phase of private and public life. Because of the enormous compass of its influence, it cannot be eradicated by "abstract and doctrinal propaganda": it must be wiped out by a social revolution.

Bakunin dealt in some detail with the origin and evolution of religion, a very popular theme in his time among both the students of culture (encouraged by the publication of Sir Edward Tylor's *Primitive Culture* in 1871) and ideologues of various socialist movements. Engrossed in the intellectual aspects of religion as specific attributes of the evolving structure of human society, he argued vehemently that religious thought is an ideological force of the first magnitude. In religion he saw the mainstay of social inequality and a force antithetical to social progress. By conceptualizing a hierarchical order in the world of divine existence, religion is readily transformed into an ideology of social inequality in the world of human existence. Religion cannot be humanized, for social equality is totally alien to it; no society can progress beyond a certain stage of development unless it eliminates religion. The glorification of God is the same as the denigration of man. In his long excursions into the social characteristics of religion, Bakunin sided with the growing body of spokesmen for various socialist and anarchist creeds who equated the evolution of morality with the growing secularization of thought and who defined religion as institutionalized ignorance.

Bakunin's discussion of religion contained no claim to academic objectivity and exhibited no original theoretical insights relevant to the evolution of human society. His negative attitude has two specific sources. In the first place, it is a mere reflection of the positivist bent of his philosophical orientation that led him to look to the full triumph of science over theology and metaphysics as the unerring sign of the future society. In this respect, his position was indistinguishable from that of Lavrov, who, however, preferred to talk about "critical thought" rather than about "science," even though he treated the two as synonyms. According to Lavrov: "The initial manifestations of human consciousness in various forms of religious behavior subordinated the needs created by society to the needs created by phantasy; they brought about an involvement in ascetism, a sacrifice of earthly goods to the otherworldly rulers, and the creation in many countries of a new estate of exploiters who served as intermediaries between man and the supernatural world. Religious activity stood in the way of a proper and harmonious satisfaction of human needs, for it slowed down the development of a conscious and critical attitude toward them; it interfered with the general development of critical thought, the main enemy of the religious world."[25] The most distinctive feature of modern time, according to both Bakunin and Lavrov, is the emergence of sociology as a science signifying the irreversible substitution of a scientific approach to the study of social evolution for the religious and metaphysical approaches. To both, the progress in the scientific study of social evolution is synonymous with the progress on the path leading to the triumphs of socialism. As positivists, both thought that religion had ceased to make intellectual contributions, the true indicators of social progress.

In the second place, Bakunin's sweeping attacks on religion are a specific reflection of the bitter attitude of the intelligentsia toward the Russian church as the chief guardian of sacred culture built upon the feudal foundations of autocracy and as the archenemy of enlightenment and political liberties. Bakunin, a more extreme representative of the rebellious intelligentsia, found in atheism the only sound response to the historical conditions that made the church a blind servant of a state structure that had outlived its usefulness and could prolong its existence only by a reliance on naked force. His sweeping statements on the universal aspects of religion are scarcely more than a generalizing of Russian experience.

Bakunin had little interest in the universal evolution of human society, the main concern of the leading nineteenth-century social theorists. A discussion of religion as a necessary phase in the development of human society marked the limit of his concern with this evolution. He endorsed Marx's view of the infrastructural significance of the economic factor in social history, but he made no effort to integrate it into his social theory. He readily accepted Marx's claim that the collapse of capitalism was unavoidable, but he felt no need to solicit the help of the objective laws of history. Marx's firm belief in the scientific predictability of social evolution (and revolution) was accompanied by an equally firm belief in the essential role of class discipline and centralized political endeavor in preparing the way for revolution. Unencumbered by a belief in historical necessity, Bakunin "put his faith in the spontaneous action of the individual workers and of such primary groups as their natural instincts for social cooperation would induce them to form as the need arose."[26] Human society, Bakunin admitted readily, is governed by objective laws. But man cannot be guided by these laws for he is ignorant of their specific nature; sociology had not been long enough in the realm of science to be in a position to unveil the universal laws of social structure and dynamics. Man is guided by a general awareness of the gradually growing domination of "reason" over "animality," the best index of the progressive unfolding of freedom. In his emphasis on reason as the true indicator of social progress, Bakunin was both a Comtian—for he relied on positive knowledge as a yardstick measuring the triumphs of reason—and a Hegelian—for he saw in reason both the substance and the logic of universal history. Like Hegel, he saw history as a dialectical process, a development through social conflict. However, he did not take the Hegelian dialectical triad seriously; to him, the "thesis" and the "antithesis" do not necessarily dissolve in a "synthesis" that preserves historical continuity.

During and after the reform era, the leading Russian theories of society, whether claiming to be scientific or openly antiscientific, were split into two major categories. Some theories considered the state the essence of society— the purest expression of sacred culture and of the universal principles of social change. The chief advocates of this theory operated on the assumption that modern Russian society was a creation of the Petrine and post-Petrine Russian state. For this reason, Boris Chicherin, the chief spokesman for the "state theory" (gosudarstvennaia teoriia), recognized sociology only as a branch of jurisprudence. To him, as to many other Russian writers, the study of society was useful only inasmuch as it enriched the study of the state. This does not mean that all the articulators of the state theory were defenders of the supremacy of the state in Russian society: while to some writers the manner in which this theory expressed the facts of history was commensurate with the ideals of humanity, to others it was antithetical to those ideals.

The second major category of theories treated society as a sociological concept much broader than the state; these theories received strong impetus from the establishment of the zemstvos and several other types of organizations dedicated, in principle, to local self-government and to transferring some of the state functions to local authorities. The "social theory" (obshchestvennaia teoriia) appealed to the intelligentsia, who viewed the autocratic state as the major force impeding the modernization of Russian society, and who dreamed of a future Russian polity in which the state, as a duly constituted agency of society, would be an instrument of legitimately instituted authority. Bakunin gave this orientation the most extreme formulation: he advocated not merely an expansion of the power and jurisdiction of society at the expense of the state but a full elimination of the latter. In formulating the most extreme theory of anarchism, Bakunin reacted to the most extreme theory of statism, firmly built into the autocratic ideology.

To Bakunin, society and the individual are the basic sociological concepts. Society, in its pure form, differs from the state in that it has no need to impose "formal, official, and authoritative" constraints on the individual, for it produces the individual in its own image: a person, according to Bakunin, is an "individualized society."[27] While the state is an artificial creation, society is the natural condition of human existence. As a natural phenomenon, society "progresses slowly, through the momentum imparted by individual institutions, not through the mind and the will of the legislator." Even though the laws that rule society may be unarticulated, they are "natural laws, inherent in the social body just as physical laws are inherent in the material world."[28]

Most modern social theories, Bakunin argued, operate from the wrong base because they isolate the individual from society. However, like Lavrov, Mikhailovskii, and other Populist theorists, Bakunin did not view the individual as a blind product of society, as a true reflection of social values and institutionalized norms of behavior. To him, too, the individual is both a product and a creator of society, although he makes it clear that only as a "product" of society can the individual be an innovator, a source of social change. Implicit in Bakunin's argumentation is the idea that the objective laws of social development alone do not explain human society, for the role of the individual innovator is equally important. Without nonconformism there can be no social change. The freedom of the individual, a popular theme in Bakunin's writings, is not a transcendental notion or a metaphysical category: it is strictly a historical phenomenon, a result of various terrestrial conditions and influences. It is "the ever-renewing result of numerous material, intellectual, and moral influences of the surrounding individuals and of the society in which the individual is born, and in which he grows up and dies."[29] The freedom of the individual is the result of the give-and-take relations between individuals within a social context, and between the individual and society. Although freedom does not exclude all limitations on the actions of the individual, it is fully incompatible with the limitations and constraints that protect institutionalized authority. The pivotal point of Bakunin's argument is that freedom is not a natural gift but a social product. He rejected social-contract theories which, by claiming that man surrenders some of his natural freedom in order to enhance his security, legitimate the institutionalization of authority, the most dangerous enemy of freedom.

Bakunin accepted, in principle, the Marxian theory of the division of modern society into two major classes: the capitalists and the proletariat. He also endorsed Marx's view of the proletariat as the architects of the socialist society of the future. However, he was less precise than Marx in defining the proletariat. On some occasions, he identified the proletariat with the working force of modern industry. On other occasions, the proletariat included all the toiling masses, the peasants not less than industrial labor. With regard to Russia, his references to the proletariat are actually references to the peasantry. In "Federalism, Socialism, and Anti-Theologism," he wrote that the initiative for a social revolution will come in the West from factory workers, and in Russia, Poland, and other Slavic countries from the peasantry.[30] He commended the international socialist movement in Italy because it embraced not only city dwellers but also the rural population. The Italian proletariat, he contended, consisted of "two to three million urban workers" and "approximately twenty million totally deprived peasants."[31]

In identifying the proletariat with the "toiling masses" and the "toiling masses" with the narod, Bakunin thought and wrote in the tradition of Russian Populism. Proudhon attracted Bakunin for the same reason that he attracted the Russian radical intelligentsia, particularly the Populists. In echoing Proudhon's attacks on the "hypocrisy" of modern democracy and his exaltation of autonomous local economic associations and the principles of cooperation, Bakunin echoed the guiding ideas of Russian Populism. In his analysis of "cooperation" and "conflict" as mechanisms of social cohesion, he thought like a typical Populist. Although he envisaged the anarchist utopia of the future as an embodiment of the purest and most versatile cooperation, he treated conflict as the propelling force of social progress. Behind the grand outlines of social progress he saw a succession of two basic types of conflict. In primordial society, man, stumbling out of the animal world, hung tenaciously to the emergent humanity to help him in his fight against the residues of "animality" that stood against culture as a man-made environment and way of life. In the fully constituted society, man relies on the "instinct of rebelliousness," the backbone of his biological constitution, to fight against all anachronistic social institutions that curb social equality, the highest principle of humanity. Bakunin consistently emphasized that man, in ascending the scale of humanity, fought both nature and civilization.[32]

In one important respect, Bakunin differed from the leading Populist theorists: he did not recognize the intelligentsia as a "classless" group engineering the course of social progress. The wheels of history, according to him, are set into motion by the spontaneous action of the instinctively rebellious masses, rather than by artificial action charted by "critically thinking individuals." He differed from the Populists also in rejecting the obshchina as a model of the communal existence of the future; he reasoned that the proliferating channels of state control had divested the obshchina of the last vestiges of the communal values of "justice" and "basic humanity."[33] In the "local autonomy" of the newly founded zemstvos he found merely another example of the hypocrisy of universal suffrage in the modern political community.

In articulating his social theory, Bakunin became both the leading nineteenth-century ideologist of peasant socialism and the most uncompromising critic of the Russian social reality steeped in institutional residues of the feudal order. His theory in general was designed more to create a revolutionary climate than either to depict and systematize the objective laws of human society or to set up the framework of a revolutionary organization. Viewed from a twentieth-century vantage point, Bakunin was much more successful in depicting the restrictions imposed by the modern state, democratic as well as nondemocratic, on the freedom of the individual than in showing the feasibility of an anarchist utopia. It may be assumed that he believed in action more than in theory merely because he thought that the world was too troubled to wait for sociology to acquire the instruments of science necessary for discovering the hitherto hidden laws of social development. "We know," he said, "that sociology as a science has just come into existence and that its principles have not yet been established. If we judge this science on the basis of other sciences, then we must recognize that it will take at least one more century until it will be fully established and will become a serious, relatively complete and self-sufficient science. So, what shall we do? Should the suffering mankind wait until a fully established sociology comes up finally with directives and instructions for a rational reorganization of life? The answer is no, a thousand times no."[34] Bakunin acted as a true disciple of Proudhon when he said that even if sociology was in full bloom it could not ascend the heights of universal abstractions, for it could never know more than a "small fragment of the truth." Proudhon's statement that "the truth in which I believe is still unknown to me" describes Bakunin's social logic as well. It may also be assumed that, in favoring action over theory, Bakunin merely followed the dictates of his troubled soul and fiery temperament.

PETR KROPOTKIN: EXPERIENCE IN SOCIAL PROTEST

Petr Alekseevich Kropotkin, unlike Bakunin, distinguished himself more as a theorist with a flair for sociological analysis and generalization than as a man of practical politics. He was not only a great believer in natural science as the most potent depository of secular wisdom and sound models for social theory but was also a practicing scientist of some repute. His geographical studies were rich in empirical detail and daring hypotheses of broad theoretical import.

Born to a family of princely lineage in 1842, Kropotkin studied at the Corps of Pages, a military school preparing children of the aristocracy for high stations in the intricate system of state counselorship. Upon graduating and entering the military service, he applied for a position in Siberia, where he spent five years (1862–67). The Siberian sojourn added vast stores of empirical knowledge to Kropotkin's involvement in such varied disciplines as physical geography, historical geology, ethnography, and frontier psychology. As an administrative assistant he acquired intimate knowledge of the rigid Siberian penal system, the incredible inflexibility of governmental bureaucracy, and the inhumanity of the sacred culture clustered around the autocratic principles of government. When the governor of the Baikal region made him a secretary of committees on prison reforms and on urban self-government, he steeped himself in relevant literature, both Russian and foreign, and spent long hours interviewing local citizens intimately familiar with the exacting problems of Siberian life. He submitted detailed projects for reforms which, like thousands of similar projects encouraged by the spirit of the Great Reforms, were buried in the files of the St. Petersburg bureaucracy.

As a participant in several expeditions exploring the riches of Siberia, Kropotkin had ample opportunity to record fresh information in physical geography and to observe life in isolated native and Russian communities. The pristine humanity of the elementary forms of cooperation with which these communities met the challenge of the Siberian environment stood in sharp contrast to the impersonality of Siberian administration, the watchdog of the empire. In Siberia, Kropotkin found more than a harsh nature, struggling settlements, and bureaucracy at its worst; he also encountered numerous members of the rebellious intelligentsia exiled for political reasons. The exiles made him aware of the heroic exploits and grievous experiences of men engaged in a determined effort to bring Russia out of the darkness of feudalism. They also provided him with the latest literature contributing to the philosophical and ideological elaboration and refinement of political resistance. In search of a realistic approach to social dynamics, he welcomed Spinoza's effort to make mathematics the basic instrument for a scientific study of society; he also expressed skepticism of Kant's theory of ethics, grounded in metaphysics rather than in science.[35] It was no accident that the last entry in his Siberian diary was a comment on John Stuart Mill's and Auguste Comte's interpretations of the social role of knowledge.[36] Kropotkin reasoned that the best way to acquire knowledge beneficial to society is to follow the methods of science and to stay with the subjects conducive to human comprehension, that is, to avoid the arid areas of theological thought and metaphysics (the traditional bastions of autocratic ideology). While in Siberia, he found time to read the scientific works of Goethe, Alexander von Humboldt, and John Herschel, and to follow the geological researches in Siberia conducted by G. P. Gel'mersen, a distinguished member of the St. Petersburg Academy of Sciences.

When Kropotkin returned to St. Petersburg, he brought voluminous notebooks of raw geographical information and a keen awareness of the incompatibility of the tsarist state with the freedom of spontaneous action, the prime mover of social progress. Imbued with the scientistic spirit of

Nihilism, he was now convinced that both the Siberian geographical challenge and the Siberian human plight needed deeper scientific explanation. The Siberian experience had prepared him to turn to science in search of a deeper knowledge of nature and society and to accept the claim of the swelling ranks of rebellious intelligentsia that the Russian "state" was the basic enemy of Russian "society," and that all revolutionary action in Russia should concentrate on overthrowing the existing political order.

During the first five years after his return from Siberia, Kropotkin was interested more in nature than in society, and more in science than in ideology. In 1867 he enrolled in the mathematical department of St. Petersburg University for the purpose of becoming proficient in the most rigorous methods of scientific inquiry. Along with university studies, he was active in the Russian Geographical Society, attending meetings and organizing his Siberian notes for publication. In the university he worked in an atmosphere permeated with the democratic ideals of the restive raznochintsy students; in the society, dominated by older men, he worked in a carefully guarded island of aristocratic Russia. The society was so pleased with his work that in 1870 it made him secretary of the department of physical geography and in 1871 funded his trip to Finland and Sweden for a study of the role of glaciers in the formation of topographic configurations. His published papers were faithful records of minute geographical observations, but they were also rich in hypotheses and theoretical propositions. He advanced a novel theory of the primary role of glaciation in the formation of Siberian landscape; he formulated a theory of plateaus as major features of Siberian topography; and he established the uniform northeast-southwest extension of the Siberian mountain ranges, indicating the role of common factors in the emergence of the major topographic features of North Asia.[37]

Meritorious work in the Russian Geographical Society produced another reward for Kropotkin: in 1872 he received permission to visit Switzerland and Belgium. Adding no laurels to his accomplishments in science, this trip marked a turning point in the evolution of Kropotkin's political ideas; it made him an ardent supporter of anarchism as a revolutionary movement. In Switzerland he came in close contact with the Russian revolutionary emigration, which at that time was divided into two major factions: the relatively moderate Lavrovists, who placed much more emphasis on political education than on the urgency of revolution, and the extremist Bakuninists, who believed more in the radical tactics of revolution than in the tedious process of political education. In Switzerland he also observed the activities of the Jura Federation, the stronghold of Bakunin's political and ideological influence. In Belgium he became acquainted with an assortment of political activists identified with the First International and divided into two major factions: the social-democratic wing, dominated by Marx, and the anarchists, led by Bakunin. In both Switzerland and Belgium he found the same hero: Mikhail

Bakunin, the articulator of an ideology that welded the social philosophy of anarchism and the strategy of revolutionary action into a political movement of considerable appeal. Kropotkin only regretted that he did not have the pleasure of personal acquaintance with Bakunin, who at that time was in Italy.

Soon after returning to St. Petersburg in 1872, Kropotkin joined a revolutionary group known as the Great Society of Propaganda, or the Chaikovskii Circle, a group of young men engaged in the study of Russia's ills and in propagandizing revolutionary ideas. While his experience in Switzerland and Belgium made him an anarchist in theory, work in the Chaikovskii Circle made him an anarchist in both theory and practice. The simultaneous identification with the Russian Geographical Society and the Chaikovskii Circle marked the beginning of a new phase in Kropotkin's eventful intellectual and political odyssey, a phase that combined an ardent attachment to science with an unceasing effort to articulate and propagandize the ideology of anarchism. The dual labors had a unifying element: a conviction that anarchist ideology was deeply grounded in science, that its roots were in a confluence of scientific theory and the spirit of humanity.

Combining a trained scientific mind with revolutionary zeal, Kropotkin was the most logical person to prepare a detailed statement on the ideological principles and political strategy of the Chaikovskii Circle. In a long manifesto entitled "Must We Concern Ourselves with an Examination of the Ideal of a Future System?" he provided a rich and forthright analysis of social and political ideas. This manifesto was important, in retrospect, more as a record of his philosophy than as a set of principles guiding the work of the Chaikovskii Circle. The first part of the manifesto unleashed a savage attack on all existing kinds of government as prime contributors to the perpetuation of inequality; it also offered an espousal of the obshchina and artel as models of a stateless society of the future. The second part elaborated the theme of social revolution as the most efficient way of laying the groundwork for a stateless society, a society built and sustained by the spontaneous action of free men rather than by the artificial and coercive action of the state. Recognizing that the peculiar historical conditioning of the Russian political order required unique revolutionary strategy, he emphasized the need for a heavy concentration on political education and recommended that no alliance be sought with international revolutionary movements.[38]

Kropotkin did not escape the vigilance of the ubiquitous political police. In 1875 he was incarcerated in the Peter and Paul Fortress, the prison for political dissidents. The Russian Geographical Society helped him ease the burden of prison solitude by meeting his requests for research material, and in 1876 it published his study on the Ice Age. He escaped from the prison hospital in 1876 and after a few months showed up in London. Western Europe was his home for the next forty years. Blessed with princely aplomb, oratorical mastery, personal charm, and boundless energy, he made his adaptation to Western life a quick and painless process.

The long years of emigration fell into two distinct periods. From 1876 to 1886 Kropotkin's revolutionary zeal surpassed his interest in science. Residing mostly in France and Switzerland, he attended and spoke at many socialist and anarchist meetings and demonstrations, elaborating the ideology and strategy of the forthcoming revolution. Although intimidated by the Russian secret police and agents provocateurs, threatened by local authorities, and hampered by the growing fragmentation of the revolutionary forces, particularly after the demise of the First International, he channelled all his energy into articulating the anarchist principles and kindling the revolutionary fire. The journal *Le Révolté*, which he published from 1879 to 1883, was his main political and ideological weapon. Occasionally an entire issue of the journal consisted of articles written by Kropotkin. *Paroles d'un Révolté*, published in 1885 by Elisée Reclus, presented a selection from Kropotkin's *Révolté* articles, clarifying the basic issues of the anarchist program and political expediency. Kropotkin believed that revolution was not only inevitable but also imminent and invincible, and that the destruction of the economic base of bourgeois society was its chief goal. The anarchist society, as blueprinted in the *Révolté* articles, had three basic characteristics: it was based on an economy of small producers, aggregated into independent associations; it recognized no state authority— it was a variety of "no-state socialism"; and it was governed not by law, artificially produced by political authorities, but by moral rules, products of spontaneous cooperation. The revolutionary verve of Kropotkin's writings was matched only by the idyllic naiveté of his sociological assumptions and the unlimited scope of his generalizations.

In 1886, after his release from a prison in Clairvaux, France, Kropotkin settled in London, his home base until 1917. At that time England faced no serious socialist agitation, and anarchism was almost completely unknown. Quick to adjust to the new environment, Kropotkin now devoted much more time to theoretical writing than to practical politics. In papers published in the French journal *La Révolte* during the 1890s he laid the groundwork for a broad theoretical approach to anarchism. In England, he said, he took advantage of living in an industrial society to acquire firsthand knowledge about the organization and dynamics of modern production and commercial enterprises and to examine the basic economic theories.[39] While during the previous period he transposed anarchism into an elaborate system of guides for immediate political action and ideological propaganda, during the London period he elaborated anarchism as a general sociology and philosophy of history, unencumbered by the political contingencies of the day. Moreover, his writing was not limited to topics related, directly or indirectly, to anarchism. He found the atmosphere in London congenial to scientific work. His scientific writings, published in *Nature, The Nineteenth Century,* and *The GeographicalJournal,* covered such diverse topics as the orography of Siberia, the application of Newtonian mechanics to the study of social life, and the "unsuspected" laboratory discoveries that unveiled the modern theories of the structure of matter. He thought that during his lifetime natural science had undergone two revolutions. The first revolution, in the middle of the nineteenth century, produced thermodynamics, unveiled the mechanical unity of electricity and magnetism, made physiology an extension of chemistry and physics, and ushered in the idea of biological evolution. The second revolution, at the end of the century, was set off by the discovery of radiation, revealing "the continual splitting and rebuilding of molecules," whether of organic or inorganic nature.[40] He was too close to the rapid succession of discoveries that unveiled the microscopic structure of matter to recognize in it a revolution in the scientific knowledge of the nature and dynamics of atoms rather than of molecules. However, he was quick to note that the combined effects of the two revolutions made it possible to achieve a new "synthetic philosophy," based on a full unity of philosophical and scientific thought, and to advance a general theory of society as a logical and methodological extension of natural science. He viewed the scientific revolution of the 1890s as a renewed triumph for, rather than as a challenge to and a denial of, the mechanistic orientation of the Newtonian legacy.

Among Kropotkin's many studies published during this period, three are particularly important, not only by the broad scope of their inquiry but also by their unique and complementary approaches to social reality. *Mutual Aid* (1902), Kropotkin's most celebrated work, is an essay in sociology. It deals exclusively with the grand problem of nineteenth-century sociology: the mechanism and inner meaning of social progress. Essentially a critique of Social Darwinism which treats conflict as the main source of social progress, *Mutual Aid* elaborates and defends the Populist concepts of "simple cooperation" (Mikhailovskii) and "solidarity" (Lavrov) as the key concepts unlocking the mysteries of progress and social integration. The book presents human society as an extension of nature and treats conflict as a nonessential feature of both nature and society. Social evolution is a progressive realization of man's natural potentialities and a gradual elimination of artificial social creations incompatible with human nature.

While *Mutual Aid* is cast in the classic mold of nineteenth-century sociology, *Modern Science and Anarchism* (1903) can best be characterized as an essay in the philosophy of history. It defines the place of anarchism in the grand course of modern social and intellectual history; it describes the compatibility of anarchism with the "synthetic philosophy" of modern thought grounded in science; and it provides a most categorical denial of the Hegelian view of the state as a liberating social force. Of all Kropotkin's works, *The Great French Revolution* (1909) comes closest to Leopold von

Ranke's conception of history as a discipline steeped in documentary material and unburdened by philosophical or sociological elaboration. In this book, Kropotkin moves slowly through the mass of documentary information and judgments of previous historians and is interested more in placing individual events into carefully documented historical sequences than in using selected historical material to illustrate preconceived philosophical and sociological schemes. This, however, does not mean that the book is totally free of the author's anarchist bias: its anti-Jacobinism, its sympathetic and relatively elaborate treatment of the role of anarchism in the organization of Paris "sections," and its positive view of the historical role of revolutions are direct reflections of Kropotkin's ideology.[41]

In June 1917, four months after the overthrow of the Romanov dynasty, Kropotkin, at the age of seventy-five, returned to Russia. After the October Revolution he moved to an isolated provincial town, where he died in 1921, but not until he had completed the first volume of his *Ethics*, a grand effort to synthesize anarchist sociology and philosophy of history. Marking Kropotkin's maximum engagement in philosophical analysis and a minimum concern with practical politics, this book provoked Viktor Chernov to label Kropotkin a "philosophical anarchist," in contrast to Bakunin as a "political anarchist" and to Tolstoy as a "religious anarchist."[42] Tracing the history of ethical ideas from the time of Plato to that of Nietzsche and Guyau, Kropotkin elaborated a theory of ethical naturalism, which regarded the instinctive basis of human social existence as the only legitimate source of morality. Only such a theory, he thought, could make ethics both a science and a weapon of social revolution. His letters to Lenin often dealt with the moral dilemmas and inconsistencies of the October Revolution—a revolution totally alien to anarchist ideals.[43] In 1918, he wrote that the English Revolution in the seventeenth century and the French Revolution in the eighteenth century were successful because they were dedicated to the achievement of high moral ideals. He added that the October Revolution could prove to be a historical success only if its leaders abandoned their blind allegiance to economic materialism and, instead, dedicated themselves to the higher ideals of humanity.[44] Marxism, according to him, is nineteenth-century socialism minus eighteenth-century humanism. It is a reversal of the humanistic trend that started in the Renaissance.

KROPOTKIN'S THEORY OF SOCIETY

To Kropotkin, anarchism is not a utopia, it is a science. Anarchism is "an attempt" to apply the knowledge obtained with the help of the inductive method of natural science to the study of human institutions. It is "an attempt to foresee the future steps of mankind on the road to liberty, equality, and fraternity, with a view to realizing the greatest sum of happiness for every unit of human society."

Anarchism, Kropotkin continued, "is the inevitable result of that natural-scientific, intellectual movement which began at the close of the eighteenth century, was hampered for half a century by the reaction that set in throughout Europe after the French Revolution, and has been appearing again in full vigor since the end of the fifties. Its roots lie in the natural-scientific philosophy of the century mentioned. Its complete scientific basis, however, it can receive only after that awakening of naturalism which brought into being the natural-scientific study of human social institutions."[45]

Kropotkin's anarchism is a socialist ideology and a scientific theory. As a socialist ideology, it has deep roots in the ideas of William Godwin, Proudhon, and Bakunin. Godwin was the first social critic to claim that, by the very reason of its existence, the authority of the state is the major hindrance to the development and improvement of moral habits and that private ownership is the main source of social injustice. Proudhon's main contribution was in connecting eighteenth-century social theory with nineteenth-century anarchism, in advancing detailed and tightly woven arguments against both the state authority and the institution of property as defined by Roman law, and in elaborating mechanisms of spontaneous cooperation. Bakunin translated the theory of anarchism into an active ideology of an internationally oriented socialist movement. Kropotkin thought that Bakunin's major contribution was in showing that a full elimination of the state was a historical necessity, that so-called universal suffrage was only a mask for rule by special interests, that the full independence of communes was the only guarantee for the freedom of the individual, and that Marx corrupted "communism" by tying it to a centralized state.[46]

Kropotkin's theory is much more than an elaboration of the anarchist legacy. As a special articulation of a scientific view of sociology and of a sociological view of science it is firmly anchored in Russian Nihilism, an orientation which owed a primary debt to Auguste Comte's positive philosophy. Russian Nihilists made three Comtian ideas the intellectual pillars of their world view. First, they accepted, in principle, the Comtian notion of philosophy as a synthesis of positive knowledge; they rejected every philosophy grounded in anthropomorphism, that is, in the habit of interpreting nature by attributing to it human qualities. They were against speculative philosophy, theological dogmatism, and mystical thought. In the second place, they adopted the Comtian view of the progressive growth of secular thought—particularly as seen in the growth of science—as the true indicator of social and cultural progress. In the third place, they endorsed Comte's arguments in favor of the ontological unity of scientific knowledge, which helped make sociology an integral part of Newtonian natural philosophy.

Kropotkin viewed the scientific study of society as an extension of the mechanistic philosophy to the realm of social behavior and organization.

According to him, "Anarchism is a world-concept based upon a mechanical explanation of all phenomena, embracing the whole of nature" and "the life of human societies and their economic, political, and moral problems." The aim of anarchism is to construct a synthetic philosophy and to embrace in one generalization all the phenomena of nature, including social life.[47] Kropotkin stood firmly on the position that such great scientists of the middle decades of the nineteenth century as Grove, Clausius, Helmholtz, Joule, and Kirchhoff had proven the unity of the inorganic and organic world; that all phenomena, including light, heat, electricity, and magnetism, are results of the same dynamics of molecules; and that "life is but a series of chemical decompositions and recompositions in very complex molecules."[48] He lauded Comte for having helped legitimatize both biology and sociology by including them in his scheme of fundamental sciences. While admitting that sociology was not yet fully crystallized as a science, he stated that the scholars who applied the scientific method to the study of human society were able to overcome the major obstacles set up by metaphysics and scholasticism.

Just as biology, according to Kropotkin, is an extension of chemistry, so sociology is an extension of biology. The Darwinian evolutionary theory has given biology an integrative principle of universal magnitude and has made it a logical component of the Newtonian mechanistic paradigm; at the same time, it has given sociology a fundamental conceptual tool for a natural-science approach to the study of the life and structure of human society. Darwin's theory has not merely provided a theory of the origin of species; it also has provided a key for the understanding of biological and social evolution.[49] "The idea of a continuous development—of a progressive evolution and a gradual adaptation of beings and societies to new conditions, in proportion as these conditions become modified—found a far wider field to work in than that of merely explaining the origin of new species .... Taking this principle, so rich in consequences, as a basis, it was possible to reconstruct, not only the history of organisms, but also the history of human institutions."[50] The concept of evolution, Kropotkin argued, was the first powerful tool in the hands of sociologists, emancipating them from their traditional reliance on metaphysics. He cited Sir Henry Maine and his followers, who in their comparative studies of primitive institutions applied the inductive method of modern biological sciences to show that the study of social evolution is no less scientifically productive than the study of organic evolution.

It is true, Kropotkin noted, that the method of evolution was applied long before the advent of Darwin's theory; the French Encyclopedists and such nineteenth-century historians as Augustin Thierry in France, G. L. Maurer and the "Germanists" in Germany, and N. I. Kostomarov and I. D. Beliaev in Russia had articulated an evolutionary approach to social institutions. But he was convinced that Darwinian evolutionism was the first development to enable scholars "to treat the facts of history in the same manner that naturalists examine the gradual development of the organs of a plant or that of a new species."[51] According to Kropotkin, Darwinian evolution as the universal and most comprehensive law of nature provided a sound methodological and philosophical basis for a full separation of social science from metaphysics—for a full emancipation of social scientists from dependence on dialectical logic, transcendental causation, and providential, teleological, and anthropomorphic explanations. It created the necessary condition for making sociology an abstract science, potentially equal with mechanics. It not only made it possible for sociology, ethics, and political economy to become indistinguishable, methodologically, from natural science, it also opened the doors for bringing the study of society in tune with the Newtonian paradigm, built upon the principles of immanent causation, ontological primacy of matter, and continuity in motion and change. Darwin, according to Kropotkin, gave sociology both a universal law of social development and a scientific method—the "inductive-deductive method." Sociological abstractions are of two kinds: generalizations derived from data gathered by the inductive method and hypotheses, or "working deductions," which are incorporated into the body of scientific knowledge only after they have been empirically verified—otherwise they are replaced by other hypotheses.

Despite his high regard for Darwin's scientific contributions, Kropotkin built much of his scholarly reputation by refuting one of the cornerstones of the theory of evolution: the conception of the struggle for existence as the prime mover of both biological and social transformation. He noted that, in the *Descent of Man*, Darwin recognized both competition and cooperation as mechanisms of evolutionary change; but he lamented Darwin's tendency to make cooperation less important than competition.[52]

Kropotkin was particularly critical of Thomas H. Huxley, who, in an effort to translate Darwin's theory of biological evolution into a sociological theory, claimed that man's instinctive endowments encouraged competition as a mechanism of social relations. In 1888, Huxley, in "The Struggle for Existence in Human Society," drew a sharp distinction between man as an animal and man as a member of society: as an animal, man is engaged in ferocious competition for survival; as a member of society, he is engaged in a constantly expanding process of cooperation. The history of civilization is a gradual substitution of culturally generated mutual peace and cooperation for the Hobbesian war of each against all as the normal state of social relations. Thus, according to Huxley, the evolution of human society expresses a gradual but inexorable curbing of man's instinctive predisposition for competition and conflict. In "Evolution and Ethics" (1893), Huxley stated: "Social progress means a checking of the cosmic process at every step and the substitution for it of another, which may be called the ethical process; the end of which is not the survival of those who may happen to be the fittest . . . but of those who are ethically the best."[53] The source of morality, as the essential attribute of human social existence, is in the denial of the instinctive nature of man.

Mutual Aid, Kropotkin's most widely read book—a book that was translated within a short span of time into most European languages—is essentially a rebuttal of Huxley's thesis.[54] Kropotkin primarily resented Huxley's efforts to show that social harmony and cooperation were results of a cultural, in contrast to a biological, evolution of man. He reasoned that Huxley's rejection of natural causation in the development of civilization gave solace only to believers in supernatural causation. (Kropotkin thought that social causation is only a variation of natural causation.) He also argued that Huxley had failed to see that mutual trust and solidarity were the chief attributes of the clan organization and tribal statelessness. He was particularly annoyed at Huxley's exaltation of the civilizing role of the state; in "The Struggle for Existence in Human Society," Huxley advocated extensive participation of the British government in the guidance and organization of formal education. Kropotkin was personally impelled to refute Huxley's claim that the modern advocates of "anarchism" sought a return to "social chaos" and "the brute struggle for existence."

In *Mutual Aid*, Kropotkin assembled voluminous information from ethnography and natural history for the purpose of providing an empirical base for his claim that "sociality" is no less a "law of nature" than "mutual struggle," and that social progress depends on the spontaneous development of the instinctive base of social solidarity. He took the clue from K. F. Kessler, an eminent Russian naturalist who, in a speech delivered in 1879 before the members of the Moscow Society for Naturalists, stated that "in the evolution of the organic world—in the progressive modification of organic beings—mutual support among individuals plays a much more important part than their mutual struggle."[55] He adduced considerable evidence to show that similar views were held by most Russian naturalists. In essence, Kropotkin's theory was not a categorical denial of Darwin's natural selection; it was merely an effort to show that "in the ethical progress of man, mutual support—not mutual struggle—has had the leading part." Its basic thesis was that while both competition and cooperation are rooted in man's instinctive endowment, it is only cooperation that ensures the "progressive evolution" of human society. Kropotkin recognized competition, or struggle, as an unavoidable component of human activity: whatever action he undertakes, man always encounters natural or social barriers which he must remove. Always indispensable, struggle is moral only in cases when it is directed against natural and social forces standing in the way of man's creative power. It is a progressive force only when it destroys the old forms of social existence in order to create new institutions that widen the base of justice and solidarity.[56] Huxley viewed human nature as a sociological phenomenon—as a product of the socialization of the human animal. Kropotkin viewed human society as a biological phenomenon—as a naturalization of human relations. The ideology of anarchism, as Kropotkin saw it, sought to free human society of all artificial elements, such as institutionalized authority, hampering the natural forces contributing to social harmony.

Kropotkin's theory of "mutual aid" or "cooperation" was closely linked to his theory of the origin and nature of the moral code. In fact, he viewed social evolution as a succession of gradual and progressive victories for social relations congruent with and derived from the instinctive base of morality. In his criticism of Comte's sociology, Kropotkin stated: "Comte had not recognized that the moral sense of man is as much dependent upon his real nature as all the physical features of his organization are; that both are an inheritance derived from an extremely long process of evolution—a process which has lasted already many scores of thousands of years.... Consequently, he could not see that the moral sense of man is nothing else but a further evolution of the mutual aid instincts evolved in animal societies long before the first man-like creatures appeared on the earth."[57] He fully endorsed J. M. Guyau's claim that "moral approval and disapproval were naturally prompted in man by instinctive justice."[58] "Guyau," he said, "understood that morality could not be built on egoism alone, as was the opinion of Epicurus, and later of the English utilitarians. He saw that inner harmony, and 'unity of being' (l'unité de l'être) will not suffice: he saw that morality includes also the instinct of sociability."[59] Bakunin shared the same view. "Science," he wrote, "has established that all intellectual and moral acts which distinguish man from animal species ... are the products of a combination of the diverse, purely physiological functions of the brain."[60] The mutual-aid instinct, in Kropotkin's view, undergoes a dual evolution: it becomes a dominant part of the sociopsychological makeup of the constantly growing proportion of the human population; and it becomes more diversified—for example, it becomes a source of compassion and justice. Mutual aid, justice, and compassion are, in Kropotkin's opinion, at the root of all ethical conceptions.[61]

In his view of social evolution, Kropotkin did not stay strictly within biological limitations; indeed, he treated social evolution as a result of an interaction of universal biological endowments, subject to mechanistic-causal explanations, and particular historical actions. expressing the purposiveness of man's behavior and social designs. His general theory of social evolution embodies four complementary principles.

First, evolution is universal. Just as organic evolution is a continuation of inorganic evolution, so social evolution is a continuation of organic evolution. As a result, sociology is an extension of biology in the same way that biology is an extension of chemistry and physics.

Second, social evolution is synonymous with progress, but progress is not an automatic realization of a preconceived plan: it is the result of a struggle between the forces which are compatible with the instinctive basis of cooperation and the forces which are derived from the instinctive basis of competition. Progress is measured in terms of the general expansion in the compass and thoroughness of cooperation. Contrary to the Hegelian philosophy of history, progress is not measured in terms of the development of the state as an organization of authority, for every institutionalized authority, past and present, is a negation of individual freedom and social equality.

Third, evolution is not an even process; sometimes it is an accelerated process, at other times it is exceedingly slow, approaching the point of stagnation, and at still other times it is a process of socially generated regression. For obvious reasons, Kropotkin treated the medieval period—the period of free cities—as an exhilarating and enormously productive phase in human history. He thought that "under the protection of their own liberties, which grew in the soil of free agreement and free initiative, these cities brought forth and developed a new civilization with a rapidity unparalleled in the entire history of man."[62] "With the exclusion of that other glorious epoch—the epoch of free cities in ancient Greece—mankind had never made such rapid progress. At no other time had man experienced such a profound change within the course of two to three centuries; nor was he so successful in establishing his mastery over the forces of nature."[63] The most outstanding achievements of modern civilization are mere elaborations of ideas produced by the creative genius of medieval cities. The emergence of nation-states in the sixteenth century robbed civilization of creative vigor and originality.

Fourth, all parts of the socioeconomic reality do not evolve at the same speed. Some parts may lag behind others and may even lead to the formation of petrified complexes reducing the vitality of individual social and cultural systems. Concerted social action, sometimes of revolutionary proportions, is needed to eliminate the pathological effects of these complexes. No social revolution, however, will produce satisfactory results if it works contrary to the laws of biological evolution and if it is not a ramification of biological evolution. Social revolution is not a historical aberration: it is an integral part of the universal evolutionary process. Revolutions are not important as mechanisms of cataclysmic changes in the fabric of society and in the hierarchy of values; they are important inasmuch as they define the main lines of evolutionary changes which take place in their wake.

In his exaltation of "mutual aid," or cooperation, as the primary index of social evolution, Kropotkin did not deviate from the well-established Russian tradition in social theory. Indeed, not a single representative of Russian sociological thought considered the struggle for existence the prime mover of social evolution. The German sociologist Albert Schäffle, the most extreme representative of Social Darwinism, who claimed that the stronger societies, that is, societies with a maximum survival potential in the struggle for existence, are also the societies with the highest level of morality, did not have a single supporter in Russia. The same goes for the Austrian sociologist Ludwig Gumplowicz, who treated military conquerors, elite ethnic groups, and the highest strata of society as the chief engineers of social progress.

Kropotkin's stress on cooperation and individuality as the most significant indices of social evolution is essentially indistinguishable from the axiomatic basis of Populist sociology. Both Mikhailovskii and Kropotkin viewed the expanding freedom and independence of the individual as the key manifestation of social progress.[64] When Kropotkin identified the "integration of labor"—that is, the consolidation of physical and intellectual work into an indivisible process—as the supreme ideal of society, he merely endorsed the idea of "simple cooperation" expressed much earlier in Mikhailovskii's "What is Progress?"[65] To both men the process of "the integration of labor" in society is tantamount to a progressive reduction of heterogeneity in the division of social labor and the corresponding growth of the internal unity of both personality and society. Perhaps the chief difference between the two was that, in the interplay of society and personality, Kropotkin gave more weight to society and Mikhailovskii more to personality.

Since Kropotkin envisaged the ideal society of the future as having neither ownership nor wages, he called his ideology "anarchistic communism," in contrast to Bakunin's "anarchistic collectivism," which had room for differential wages and collective ownership. In elaborating the theory of "anarchistic communism" (or "pure communism"), Kropotkin felt obliged to define his position vis-à-vis the social theory of Karl Marx. Unlike Bakunin, he experienced no passing infatuation for and made no compromises with Marxism.[66] He treated Marxist theory as a classic ideology of "state socialism"—an ideology of mass economy inimical to the autonomy of local economic associations and favoring a centralized state apparatus. The Marxist designs for "state socialism" were, in his view, an unnatural adaptation of socialist ideals to the rigidly centralized German state. Kropotkin rejected Marxism not only as an ideology but also as a science; he was particularly critical of the dialectical method, the cornerstone of the Marxist "science" of nature and society. He made his position clear and forthright:

We have heard much of late about "the dialectical method," which was recommended for formulating the socialist ideology. Such a method we do not recognize, neither would the modern natural science have anything to do with it. "The dialectical method" reminds the modern naturalist of something long since passed—of something outlived and now happily forgotten by science. The discoveries of the nineteenth century in mechanics, physics, chemistry, biology, physical psychology, anthropology, psychology of nations, etc., were made not by the dialectical method but by the natural-scientific method, the method of induction and deduction. And since man is part of nature, and since the life of his "spirit," personal as well as social, is just as much a phenomenon of nature as is the growth of a flower and the social life among the ants and the bees, there is no cause for suddenly changing our method of investigation when we pass from the flower to man, or from a settlement of beavers to a human town.[67]

Kropotkin rejected the dialectical method not only as a method of scientific inquiry but also as an explanation of social revolutions. He claimed that social revolutions cannot be defined in terms of sudden, qualitative changes of large proportions; just as one form of existence (a star, or a bird, for example) cannot suddenly change into another form of existence, so a form of society cannot be suddenly transformed into another form of society. Revolution, an important notion in Kropotkin's social theory, is not a sudden emergence of a new quality from a unique "synthesis" of a "thesis" and an "antithesis" but is merely "accelerated evolution" leading to a drastic reduction, or full elimination, of specific processes working against the "natural" or "scientific" growth of social relations. He admitted that every society experiences two conflicting "tendencies": the natural tendency leading to a reinforcement of institutions upholding solidarity and mutual aid and the unnatural tendency on the part of dominant groups "to strengthen their authority over the people."[68] The imminent goal of anarchist revolution, according to him, is not to install a new type of social relations but to eradicate the unnatural institutional arrangements working against the full realization of the social potential of human nature.

In his own words, Kropotkin's social theory is a search for "a realistic moral science," "a science as free from superstition, religious dogmatism, and metaphysical mythology as modern cosmogony and philosophy already are, and permeated at the same time with those higher feelings and brighter hopes which are inspired by the modern knowledge of man and his history."[69]

Mikhailovskii thought that sociology could acquire the status of a science only if it relied on a subjective method which, while of no use in natural science, could alone reach the depths of human motivations, goals, and moral ideals. To Kropotkin, on the other hand, sociology could produce reliable information only if it relied totally on the objective method of natural science that had no room for metaphysical prejudgment and mysticism. But while they differed on the finer points of epistemology, they were united in ideology; both looked for a way out of the oppressive atmosphere of a social system laden with residues of feudal institutions and dominated by political despotism. Their "scientific" views of future society may or may not have been fully congruent with the modern achievements in science, but they were a categorical negation of the values supporting the sacred culture of autocratic Russia. Their ideals of individuality, independent local economies, politically autonomous communities, and secular morality may or may not have been realistic—or scientific—indicators of the future stages in the evolution of human society, but they were undeniably an unqualified negation of the dominant values of contemporary Russian society. Kropotkin's, like Mikhailovskii's, realistic comprehension of the existing society was matched only by a utopian dream about the ideal society of the future.

In his search for a scientific sociology, Kropotkin acted more as a champion of the scientific world view than as a scientist. As a scientist, he worked successfully in physical geography, but there was no connection between his work in natural science and sociology. To sociology he brought not the method of rigorous inquiry but a commitment to a scientific world view: a belief that science is the mainspring of civilization and the source of objective designs for a future society embodying the principles of mutual aid and harmonious development of personality. His work clearly showed that an exaltation of the scientific world view was not a guaranty for scrupulous application of the scientific method and a careful scrutiny of the dominant trends in the development of scientific thought. The basic weakness of his scientific stance was that it made science subservient to ideology. He looked at the development of modern science as a process congruent with his ideology and felt no need to undertake a systematic analysis of the inner logic of the growth of scientific thought. In this respect his position was typical of the Russian intelligentsia—whether they carried the banner of Nihilism, anarchism, Populism or Marxism—whose enthusiasm for science and its social power far outran their familiarity with the major trends in modern scientific thought and who often defended a scientific world view by relying on antiquated or distorted scientific ideas.

Kropotkin's scientific world view was dominated by two notions: the universality of the Newtonian mechanistic paradigm and the growing "individualization" of scientific research, that is, the increasing concern of modern science with individual (or specific), rather than general, natural phenomena. At the time when Kropotkin was trying to make sociology a science by incorporating it completely into Newtonian science—dominated by the notion of the material unity of the world, the denial of teleology as an explanatory principle, and the idea of universal continuity in natural and social change—a new scientific paradigm was beginning to challenge most of the pivotal principles of the mechanistic legacy. He was making sociology a mechanistic science at the time when physicists were trying to expand the horizons of their discipline far beyond, and in opposition to, the Newtonian conception of natural philosophy.

Kropotkin argued that the process of "individualization" was the dominant trend in the development not only of modern society but also of modern science.[70] Modern astronomy has abandoned its traditional concentration on the general unity of the universe and has made individual planets and stars its main concern; modern physics gives precedence to the individuality of atoms over the generality of matter; modern botany and zoology concentrate on the individual forms of life and their adaptation to the environment; and physiology has embarked on the study of "the autonomous cells" of the blood, tissues, and nerve centers. In the same way, modern sociology has finally recognized that the process of "individualization"—of a progressive affirmation of the individual as the pivotal force of history—must be the focus of its inquiries.

A discerning student of the history of modern science would have no difficulty in recognizing that Kropotkin's statements were an expression of a world outlook rather than an accurate assessment of the status of scientific thought. In his eagerness to emphasize the search for "individuality" across the entire spectrum of natural science, he overlooked the modern search for a grand synthesis in various branches of knowledge—such as the Maxwellian synthesis in physics, the Mendeleevian synthesis in chemistry, and the Darwinian synthesis in biology—and the triumphs of structural approaches in organic chemistry, physiology, crystallography, and sociology. These synthetic efforts sought to establish universal entities of nature and society irreducible to the compositions, actions, and behaviors of individual constituents. In sociology, the theory was dominated by schools best typified by Durkheim's structuralism, which assumed the ontological irreducibility of "collective representations" to "individual representations," and the Simmelian search for pure forms of social relations revealing the larger principles of the integration of human society. Kropotkin was too busy criticizing the discrepancies in the sociological systems of Comte, Spencer, and Marx to take a closer look at the more modern developments in social theory.

Despite his relentless attacks on Darwin's principle of the struggle for existence as a motive force of evolution, Kropotkin dedicated his life to building a sociology upon two pillars of Darwin's legacy: a historicism that had no room for providential interference in the development of society and an inductionism that provided logical safeguards against the intrusion of metaphysics and mysticism into the study of social reality. His view of society as a natural phenomenon built upon the instinctive base of "mutual aid" did not prevent him from concentrating on social relations as historical phenomena—a man-made reality. The sociologist must depict the biological endowments of society but he must also formulate plans for their most effective realization. The sociologist studies society in order to change it.

As a social evolutionist, Kropotkin adhered closely, though not consistently, to the rule that the development of human society must be understood in terms of efficient causes (the only legitimate concern of science) and not final causes (the way of metaphysics). Although he believed in a future society unrestrained by the state apparatus, he did not view this society as a predetermined final goal but as a system of social relations created by man in full agreement with the instinctive base of morality. To Kropotkin, social evolution is not an automatic unfolding of a preconceived plan but a conscious search for better methods of creating social relations harmonious with human nature. He did not present the details of an anarchist utopia; his main job was to adduce scientific arguments in favor of modern man's search for a society unfettered by the impersonality of the modern state structure. But despite his natural science bias, his predictions of the future development of society were warranted more by the ideals of moral desirability than by the rigor of causal necessity. Despite the forcefulness of his arguments and the astuteness of his criticism, he won the day not by the power of his science but by the rich humanity of his dreams. As a recorder of the compounded moral dilemmas of civilized society he was one of the noblest and most perceptive figures in modern social theory. Kropotkin's social thought was a passionate counterpoise to two major trends in the history of modern society: the growing subjugation of the individual to the insatiable power of government authority, whether it be absolutist or democratic, and powerful movements that view centralized political action as the only safe path to socialism.[71]

4. The Philosophy of History and Social Theory

The Theory of Cultural-Historical Types: N. Ia. Danilevskii

The regularities in social change—in the historical process—were the dominant topic of nineteenth-century sociology. In the *Philosophy of History as Sociology*, published in 1897, Paul Barth surveyed the development of nineteenth-century sociology and related disciplines (such as cultural anthropology) concerned with the universal laws of social evolution. The main thesis of his book was that sociology and the philosophy of history were essentially the same discipline: while the leading philosophers of history produced tightly conceptualized theories of society, the leading sociologists devoted much of their time to articulating broad philosophical interpretations of history.

There are three major types of the philosophy of history. The first type is essentially ontological; it is concerned with the universal prime movers of the historical process and with the periodization of social evolution. It deals with the patterning of the substance of history and with the predictability of changes in social structure. The second type is essentially epistemological; it deals with the nature of historical knowledge and tries to answer the question of whether the historian should follow the general method of the natural sciences, the specific method of the social sciences, or the traditional rules of humanistic inquiry. The third type is essentially sociological; it deals primarily with the general laws of social structure and social dynamics, with the essential attributes of societies representing discrete phases of the universal socioeconomic evolution.

The most original and erudite Russian philosopher of history of the nineteenth century was Nikolai Iakovlevich Danilevskii. His complex and intricate system of philosophical-historical thought is an elaborate and tightly woven combination of ontological, epistemological, and sociological approaches. Very few Russian thinkers of the nineteenth century matched the originality of his thought and his aloofness from Western philosophical models. The reason for a generally unsympathetic reception of his ideas by contemporaries as well as succeeding generations was not so much in the inner logic of his thought as it was in the unpopularity of his ideological views.

Danilevskii was born in 1822 to a family of military distinction. In 1837 he enrolled in the Tsarskosel'skii Lycée, a school accessible only to young men of aristocratic origin. From 1843 to 1847 he studied the natural sciences at St. Petersburg University, whose academic staff included several internationally famed members of the St. Petersburg Academy of Sciences. Particularly renowned among these scholars was Karl von Baer, the leading embryologist of pre-Darwinian vintage, a modern pioneer in physical anthropology and a seasoned geographer-traveller. In 1849 Danilevskii received a master's degree in botany; his dissertation dealt with the flora of Orel province. In 1850, the police ordered him to leave St. Petersburg because of his association with the Petrashevskii circle—a group of young critics (including Dostoevskii) of the Russian political system—and his sympathetic interest in Fourier's socialist designs. During the next three years he worked in the offices of the governors of Vologda and Samara.

Shortly after his return to St. Petersburg in 1853 he was selected by Karl von Baer to take part in his scientific expedition to the Black and Caspian seas for a study of fishing resources. The expedition completed its work in 1857 and Danilevskii wrote the volume summarizing the major findings. During the remainder of his life he worked primarily in organizing and leading research expeditions engaged in economic studies of fishing resources in European Russia. He died in 1885 while searching for the causes of the decline in the fishing resources in Caucasian lakes.

Danilevskii also found time to write on more general topics not related to his professional work. The most important among these was *Russia and Europe* (1869), a major treatise in the philosophy of history. It represents a skillful intertwining of all three basic approaches in the philosophy of history: while the brunt of his argument is of an ontological nature, he also makes extensive use of epistemological and sociological analyses.

The basis of Danilevskii's ontological approach to the philosophy of history is the assumption that there are three basic ingredients of which the world is made: matter, motion, and spirit. Since matter is studied by chemistry, motion by physics, and spirit by psychology, these are the only sciences which can formulate valid laws of universal applicability. An important product of Danilevskii's philosophy of science is the assumption that history (and all the social sciences) has no ontological license to search for universal laws. All efforts to discover a general line in the evolution of mankind are intellectually fraudulent. Not only Hegel with his idea of the universal unveiling of the powers of reason, and Comte with his three-stage formula of the universal development of human society, but also the Darwinian sociologists who found in biological transformism a general model of universal social and cultural evolution extended themselves far beyond the ontological limits of historical knowledge. If the study of sociocultural history is to be scientific, it must be confined to the formulation of laws that are limited in time and space.

In propounding his thesis of the limited nature of historical generalizations, Danilevskii relied on selected antitransmutationist theories in biology. Biology, like history, has no ontological basis for the formulation of universal laws; all biological theories that advocate unilinear development and the emergence of new species by a transformation of the existing ones go beyond the limits of their competence by introducing "artificial systems" of nature. A follower of Cuvier's theory, according to which no transformation in living forms extends beyond the fixed limits of specific biological types, he advocated a return to the theory of "natural systems" in the living world, a theory which recognizes the discreteness, discontinuity, and morphological individuality of a small number of biological types. Relying on a biological analogy, he found "scientific" support for his contention that human societies, too, are discrete, discontinuous, and individualized and that a scientifically rigorous history must deal exclusively with "natural systems" in sociocultural formations. A society, like a biological species, must be studied as a unique morphological phenomenon, as a historical culture sui generis. Just as there is no universal biological evolution, there is no universal history in the strict meaning of the term. And just as there is no "theoretical comparative physiology" and "theoretical comparative anatomy," for each type of living form has its own physiological and anatomical plan, there is no theoretical sociology as a discipline of the universal laws of social development.

To the ontological foundations of his philosophy of history Danilevskii gave elaborate epistemological support. All human knowledge, he argued in the spirit of Kantian philosophy, is subjective: science deals with nature in the way man perceives it, not in the way it exists independently of man. By relying on rigorous methods of inquiry, the natural sciences can reach a high level of objectivity; however, no methods can free history and the social sciences of their essentially subjective nature. The most important subjective bias built into historical knowledge has a national origin and identification. While chemistry, physics, and the other natural sciences are international in the main body of their knowledge, history, political economy, and sociology are predominantly national. Chemistry must be judged in terms of the acceptance of its theories and facts by the international community of scientists; history and the social sciences must be judged primarily in terms of their national significance and setting. Thus, on epistemological grounds, too, Danilevskii rejected the feasibility of a universal history.

Danilevskii elaborated his epistemological views on the subjective nature of scientific knowledge into a carefully thought out and rather impressive discussion of the differential roles of various nations in scientific creativeness. In the development of every science he recognized five distinct phases. In the phase of unsystematic empirical wisdom, science consists of accumulated aggregates of data which are not integrated into theoretical systems. In the phase of artificial systems the chaotic mass of empirical data is subsumed under general principles which, while not true representatives of reality, help give a broad picture of nature. Ptolemaic astronomy was an artificial system, for "it did not express the essential meaning of phenomena and did not conform to them; it was merely an auxiliary instrument helping reason and memory to orient themselves in the mass of particular phenomena."[1] In the phase of natural systems, the general principles of science are in full accord with the mass of phenomena covered by them. The Copernican system belongs to this phase, for it correctly identifies the real place of every celestial body. In the phase of partial empirical laws, particular generalizations are deduced from the natural system. However, while these generalizations show the relations between various phenomena, they do not explain them. Kepler's laws offer the most graphic illustration of this phase. The phase of a general rational law is best illustrated by Newton's law of gravitation, which both unites and explains all partial empirical laws. This is the crowning, and the last, phase in the development of a particular science. After a science reaches the phase in which it is dominated by a general rational law, it can advance only by discovering new facts (new planets and comets, for example), by refining the inner logic of explanatory principles, by improving research techniques, and by embracing other systems of natural phenomena. The basic law of one science could also be combined with the basic laws of other sciences. But once the knowledge of a science is integrated into a general rational law it has exhausted its generalizing power and cannot produce another general rational law.

By combining the thesis of the essentially subjective nature of scientific knowledge with the theory of the five-phase development of individual sciences, Danilevskii undertook to explain the differential participation of individual nations in the development of scientific thought. His aim was to show that even the most exact sciences bear a definite imprint of the unique psychological makeup of individual nationalities—that even the most exact sciences are reflections of the national character. He argued, for example, that while the English distinguished themselves by their contributions to all four phases (discounting the phase of unsystematized empirical knowledge), the French excelled primarily in helping individual sciences enter the phase of partial empirical laws. The Germans share honors with the English of having been statistical leaders in raising individual sciences to higher levels of development; however, they differ from the English in that they have not raised a single science to the level of natural systems.[2] Hidden in Danilevskii's argumentation is the tacit acknowledgment that the Russians had not produced a single scientist credited with having raised a science to a higher phase of development. It is worth noting, however, that in 1869, the year of the publication of *Russia and Europe*, D. I. Mendeleev announced his discovery of the periodic law of elements, the most comprehensive law in chemistry formulated in the nineteenth century.

The national character finds a graphic expression not only in the differential participation of individual nations in raising individual sciences to higher phases of development but also in the selection by nations of particular sciences for special emphasis. "For example," Danilevskii states, "in the love for, and the utilization of, pure and applied mathematics the first place without any doubt belongs to the French. In this field they alone have produced more outstanding scholars than all other European nations together: Pascal, Descartes, Clairaut, D'Alembert, Monge, Laplace, Fourier, Legendre, Poisson, Cauchy, Leverrier—all are French."[3] Germany, on the other hand, has excelled in linguistics and comparative philology. France has had almost no competitors equal to such famous German names in these fields as A. F. Pott, Wilhelm von Humboldt, Jacob Grimm, Christian Lassen, August Schleicher, and Max Müller. England, too, has had its beloved science: geology which, in all its major developments, owes a primary debt to British scholarship.

The "national character" makes an indelible imprint not only on individual sciences but also on specific theoretical orientations. The love for independent activity and the search for a versatile development of "personality or individuality," which results from a continuous struggle against all external hindrances, are, according to Danilevskii, "the dominant traits of the English national character." "Struggle and unlimited rivalry are the life of an Englishman: he accepts them in all their ramifications, treats them as his rights, tolerates no restriction on them . . ., and sees them as a source of enjoyment."[4] Hobbes's view of the paramount role of the principle of *bellum omnium contra omnes* in the formation of human society, Adam Smith's economic theory of free competition between producers and consumers— and among producers themselves—as the basic source of economic harmony, and Darwin's theory of evolution based on the struggle for existence are the best known and most graphic scientific expressions of the English national penchant for continuous struggle.

Danilevskii noted that a profound feeling in favor of state control over the actions of individuals was deeply rooted in the French national character. True to the bent of the national character, the three major French economic schools—mercantilists, physiocrats, and the right-to-work advocates— sought state protection for a full implementation of their plans. Saint-Simon and his school created a complex plan for a society in which the government would exercise close control over social labor and the distribution of wealth.

Danilevskii conceded that all sciences are not equally open to unique national influences. Nationality finds the least expression in mathematics and the oldest physical sciences (typified by astronomy), which have evolved the most exact methods of inquiry. The less amenable a subject of inquiry is to exact scientific treatment, the more likely it is to invite a national bias. The social sciences and the humanities command the least rigorous methods and are permeated with a maximum of national sentiment. The "difficulties" are compounded by the fact that even the subject of inquiry is often of predominantly national significance; thus the social sciences are national both in their cultural bias and their subject of inquiry.[5]

So far we have looked into two arguments used by Danilevskii in support of his theory of the discreteness and discontinuity of the types of national cultures. The ontological argument convinced him that human societies do not have a common and universal substratum. The epistemological argument provided him with illustrations for the unique cognitive attributes, or epistemological biases, of individual national types. He was particularly eager to show that the substantive and cognitive limitations of the social sciences and the philosophy of history are significant proof of the qualitative, "morphological" differences between national cultures, and therefore of the noncomparability of national cultures and the nonexistence of universal laws of social structure and social evolution.

But he did not rest his case there. Next he examined the sociological arguments in favor of the theory of the discrete nature of national cultural types, rejecting all notions of the basic unity of culture and of the unilinearity of social evolution. He relied on the conception of the "cultural-historical type" as the basic sociological unit in the history of man. "Cultural-historical types" can be synchronic but more commonly are diachronic. They are not necessarily coterminous with individual national groups; more often than not they are aggregates of ethnic groups united by a system of specific values—each type has a unique cultural morphology and forms a "natural system." As "natural systems," cultural-historical types are unique and cannot be projected on a single line of development. With the rejection of unilinear evolutionism. Danilevskii rejected, at least in theory, the idea of progress, the value judgment widely shared by nineteenth-century social theorists.

Danilevskii made it clear that it is not the fate of every national group to become an integral part of a cultural-historical type. Some peoples remain at the level of "ethnic material" and fail to achieve the morphological integration necessary for the emergence of a cultural-historical type. Other peoples may perform the role of "historical spoilers," expediting the downfall of dying civilizations. The Huns, Mongols, and Turks belonged to this group. The periodic rise of these "negative" types to historical prominence, as well as the chronic existence of stagnant "ethnographic materials," helped Danilevskii reinforce his attack on the notion of the universality, unity, and continuity of social evolution. He also recognized the existence of two cultural-historical types—the Peruvian and Mexican—whose latent resources were not fully developed because of destructive forces of external origin.

Danilevskii recognized ten fully developed cultural-historical types: Egyptian, Chinese, Assyro-Babylonian-Phoenician-Chaldean or ancient

Semitic, Hindu, Iranian, Hebrew, Greek, Roman, neo-Semitic or Arabian, and German-Romanic or European. The critics of Danilevskii's theory have noted that, while explicitly rejecting the notion of a "universal history" because of the substantive incommensurability of diverse cultural-historical types, he implicitly endorsed a concept of universal sociology by elaborating a set of general laws codifying the formal commensurability of the inner mechanisms in the development of all cultural-historical types.[6] The pronounced dissimilarity of historical cultures did not prevent him from recognizing a set of broad principles of sociological unity.

Indeed, he formulated five basic laws governing the emergence and development of the cultural-historical types: (1) a people, or an aggregate of peoples, can form a cultural-historical type if it has a basic linguistic affinity, is spiritually capable of historical development, and has passed through the stage of childhood; (2) no people can advance to the state of civilization characteristic of a cultural-historical type unless it has achieved political independence; (3) the principles of the civilization of a cultural-historical type cannot be mechanically transmitted to the peoples of another type, for each type elaborates its own civilization even though it may depend to a greater or lesser degree on the influences of alien civilizations; (4) the civilization indigenous to a given cultural-historical type achieves its full development only when the diversity of its ethnic elements is not crushed by rigid political unity—only when it forms a federation or a union of states; and (5) the growth period of a cultural-historical type is indefinitely long, but the period of blossoming and fruit-bearing is relatively short.

The basic characteristic of cultural-historical types is their uniqueness, their unrepetitiveness. Even when cultural material is "transmitted" from one civilization to another, it acquires a new meaning or a different emphasis in the borrowing civilization. Science, for example, represents a central cluster of values in the European type; in the Slavic cultural-historical type it is merely borrowed material unaffiliated with the primary values.

In his discussion of the principles which give each cultural-historical type a unique morphology, Danilevskii was led to a search for a universal sociological explanation of the primary clusters of values which, in their totality, embrace all the modes of cultural integration. He recognized four major "cultural activities" that provide the means for the integration of individual cultural-historical types: religion, culture in the narrower meaning of the term (aesthetics, science, technology, and so on), politics, and socioeconomic organization. Individual types do not necessarily elevate all four activities to the same high level of emphasis and elaboration. The Hebrew type, for example, was preoccupied with religious activities, the Greek with aesthetic modes of expression, and the Roman with politics. The European type, in contrast, had two emphases: politics and science. In his Pan-Slavic exuberance,

Danilevskii proclaimed the burgeoning Slavic civilization to be more complete and symmetrical than any previous or coexisting cultural-historical type.

In elaborating the sociological principles of his theory of cultural-historical types, Danilevskii was quick to recognize Darwinism as an antithetical force of the first magnitude. Indeed, he wrote a two-volume study attacking every basic proposition advanced by Darwin's scientific legacy. The book was noted by his contemporaries as a comprehensive compilation of current anti-Darwinian arguments rather than as an original and carefully documented treatise. Its nomination for a prize by the St. Petersburg Academy of Sciences was turned down by a committee of judges who contended that it contained gross distortions of Darwin's theoretical propositions and offered few original ideas.[7] Danilevskii rejected Darwin's theory on philosophical, biological, and sociological grounds. Posing as a defender of science, he claimed that Darwin's basic aim was not to add to scientific thought but to advance a materialistic philosophy of science which viewed the universe as a mechanism totally independent of a supreme intelligence.[8] In his criticism of the scientific foundations of Darwinism, Danilevskii relied heavily on the arguments advanced by the leading opponents of both natural selection and the transmutationist idea. From Karl von Baer he borrowed the idea of the paramount role of final causes (teleology) in the world of organic nature, from Kölliker the rejection of gradualism as the true description of evolution, and from Louis Agassiz the notion of the incompatibility of modern paleontological information with the principle of transmutation. He also relied on an assortment of criticisms advanced by some of the leading physiologists, embryologists, botanists, and zoologists of the time.

In his criticism of the current sociological elaboration of the Darwinian theory, Danilevskii concentrated on the incompatibility of the "materialism," "determinism," and "pseudo-teleology" (shown most clearly in the treatment of adaptation as the goal of evolution) of evolutionism with the moral code as the most sublime expression of humanity. Here again he relied heavily on the two most common assumptions of the critics of the sociological theory based on Darwinian evolution: first, the total incompatibility of the struggle for survival with the moral order in human society, and, second, the total incompatibility of the principle of natural causality with the religious substratum of the ethical code. Danilevskii viewed Darwinism as a pseudo-scientific plan to destroy the religious and moral foundations of modern society.

Underlying Danilevskii's long excursions into the ontological, epistemological, and sociological attributes of civilizations was a pronounced ideological commitment. He was the chief ideologue of Pan-Slavism, an ultraconservative movement which sought Russia's active engagement in a war for the liberation of all Slavic peoples and the formation of a Slavic federation with Constantinople as its capital. The movement was an elaboration and modernization of Slavophilism. N. N. Strakhov called *Russia and Europe* "the catechism and the code of Slavophilism."[9] K. N. Bestuzhev-Riumin regarded the book as a grand systematization of Slavophile views and a turning point in the growth of Russia's search for national "self-understanding."[10] Several writers claimed that the book's real strength was in rebuilding the Slavophile philosophy upon a "solid scientific basis." Dostoevskii was impressed with the work as a synthesis of unassailable arguments against all theories which regarded the Russian way of life and values as an extension of Western culture.[11] Dostoevskii was under the spell of Danilevskii's philosophy of history when he asserted that science may be a source of great wisdom but that it is not Russian. He acknowledged the social usefulness of science and said that Russia should take full advantage of modern developments in experimental science, but he insisted that the true genius of Russian culture lay not in secular wisdom and positive knowledge but in religious contemplation. He lauded *Russia and Europe* as a storehouse of incontrovertible proofs for his own contention that "the Russian Christ," as embodied in the Orthodox church, was the essence of Russian culture and the most powerful source of Russian contributions to the good of humanity.

Danilevskii accepted the Slavophile notion of the cultural uniqueness of Slavic culture, but he resented the heavy reliance of Khomiakov and other leading Slavophiles on Western philosophical thought in the articulation of their views. He also rejected, but not with unimpeachable consistency, the Slavophile notion of the universal appeal and messianic value of the Eastern Orthodox religion and of the future role of the Russian church in the salvation of mankind from the accumulated sins of bygone centuries. Vladimir Solov'ev stated that the Slavophile view of Russian society as the carrier and embodiment of universal enlightenment and religion was much closer to true Christianity than Danilevskii's view of localized religions identified with individual cultural-historical types.[12] As attested by his views on the burgeoning Slavic civilization as the most complete and symmetrical culture, Danilevskii was not immune to the notion of the superiority of unheralded Slavic values, attitudes, and social institutions; actually, however, the main thrust of his speculation was in the effort to show the full cultural autonomy of Slavdom and to refute claims of the advocates of the superiority of Western civilization.

Danilevskii found it much easier to claim structural uniqueness for Slavic civilization than to spell out its concrete attributes. He anticipated a future Slavic polity in which religion would be dominated by a dedication to the preservation of pristine Christianity, the political life by an organic synthesis of autocracy and individual freedom, the economic organization by the obshchina as the community closest to the welfare of the masses, and the cultural sphere by the aesthetic rather than intellectual mode of expression and creativeness. The noted historian P. N. Miliukov stated cogently that some of these characteristics were echoes of past beliefs, while others hung in the clouds of obscurity and indefiniteness.[13] The interpretation of obshchina, for example, did not go beyond the endorsement of a Slavophile idea, while the view of the future political organization was a vague "synthesis" of "freedom" and "autocracy."[14] Modern history has proved Danilevskii a poor prophet not only in his claim that the Russians would not play a creative role in the advancement of scientific knowledge but also in his bold assertion that the essentially conservative bent of the Russian mind would foredoom any revolutionary upheaval.

During the 1890s, the liberal intelligentsia, including a solid contingent of academics, looked at Danilevskii as the chief codifier of an ideology dedicated to the preservation of autocracy and to an isolation of Russia from Western thought, if not from Western technology. Miliukov, a typical member of the liberal intelligentsia, presented the most complete and systematic critique of the theory of historical-cultural types.[15] He took great pains to show that, despite its strict scientific decorum, Danilevskii's theory of history was an exercise in the philosophy of historical providentialism. Miliukov had little difficulty in unmasking Danilevskii's uncritical reliance on the outmoded morphological principles of G. Cuvier and K. von Baer and in showing that the theory of cultural-historical types was an echo of the Slavophile portrayal of the Russian national character. Danilevskii followed the Slavophiles in identifying certain universal characteristics of culture as exclusive traits of the Russian people, in overgeneralizing the unique sociocultural characteristics of individual historical periods, and in elevating ideological biases to the level of scientific facts.[16]

Miliukov asserted correctly that the theory of cultural-historical types was based on the ideology of Pan-Slavism and that it gave comfort only to the reactionary forces advocating an extension of Russian political control over other Slavic peoples. *Russia and Europe* advanced an elaborate philosophy of history in support of the rising forces of Russian imperialism, which advocated a "Slavic federation," ruled from Constantinople, as the most effective solution of the Eastern question.[17] Danilevskii's philosophy marshals support for the thesis that the Slavic nations under foreign rule should not seek help in the West, dominated by materialistic science and Protestant democracy, but in Russia, the homeland of autocracy, nascent Christianity, and spiritualist philosophy. Although Miliukov's analysis was scrupulously thorough and carefully documented, it was not a model of scientific detachment for it was part of a campaign to advance and consolidate a liberal ideology of constitutional government.

Despite an ideological commitment that did not please the typical (liberal) members of the intelligentsia of his time and despite vexing inconsistencies in his philosophy, Danilevskii was one of the most original Russian sociologists of his time. His theory of cultural-historical types was a unique and on the whole an original sociological theory. V. Solov'ev's charge that it was scarcely more than an elaboration of a theory sketched by Heinrich Rückert in an appendix to his *Lehrbuch der Weltgeschichte in organischer Darstellung* (1857) was refuted carefully and convincingly by N. N. Strakhov.[18] While his dreams of a Slavic utopia in the near future were open to broad criticism and refutation, his dramatically expressed annoyance at Western historians and philosophers who viewed Western culture as the summit of man's achievements and who relegated all other cultures either to oblivion or to the level of abortive—or as yet incomplete—efforts to emulate the West should not be disregarded. He was correct in identifying the notion of unilinearity in Western interpretations of universal history as a tool of Western intellectual imperialism. He erred, however, in basing his own concept of discrete cultural types on outdated biological concepts of the pre-Darwinian vintage.

Danilevskii did not reject the notion of cultural progress altogether for he saw no reason why individual cultural-historical types should not borrow cultural material from other civilizations. But he was adamant in his claim that the idea of progress cannot explain the quintessence of individual civilizations as special arrangements of values that guarantee each cultural-historical type a unique place in man's history. The crux of his thought is that sociology will remain a sterile science as long as it does not place the major emphasis on a systematic and intensive study of the unique structural and substantive characteristics of individual societies. A vast majority of Russian sociologists, from the Nihilists to the Marxists, looked on the evolution of Russian society through the prism of a universal social evolution; Danilevskii, on the other hand, took a broad and critical view of the notion of "universal history" from the point of view of Russian civilization. In the process, according to P. A. Sorokin, he offered "several of the most important generalizations of contemporary sociology and anthropology concerning the diffusion, migration, expansion, and mobility of culture." He also set forth "the theory that technological or material culture tends to diffuse only within its own area and cannot spread over various cultures except in its elements."[19] He erred in trying to squeeze the broad potentialities of Russian culture into a narrow and rigid mold of Slavophile thought.[20]

NEO-KANTIAN HISTORICISM

In 1865, the German philosopher Otto Liebmann published *Kant und Epigonen*, a major study dedicated to a revival and modernization of the basic principles of Kant's theory of knowledge. His prophetic call of "Back to Kant" made Liebmann the forerunner of neo-Kantian philosophy, which reached maturity in the 1890s and the first decade of the twentieth century. Its leading representatives were grouped around two centers: the Baden school, dominated by Wilhelm Windelband and Heinrich Rickert, and the Marburg school, dominated by Hermann Cohen and Paul Natrop.

In the rich legacy of neo-Kantian philosophy three ideas received particularly detailed elaboration.

First, the neo-Kantians postulated the epistemological unity of scientific knowledge. This idea was a logical derivation from the general proposition that all human knowledge is subjective in origin, that it is a product of the human mind, which frames a posteriori cognitive material (data obtained by sense organs) within a priori categories of thought, which are inborn and independent of experience.

Second, the neo-Kantians elaborated the principle of logical and methodological differences between the natural sciences and the social sciences. They viewed the natural sciences as essentially nomothetic; to these sciences, the natural phenomena are important only inasmuch as they illustrate the working of general laws of nature. The social and humanistic sciences, on the other hand, are mainly idiographic; individual social-cultural phenomena are important scientifically more by their unique characteristics than as examples of the working of universal laws. Ernst Troeltsch made it clear that the notion of the "individuality" of phenomena, as viewed by Windelband and Rickert, stands strictly for "the uniqueness and nonrepetitiveness of a historical subject, whether it be an epoch, a state, a people, a mood of the masses, a class orientation, or an individual person."[21] Rickert, one of the main spokesmen for the methodological dichotomy of the sciences, does not claim that all the natural sciences must be nomothetic and that all social and humanistic sciences must be idiographic, for he readily admits that there are natural sciences which are idiographic and social sciences which are nomothetic. What he means is that the true strength of natural science is in a nomothetic, or generalizing, orientation and that the social sciences are at their best when they are oriented idiographically. According to Rickert, the empirical reality becomes nature when it is examined with the help of a generalizing method, and it becomes history when it is examined with the help of an individualizing method.[22] The emphasis on the primacy of the idiographic orientation in the social sciences is equivalent to the admission that human society is essentially a historical phenomenon.

Third, the neo-Kantians claimed that, while natural phenomena could be fully understood within the framework of causal explanations, social phenomena require both causal and teleological explanations. This proposition led a typical neo-Kantian philosopher to claim that social reality must be split between two distinct modes of inquiry: one concerned with society as "being" (as a historical phenomenon), and the other with society as "duty" (as a moral phenomenon). While idiographically oriented social sciences study society as "being," philosophy alone can explore the depths of society as "duty." The social sciences stay in the world of social causation; philosophy dwells in the world of social purposiveness. The ultimate goal of moral philosophy is to lay bare the complex reality of "pure will" or "absolute morality," conceived as the ethical law transcending the limits of space and time. The neo-Kantians were as eager to emancipate moral philosophy from metaphysical interference as they were to surrender to it the essential domains of sociological inquiry. Cohen went so far as to claim that moral philosophy must ground its methodology in mathematics, not necessarily as a system of procedures for quantitative measurement but as a symbol of most accomplished and rigorous logical analysis. However, Cohen was more interested in pointing out the cognitive limitations of science than in advancing the scientific precision of philosophy.

Neo-Kantianism did not evolve into a closed system. It produced a new generation of astute students of society dedicated to helping empirical science incorporate the wide areas of social reality which their teachers had surrendered to philosophy. The rebellion of the new generation received powerful impetus from the sociological work of Max Weber, the giant of modern sociology, who made a bold and eminently successful effort to widen the scope of the scientific study of society by making moral "purposiveness" a variety of social "causality" and by bringing "being" and "duty" under the common roof of science. An elaborate logical analysis of the links between collective concepts and concrete human action convinced Weber that a cross section of value judgments, underlying the dominant points of view, elevated social action above the amorphous mass of daily experience. A critical examination of value judgments helped science become a technique for establishing multiple links between social ideals and social action. In subordinating value judgments to scientific scrutiny, Weber abandoned the neo-Kantian notion of "absolute morality." But he retained the neo-Kantian rejection of neopositivism. While neopositivists sought to resolve the dilemma of the logical incompatibility of "being" and "duty" by recognizing only those values that have a source in, or are compatible with, science, Weber sought to construct a logical and methodological apparatus for distilling "objective" and "rational" meanings from "subjective" and "irrational" values. According to him, the fact that values, in their inner makeup, may be incompatible with the rationality of science does not make them inaccessible to scientific treatment.

The Russian articulators of neo-Kantian philosophy as applied to the study of society belonged generally to four distinct groups. The first group embraced the neo-Populists, who saw in some of the leading neo-Kantian ideas a general confirmation and elaboration of the epistemological legacy of Mikhailovskii's and Lavrov's sociology. Viktor Chernov culled many citations from the works of Dilthey, Windelband, Simmel, and Rickert that supported the claims of Populist leaders that sociology could not rely on natural science models, for its data were essentially subjective: they reflected the purposiveness of social action, the ethical distinctness of human existence, and the freedom of will. He pointed out that Rickert's identification of the historical approach as teleological differed in no way from Mikhailovskii's treatment of "subjective ideals" as the motive force of history.[23] Both Mikhailovskii and Rickert were extremely careful in protecting the teleological orientation in historical and social inquiry from the lures of metaphysical speculation and excursions into the world of supernaturalism.[24] While extremely critical of current efforts to blend the "subjectivism" of Kantian philosophy with the "objectivism" of Marxian theory, Chernov was not averse to blending the "subjectivism" of the Russian sociological school and neo-Kantianism with the "objectivism" of neopositivist philosophy , particularly of "Avenarius's school."[25] His notion of sociology as a combination of "objective" and "subjective" studies betrays an influence of the neopositivist interpretation of historical investigation as a distillation of objective knowledge (that is, knowledge revealing regularities in the historical process) from the subjective experience of historical actors. More than other Russian sociologists, he argued that the subjective approach in sociology supplements, rather than replaces, the objective approach modeled on the natural sciences. However, Chernov was too preoccupied with elaborating the subjective side of the sociological equation to give the objective side more than a minimum of attention.

The second group consisted of young Marxist renegades, led by Petr Struve and N. A. Berdiaev, who looked for a middle course between Kant's moral philosophy and Marx's sociological theory. Influenced by Rudolf Stammler's *Economy and Law* and Eduard Bernstein's *Evolutionary Socialism*, they tried to modulate the most categorical and inflexible propositions of Marxian theory in the spirit of Kant's philosophical legacy.[26] They viewed sociology as a synthesis of historical materialism and the ethical absolutism elaborated in Kant's *Critique of Practical Reason*. In essence, however, they treated sociology as a philosophy of values concerned primarily with the universal laws of social integration, which are not distilled from empirical material but are constructions of pure logic. Most ex-Marxists were at first critical of, and published essays against, a coalescence of Kant and Marx.[27] For most of them the engagement in neo-Kantian philosophy was a temporary pause on the way to idealistic metaphysics.

The third group consisted of the chief representatives of the modern Russian school of natural law, who claimed that the overconcern with specific and concrete social attributes of the law prevented legal scholars from trying to reach the depths of universal justice, that is, the quintessence of the ethical foundations of law. Reacting critically to the empirically oriented sociology of law, the advocates of natural law advanced a normative approach to law as a specific branch of philosophy. Led by P. I. Novgorodtsev, they argued that the moral aspects could be fully comprehended within a teleological framework of moral philosophy rather than within the causal framework of science. According to Novgorodtsev, science studies the ephemeral aspects of law, while philosophy concentrates on the absolute, immutable, and universal attributes of law.[28] The raison d'être of moral philosophy is in the incompetence of science to treat ethical problems. Kant's greatest contribution, according to Novgorodtsev, was in showing that scientific explanation, based on the principles of necessity, causality, and predictable regularity, did not reach moral freedom, the essence of social reality. "Moral metaphysics," rather than "social physics," provided the true methods for the study of the structure of human society.

The fourth group found its most erudite representative in B. A. Kistiakovskii, a friend of Max Weber and a man who combined a strong ideological commitment to parliamentary democracy with a deep concern with the interaction of law, as a normative system, with total society.* The far-ranging social consequences of the rapid politicization of Russian society at the turn of the century made it clear that to reject values (or value judgments) as a field of scientific inquiry was to take science away from the most acute realities of Russian society. Like Weber, Kistiakovskii categorically refused to accept the much circulated view of the "crisis of science" which encouraged metaphysical encroachment on the most vital domains of scientific inquiry. Instead, he dedicated his work to widening the orbit of the scientific study of society and to bringing the study of "causal" and "purposive" social complexes into complementary relationship. By accepting "causality" as an important principle of social science explanations, he rejected the current views of the total uselessness of natural science models in sociological theory. Unlike Chernov, he gave much attention to the natural science side of the sociological equation.

A. S. Lappo-Danilevskii: Varieties of Historical Inquiry

Among the Russian followers of neo-Kantian philosophy interested primarily in the historical nature of social theory, A. S. Lappo-Danilevskii stood out by the depth of his theoretical analysis and the sweep of problems which he brought under critical scrutiny. No Russian historian of his age matched the versatility of his interests in the relationship of historical inquiry to the basic problems of social theory. Working outside the main currents of Russian neo-Kantianism, he claimed no direct contact with the Populist tradition and no affiliation with the group of disenchanted Marxists in search of a more

---

*The social theory of Kistiakovskii is the subject of chapter 5.

flexible and humanistic philosophical position. The contemporary revival of natural law theory did not attract his attention; nor did he join the small group of Russian scholars ready to meet the massive challenge of Max Weber's sociological interpretation of history and historical interpretation of sociology.

Born in 1863 in a village in Ekaterinoslav province, Lappo-Danilevskii belonged to an old aristocratic family of high economic status and wide intellectual interests.[29] As a high school student he was much impressed with G. H. Lewes's *History of Philosophy*, which provided an easily digestible review of the main currents in Western thought and which presented the growth of philosophy as an essential part of the inexorable progress of both human mind and human values. Comte and Spencer attracted him by their bold searches for the universal laws of social evolution. George Grote's *History of Greece* impressed him partly as a work dedicated to the principles of democracy and partly as a model scientific study of history combining a careful scrutiny of documentary sources, a general knowledge of political theory, and an elaborate philosophical view on the universal evolution of moral principles. As a student at St. Petersburg University, he was one of the most active members of the Scientific and Literary Society, an organization dedicated to encouraging promising students to pursue scholarly activities. In addition to having sponsored his first research ventures, the society gave him valuable experience in collective research projects and introduced him to the rapidly growing literature on the theoretical and methodological foundations of modern historical studies. In 1885, the society was the home base of a circle involved in the study of Herbert Spencer's sociology and psychology. Lappo-Danilevskii's constant search for more perfect methods of scientific inquiry prompted him to take all the courses in mathematics offered at St. Petersburg University and to work on a system of mathematical notations applicable to historical research.[30] According to one of his contemporaries, he thought that mathematical procedures would help him to discover the symmetry of universal history as a special feature of the symmetry of the universe.[31] He also studied physics, chemistry, and astronomy, all contributing to the formation of a well-knit sociological orientation in the realm of the humanities.[32]

Lappo-Danilevskii graduated from the university in 1886 and a year later was appointed a docent at his alma mater on the strength of his master's dissertation that dealt with direct tax assessment in seventeenth-century Russia—a treatise that placed him immediately in the forefront of contemporary Russian historians.[33] Most of his historical studies were on economic and intellectual topics and were united by a heavy concern with the interrelationship of the state and society and by a search for historical regularities that expressed the structural unity of Russian society and the distinct phases in the evolution of Russian culture. Although Lappo-Danilevskii identified most of his studies as monographs on the economic history of Russia, he actually concentrated on the role of economic processes in "the emergence and development of new forms of social organization" and their reflection in legal norms. [34] He was particularly interested in the role of law as a catalyst of modernization. He enriched historical scholarship primarily by pointing out the importance of a systematic study of the interaction of major orders, or institutionalized systems, of social relations. In previously unused documents belonging to the vast category of private law he discovered a particularly rich source of information of vital sociological significance. [35] It came as no surprise to the rapidly expanding community of Russian historians when, in 1905, the St. Petersburg Academy of Sciences elected him to its regular membership.

Securely settled at the top of the academic ladder, Lappo-Danilevskii, without abandoning his work in Russian history, devoted much time to the theory of history. For many years he conducted a seminar on topics related to historical methodology. He made a strict distinction between "methodics" and "methodology": the former examined and systematized the technical rules of research and the latter the vast area of the ontological, epistemological, and logical aspects of historical inquiry. To distill the essential principles of historical methodology from the vast and unwieldy mass of modern philosophical thought, he devoted entire seminars to such specific topics as the theory of evolution, the role of values in the formation of social entities, the relevance of the theory of probability for discovering scientific regularities in the random occurrence of historical events, and the classification of the sciences. [36] The result of this engagement was the *Methodology of History*, a monumental effort to delimit the scientific boundaries of historical research and to formulate a systematic and comprehensive theory of historical knowledge. [37] In 1915, the academy made a logical choice when it appointed him to serve on the committee entrusted with preparing a historical survey of Russian contributions to science, modelled on the Paris Academy of Sciences' *La science française*. In 1919, the St. Petersburg Academy recognized his erudition in sociology by asking him to deliver a eulogy for Emile Durkheim.

Although Lappo-Danilevskii showed aristocratic detachment from the political fermentation during the waning years of the autocratic rule, he expressed a distinct preference for constitutional monarchy as the best form of government for Russia. This, however, did not prevent him in 1917, immediately after the downfall of the monarchy, from accepting the provisional government's appointment to serve on the committee entrusted with the preparation of the electoral law for the Constituent Assembly. [38] He accepted the philosophy of the new government and was deeply disappointed when the October Revolution brought the process of political liberalization to an abrupt end. He died in 1919 at the age of fifty-six.

Lappo-Danilevskii's complex theoretical structure is a detailed and scrupulous elaboration of the idea that a satisfactory theory of society could be built only upon the scientific foundations of historical inquiry. In his search for a theory of society, as a theory of history, he operated primarily on an epistemological level. He wrote: "It is impossible not to recognize the very close ties between the theory of knowledge and the methodology of science: only from a definite epistemological point of view is it possible to construct an integrated theory depicting the tasks and procedures of scientific methodology."[39] Epistemology, he stated, elucidates such questions of essential methodological significance as the interrelationship of a priori and a posteriori categories of knowledge, the general conditions and limits of knowledge, the nature of "generalizing" and "particularizing" conceptions, and the need for differential methodological approaches to various types of reality. Logic provides a genetic explanation of the nature and development of generalizations and abstractions, and it specifies the formal procedures for the integration of scientific knowledge. But in order to make a most effective choice of methods, it is necessary to undertake an epistemological analysis of the unique characteristics of the cognitive material handled by individual sciences. "Without methodological considerations, no science could achieve conceptual unity." But, on the other hand, no methodology can become an effective instrument of science unless it is grounded in epistemology. Only with the help of epistemology, he said, can a science elaborate specific principles and methods for the purpose of integrating the facts of experience and arriving at a system of scientific concepts.[40] Methodology is an indispensable tool for the advancement of science, and epistemology is the basis upon which methodology should be built.

Lappo-Danilevskii's epistemological position is based on an acceptance, in principle if not in detail, of Windelband's (and Rickert's) claim that the sciences are faced with two general types of knowledge—one conducive to universal abstractions, and another steeped in the qualities of nonrepetitiveness and individuality, limited to a low level of generalization. In one type of knowledge each individual object of inquiry acquires its real meaning when it is viewed as a true representative of the universe of phenomena to which it belongs; in the second type of knowledge, individual objects of inquiry lose their true meaning when they are regarded as representatives of a universe of phenomena. Some sciences—identified as nomothetic—are concerned primarily with the first category of knowledge. Other sciences—labeled idiographic—deal primarily with the second category of knowledge.

In a long essay on the philosophical presuppositions of Auguste Comte's sociology, Lappo-Danilevskii made his initial attack on the efforts to make sociology a pure nomothetic science. Comte, he claimed, had failed in his effort to lay the scientific foundations of sociology as a generalizing science, for he had oversimplified social reality. In the first place, he ignored the individual as a social unit and submerged him fully into collective existence. Indeed, Comte denied the importance of the individual not only as a sociological but also as a psychological phenomenon: to him psychology was fully subsumed within physiology. In the second place, he made the intellectual evolution of man "the supreme principle of the total development of mankind."[41] For this reason, he viewed the succession of the three stages of intellectual growth (theological, metaphysical, and positive) as the fundamental law of social evolution. He tried to make sociology a science by building it upon "metaphysical" foundations.

In addition to gross oversimplifications, Comte's sociology, according to Lappo-Danilevskii, suffered from far-reaching inconsistencies, mainly of a philosophical nature. For example, Comte made no effort to reconcile epistemological relativism (based on the assumption of the essential subjectivity of knowledge) and methodological absolutism (based on the assumption that the scientific method produces knowledge that is absolute in validity and universal in applicability). He identified sociology as "social physics"—a science of social causation; however, he built it upon a teleological basis, for he considered the "positive stage" to be the ultimate point, the goal, of social evolution.[42] The theological and metaphysical stages were merely transitory phases of a gradual but inexorable affirmation of the positive stage. The ideal of positive society led Comte to shift the focus of his sociological analysis from causal explanations to teleological evaluations. The teleological element, in turn, led him to define social progress as a process of moral advancement and to place a veil of ontological obscurity around the three-stage intellectual progress.

Comte, according to Lappo-Danilevskii, was engaged as much in the search for the fundamental principles of sociology as he was in the search for a deductive philosophy of history. In both efforts he failed to operate from an empirical base; he completely ignored such disciplines as economics and ethnography, which were in command of vast stores of concrete information. He took a dim view of Quetelet's efforts to quantify empirical data of sociological significance, and he rejected the theory of probability that was considered by a growing number of social scientists as the most effective mathematical method for detecting significant regularities in mass behavior.[43] Although he talked with great animation about the laws of sociology, he did not discover a single one of them; "only in passing did he touch upon particular laws of social interaction or social differentiation and integration."[44]

The example of Comte, Lappo-Danilevskii concluded, should serve as a warning to all those who try to set up a science of society without having a clear idea of its foundations. In his determined efforts to spell out the epistemological and methodological weaknesses of Comte's social theory, Lappo-Danilevskii neglected to explain the enormous influence of the

French thinker on modern sociological thought, in Russia not less than in Western Europe.

In the *Methodology of History*, his main theoretical work, Lappo-Danilevskii made a critical survey of the major nomothetic orientations in the social sciences which, in his opinion, disregarded the unique attributes of sociohistorical knowledge and which did not tie the elaborate systems of abstract formulations to an empirical base. He made an impression on his contemporaries, particularly with his detailed analysis of the three major categories of the modern nomothetic orientation in social science and social history.

The first category included the work of historians who relied on two major explanatory principles of Newtonian mechanics—causality and continuity of motion—to achieve a scientific ordering of historical knowledge. For the students of world history this invitation to nomothetic heights was particularly inviting: pressured by the unwieldy nature and massive proportions of rapidly growing documentation, they found it expedient to rely on abstract schemes as a way of separating the "significant" from the "ephemeral," the "regular" from the "irregular," and of producing a readable, comprehensive, and manageable work of scholarship. If in all this they turned to the natural sciences for models of conceptualization and theoretical integration, the reason was that the nineteenth century was the century of the rapid expansion of scientific knowledge and of the areas brought under scientific scrutiny.

Lappo-Danilevskii noted the growing interest in the application of natural science models in the writing of national histories. He referred, for example, to W. H. Riehl's interpretation of the "natural history of the German people" as a constant search for equilibrium in the battle between two historical forces: "the force of inertia" and "the force of motion."[45] He was particularly interested in H. T. Buckle, the author of the famous *History of Civilization in England*, undoubtedly because of his strong influence on the development of modern social theory in Russia, particularly during the 1860s. He said that, under the influence of Adam Smith and John Stuart Mill, Buckle asserted that history should seek to formulate empirical generalizations as the first step in a search for universal laws.[46] The search for regularities in history, according to Buckle, is based on the law of causality, according to which the same conditions are likely to produce the same results in human history no less than in natural history. Relying on an extensive use of statistics, the comparative method, and various historical "laws" enunciated by earlier historians, he made bold efforts to show that civilizations develop in accordance with certain general laws. He claimed, for example, that the earlier phases of a civilization are characterized by the dominance of the influence of nature—particularly climate—on man, while the later phases are characterized by a rapidly increasing influence of man on nature. Also: the rapid development in higher civilizations is manifested in intellectual activities and achievements, not in moral life. To Buckle, these are not passing generalizations but scientific abstractions helping in the selection, interpretation, and integration of historical knowledge.

The second category of scholarly efforts to transform the study of history into a rigorous science included the sociological elaborations of the Darwinian theory of evolution. This orientation introduced a grand scheme of evolutionary phases through which all societies pass—at different speeds and with local cultural adaptations, to be sure—in their march from primitive obscurity to the highest levels of civilization. Societies not only pass (unless they become ossified) through the same evolutionary stages, but they are also propelled by the same force: the struggle for existence. Social evolution is part of natural evolution and both are basically independent of the human will.[47] Aside from the monstrous abuse of biological analogies in the search for the universal principles of social change, these theories are also guilty of a parochial bias, for all regard the European nations—with the predictable omission of Russia—as the only groups which have passed through all phases of evolution, and which alone are destined to guide mankind to the higher, as yet unscaled, rungs of cultural accomplishment.[48]

The third catagory—to which Lappo-Danilevskii devoted a great deal of attention—included economic theories of history, among which the Marxian sociological theory occupied the first place. No other Russian scholar of the pre-Soviet era had produced a more systematic, comprehensive, and incisive critique of the philosophical and sociological content of economic materialism. He contended that, although economic materialism had made a major contribution to a general theory of history, it provided the most graphic example of the epistemological, logical, and methodological weaknesses of the nomothetic orientation.[49] Marx himself recognized the limitations of an inflexible and unmodulated nomothetic orientation in social science and tried to make concessions to the idiographic view. According to Lappo-Danilevskii, Marx made use of an individualizing or idiographic approach to the study of historical processes, conditions, and periods. For example, Marx noted the fortuitous role of demographic factors in social evolution; he recognized social revolution as a deviation from the universal law of continuity in social change; and he attached considerable importance to local influences on the historical process. Marx was critical of those who ignored historical differences among societies at the same level of structural development; he discussed the unique social conditions which characterized the earlier periods of human development and which could never return; and he opposed those who viewed all aspects of modern society as expressions of the bourgeois system.[50] In his claim that every socioeconomic formation had unique laws of internal organization and development, Marx was much more idiographic than most leading bourgeois political economists. Relying on direct citations from the writings of Marx and Engels, Lappo-Danilevskii noted concessions by the founders of economic materialism to the relative independence of ideology as expressed in human behavior and various components of the social superstructure. Lappo-Danilevskii was ready to admit, however, that Marx attached only a secondary importance to the idiographic approach, that he used it only to trace deviations from the norms of the "natural law of social development" and to dissect the forms of social relations indicative of the gradual disintegration of the capitalist system.

The best proof of the intrinsic weakness of the nomothetic commitment of Marx's approach to the study of social history was the widespread search for modifications and elaborations of his legacy. Most leading followers of Marx's theory worked to straighten out its inner logic, to bolster its effectiveness as both a research tool and an ideology, and to widen its theoretical horizons. Some followers, typified by Dietzgen ("officially recognized as the philosopher of the doctrine"), worked on the refinement and reinforcement of the ontological basis of Marxist theory; they sought to effect a coalescence of historical materialism and historical idealism (unburdened by metaphysical exaggerations) into a unified and comprehensive theory of society.[51] A particularly strong faction of Marxists, typified by A. Labriola, tried to modernize Marxian epistemology by going beyond the original Marxian preoccupation with the economic genesis of thought and by attributing greater autonomy to the superstructure.[52] Lappo-Danilevskii also took note of the widespread efforts to blend Marxian and neo-Kantian philosophies, particularly of the Marburg variety, which led first to revisionism and then to massive drifting away from economic materialism.

Lappo-Danilevskii was particularly eager to show the role of Russian Marxists in modifying and revising the philosophical and sociological foundations of economic materialism and in illustrating the indefensibility of this specific brand of nomothetic orientation. Even G. V. Plekhanov, the most consistent orthodox Marxist in Russia, was compelled to admit that, although man is a "product of history," he is untiring in his efforts to fit history into his own world in order to make it more intelligible.[53] P. B. Struve's and M. I. Tugan-Baranovskii's efforts to reconcile economic materialism and ethical idealism led them into the camp of revisionism. A. A. Bogdanov's efforts to reconcile Marxism and neopositivist theories of knowledge led him to a position of eclecticism with little resemblance to dialectical materialism.[54]

Lappo-Danilevskii built his theory of history on the idea that all sciences are actually combinations of nomothetic and idiographic approaches; a science is called idiographic not because it excludes generalizing approaches altogether but because it is involved primarily in a search for unique aspects of nature and society. Although he recognized the essentially nomothetic nature of sociology, he was very critical of sociologists who in their eagerness to formulate the laws of universal social development ignored the uniqueness of historical experience; who, in building the nomothetic edifices, found no use for factual material obtained with the help of idiographic methods. On the other hand, he was careful to emphasize that even though history is mainly an idiographic science, it should not abandon a constant search for generalizations. According to him, a historian who steers away from the abstract notions of change and cultural integration is only touching the surface of his academic field. History, as a nomothetic discipline, searches for universal laws of social development; history, as an idiographic discipline, tries to tie individual historical events to cultural totalities welded by unique values. Nomothetically oriented history studies the influence of the environment (primarily social and superorganic environment) on the individual. It searches for regularities in psychic responses of individuals to similar environments: it seeks to formulate the laws of social behavior. Idiographically oriented history, on the other hand, concentrates on the socially significant influence of the individual on the environment.[55] The two types of science study the same reality from two different but complementary vantage points. The two can be fully separated only in theory; in practice, they are paired in multitudes of combinations depending on the nature of the subject of inquiry and the interest of the investigator.[56]

Whether idiographic or nomothetic, or both, history (as well as the other social sciences) possesses distinct attributes which clearly separate it from the natural sciences. The natural scientist examines sequences of causally linked events reducible to direct observation and empirical verification for the purpose of arriving at the laws of nature. Historians and social scientists examine human experience—psychic phenomena—irreducible to direct observation and empirical verification. They can generalize only by concentrating on the meaning of human experience, on the purposive direction of social action. In neo-Kantian terminology, while the natural scientist aims at *explaining* the work of nature, the social scientist concentrates on *understanding* the work of society. In this enterprise, he is helped by two fundamental assumptions: the psychic unity of mankind (the reliance of all human beings on the same innate capacities that make possible the conceptualization and the ordering of human experience) and the ethical unity of mankind (the absolute values that guide the universal social evolution and define social progress). The law of the psychic unity of mankind, of the fundamental unity of my "I" and the "I's" of other persons, supplies the basic condition without which the objectification of historical knowledge could not be achieved and history could not rise to the level of a science. The psychic unity of mankind makes it possible for individual cognitions to coalesce into a "general cognition." The law of the ethical unity of mankind, of the absolute values toward which all societies strive, provides the basic condition without which the idea of progress could have no scientific validity as the most general principle of historical interpretation. In his eagerness to delineate the precise borderlines of the social sciences, Lappo-Danilevskii found himself among the neo-Kantians of the Marburg School who fought a valiant battle to save the notion of absolute moral values as an explanatory principle of social behavior without falling into the trap of idealistic metaphysics. He found the problem exceedingly difficult and left it generally unsolved.

A closer look into his laborious theory of history reveals that Lappo-Danilevskii recognized three distinct types of historical studies. The first type embraces the scholarship concerned with historical events, that is, with history in the classical meaning of the term. No Russian historian had emulated Lappo-Danilevskii's efforts to widen the empirical base of historical studies and to sharpen the tools of documentary analysis. He taught his students the use of various modern techniques, including rigorous linguistic analysis, to distill historical wisdom from scattered documents covering the vast domain of "private law," cadastral materials, court actions, and intermanorial relations. He made a concerted effort to ground historical analysis in statistical computations and to replace "primitive observation" by a search for mathematical "averages." His studies of political, economic, and intellectual developments during the age of Catherine II are masterworks in depth analysis of rich, and previously unused, sources. In these studies the emphasis is on distilling facts from chaotic documentary sources and letting the facts reveal the course of history.

The second type of history writing has all the earmarks of sociology, even though Lappo-Danilevskii refrained from using that label. Concerned with collective individualities, sociology formulates generalizations about such social entities as estates, economic groups, regional communities, and nations. These generalizations are essentially idiographic: they are not universal laws but empirical generalizations limited in space and time. Products of distillations of sociological uniformities and regularities from enormous quantities of "discrete" and "nonrepetitive" historical events, they express both the trends of social evolution and the principles of structural integration. Lappo-Danilevskii's periodization of eighteenth-century Russian history is actually such an empirical generalization. After a long and comprehensive study of political, economic, and intellectual developments, he concluded that the history of Russia in the eighteenth century could be divided into four periods, each covering approximately a quarter of a century and representing a distinct sociological category. The unlimited power of the government gave the first period its most distinguishing feature. The second period saw a weakening of government authority and a strengthening of estates (particularly the aristocracy). A growing interaction of the government and society, a gradual emancipation of the estates (particularly the aristocracy) from obligations to the state, and the emergence of public opinion as a political factor depicted the real dynamics of the third period.

A serious rupture in the interaction of the government and society was the chief feature of the fourth period. In his search for sociological categorizations, Lappo-Danilevskii adhered to the principle that one of the basic duties of the historian is to establish empirically verifiable links between history, as a series of "discrete" events, and society, as an integrated system of institutional complexes. At the sociological level, the historian is ready to move from an "individualized" study of historical details to a "typological" treatment of structural developments.

Lappo-Danilevskii found the sociological or typological approach to history particularly suitable in the study of the diffusion and influence of Western ideas in Russia. In the initial phase of the Westernization of Russia, for example, he recognized a smoldering battle between two Western theories of the state: Hobbes's theory, which fully subordinated the individual to the state, and Pufendorf's and Grotius's theories, which advocated active citizenship and limited government controls.[57] In the diffusion of both theories he saw an unmistakable sign of the rapid secularization of Russian culture and politics; it showed that the influential Russians of both theoretical persuasions had substituted an "immanent" view of the state for the "transcendental" view that had dominated the thinking of the preceding generations. The "immanent" view, which eliminated divine interference from the evolution of political institutions, dominated various theories of natural law built on natural science models.[58] Lappo-Danilevskii saw in the diffusion of the ideas of Pufendorf and Grotius the beginning of a long process of the modernization of Russia, expressed in a gradual emergence of the individual as the nerve center of the complex fabric of sociopolitical reality. In the growth of citizenship as an active sociological category he saw the very essence of the evolution of modern Russian society.

The preoccupation with the idea of the increasing role of the individual in Russian history led Lappo-Danilevskii to an appreciative appraisal of Populist sociology. He endorsed both Mikhailovskii's formula of progress as a gradual realization of the "wholeness of the individual" and Lavrov's identification of progress with growing social solidarity. According to him, the inner unity of the individual, as the basic prerequisite for the inner unity of culture, is a historical phenomenon; like Simmel, he reasoned that man's continuous effort to reconcile within himself the expanding diversity of group expectations leads to a more conscious unity of the age. He added the concept of collective personality to the usual category of individual personality and viewed the idiographic nature of history as a study of national individualities. He identified evolution as a gradual harmonization of national individualities with the individuality of mankind. To him "individuality" stood for a unity of values that ensures solidarity and cooperation as the basic ingredients of human existence.

Like K. D. Kavelin and the Populists, Lappo-Danilevskii argued that the gradual emancipation of the individual was the essence of Russian history. He noted: "Even though they did not recognize the individual as an independent unit of society, the reforms of Peter the Great cleared the ground for his future development. In new social relations and intensified and improved economic activities, the Russian man of the eighteenth century found spiritual and material support for personal initiative and autonomous activity."[59] In the diffusion of legal ideas under the influence of the philosophy of natural law he saw a profound search for the recognition of "man's proprietary and personal rights." He thought that the growing recognition of the individual led to the transformation of estates into groups protecting the rights of each member, the first step on the road to the achievement of civil rights.

A profound concern with the idea of progress led Lappo-Danilevskii to the third type of historical study—the philosophy of history, dominated by a theoretical study of "progress" as "the elaboration of a harmonious conception of the world."[60] He reasoned that an individual society could contribute to the gradual realization of world harmony only if it had achieved an internal integration of its moral, intellectual, and social principles. He saw the future of universal harmony in the increasing complementarity of unique national cultures rather than in the creation of a uniform culture of the world. This was his way of reconciling the diversity of national societies with the unity of the cosmic evolution of human existence.

N. Ia. Danilevskii and A. S. Lappo-Danilevskii: A Comparison

N. Ia. Danilevskii argued vehemently that the future of Russia was in the predestined development of her own value system, social commitments, intellectual priorities, and organizational principles. Lappo-Danilevskii, on the other hand, expressed a more realistic view: he recognized that the evolution of modern Russian society was dominated less by a search for national values than by a massive, and often uncritical, borrowing of Western ideas and practices. Russia, he said, has a borrowed culture and a culture without internal unity. He thought that the emergence of Russian nationalism in the nineteenth century—particularly of the movement for national self-understanding in the 1860s—marked the beginning of a wide search for cultural integration. He gave credit to the Slavophiles and Danilevskii for their bold efforts to identify the pivotal values of Russian society, but he rejected their efforts to interpret Russian culture as a negation of Western culture and to isolate Russian culture from the universal evolution of humanity. In his opinion, Russia could enter the path of progressive development not by a denial of borrowed cultural elements and habits but by an integration of this material into an internally consistent system of values. He admitted, however, that a cultural integration of Russia, without which she could not "act for the good of humanity," could be achieved only "under liberal political conditions."[61] Only free work in all forms of creative expression—from religion and the arts to philosophy and science—could give a modern culture a purposeful unity and a progressive place in the universal scheme of sociocultural progress. The study of the diversity of national histories is, according to him, the only sound path leading to an understanding of the unity of humanity. He never abandoned the neo-Kantian dictum that the ultimate function of the historian was to trace the confluence of myriads of local and national individualities into the "grand individuality" of mankind as the purest and most universal expression of ethical ideals and values.

Lappo-Danilevskii's philosophy of history elaborates and combines the notions of "progress" as the pivotal element of social "evolution" and of local or national history as a unique expression of universal progress. Because of his concern with cultural progress, the local historian does not deal with all events; he concentrates on those that, as organic parts of broader historical currents, reveal the universal development of culture.[62] Lappo-Danilevskii gave credit to N. I. Kareev for having written a very general study of social evolution and progress and highly individualized studies of Western European societies. He lauded Kliuchevskii for having matched an interest in the general principles of sociology with an "individualized" conception of Russian history.[63]

Among the scholars of the post-Reform era who claimed that their philosophies of history were cast within a framework of science, N. Ia. Danilevskii and Lappo-Danilevskii occupied the leading positions. They were also the most typical representatives of philosophical approaches to Russian history. They shared several views of a general nature. Both, for example, adhered to epistemological relativism, according to which human knowledge is not a true copy of objectively existing reality but is a product of a subjective reworking and processing of sensory material and is open to specific cultural and historical influences. Both combined a theory of history with a distinct sociological orientation, and both opposed materialism as a basis upon which science is built.

Beyond these general similarities, which allowed for many variations in the interpretation of significant details, there were differences, primarily in the clusters of problems selected for emphasis and systematic elaboration. Danilevskii's basic interest was ontological: he concentrated, first, on the values which give a cultural-historical type a unique configuration, and, second, on comparing the basic cultural contents of the more recent types of civilizations. Lappo-Danilevskii worked primarily from an epistemological position: he provided an original elaboration of neo-Kantian views on the unique attributes of the social sciences, as historical disciplines, irreducible to natural science models. According to Danilevskii, the social sciences are unique because they are subjective, and they are subjective because they unavoidably express strong national biases encrusted in unique systems of values. According to Lappo-Danilevskii, the social sciences are subjective in their preoccupation with human motivations and the "will" of "individualities" in the historical process.

Danilevskii and Lappo-Danilevskii gave different responses to the idea of social progress, which dominated much of the nineteenth-century sociological theory and was the central theme in the work of such progenitors of modern sociology as Adolphe Quetelet, Comte, Marx, and Lewis H. Morgan. Danilevskii echoed the official view of Russian autocracy and the Orthodox church as the true embodiments of all structural and ideological ingredients of an ideal society. He saw the future of Russia in its shedding of the artificially grafted materialism allied with science and democracy and its returning to the patriarchal regime and religious philosophy of pre-Petrine Russia. Lappo-Danilevskii, who belonged to the diffuse group of academic liberals that saw the future of Russia in constitutional monarchy, viewed history as a record of the progressive and inexorable expansion of solidarity in relations of man to man and society to society. His idea of progress did not differ essentially from Mikhailovskii's notion of parallel developments in the unity and diversity of labor, Comte's notion of "social consensus" as the basic source of social unity, and Durkheim's view of social evolution as a gradual substitution of "organic solidarity" for "mechanical solidarity." Defined in the vague terms of the nineteenth-century faith in the idea of progress, Lappo-Danilevskii's conception of solidarity stands in sharp contrast to the disciplined concreteness of his historical research and the empirical grounding of his sociological generalizations. The most distinctive and impressive feature of his scholarly work was that it combined "a rigid discipline of scientific inquiry" with a "lyrical feeling" of world unity.[64] As a true neo-Kantian, he interpreted the moral order as the main depository of universal human values and identified the evolution of the moral order in terms of a gradual retreat of necessity and causality before the forces of freedom and purposive social action. As a positivist, he measured cultural progress in terms of the accumulation of secular wisdom and of a gradual shifting of humanity from the rule of instinct and passion to the rule of reason. To him, the growing power of science and the expanding compass of moral rules were closely related parts of the universal progress of culture.

As a historian, Lappo-Danilevskii distinguished himself by elaborate research techniques, meticulous scrutiny of documentary sources, and consistent efforts to place discrete events into broader historical currents. As a sociologist, he sought to unveil the general characteristics of Russian society, concentrating on the major stages of social evolution and on the structural principles of social unity. As a philosopher of history, he endeavored to discover the kernel of universality in every culture, representing the highest ideals of mankind. In the process of identifying the substance of his philosophy of history, he transcended the limits of science to give vent to his preoccupation with the attributes of a perfect society. His work showed clearly that the study of history could benefit from adhering to the standards of scientific scholarship; however, it also showed that the idea of progress, as a basic principle of historical explanation, was only a bridge between scholarship and ideology. Like most Russian social theorists, Lappo-Danilevskii looked at the gradual realization of moral ideals as the essence of history.

5. A Sociological Synthesis:
B. A. Kistiakovskii

The life story of B. A. Kistiakovskii is particularly important because it provides a classic picture of the basic dilemmas and unique interests of Russian sociology. The details of his life bring into relief the harried existence of a large contingent of Russian sociologists forced into an unceasing search for a reconciliation of science and ideology, scholarship and politics. Kistiakovskii was a typical Russian sociologist: he had a discernible ideological commitment; he was an active participant in politics and served several prison terms for illicit political activities; he had a keen interest in the epistemological debate centered on the possibility and nature of a scientific study of society; he was engaged in extensive journalistic activity; and he had an academic career dominated by insecurity and restricted employment possibilities. In one important respect, however, Kistiakovskii was atypical: his contributions to sociology were recognized in the West before they were noted in Russia.[1]

Kistiakovskii was born in 1868 to an academic family: his father, A. F. Kistiakovskii, a professor of law at Kiev University, was widely known through his textbook in criminal law and his original legal studies of the death penalty and juvenile delinquency. The senior Kistiakovskii was an ardent advocate of historical and comparative approaches in jurisprudence and pleaded for a systematic study of the rich legal resources of customary law. As a high school student, the junior Kistiakovskii belonged to various clandestine circles engaged in reading illegal works on Ukrainian history and culture. Expulsions, or threats of expulsion, forced him to move from one high school to another, and from one Ukrainian city to another. The same fate followed him to the university: he began as a student at Kiev University, continued at Khar'kov University, and finally enrolled at Dorpat University, dropping out before the completion of undergraduate studies. After joining a Marxist circle in Dorpat, he spent summer vacations in the Ukraine propagandizing for an ideology that interpreted the vital social and cultural interests of the Ukrainian people from the vantage point of a revolutionary socialist theory.

In 1892, Kistiakovskii was imprisoned for illegal political activities in Volynia. Involuntary confinement gave him the time to read the works of

Kant, Hegel, Lorenz von Stein, Wundt, Taine, as well as the more modern philosophers. His dedicated mother provided him with a continuous supply of books and journals. Upon his release from prison in 1893, he was ordered to report to the police at regular intervals until 1895. As soon as the parole obligations ended, he went to Germany and enrolled at Berlin University, where Georg Simmel lectured in sociology and Kantian philosophy. He also spent some time in Heidelberg and Paris, attending lectures on topics from modern philosophy and social theory and working in the leading libraries. The reputation of the philosopher Wilhelm Windelband attracted him to Strasbourg University, where he completed his doctoral dissertation, *Society and the Individual* (1899), a tightly woven system of ideas that marked his irrevocable break with Marxism. Like the leading neo-Kantian philosophers, he showed a profound interest in the epistemological and methodological foundations of the social sciences.

In the same year Kistiakovskii returned to St. Petersburg. At a meeting of the Philosophical Society, he read a methodological paper dealing with the interlacing of the categories of "necessity" and "justice" in social theory. The paper reaffirmed his transition from "philosophical materialism" to "philosophical idealism." In the following year the police arrested his wife for illegal work in the Ukrainian nationalist movement. Although released immediately, she received a relatively heavy penalty: she lost the right to reside in St. Petersburg, Moscow, or Kiev and was later exiled to Vologda. In 1901 Kistiakovskii was back in Germany, in Berlin and Heidelberg. He was well received in German academic circles on the strength of the glowing reviews of *Society and the Individual* in such leading journals as the *Zeitschrift für Socialwissenschaft* and *Kantstudien*.[2] The venerable Georg Jellinek took note of his work in the later editions of the *Allgemeine Staatslehre*. Kistiakovskii's ideas figured prominently in Hans Kelsen's noted effort to articulate the differences between "legal" and "sociological" attributes of the state.[3]

At this time Kistiakovskii established close contact with political refugees gathered around P. B. Struve, an ex-Marxist of dynamic personality and mercurial political convictions. He helped Struve edit the journal *Liberation* and played an important role in the publication of the political works of M. P. Dragomanov, an influential leader of the movement for Ukrainian cultural and political autonomy. He was among the representatives of various groups of liberal intelligentsia who met in Schaffhausen, Switzerland, in August 1903, to lay the groundwork for a Russian constitutional movement.[4] In Berlin, he also belonged to a group of young Russian scholars deeply engaged in the study of modern philosophy. Among his new friends was A. A. Chuprov, a modern pioneer in mathematical-statistical analysis of empirical data of demographic and sociohistorical relevance. In his search for the mathematicization of social science, Chuprov pointed out the need for building upon the ideas presented in Laplace's *Essai philosophique sur les probabilités* and the mathematical work of Cournot.[5] A few years later, Kistiakovskii wrote a favorable review of Chuprov's classic work, *Essays on the Theory of Statistics.*[6] P. I. Novgorodtsev, another member of the Berlin group, was the editor of the symposium *The Problems of Idealism*, published in 1902, to which Kistiakovskii contributed a critical essay on the philosophical foundations and ideological involvement of Populist sociology.[7]

In 1904, an amnesty ended Mrs. Kistiakovskaia's exile, and soon the family journeyed to Germany. The echoes of the 1905 revolution, which heightened the hopes and political aspirations of refugee organizations, brought Kistiakovskii into closer contact with Ukrainian nationalist groups. This, however, did not take him away from a stimulating and mutually beneficial association with Max Weber, whose star was just beginning to reveal its extraordinary brilliance, and with whom he shared many novel and challenging ideas in sociological theory and methodology. With Kistiakovskii's encouragement and acknowledged assistance, Max Weber wrote two long essays dealing with the politics and agrarian problems of contemporary Russia.[8] Kistiakovskii's wife produced a Russian translation of Weber's "Zur Beurtheilung der gegenwärtigen Entwicklung Russlands."

In 1906, after the revolution, Kistiakovskii settled in Moscow and was appointed a member of the teaching staff of the Institute of Commerce. In 1909, he earned a magister's degree in law from Moscow University and was appointed private docent, a nontenured position, at the same institution. In 1911, along with many other liberal professors, he resigned from his teaching position in protest against the dismissal of the rector of the university by L. A. Kasso, the ultraconservative minister of national ecucation. He promptly accepted the invitation of the Demidov Lycée at Iaroslavl' to join its teaching staff, a post he held until 1917 and one which did not prevent him from spending long stretches of time in Moscow. At Iaroslavl' he offered courses in the philosophy of law and political science.

Teaching was only one of Kistiakovskii's many activities. In rapid succession, he published articles dealing with both the current political issues and the philosophy and sociology of law. He was a noted contributor to such new periodical publications as the *North Star*, *Moscow Weekly*, and *Law*. For a while he was the editor of *Critical Review*, a journal covering a wide range of topics from the modern developments in post-Newtonian physics to literary essays. In addition to his scholarly studies, he published popular articles on themes of current intellectual interest as well as articles of an ideological nature. He contributed an article to the symposium *Vekhi* (*Signposts*), most of whose contributors were ex-Marxists who saw the chief source of Russia's national and social plight in the unrealistic and irresponsible work of the intelligentsia. He differed from most other contributors in that he did not deny the paramount historical role of the intelligentsia as an agent of secular thought, even though he reasoned that the time had come for the intelligentsia to substitute self-examination for outward directed activities.[9] The *Vekhi* authors, all idealists, were divided into two irreconcilable groups: the group typified by N. A. Berdiaev and S. N. Bulgakov, who regarded the intellectual imperialism of "materialist" science as the main source of decadence in modern society, and the group, typified by Kistiakovskii, who saw in a philosophical reconciliation of modern science and idealistic theory of knowledge a sure path to restoring the health of modern civilization.[10]

In 1912, Kistiakovskii became the editor of the revived *Juridical Messenger*, restoring its reputation as the country's leading sociological journal. In all his writings, editorial comments, and popular lectures he expressed confidence in the possibility of placing scientific foundations under the study of society. He thought that, in its search for scientific status, sociology must face the realities of a modern industrial society and must seek to decode the growing complexity of the role of the individual in the network of social relations. No Russian sociologist had surpassed his measured and carefully articulated detachment from cultural parochialism.

In 1916, Kistiakovskii published *The Social Sciences and Law*, consisting mostly of articles published during the preceding ten years but welded into a rigorous and very complex system of philosophical and methodological principles linking jurisprudence to the social sciences, particularly sociology. In the same year, this book earned him a doctorate from Khar'kov University. No Russian sociological work of pre-Soviet vintage matched Kistiakovskii's magnum opus in the compass of examined problems, the depth of epistemological analysis, and the logical elaboration of methodology. His basic sociological orientation was the same as that of his friend Max Weber: both argued that the social scientist could neither ignore causality nor accept dogmatically the natural science models of causal explanations; he had to recognize the key methodological value of causality but also adapt it to the specific needs of social science inquiry.

After the collapse of the monarchy, Kistiakovskii settled in Kiev and helped in preparing plans for the founding and organizing of the Ukrainian Academy of Sciences. At the same time, he was appointed professor of law at Kiev University, and in 1919 he was elected to the Ukrainian Academy of Sciences, which at that time symbolized the unity of revitalized Ukrainian cultural identity and the world of modern scholarship, the two guiding forces of Kistiakovskii's intellectual life. He died in 1920, at the age of fifty-two.

THE FOUNDATIONS OF SOCIOLOGICAL THEORY

A student of Wilhelm Windelband, Heinrich Rickert, and Georg Simmel, Kistiakovskii began his scholarly career by joining the growing group of

German scholars who contributed to the emergence and consolidation of the various schools of neo-Kantianism and who gave much attention to both the relations between science and philosophy and to the differences between the natural and social sciences. His philosophy of social science occupied a middle ground between the positivist commitment to a search for universal laws of social structure and change, and the neo-Kantian claims that the social sciences—as the *Geisteswissenschaften*—must examine the unique characteristics of individual societies and historical periods rather than search for general laws. The scientific study of society, according to him, must be both nomothetic and idiographic. In this respect, too, his ideas were similar, in principle, to those of Weber.

Kistiakovskii was firmly convinced that the achievements of modern natural science are "so great, vital, and exhilarating" that the contemporary crisis in physics, precipitated by a series of laboratory results which challenged the exclusive authority of the Newtonian mechanistic model of the universe, should be no source of dismay. This crisis, he said, was more epistemological than substantive.[11] In search of arguments supporting his thesis, Kistiakovskii subjected two contemporary philosophical orientations—William James's pragmatism and N. A. Berdiaev's ethical mysticism—to sweeping and relentless criticism. In James's commitment to pragmatic relativism he saw an unwarranted and overextended elaboration of utility as the prime criterion of truth and a denial of the existence of objective, universal, and permanent truth.[12] The basic weakness of pragmatism, he thought, is that it "lowers scientific knowledge to the level of hypotheses" and that it denies scientific truth the attributes of "stability, immutability and constancy."[13] James erred in his *Varieties of Religious Experience* in recognizing no differences between the religious experience of mystics and the experiments of physicists and chemists. He noted that James's pragmatic relativism limits the intellectual power not only of science but also of religion.[14] All this, however, shows that Kistiakovskii was not aware of James's pioneering work in laying the foundations of scientific psychology and that he did not realize that epistemological relativism was not an exclusive attribute of pragmatism but that it was rapidly becoming the major philosophy of modern science.

N. A. Berdiaev, Russia's most determined opponent of the scientific mode of inquiry, differed from James (according to Kistiakovskii) in one important respect: while denigrating scientific knowledge as relative, limited, and transitional information, he extolled religious truth as absolute, limitless and eternal wisdom. The modesty of scientists in their intellectual claims is, according to Berdiaev, only a cover for the intrinsic weakness and ephemeral validity of scientific thought.[15] Scientific knowledge, he argued, is a denial of the freedom of will, while religious belief is the highest triumph of human freedom. While scientific knowledge stands on the thin surface of rational phenomena, religious belief takes man into the essence of reality. In rejecting this interpretation, Kistiakovskii argued that, at least on philosophical (particularly epistemological) grounds, religion and science are noncomparable: each relies on a unique human endowment in its search for wisdom, and the "truths" of one cannot be judged by the "truths" of the other. Berdiaev dreamed of a culture in which scientific thought would be ancillary to religious thought; Kistiakovskii saw the strength of future societies in the full autonomy of science and religion as distinct sources and repositories of wisdom.

Berdiaev recognized the natural sciences as legitimate fields of intellectual endeavor even though he emphasized the superficial nature of their accumulated wisdom. However, he denied any value to the social sciences, particularly to sociology. Societies, according to him, are primarily moral phenomena, and morality is a divine creation transcending the vicissitudes of history and limitations of social space. To Kistiakovskii, on the other hand, sociology has all the logical, methodological, and epistemological resources at its disposal to operate as a legitimate and independent science. Berdiaev sought an escape in the world of unreality dominated by Eastern Orthodox mysticism and Slavophile *sobornost'*; Kistiakovskii endeavored to present the picture of a real world dominated by a constant search for measurable knowledge of practical social value. Behind Berdiaev's espousal of religious mysticism was an aristocratic view of the world; behind Kistiakovskii's scientific orientation was an unmistakeable attachment to democratic ideals.

During the early years of the twentieth century, Russian social, ideological, and philosophical thought was influenced by a profound resurgence and popularity of idealistic philosophy. The publication of the symposium *The Problems of Idealism* in 1902 and the massive discussion that it generated brought the ideas of the new philosophy to the attention of a broad stratum of the intelligentsia. The book was reviewed in all popular journals and was treated extensively in special symposia. Soon it became clear that idealistic philosophy was actually split into two major orientations with no shared commitments or values. One orientation was metaphysical and mystical and had its historical roots in the philosophies of Slavophilism and Vladimir Solov'ev. Its most productive and belligerent spokesman was Berdiaev. In Kistiakovskii's opinion, "mystical and metaphysical idealism is an escape from the realities of human experience."[16] It is an escape into the vague suppositions that, while reflecting personal predilections, have nothing in common with the facts and the spirit of science. The second orientation was popularly known as scientific idealism and was essentially antimetaphysical, epistemological, and proscientific. It was in turn divided into two major subdivisions. One group, inspired by the philosophical ideas of Ernst Mach and Richard Avenarius, assumed that no critical epistemological attributes separated the social sciences from the natural sciences and that the intellectual realms of philosophy and science are coterminous, that is, that philosophy has no concerns transcending the power and the jurisdiction of science. The second group espoused the neo-Kantian philosophy which claimed that definite epistemological attributes separated the social sciences from the natural sciences and that philosophy is not coterminous with science—that it can reach the parts of reality inaccessible to science.

Although Kistiakovskii was a leading articulator of the neo-Kantian branch of scientific philosophy, he was not a mere imitator of Western models; while subscribing to the basic postulates of Kantian phenomenology (which makes the phenomena, not the noumena, the subject of scientific treatment) and to Windelband's and Rickert's epistemological, methodological, and logical differentiation between the natural sciences and the "cultural" sciences, he showed considerable originality in examining the philosophical foundations of sociology and in advancing an elaborate scheme of sociological principles. Recurrent throughout his work are a number of basic assumptions which show clearly that he was strongly influenced by Georg Simmel's efforts to build the scientific foundations of sociology. Like Simmel, he argued that the field of sociology must be narrowed by surrendering to philosophy the areas of social behavior not conducive to scientific treatment. The function of sociology is not to replace social philosophy and the philosophy of history but to supplement them. Only by recognizing its epistemological limitations, and by avoiding ontological involvement, could sociology succeed in establishing itself as a legitimate science. Sociology should add a concern with the basic forms of social integration to its traditional search for substantive generalizations of various levels of abstraction.[17] He was one of the chief Russian spokesmen for so-called formal sociology.

In building the theoretical foundations of sociology, Kistiakovskii concentrated mainly on two topics: the leading orientations in the Russian sociological tradition and the basic epistemological and methodological differences between the natural sciences and the social sciences (particularly sociology).

In subjecting various theories of society, strongly represented in Russia, to penetrating criticism, Kistiakovskii was interested chiefly in unraveling the epistemological difficulties and dilemmas of modern sociology. He concentrated on three major orientations: the organicist school, Marxist theory, and Populist subjective sociology. Behind his criticism was a determined effort to establish the epistemological basis and methodological tools of a modern sociology—a sociology that would take into account both the current developments in the philosophy of science and the rapidly growing complexity of the modern industrial society.

In *Society and the Individual*, he attacked the organicist theory in sociology, most resolutely defended and elaborated by Paul Lilienfeld, on the ground that it ignored the essential attributes of social reality.[18] In order to make sociological knowledge a part of natural science, this orientation oversimplified the moral principles of social integration and the complex psychology of social behavior. Kistiakovskii emphasized repeatedly that he did not rule out completely the use of natural science models in the social sciences; what he ruled out categorically was the notion of sociology as an extension of biology, as a natural science completely dominated by the mechanical laws of causality, equilibrium, atomic attraction and repulsion, and continuity in motion. Lilienfeld translated sociology into a complex neurophysiological system based on the laws and principles of Newtonian mechanics. Kistiakovskii adduced ample evidence in support of his contention that most schools in sociology contained a strong organicist bias. He thought that various organicist orientations were useful only inasmuch as they revealed the major intellectual causes of the crisis in modern social theory. While the current crisis in natural science was not really a crisis in science but in epistemology, the crisis in social science was a crisis in both science and epistemology.

Kistiakovskii credited Marxism with two contributions to the scientific study of society: it recognized the epistemological and methodological uniqueness of social science, and it brought many previously ignored aspects of social reality to the attention of scholars.[19] However, this did not stop him from subjecting Marxism to extensive criticism. He thought that while the organicists tended to exaggerate the role of natural science models in the social sciences, the Marxists, despite their adherence to a monist ontology, tended to replace all natural science models by pure social science constructions. He also claimed that Marxist sociologists were history-centered, which prevented them from forming scientific concepts transcending the limitations of space and time; according to him, neither sociology nor any other body of systematic knowledge could become a science as long as its conceptualization was limited in terms of space and time.[20] The Marxists were too preoccupied with the narrow historical category of "social class" to give sufficient attention to the broad sociological category of "social group." Kistiakovskii also attacked economic reductionism, which, he thought, failed to recognize that there are social processes that are independent of economic and material conditions even though a generalized connection between them could be established. Marxist sociologists, he thought, do an acceptable job as long as they study social phenomena directly linked with the economy and the organization of production, but they are on shaky ground when they apply economic reductionism to sociocultural phenomena that are essentially independent of economic determinants.[21] The Marxists also err in treating causality as a universal principle of sociological explanation. Indeed, the Marxists committed a double error: they assumed that causal explanations are coterminous with scientific explanations and that all causal explanations must be derived from, or reduced to, the same categories of phenomena. Of all monist systems, Marxism "is founded on the most uncritical views on the forms and elements of scientific thought."[22]

Kistiakovskii concentrated his heaviest criticism, however, on subjective sociology, which he labeled the Russian sociological school. He did not challenge the democratic ideals and the humanistic orientation of subjective sociology; he dealt exclusively with its logical and epistemological foundations. While the Marxists, according to him, exaggerated the role of causality as an explanatory principle in science and distorted the meaning of causality by making it a monistic, and therefore a predetermined, principle, the subjective sociologists ignored the role of causality altogether. While the Marxists created a pseudo-science, the proponents of subjective sociology completely abandoned the realm of science.

Mikhailovskii, according to Kistiakovskii, committed the unpardonable error of denying causal necessity a place in the epistemological base of sociology, thus rejecting any similarity between sociology and the natural sciences. Mikhailovskii was led to this position by his consistent emphasis on the uniqueness and nonrepetitiveness of individual behavior and his unwillingness to face the regularity and repetitiveness of causally linked modes of group behavior; he exaggerated the role of the freedom of individual expression and creativeness by ignoring the role of social determinants. Mikhailovskii opposed the objective method in sociology on the ground that no social theorist had found a fruitful application for it.[23] Kistiakovskii, on the other hand, equated Mikhailovskii's subjectivism with a denial of the possibility of universal generalizations in the social sciences. Mikhailovskii recognized only "conditional truths" as the legitimate realm of social science.

Instead of objective causes—or causal necessity—Mikhailovskii, according to Kistiakovskii, concentrated on the role of possibility in social development. The social process, as viewed by Mikhailovskii, is mainly a realization or non-realization of various possibilities.[24] Mikhailovskii constantly referred to the possibilities open to Russia for averting certain phases of development, such as capitalism, conceptualized by sociologists, political economists, or philosophers of history. Moreover, he and his followers were not satisfied with a mere substitution of the category of possibility for the category of necessity; they were also quite explicit in their identification of "possibility" with "desirability." A sociologist must be able to differentiate between the desirable and the undesirable; but he must also search for the most advantageous conditions for the advancement of the desirable and the elimination of the undesirable.[25] Thus, to subjective sociologists everything that is socially desirable is also historically possible. Kistiakovskii categorically opposed the idea of making sociology ancillary to ideology. He was undeniably correct in claiming that the two dominant Russian sociological orientations—economic materialism and subjective sociology—were motivated much more by ideological contingencies than by scientific impartiality. Mikhailovskii treated "necessity" and "possibility" as mutually exclusive; Kistiakovskii, on the other hand, argued that they were not mutually exclusive, that "necessity" may often present several "possibilities." He claimed that Mikhailovskii regarded these categories as nonrelated because he operated on the assumption that "possibilities" are determined not by objective causal necessities but by subjective criteria of desirability. Mikhailovskii tied his views on social progress to the subjective goals of Populist ideology and not to the objective alternatives, or possibilities, presented by the laws of social development. In the bitter conflict between the orientation which sought a causal explanation of social phenomena (that is, necessary phenomena) and the orientation which placed the emphasis on the purposiveness of social action—on the selection of human activities in accordance with cherished ideals and accepted duties—Mikhailovskii sided with the latter. While the Marxist sociologists placed overwhelming emphasis on causally determined universal laws of social development, the Populist sociologists, led by Mikhailovskii, stayed completely within the realm of human ideals and duties.

Although Kistiakovskii viewed the categories of "possibility" and "desirability" as residues of metaphysical obscurantism, he was not ready to dismiss subjective sociology altogether. He acknowledged that even in his passion for "possibilities" and "desirabilities," Mikhailovskii had the good sense to avoid unfounded generalizations. When he denied the possibility of a capitalist stage in the development of Russian society and economy, he referred to capitalism as a pure or universal socioeconomic category; this, however, did not deny the possibility of Russian capitalism as a unique historical category.[26]

Kistiakovskii claimed that most Russian theories of society were embraced within three distinct orientations: the mystical metaphysicists, led by N. A. Berdiaev, who denied the legitimacy of sociology as a scientific discipline on the ground that it usurped a domain of inquiry which transcended the power of science; the Populists, who refused to tie science in general and sociology in particular to the law of universal causality and who placed the freedom of man above the force of causal necessity; and the Marxists, who cast their sociological theory within the mold of objective and universal causality and subordinated the will of man to the laws of social organization and development. In criticizing the main currents in Russian sociological thought, he was guided by the notion that in order to become a science, sociology must first of all cease to be a tool of ideology. He reasoned that the metaphysicists' unrestrained attack on the scientific and this-worldly claims of sociology gave comfort only to the ideologues of autocracy; that the Populists' reliance on sociology to justify their dreams of humanitarian and libertarian society and to extol the cultural and historical role of personality was part of the search for an antibourgeois, obshchina-oriented polity; and that the Marxists' deterministic sociology was in the final analysis a "scientific" justification of revolutionary upheavals as the only way for Russia to achieve a higher level of civilization.

Kistiakovskii's critique of the Russian sociological tradition was part of a broader effort to define sociology as a legitimate area of scientific inquiry. He viewed science as a generic concept for growing branches of systematic knowledge integrated with the help of empirically verifiable abstractions. The aim of every science, whether it deals with natural or social phenomena, is to subsume a maximum of empirical knowledge under a minimum of abstract principles. In the search for abstract categories, science must rise above the limitations of space and time; only in the search for empirical diversity of phenomena covered by individual abstractions are the scientists expected to consider time and space as reference points. Universal abstractions denote the *qualitative* side of science; empirical knowledge denotes merely *quantitative* diversity of time-bound and space-bound knowledge subsumed under universal abstractions. General concepts, according to Kistiakovskii, are not ontological propositions but logical abstractions that reduce the work of sociology to "a limited sphere of social phenomena" unbounded by space and time. They have three general characteristics: first, they are essentially psychological, that is, they depict the basic psychological mechanism—such as Tarde's imitation—of social processes; second, they designate pure forms of social interaction, such as subordination, domination, and assimilation; and, third, they are heuristic, that is, they are not identifications of social interaction but sets of explanatory principles. General concepts, in turn, must be firmly grounded in empirical generalizations based on an intensive study of the "social attributes" of the entire spectrum of institutionalized activity.

In its search for both empirical generalizations and universal abstractions, sociology is committed first of all to a search for causal links or conditional necessities in the work of society. However, Kistiakovskii made it clear that causality as a cardinal epistemological principle of sociology, as well as of science in general, does not express the concrete world per se but is a prism through which we look at the world; causality is a means, not a goal, of scientific inquiry.[27] Causality, as employed by a scientist, is more a human convention of heuristic significance than a concrete attribute of the objective world. In its search for causal explanations, sociology must avoid two major pitfalls of traditional sociology.

First, it must abandon all efforts to reduce social action to a number of key causes operating from an arbitrarily selected social substratum. Kistiakovskii was against every determinism, and, instead, emphasized the need for precise empirical studies of the multiple systems of intertwined causal relations. The various deterministic orientations in sociology were to him only components of a more complex network of causality. For example, the sociological orientation which gives primacy to "the material-productive processes" and the sociological orientation which leans toward psychological reductionism are tolerable only inasmuch as they are treated as components of a more comprehensive system of conceptualization.

Second, sociology must not derive its causal explanations from general concepts which merely designate specific domains of scientific inquiry. "Evolution" is one such concept. It designates a special field of biological study and is not an explanatory principle. Many sociologists, led by Spencer, have erred in using evolution as a key for explaining the dynamics of human society rather than as a specific topic of specific inquiry. For this reason, they viewed evolution as a teleological process, essentially independent of causal explanations. Evolution helped sociologists in their efforts to build their discipline on a natural science model. It helped them to translate the natural science search for regularities in nature into a social science search for regularities in society. However, in adopting evolution, many social scientists have failed to recognize that, while the natural scientists could undertake only an indirect study of regularities in nature, sociologists could undertake a direct study of regularities in society: they could extract "regular" or "repetitive" elements in social behavior from the mass of unique, unrepetitive social phenomena.

Natural scientists rely on the calculus and allied branches of mathematics to detect and formalize apparent regularities and continuities in nature. But on what method should a sociologist rely in his effort to transform apparent irregularities and discontinuities in social behavior into logical continuities and regularities conducive to scientific treatment? Encouraged by the writings of German physiologist I. von Kries and the Russian statistician A. A. Chuprov, Kistiakovskii was optimistic about the great prospects for an extensive use of statistical methods in sociological research. The peculiarity of the statistical method, according to him, is that it does not treat unique phenomena as "unconditionally unique" but as parts of integrated systems of action—the so-called statistical "totalities," "groups," or "masses." In order to recognize the elements of uniformity and repetitiveness in the aggregates of unique and apparently unrepetitive phenomena, the sociologist must resort to the tools of the mathematical theory of probability. This procedure makes it possible to "establish" a causal nexus between individual phenomena without resorting to a direct search for uniform causes. The imminent function of mathematical procedures is not to transform sociology into a thoroughly formalized system of theoretical principles but to facilitate the description of empirical regularities.

Like Max Weber, Kistiakovskii contended that causality as applied in sociology is not an epistemological and logical carry-over from the natural sciences but a distinct principle identified more in terms of "objective possibility" than in terms of "unconditional necessity."* Both were sensitive to the pressing need to rid causality of all anthropomorphic and metaphysical admixtures. They argued that "objective possibilities" in social reality should not be confused with "desirable possibilities" as postulated by individual sociologists in accordance with their ideological commitments or inclinations. They agreed in equating "objective possibility" with "adequate causality" in the study of social action, but they disagreed on specific details in the application of modern statistical methods in the study of causal relations. Weber commended Kistiakovskii's critique of the Russian subjective school's identification of "possibilities" with ideological goals and presented a detailed analysis of the theory of "objective possibility."[28] While Kistiakovskii and Weber sensed the need for making mathematical statistics a basic tool of sociological inquiry, their own research was neither mathematical nor statistical. They were mostly prophets of future developments in sociology. Both were interested more in the logical and epistemological foundations of mathematical statistics as applied in social research than in its operative mechanisms.

Kistiakovskii contended that the similarities between the social sciences and the natural sciences are purely formal: the two families of sciences share only a search for general concepts and causal explanations. The differences between the two are as essential as the similarities. The natural sciences give logical primacy to general over individual phenomena; the social sciences give primacy to individual over general phenomena. The natural sciences operate in terms of absolute causality; the social sciences operate in terms of probabilistic causality. The natural sciences investigate a reality that falls completely within the domain of causality; the social sciences face a reality which falls within the domains of both empirical causality and moral purposiveness.

In *Society and the Individual*, Kistiakovskii relied on the causality-purposiveness dichotomy in advancing a general theory of the state. The state, according to him, appears in two different forms: as "the state in a juridical sense" and as "the state in the sense of society."[29] While the latter calls for an empirical study of causal relations within and between social groups, the former requires an interpretive study of the purposiveness of "normative ideals."[30] Although the two studies are qualitatively different, they are not mutually exclusive: they approach the same reality from different vantage

---

*According to Talcott Parsons: "The concept 'objective possibility' plays an important technical role in Weber's methodological studies. According to his usage, a thing is 'objectively possible' if it 'makes sense' to conceive it as an empirically existing entity. It is a question of conforming with the formal logical conditions. The question whether a phenomenon which is in this sense 'objectively possible' will actually be found with any significant degree of probability or approximation, is a logically distinct question" (In Max Weber, *The Theory of Social and Economic Organization*, p. 149 n).

points.[31] Most of Kistiakovskii's work in social and legal theory was dedicated to a logical and epistemological refinement and amplification of this view. However, he did not make a serious effort to combine the two approaches into a unified method. He resolved the dilemma simply by assuming that the two different aspects of social reality call for two distinct approaches to the complex nature of society: the sociological approach and the normative approach. The sociological approach deals with the *real* social existence. The normative approach deals with the *ideal* world embodied in moral duties. Like Georg Simmel, Kistiakovskii assumed that the normative study of social reality requires extensive assistance from moral philosophy unfettered by metaphysical obscurantism. The sociological approach can add to the understanding of, but cannot resolve by itself, the profound epistemological conflict between the causally determined social phenomena and man's active participation in the social process, which calls for a conscious selection of activities in accordance with accepted ideals and moral duty. Kistiakovskii was careful to emphasize that the normative approach to social reality should not be reduced to mere recitations of universal ethical principles, immune to the whims of evolution, but that it should concentrate on the historical embodiments of these principles in unique "cultural communities."[32] The normative approach should concentrate not on taking an inventory of ethical rules but on analyzing the multiple ramifications of morality in action.

In his appraisal of Mikhailovskii's sociological theory, Kistiakovskii followed mainly a line of negative criticism; however, the similarities between the two theoretical orientations are much more profound than the differences. Although inspired and guided by the ideas unleashed by neo-Kantian philosophy, particularly on the differences between the natural sciences and the social sciences, he had failed to note that these ideas had been anticipated by Lavrov and Mikhailovskii, the leaders of the subjective school. N. I. Kareev, a codifier of subjective sociology, has provided a pertinent and generally correct summary of the philosophical views which served as the meeting ground for the two orientations.

B. A. Kistiakovskii, a confirmed follower of Kant, is one of the first writers who applied the epistemological principles of critical [i.e., Kantian] philosophy to the methodology of the social sciences, as attested by his *Society and the Individual*, published in 1899. A Kantian in the study of social phenomena, he treats both the category of absolute causality and the category of duty; thus he is a realist and an idealist at the same time. However, since his idealism has neither metaphysical nor mystical character, he could be called a positivist in the broadest meaning of the term. While narrow positivism does not go beyond the categories of necessity, causality and regularity, and is characterized by strict objectivism, B. A. Kistiakovskii's introduction of the notions of duty and justice into the study of social phenomena makes him a kin to the "Russian Sociological School," which some fifty years ago came to be known as sociological subjectivism and which he has subjected to unjust or, at least, unwarranted criticism. That society, law, and the state exist not only as an essential reality but also as a duty is a thesis advanced by the subjective school in Russian sociology with whose literature he is not well acquainted. To appraise these ideas in their fullness, he should have studied not so much the work of N. K. Mikhailovskii as the work of P. L. Lavrov, who was much more interested in philosophy in general, and in epistemology, logic, methodology, and ethics, in particular. Kistiakovskii differs from positivists-objectivists who view the historical process strictly as a mechanical or organic evolution—the point of view, which has been accepted, among others, by the Russian economic materialists during the 1890s—in that he recognizes the creative role of the individual in social life. This, too, brings him close to the views of the Russian Sociological School.[33]

In one important respect, Kistiakovskii stood apart not only from subjective sociology but from most other leading Russian sociological schools as well: he argued with remarkable consistency that the sociologist is not an authority in social policies, that his task is to understand and not to regulate or change human society. He was also the most convincing and eloquent spokesman for the school of thought which claimed that the sociologist, regardless of his heavy reliance on philosophy, must never abandon the search for firmer scientific foundations of his discipline. His world view was an original reworking of neo-Kantian thought in the spirit of scientific positivism and philosophical humanism.

Sociology and the General Theory of Law

To Kistiakovskii, sociology is not only a general social science, concerned with the epistemological, logical, and methodological problems of a scientific search for the universal laws of social reality. It is also a special social science—or a special approach to social reality. His elaborate search for a comprehensive study of law provided him with an opportunity to subject the idea of sociology as a special social science to detailed elaboration and refinement. In *Social Sciences and Law* he expanded the two-faceted general theory of the state into a four-faceted general theory of law, an original synthesis of several leading orientations in modern jurisprudence and an elaborate effort to spell out the specific nature of the sociological approach to social reality as one of the several possible major approaches. In elaborating his general theory of law, Kistiakovskii relied heavily on a critical examination of four dominant Russian orientations in jurisprudence: the analytical orientation which considered the inner logic and the formal principles of legal systems the main task of the general science of law; the

sociological orientation which treated law exclusively as an instrument of
social cohesion and social evolution; the psychological orientation which
sought to decode the universal instinctive and emotional foundations of legal
behavior; and the normative orientation which viewed law as a supreme
embodiment of the universal and transhistorical values of human existence.
Kistiakovskii's critical assessment and use of these orientations deserve
closer scrutiny.

The analytical orientation, the strongest in Russia, treated law as the
totality of norms safeguarded by the coercive power of the state.[34] It equated
the study of law with a description and schematization of the component
parts of legal systems. While recognizing that this orientation made a major
contribution to the conceptualization of the general principles of the legal
structure of the state and to the scientific study of the organizational
principles of legal systems, Kistiakovskii contended that it had a major
weakness: it was inapplicable to the study of a large part of constitutional
law and of international relations whose legal structure was not conducive
either to high levels of abstraction or to precise logical formulations. The
jurists who belonged to this school tended to undervalue the legal character
of customary law and to rely on "sheer sophistry" in producing elaborate
legal schemes. This approach found the staunchest support in various
positivist schools, committed to a search for logical similarities between
scientific laws and juridical norms.

The sociological orientation, a relatively new development, dealt with law
as an instrument of social integration and a mechanism of social change.
The Moscow Juridical Society, founded in 1863 and inspired by the spirit of
the Great Reforms, gave this orientation an institutional support and
philosophical guidance. The dominant figure in the society was S. A. Muromtsev, a professor of law at Moscow University from 1877 to 1884, when
he was dismissed by the minister of national education for illicit political
activities. After 1884, he worked intermittently as a lawyer, a journalist, and
a law professor at the Shaniavskii University, a Moscow institution sustained
exclusively by a private financial endowment. A rich experience in the work
for the Moscow City Duma, the zemstvo movement, and the Central
Committee of the Constitutional-Democratic party prepared him for the role
of the chairman of the First State Duma (1906) in which he displayed
courageous dedication to the democratic process and a proclivity for strict
parliamentary procedures. In 1907, he received a three-month jail sentence
for his participation in an "illegal" conference of a group of the First State
Duma deputies, held after the first Russian parliament was officially
dissolved, and for signing the Vyborg Appeal, which encouraged opposition
to the government's efforts to cut the roots from under the burgeoning
institutions of political democracy.

Kistiakovskii considered Muromtsev the founder of the sociology of law as a distinct discipline and lamented government interference which hampered its development.[35] In 1878, Muromtsev became the editor of the society's *Juridical Messenger*, and transformed it immediately into a journal of "practical jurisprudence," relying heavily on zemstvo statistics, and into "the only Russian journal devoted to social theory in the broadest meaning of the term."[36] While giving increasing attention to the developments in Western legal theory, the society worked intensively on the preparation of projects for legislative reforms. The Juridical Society, wrote one of its members, built a bridge between law and politics and "played a major role in the diffusion of constitutional ideas in Russia." Its meetings were "a school of civic education."[37]

Muromtsev presented his sociological ideas in general statements and methodological hints scattered throughout his many writings, rather than in a conceptually integrated general treatise. His best-known works are *Essays on the General Theory of Civil Law* (1877) and *Definition and Basic Divisions of Law* (1879). His *Sociological Essays*, written as journal articles, remained uncompleted. He was the first Russian scholar to advocate a science of law combining a general sociological theory (he was particularly impressed with the theoretical models provided by Comte, Spencer, Tylor, and Lubbock) and a concrete historical analysis of legal norms in their social and historical context. The study of law, he wrote, must take into account both the uniformity of the universal attributes of law and the uniqueness of the legal experience of individual societies.[38] While only general theory can explain the inner logic in the development of law, empirical studies are indispensable for an understanding of the unending communal search for more perfect ideas of justice.[39] In its essence, law is a system of social relations.[40] According to Muromtsev, the origin of legal norms must be sought in social resolutions of conflicts between various groups. Alluding to Russian realities, he claimed that societies torn by inequality and disharmony face especially difficult conditions in promulgating and enforcing laws that sustain cooperation as the pivotal force of social integration. In a special study of the forces which link the individual to the total society as a system of multiple forms of cooperation, he elaborated "sociality" as a concept denoting the cultural and psychological predisposition of the individual to become an integral part of various processes of cooperation.[41] Rudolf von Jhering, in Muromtsev's opinion, should be considered the founder of the "positive" orientation in jurisprudence, for he was the first to elaborate the idea of law as a product of the activities of individuals in search of socially sanctioned avenues of cooperation. The recognition of the individual as the ultimate source of law meant the recognition of the inseparability of the study of law from the social sciences concerned with the theoretical aspects of social structure, cultural values, and personality.[42]

Muromtsev contended that the basic weakness of contemporary studies of law was in the reification (he called it objectification) of abstract legal principles. In such handy abstractions as "national character," "legal organism," and "organic development of law," freely used by the representatives of the historical school in jurisprudence, he saw figurative expressions that contributed only confusion to the study of the "real" processes in the formation and evolution of law. He argued that it was much easier, but less productive, to study legal reality by relying on convenient analogies than by undertaking tedious historical research and social analysis. In his opinion, a considerable confusion in the general theory of law stemmed from a totally unwarranted identification of law as a system of legal norms with law, as a scientific statement on regularities in nature and society. To state that legal theory covers the gradual expansion of "justice" is to state a moral principle, not a scientific law. This identification made legal theorists a mixture of moralizers and theorists. They concentrated much more on the automatic unfolding of legal principles than on the everyday realities of law. Under Muromtsev's influence, a solid group of jurists conducted detailed studies of the social and political attributes of Russian law, without ignoring the pressing need for a scientific study of the development of law as a vital component of the universal evolution of human society. It was also under his influence that an increasing number of jurists recognized two types of jurisprudence: theoretical jurisprudence concerned with detecting regularities, limited though they may be, in the development of law and applied jurisprudence, concerned with practical designs for the use of law in paving the way for social progress. [43]

Kistiakovskii was not satisfied with a mere endorsement of Muromtsev's view of law as a social phenomenon; he surveyed modern literature in the field in order to give his own sociology of law more precision and depth. He took a closer look into two more current views on the relation of law to society.

The champions of the first view argued that since law can exist only in, and as determined by, society, it can be studied exclusively as part of social structure; in their opinion, the sociology of law is the most fundamental science of law. Kistiakovskii could not endorse this view. He argued that the isolation of specific components of nature and society from the total context of reality is a basic logical prerequisite for scientific studies in depth. He noted also that the nonsociological studies of law have proven their usefulness by producing valuable material long before the emergence of the sociology of law. The sociology of law, in his opinion, could perform a useful role only if it recognized that it represented but one of several approaches to law.

The articulators of the second view, headed by Rudolf Stammler, argued that society is more a product of law than law is a product of society. Kistiakovskii followed Max Weber in subjecting this orientation to a thorough and devastating criticism. Identifying the logical processes of scientific abstraction with the real processes of life, Stammler (according to Weber and Kistiakovskii) insisted that the social life of man can be scientifically investigated only when it is treated within a legal context and as an objectification of legal norms. Kistiakovskii, relying on Muromtsev, rejected Stammler's theory on three grounds: first, it provided only for a legalistic study of society rather than for a social study of law; second, it was too concerned with the legal system (law as stated in legal books) to allow for the adequate consideration of legal relations (law as carried out in practice); and, third, it did not make room for a study of the interaction between the objective law of the state and the subjective experiences and proclivities of individuals.[44]

Kistiakovskii pointed out that a sociological study of the substance of law was a sure path to criticism of the institutional sources of inequality and, particularly in Russia, to government retaliation. The sociology of law, he thought, must have a theoretical and a practical goal: it must contribute to both the enrichment of the general theory of society and the maintenance of the substantive unity of "law" and "justice."[45] The task of the student of the social attributes of law is not only to arrive at theoretical formulation of a scientific nature but also to help in making law an unrestricted expression of justice.

In 1880, Muromtsev was the leader of a group of twenty Moscow citizens who sent a memorandum to M. T. Loris-Melikov, the head of the Supreme Commission for Safeguarding the State Order and Social Peace (founded in 1880), noting the "growing opposition" to the government and suggesting that "an independent assembly of zemstvo representatives" be invited to participate in government affairs for the purpose of ensuring "the rights of the individual to the freedom of thought and expression."[46]

In 1884, Muromtsev was dismissed from his university position by a direct order of the minister of national education.[47] In 1892, in response to intensified government censorship, the Moscow Juridical Society decided to terminate the publication of the *Juridical Messenger*, the stronghold of Muromtsev's influence on legal scholars. In 1899, the government ordered that the society terminate all its activities.[48] The government's determined effort to suppress the type of sociological study of law inaugurated by Muromtsev compelled the academic community to abandon the study of the interaction of law and society and to resort to the treatment of law as an abstract category standing above the social and political realities of the day.

The psychological orientation, particularly as elaborated by L. I. Petrazhitskii, was the most notable academic adaptation to the government's determination to suppress the study of the concrete social and political attributes of law in general and Russian law in particular.

A professor of law at St. Petersburg University, Petrazhitskii claimed that neither philosophy nor sociology offered satisfactory tools for the understanding of the fundamental principles of law.[49] He rejected the "positivist" view of law as an "external" phenomenon, created and imposed on the individual by society and its agencies. The state or any other political authority, he said, is not a creator but a product of law. Instead, he argued that law is an "internal" phenomenon, that its foundations are in man's psychic constitution.[50] Of the three basic human endowments—cognition, volition, and emotional impulses—he considered the last the basic source of social behavior in general and legal behavior in particular.[51] As specific neurophysiological reactions to biological and cultural stimuli, "legal emotions" are the universal substratum of law and morality. In one important respect, the evolution of legal and moral norms is fundamentally similar to the evolution of living forms as interpreted by Darwin: in both evolutions, adaptation to new conditions and the struggle for existence play the primary role. Only legislation attuned to legal emotions can assure the progress of human society; history is laden with examples of cultural regress caused by misguided legislation.

In order to protect it from ideological infusions, Petrazhitskii sought to elevate legal theory to the highest level of scientific abstraction, an effort for which he received plaudits from a solid contingent of academic contemporaries.[52] At one point in his career, he asserted that jurisprudence, as a general social science, needed its own law of gravitation; he responded to the self-imposed challenge by matching a law of universal psychic attraction generated by legal impulses with Newton's law of universal physical attraction. In his opinion, an elaborate formulation of explanatory principles and conceptual nomenclature should precede the substantive study of law.[53] In "introspection" he saw the basic "experimental" method for disentangling the knotted strands of culturally elaborated and diversified legal emotions; introspection, in turn, may be supplemented by data produced by "external observations" of symbolic meanings of social communication expressed in words, rituals, and specific formulations of normative material.[54] Petrazhitskii argued that emotional psychology, like physics and other natural sciences, searched for basic scientific laws not by amassing endless empirical data but by establishing causal links between limited numbers of typical phenomena selected for intensive study. He was particularly critical of contemporary jurists interested in making the study of law an empirical discipline. While the sociological school in jurisprudence made the Russian legal reality the central subject of inquiry, Petrazhitskii worked on the assumption that Russian (or German, or any other) law and society, as specific "empirical " cases, were of no particular scientific significance. He often noted that the practical goal of his complex legal abstractions was to contribute to raising the legal consciousness of all segments of society to higher levels and to laying the groundwork for a practical science which he named "the politics of law" or "legislative politics."[55] However, he was too busy elaborating endless schemas of legal logic to deal seriously with the practical potentials of his theory.

Although he was involved in constructing legal theories of the most abstruse variety, Petrazhitskii did not shun active participation in politics. He was a member of the Constitutional-Democratic party and a deputy to the First State Duma. Pressured by friends, he signed the Vyborg Appeal, which brought him a short imprisonment and a temporary break in teaching at St. Petersburg University. This unpleasant experience was instrumental for his full withdrawal from politics and, perhaps, for his loss of interest in empirical jurisprudence and the legal realities of autocratic Russia.

Despite his heavy concern with the minutia of emotional psychology and the psychological theory of law, Petrazhitskii did not ignore the sociological aspects of law altogether, at least during the early phase of his academic career.[56] His analysis of differences between positive law and intuitive law is both challenging and refreshingly new. Positive law always relies on external authority, whether it be a codex of law, an ancestral dictate, or an institutional charter. Intuitive law, on the other hand, relies only on internal authority—on legal emotions or the legal consciousness of individuals and groups. It consists of myriads of ever-changing experiences crystallized into distinct group attitudes, "legal convictions," and value orientations. In many "wide areas of social activity," intuitive law plays a more important role than positive law; the real basis of every legal order is in intuitive law. When a segment of intuitive law becomes a fully developed norm of social behavior— a social sense of justice—it flows into positive law, making room for the emergence and confluence of new spontaneous manifestations of intuitive law. Since positive law does not resolve all conflicts, every society makes use of intuitive law, and it is through this use that intuitive law enriches both positive law and legal theory. Positive law specifies resolutions for typical conflicts; whenever a conflict is atypical it requires help from intuitive law. When the two types of law collide, intuitive law emerges victorious. In times of crisis, political efforts to suppress the vital complexes of intuitive law invite social revolutions.

The historical role of intuitive law is not to replace positive law but to enrich it and to enhance its responsiveness to emerging social needs. However, this does not apply to every kind of positive law. Petrazhitskii recognized two major types of positive law: legislated or "conscious" law and customary or spontaneous law. While the former transforms the "spontaneous" and "empirical" intuitive law material into "deliberate" and "rational" law, the latter is made up of petrified residues of intuitive law. Legislated law, the epitome of rationality and conscious action, is a primary index of social and cultural progress; customary law, on the other hand, is a vehicle of social stagnation and even pathology. Contrary to the views of the typical representatives of historical jurisprudence, customary law is not the embodiment of values depicting a "national character" for it is too rigid to serve as an expression of the dynamics of constantly changing collective behavior. The legal power, or normative authority, of customary law, he said, does not depend on perceptions and judgments reflecting new currents in social life and thought; on the contrary, the older the customs the more unbending their authority and the more oppressive their influence on society.[57] The more advanced a society is, the more rational and deliberate are its legislated laws and the more limited is the authority of customary law. The future of sociocultural evolution belongs to enacted law; the time will come, according to Petrazhitskii, when customary law will be of interest only to archeologists and other students of primitive culture.[58] Customary law is an enemy of democracy for it perpetuates rigid class differences, economic exploitation, and an unequal distribution of cultural values and benefits. He hinted that the staggering scope and power of customary law in Russia was the mainstay of the forces working against a democratization of Russian political institutions and a rationalization of Russian economy.[59] He thought that the most compelling task of the legal theorist should be to help accelerate the process of replacing the petrified complexes of customary law by conscious efforts to achieve the "grand ideals" of humanity.[60]

In one respect, Petrazhitskii's theory of intuitive law resembles Mikhailovskii's subjective sociology: both regard the individual as the ultimate creator of all social norms and relations. Petrazhitskii's intuitive law, in the words of a contemporary interpreter, "has an individual and adaptive character, and is determined by special conditions in the life of every person—his character, education, social status, profession and acquaintances."[61] Individual experiences of common conditions produce the intuitive law of all social groups, from individual families to entire social classes; and this law synchronizes the propensities of individuals with the needs of various groups.[62] As a progressive affirmation of individuality, the evolution of intuitive law is the chief mechanism of cultural progress. Petrazhitskii's customary law, on the other hand, allows a minimum expression of individuality and legal flexibility; as a foe of individual variability in the interpretation of values, it is the very antithesis of progress.

A comparison of positive law and intuitive law with positive morality and intuitive morality helped Petrazhitskii to formulate a system of multiple links between legal and ethical norms. However, instead of exploring the broad perspectives of his elaborate sociological schema, he turned his attention to the philosophical and logical problems of law, which took him away from both the sociology of law and "the politics of law." In his view, the universal sources and manifestations of legal consciousness and moral laws are beyond the reach of sociology, which he identified as an empirical science deeply entangled in a morass of historical details.

Petrazhitskii appealed to liberal professors and other intellectuals by his professed aim to formulate a theory of law as a general theory of society that would stand clearly apart from both ideology and metaphysics—a theory that would belong exclusively to the domain of science. He was not completely successful in either of the two endeavors. His theory of law was an intellectual force behind the constitutionalist movement in Russia, strong particularly among university professors. This theory treated law, enacted by representative legislative bodies, as the most powerful instrument of social progress, an instrument that could free Russia from the crippling burden of the feudal past without causing social ruptures of cataclysmic proportions. Petrazhitskii's theoretical work was also an attack on the schools of thought, represented in Russia by Boris Chicherin, V. S. Solov'ev, and Evgenii Trubetskoi, which built their reputations on extravagant claims that the general theory of law cannot be confined within the limits of science but must belong to the realm of metaphysics. However, in his effort to place the general theory of law on scientific foundations, Petrazhitskii succumbed to the lure of an outdated mechanistic model in physics that treated the universe as a clockwork consisting of elaborate wheels and pulleys and that led him to substitute logical deductions from ontological presuppositions for both the experience of history and the experimentation of science.

Kistiakovskii recognized the perceptive depth of Petrazhitskii's theory and saw many advantages in his cogent analysis of differences between morality and law.[63] While moral norms, as defined by Petrazhitskii, are "unilateral" phenomena of purely "imperative" nature, legal norms are "bilateral" phenomena, for they are both imperative and attributive: they represent an indissoluble link between legal obligations and subjective rights. This definition, Kistiakovskii noted, has an advantage over the traditional view of law as a coercive instrument of the state or as a result of a "general will" or "universal consensus" in that it opens the door for the study of the previously unexplored role of motivation in legal behavior and brings together legal psychology and legal pedagogy.[64] However, this did not deter him from subjecting Petrazhitskii's theory to relentless criticism. He noted that, instead of grounding his elaborate theory in social psychology, Petrazhitskii operated strictly within an anachronistic individual psychology which failed to explore the links between personality and society. Moreover, Petrazhitskii operated within the slightly modified framework of the old and worn-out associationist psychology which corresponded to the atomistic orientation in the natural sciences and fully disregarded the role of culture in the development of personality. He was concerned more with categorizing the varieties of legal behavior than with exploring its dynamics; he was interested more in cataloging the psychological aspects of law than in setting up logical and methodological procedures for a systematic, in-depth study of legal action and the vital links between law and society.[65] In a sense, he advanced a general theory of legal mentality rather than a psychological theory of law: he was too preoccupied with the inner logic of legal mentality to concern himself with legal behavior as part of social action. He dealt with law as manifested in the behavior of the individual rather than with law as realized in social institutions.[66] Kistiakovskii reasoned that only legal psychology concerned with the social nature and institutional setting of law can enrich general jurisprudence and that no legal psychology, regardless of its scientific merit, can rise to the level of a general theory of law.[67]

The normative orientation in jurisprudence blossomed in Russia during the late 1890s and the first decade of the twentieth century and was closely connected with the revived interest in natural law. It, too, was a specific adaptation of the community of law experts to the determined efforts of the government to prevent a critical examination of the legal aspects of Russian society and of law as an instrument of social and political change. P. I. Novgorodtsev, a professor of law at Moscow University, was the most erudite and influential representative of this orientation. He too was a Constitutional Democrat and a deputy to the First State Duma; he too signed the Vyborg Appeal, for which he served a short prison term.[68] In his earlier work, he viewed the modern theory of natural law, particularly as advanced by Rudolf Stammler in *Economy and Law*, as an effort to rid the traditional conception of natural law of metaphysical and transcendental elements and to reconcile it with the views of modern historical jurisprudence. The theory of natural law, according to him, recognizes the existence of regularities in the development of legal norms and calls for a "critical examination" of present-day social realities from the vantage point of universal ideals embodied in "legal consciousness."[69] The universal values built into the complex edifice of natural law create the "atmosphere" in which the concrete legal norms are forged, chart the course of social evolution (and progress), and serve as the theoretical basis for a comparative study of social institutions in general and legal institutions in particular.

In his subsequent work, Novgorodtsev showed growing sympathy for the normative orientation of natural law theories and their opposition to the positivist orientation of historical jurisprudence. While in his earlier studies he accepted the idea of jurisprudence as a social science combining the historical and normative approaches, in his later work he tried to show the limited productivity of all efforts to subject legal norms—the core of legality—to scientific treatment. Law is inseparable from morality and "the moral problem cannot be resolved by historicism, and it is fully inaccessible to the positive method."[70] He argued that all efforts to bring together "reality" and "morality" have led inevitably to a distortion of both.[71] Science, as a study of "reality," handles only the limited area of experimentation and causality; "it does not go, and must not go, beyond limited facts derived from observation."[72] Science cannot unveil the inner meaning of law because "from the very beginning of its existence, law is not only an external and mechanical organization of society, but also a moral guide of social forces, for it regulates both the subordination of these forces to a higher authority and the discharge of particular duties."[73] In his later work

Novgorodtsev concentrated on making a philosophical study of the moral foundations of law the basic branch of jurisprudence. He particularly opposed the sociology of law, which he considered quite superficial. The more he wrote, the more he was inclined to view law as a system of "self-governed" moral norms, not conducive to historical explanation. Unwavering in his opposition to the scientific study of law based on "historicism" and "sociologism," he fought for philosophical jurisprudence grounded in abstract morality and "will."[74] Like Hermann Cohen, he argued that, while logic is an expression of pure thought, ethics is an expression of pure will.

Novgorodtsev and his Russian followers identified the normative approach as a "general theory of law," not complementing but transcending the sociological and psychological approaches. The legal norms which interested the normativists are pure rules of behavior emptied of all historically forged social content and psychological attributes. Without a substantive basis, they are not conducive to scientific treatment and invite logical constructions of a philosophical nature. Kistiakovskii, on the contrary, argued that the "empirical" part of law could be adequately treated on a scientific level (the level of causation), but that the "normative" part of law demanded philosophical analysis (the level of purposiveness).

Both Kistiakovskii and Novgorodtsev worked under the banner of "philosophical idealism" to which they gave completely different meanings: while to Kistiakovskii "philosophical idealism" stood for a specific epistemological elaboration of the unique scientific features of sociology, to Novgorodtsev it stood for a metaphysical denial of both sociology and psychology as legitimate sciences of law.[75] While Kistiakovskii tried to improve the methodology of the empirical study of society, Novgorodtsev worked with equal determination to show its limited scope and superficiality. Both Kistiakovskii and Novgorodtsev were strongly influenced by neo-Kantian philosophy; however, while Kistiakovskii was closer to the Baden school (particularly to Rickert), which was dominated by a search for unique philosophical and methodological foundations of the social sciences, Novgorodtsev was closer to the Marburg school (particularly to Stammler and Cohen), which was dedicated to developing a codified system of moral norms transcending both the limits of history and the power of scientific scrutiny.[76] He claimed that Kant's greatest single contribution to modern thought was in showing that the moral code did not fall into the area of scientific inquiry.[77] Kant had pointed out that, in contrast to scientific inquiry, which is limited to the world of cognizable causation and is propelled by skepticism, moral inquiry rises above every determinism and agnosticism. While morality is separable from science, it is inseparable from religion.

Novgorodtsev's theory was more than an accommodating response to the concerted efforts of the government to wipe out all branches or orientations in empirical jurisprudence that subjected the country's legal system to critical examination: it was also a reflection of the growing reaction of both scientists and philosophers to the use of mechanistic models in the study of society. Sociological positivism, which Novgorodtsev criticized, came under attack from many scientific quarters as an extension of Newtonian mechanics to the study of society; this occurred at the time when the rigid mechanistic orientation was also under attack in physics, chemistry, and biology.[78] Novgorodtsev's criticism, like that of many scientists, had a measure of validity, especially in view of the complex epistemological problems presented by the social sciences. However, guided by the idea that "the question of morality is beyond the reach of both historicism and the positive method," he substituted metaphysical expediency for epistemological elaboration and renounced any serious attempt at a scientific study of the foundations upon which human society is erected.[79] He claimed that the sociologists engaged in idle talk because they "undertook more than they could handle," were limited by a strict adherence to "moral relativism," and did not take advantage of the limitless potentialities of "philosophical idealism." Novgorodtsev accepted science only insofar as it recognized the comparatively narrow scope of its competence and the relative value of its findings.[80] He belonged to the group of intellectuals who thought that sociology asked too many unpleasant questions about the realities of social existence to be tolerated either as a science or as an academic discipline. Law, according to him, should be studied not as a historically molded specific social reality but as an embodiment of the "highest essences and ideal predestinations" of the universal course of human society.[81]

Kistiakovskii's criticism of existing legal approaches was neither sweeping nor categorical. He criticized individual approaches only inasmuch as they tended to be reductionist in causal explanations, asymmetrical in the treatment of the complex fabric of law, and intolerant of other approaches.[82] He looked for a unified theory of law which could be built only if each juridical school treated *all* aspects of law from its specific vantage point. For example, the sociological approach would be unsatisfactory as long as it did not throw specific light on the logical, psychological, and normative aspects of law. He realized that this was a challenge of enormous proportions and complexity and that legal theory had not yet reached the requisite level of maturity to meet it with measurable success. The general theory of law could be built only upon the principle of the complementarity of specialized approaches.

Kistiakovskii thought that a widening of the substantive base and a sharpening of the theoretical focus of the sociological approach was particularly essential for the development of a general theory of law. The basic concern of the sociology of law, in his opinion, is not law per se but legal norms working in society. The essence of legal norms, in contrast to aesthetic norms, is not in their intrinsic meaning but in their "continuous and regular effectuation in society." To Jhering's statement that law is not simple duty but also a historical fact, Kistiakovskii added that law above everything else is a social fact.[83] To understand the social attributes of juridical norms, it is necessary to study the embodiment of law in "legal relations." "Law" consists of juridical norms as these are written down and codified; "legal relations" refer to the work of law in real social situations. Written law consists of general, impersonal, and schematic regulations; legal relations are made up of unique, concrete, individual situations. Written law is stagnant; if it changes, it does so spasmodically, discontinuously. Moreover, in order to change law, it is necessary to put a complex machinery in operation. On the contrary, legal relations are in continuous motion, in constant flux; new legal relations emerge on the ruins of old ones. The function of a sociological study of law is to trace the translation of law into legal relations and to ascertain the multiple adaptations of juridical norms to the contingencies of everyday existence. Law may be an instrument of social change, but more often than not it is an instrument for preserving the existing social order. It is through legal relations that law is forced to make adjustments to the need for change. The traditional theories were built upon the notion of the omnipotence of law; the modern sociology of law claims that limitations in the power of law hold the key for the understanding of the evolution of institutionalized justice.[84] Kistiakovskii criticized legal positivists who tended to identify the laws of justice with the laws of science by treating both as equally intolerant of exceptions. In his opinion, it is primarily through "exceptions," created in the process of making law a functioning element of society, that the path is blazed for social innovations. It was essentially for the same reason that he criticized the jurists of the historical school who denigrated the role of the personal proclivities of legislators in enacting law and who had little use for the role of the courts in transforming law from a static to a dynamic component of social reality.

All this does not mean that Kistiakovskii denied the existence of a residual element in law which transcended the vagaries of history and embraced the universal elements of humanity. The ultimate purpose of the sociology of law is to discover the common denominators of law; but to achieve this, it must first concentrate on empirical methods for the study of multitudinous variations in the work of law. General abstractions in the sociology of law must meet the same criteria of scientific rigor as those of general sociology: they must rely on a mathematically rigorous statistical treatment of empirical data as the only way of establishing causal links and on philosophical analysis for elucidating the purposive nature of juridical norms.

Kistiakovskii was convinced that, despite its dedication to the ultimate search for universal laws of social behavior, sociology could explain only one basic component of law: regularities in the evolution of the interaction of juridical norms and society. He was annoyed with the theories of Petrazhitskii and Novgorodtsev not because they elaborated the psychological and normative approaches to law but because they ignored the interaction of law and society in everyday life. They led jurisprudence away from the study of the role of law both in official efforts to preserve the anachronistic features of the old regime and in social stirrings in favor of basic changes in the Russian polity. Novgorodtsev, in particular, did not merely ignore the empirical sociology of law; he led a sharp and bitter campaign against it.

Kistiakovskii worked diligently to separate sociology from ideology. He was unbending in his disapproval of the Russian sociological school on the ground that it treated sociology as a tool of ideology. He criticized the efforts of leading Marxists to place sociological theory behind the revolutionary movement in which they were involved. In several attacks on the integrity and usefulness of sociology, he detected a defense of the social and political status quo. But despite his efforts and cultivated dedication to the ethos of scientific objectivity, he did not achieve a full scholarly detachment from ideological interference. Behind many of his subtle thoughts, abstract inferences, and concrete examples, one can detect a dedication to an ideology of economic individualism, political freedom, scientific rationality, and technical management—an ideology which saw the immediate future of Russia in the evolution of representative government, anchored in industrial society and antithetical to Populist communalism and autocratic patriarchalism. In his opinion, only the choice of a representative government would make Russia a "legal state" (*pravovoe gosudarstvo*), such as a constitutional monarchy. He criticized the Russian "revolutionary parties"—including both the Social-Democrats and the Populists—which, preoccupied with the dreams of a "new society," disregarded the residues of the constitutional tradition in Russia as a basis upon which a new state could be built.[85] The "legal state," he thought, was not the crowning point of political evolution: it was a necessary precondition for the emergence of a socialist state, a conception which Kistiakovskii left unexplored but for which he was labeled an advocate of "juridical socialism."[86] His basic argument was that, even when it was "bourgeois" in a social sense, the state might be a great school of democracy in a political sense.[87] The essence of his argument was that political democracy was the most essential prerequisite for the emergence of a new Russia, free of the burdensome legacy of antiquated political institutions. Despite all this, his ideology, presented in scattered and unelaborated thoughts, hidden in the intricate fabric of sociological abstractions, detracted little, if any, from the power of his scientific arguments and the depth of his involvement in the epistemological and logical foundations of social theory.[88]

6. Comparative History and Sociology: M. M. Kovalevskii

Social history—the history of social institutions, social classes, communities, the social organization of economic activities, and the social background and role of politics—was a flourishing discipline in Russia, particularly after 1860. Some social historians operated on a purely descriptive or "ethnographic" level, concerned more with marshalling documentary evidence of historical relevance than with the search for broad generalizations. Others looked for trends behind the myriads of historical events but were reluctant to undertake a more complex and intricate sociological analysis of data and to enter the domain of theoretical constructions. The third group included the scholars who made deliberate efforts to combine historical research with systematic sociological analysis and who advanced original, even though not always elaborate, sociological theories. The most prominent and best-known representative of the third group was Maksim M. Kovalevskii.

Kovalevskii was a historian among sociologists and a sociologist among historians. The enormous scope of his scholarship included local histories of individual institutions, synthetic institutional histories of national proportions, carefully documented essays in comparative history, ideologically involved journalistic accounts of the development of sociology, biographies of leading social theoreticians from Condorcet to Lester Ward, and efforts to systematize modern sociological thought. In the words of Miliukov, an unusually wide compass of encyclopedic knowledge and a recognition of the complementarity of diverse scientific theories were among Kovalevskii's most outstanding personal traits. In a dedicated effort to search for common denominators in what appeared to be irreconcilable social and political views and currents lay one of his major contributions to modern sociological thought.[1] His work was a point of convergence for the historical and juridical currents of Russian scholarship committed to the search for a general science of society.

In his most widely acclaimed studies, Kovalevskii examined the evolution of economic, political, and legal institutions in Russia in the light of an eclectic and rather flexible social theory of Western vintage. According to the French sociologist René Worms, Kovalevskii was viewed in the West as Russia's most outstanding social scientist, and in his native country as an accomplished representative of "the best in Western thought."[2] Western scholars appreciated the actual data assembled in Kovalevskii's studies, which were of great value to evolutionary ethnographers and comparative historians. Herbert Spencer accepted Kovalevskii's views on the emergence of private property in land as a result of successive partitions of land originally owned by individual clans. Fouillée relied on Kovalevskii's evidence in his effort to refute Fustel de Coulanges's theory of the prehistorical origins of private property. In the *Origin of Private Property, Family, and the State*, F. Engels borrowed many examples from Kovalevskii's writings supporting his theory of unilinear social evolution from "primitive communism" to capitalism. Russian scholars were most impressed with his theoretical analyses of Russian society and culture; they also admired his ability to range over the entire spectrum of sociology, from personal fieldwork to the search for a grand theory of society.

According to a contemporary critic, Kovalevskii created a system of sociology which was derived not from a grand philosophical assumption but from factual material supplied by ethnography, history, and so-called sociocultural paleontology (studies of the earliest forms of social life). He did not engage in philosophical debate on the nature of society; his attention was focused on the forms which human society assumes in various phases of its development.[3]

Born in 1851 in the Khar'kov province, Kovalevskii came from an aristocratic family of substantial means. As a child, he learned French and displayed an unusual interest in history and literature. As a student at Khar'kov University, he was strongly influenced by D. I. Kachenovskii, whose lectures in the history of international relations and in the history of state institutions made it possible to create "a unitary view of the progressive course of the development of sociopolitical forms in all their major and essential characteristics."[4] It was at Khar'kov that he was exposed to the social philosophies of Comte and Proudhon.[5] Kovalevskii admitted, however, that most of the law professors travelled the futile road of metaphysics.

After graduating from Khar'kov University's law school in 1873, Kovalevskii was invited by his professors to undertake graduate studies as a "professorial aspirant."[6] He went to Western Europe, spending most of his time in France, where, in addition to attending lectures at the Sorbonne, he conducted research in the history of French administrative law, a project that took him to the archives of the cities of Lyon, Rouen, Montpellier, and Aix. It was in Paris that he met Professor I. V. Luchitskii, who at that time was deeply involved in the study of Calvinism. From Luchitskii, who helped him find his way through the rich resources of the Bibliothèque Nationale, he learned to appreciate the need for constant improvements in techniques of historical research and methods of historical analysis. Many years later he recorded that he admired Luchitskii because he combined "the rigorous method of science and an unqualified opposition to mysticism and metaphysics with strict professionalism, consistently correct relations with students, and inability for political compromise."[7] In England, where he spent one year, he met Sir Henry Maine, a pioneer in comparative historical studies of village communities, and Karl Marx, under whose influence he learned to appreciate the extensive role of economic relations in social and political change. He saw in Marx a man of powerful intellect and a scholar of the first order: he thought that Marx was a dispassionate and dedicated scholar and, at the same time, a stubborn and excessively passionate politician.

In 1876, Kovalevskii returned to Russia where his career advanced rapidly. In 1876, he published a monograph on the dissolution of communal agriculture in a Swiss canton. In 1877, he earned a master's degree in law from Moscow University on the basis of a dissertation dealing with the history of political courts in premodern England. In the same year, he was appointed a docent of constitutional law at Moscow University's law school. In 1880, a study of the structure of English society at the end of the Middle Ages brought him a doctorate from, and a full professorship at, Moscow University. He acquired a strong academic following not only because of his innovations in historical methodology but also because of his mastery as a lecturer. However, the government looked with much disfavor upon his course in comparative constitutional law, which threw favorable light on Western democratic institutions and gave indirect support to domestic movements favoring a constitutional government for Russia. The government was also apprehensive of the young professor's concern with the amelioration of Russian social and economic conditions. The authorities were much concerned with his close association with S. A. Muromtsev, the editor of the *Juridical Messenger*, who encouraged a sociological analysis of Russia's legal realities as part of an effort to accelerate the diffusion of modern political ideas among all segments of the population. In 1887, Kovalevskii was compelled to resign from his teaching position.[8]

In the same year, at the invitation of Stockholm University, Kovalevskii delivered a series of lectures on the most recent achievements in comparative historical studies on the origin of the family, the evolution of property, and the patriarchal community. These lectures were extremely important in making Russian ethnographic materials available to evolutionary ethnographers all over the world. During the following years Kovalevskii lectured at Oxford University, the Free College of Social Sciences in Paris, the Free University in Brussels, and the University of Chicago, concentrating on the description of traditional Russian institutions in the light of modern comparative history. He also wrote extensively on the major trends in the development of Western economic and political institutions.

During the long years of exile, Kovalevskii maintained personal contact with such leading French sociologists as G. Tarde, E. Durkheim, and

R. Worms. He was one of the founders of the International Institute of Sociology; in 1895 he was elected vice-president and in 1907 president of this organization. Personal charm, enviable erudition, and unsurpassed knowledge in the history of Russian political, legal, religious, and economic institutions combined to open many academic doors for him. At the newly instituted international congresses of sociologists, he was among the busiest and most sought after individuals. He was particularly in favor with evolutionary sociologists, who appreciated previously untapped ethnographic and historical materials that illustrated their theoretical constructions.

A prolonged Western odyssey did not estrange Kovalevskii from Russia. He continued to send articles to Russian journals and saw most of his works quickly translated into Russian. In 1901 he played a leading role in founding the Russian School of Advanced Social Studies in Paris, an institution that operated for five years and reached hundreds of young Russians who came to Western Europe as students or political refugees. Since the school's permanent faculty included only a few persons, it relied heavily on visiting Russian scholars and political leaders. The comparative pathologist Ili'a Mechnikov, a leading member of the Pasteur Institute in Paris and a champion of the scientific world view, headed the list of guest lecturers, which also included Lenin, Petr Struve, M. I. Tugan-Baranovskii, K. A. Timiriazev, and P. N. Miliukov.[9] During the 1901–2 academic year the school had 13 lecturers and 320 regular students.[10] Baited by overzealous students, intimidated by the constant surveillance by the Paris police, annoyed by the clandestine agents of the Russian police, and threatened by financial disaster, Kovalevskii and his friends could not make the new school a dynamic institution with a rich and symmetrical curriculum. Despite its many shortcomings, it was the only Russian educational institution at the time to offer courses in Russian social, economic, and political institutions from the standpoint of Western democratic ideologies.

The Paris school was the first Russian institution of higher education to offer courses in sociology. This task was entrusted to E. V. de Roberty, a pioneer in Russian sociology and the creator of an original system of neopositivist social theory. His lectures apotheosized the secularization of wisdom as the most trustworthy index of social progress and presented an elaboration of the Durkheimian idea that sociology must treat society as a reality sui generis, irreducible to individual behavior. During the 1901–2 academic year, de Roberty delivered sixteen new lectures on general sociology, concentrating on the comparative analysis of modern sociological systems. While Kovalevskii concentrated on the sociological interpretation of Russian social history, de Roberty preferred to explain the existence of diverse systems of social behavior within single societies. In 1903, the French authorities informed de Roberty that he would be allowed to reside in France only if he discontinued all relations with the Russian school. They took this action in response to a request from the Russian minister of the interior, who had been informed by Russian secret police in Paris that the school was a "seminar in revolution."[11] Resigning from the school, de Roberty left France and was appointed a professor at the Free University in Brussels.

The 1905 revolution precipitated Kovalevskii's (as well as de Roberty's) return to Russia. He was immediately elected a professor of the St. Petersburg Polytechnical Institute, but he also lectured in the Psycho-Neurological Institute, a private university founded by the neurophysiologist V. M. Bekhterev and dedicated to the proposition that higher education should be open to all persons regardless of their ethnic, religious, or social background, and that the curriculum should be so designed as to ensure a symmetrical development of personality. At this institute Kovalevskii taught the first systematic course in sociology to be offered at an institution of higher education in Russia. He also worked on the staffs of several journals and for several years edited the highly respected *Messenger of Europe.*

During this period his scholarly work continued unabated—if anything, it was more diversified than before. However, most notable were his efforts to present an integrated picture of sociology as a distinct science, as well as his published reminiscences giving an account of his personal contact with many leading men of Western social thought. In *Modern Sociologists* (1905) he presented an ambitious survey of leading orientations in contemporary sociological thought and their most eminent representatives. The book marked the first Russian attempt at a systematic presentation of modern theories of society. It is rich in subtle criticisms and cogent observations, and it is comprehensive in its coverage of theoretical systems. In *Sociology* (1910) he outlined the major features of a general theory of society. The function of sociology, he said, is to synthesize the empirical generalizations that are produced by specialized social sciences and that contribute to the understanding of the universal attributes of human society. He emphasized the complementarity of various deterministic orientations and the particularly vital role of sociology in the study of the origin of institutional complexes. Together with de Roberty, he edited the first four symposia of *New Ideas in Sociology,* designed to inform Russian readers about the dominant currents in twentieth-century sociological thought.

Equally impressive was Kovalevskii's record in active political life. In 1906, the Khar'kov province elected him to the First State Duma. In 1907, his candidacy was rejected by the same electorate, but the Academy of Sciences and the universities elected him to represent them in the State Council, of which he was one of the most eminent members, widely known by his oratory. A founder of the middle of the road Party of Democratic Reforms, he served on many legislative committees. He opposed Stolypin's land reforms on the ground that they would unduly accelerate the process of the disintegration of the obshchina and would precipitate a rapid pauperization of the peasantry. This position showed an inner conflict between Kovalevskii the scholar and Kovalevskii the politician; as a scholar, he contended that the obshchina, as a relic of an earlier evolutionary phase, was headed for inescapable extinction; as a politician, he tried to capitalize on the popularity of the romantic notion of the obshchina as a community epitomizing pristine democracy.

Kovalevskii's career does not fall readily into clearly demarcated phases of scholarly endeavor and methodological orientation; throughout his life he combined various genres of writing and moved freely from one academic interest to another. To fully understand his place in the development of social theory in Russia, it is necessary to take a closer look into two major types of his writings: comparative history and sociology.

COMPARATIVE HISTORY

During the 1860s the foundations were laid for what soon became known as comparative history. Pioneered by historians of legal institutions, the new orientation combined a sensitivity for the discrete nature of historical events with a search for regularities in the historical process. During the 1870s the foundations were laid for the modern ethnographic approach, thanks to the labors of such great ethnologists as Sir Edward Tylor and Lewis H. Morgan. This approach was concerned with fitting the "unique" material of tribal cultures, contained in myths, rituals, and customary law, into the grand scheme of universal evolution. The combination of comparative history and ethnographic approaches meant in practice a coalescence of an approach based on written documents and an approach based on cultural data collected by skillful field workers. While in his earlier work Kovalevskii depended primarily on written documents, soon after his first return from the West he made a move in the direction of ethnography. In the 1880s he spent several summers among the Ossets and several other native groups in the Caucasus in order to gather ethnographic data on so-called "legal customs"—the unwritten or customary law—sustained, mostly indirectly, by the coercive power of the state. He collected enough material for a series of articles (some published subsequently in the British *Archeological Review*) and two major works: *Modern Customs and Ancient Law* (1886) and *Law and Custom in the Caucasus* (1890).

At the same time, Kovalevskii became interested in the obshchina, the Russian rural community formerly praised by the Slavophiles as the purest embodiment of the unique values of Russian culture. Even some of the leading Populists were convinced that a regeneration of the obshchina would help Russia bypass the capitalist phase of development. Kovalevskii declared that the time had come to abandon all sentimentality in the study of the obshchina, and to introduce a "positive" approach.[12] His criticism of the "theological" and "metaphysical" interpretations of the obshchina, as well as his espousal of a positive interpretation, made it abundantly clear that he was under the spell of Comtian philosophy. He was interested not only in an objective critical study of rural communities and institutions but also in refining and consolidating the scientific foundations of comparative history and ethnography. As a professor of constitutional and comparative law, Kovalevskii was much more interested in the social dynamics of law than in distilling general juridical patterns from the mass of legal norms. As a writer, he was gradually attracted to evolutionary sociology, which placed primary emphasis on dominant forms of communities and institutions during specific phases of the grand evolution of human society. This became clear with the publication of the *Tableau des origines et de l'évolution de la famille et de la propriété* (1890), containing his lectures delivered at Stockholm University.[13] This book was an effort to substantiate and enrich Lewis H. Morgan's notion of a unilinear evolution in which the patriarchal society was preceded by a matriarchate and in which kinship bonds of social integration antedated territorial bonds. For several decades it was considered a major work in evolutionary sociology.

After testing his research skills and methodological tools on preindustrial Western societies, Caucasian folk societies, and the Russian obshchina, Kovalevskii undertook several comparative studies of the origins of modern European political and economic institutions. The effort produced such monumental works as *The Origin of Modern Democracy* (in four volumes, 1895–97) and *The Economic Growth of Europe Prior to the Emergence of Capitalist Economy* (three volumes, 1898–1903).[14] Since both works are "historical" rather than "ethnographic," they make little use of the theory of unilinear evolution and their weight is more in historical substance than in sociological deduction. At this time, Kovalevskii was more a social historian than a sociologist, and he did not allow theoretical considerations to limit his selection and interpretation of substantive data.[15]

In *The Economic Growth*, which was most typical of his scholarship during this period, Kovalevskii spelled out his theoretical position in the introductory chapter for the sole purpose of helping the reader recognize the more general social and economic trends behind the maze of information presented. The classification of socioeconomic systems was placed into a logically integrated pattern, determined primarily by population density. He consistently defended the thesis that changes in the density of population generated changes in economic activities and organization; however, he rejected the various brands of economic materialism that viewed society and culture as a superstructure erected upon a given economic arrangement. While advocating singular causation for economic change, he advocated multiple causation for social and cultural change in general. During this period he also wrote a detailed monograph on Russian economic institutions.[16] His articles appeared in French, English, and Russian journals.

Kovalevskii's early acceptance of comparative history as the most trustworthy source of empirical generalizations based on social and cultural data marked the beginning of his systematic search for a "concrete sociology" upon which a "general sociology" could be built. Several distinct influences led him into the field of comparative history. From A. O. and V. O. Kovalevskii, K. A. Timiriazev, and I. I. Mechnikov, four of the greatest Russian naturalists, he learned the value of the comparative method in constructing scientifically verifiable generalizations.[17] From V. F. Miller, with whom he conducted ethnographic fieldwork in the Caucasus, he learned the generalizing value of comparative linguistics in reconstructing the cultural history of neighboring peoples. In the work of Sir Henry Maine, he found the most impressive model for a comparative study of rural communities and their institutions and normative systems.

Kovalevskii did not adhere to a clearly defined and uniform view of the comparative method. In some writings, he defined the comparative method as an analysis of information describing a specific type of institution or community but obtained with the tools of various complementary sciences. In his Caucasian studies he made rather original efforts to blend the information supplied by ethnography, legal history, linguistics, and archeology. In using these approaches, he was guided by a view of social history that combined the German concern with the historical individuality of human societies and institutional complexes and the English search for an extension of the scientific method to the study of social history.

In other, mostly theoretical, studies, Kovalevskii viewed the comparative method as the scientific tool for comparing institutions or communities existing in different societies but representing the same phases of universal evolution. He thought that Spencer erred in applying an organismic model to the study of human society but was absolutely correct in emphasizing the great scientific potential of the comparative method, the safest path to a scientific explanation of "the origin and development of human society." The basic weakness of the comparative method, as employed by both Spencer and Kovalevskii, was that it used "empirical evidence" exclusively as illustrative material for a priori abstractions and that it relied heavily on an uncritical use of social and cultural "survivals." Kovalevskii viewed "survivals" as incontrovertible historical material helping to explain both the earlier and present-day societies, but, above everything else, providing the key for unlocking the mysteries of continuity as the basic attribute of social evolution. In selecting social and cultural complexes to be identified as "survivals," he relied less on the weight of historical proof than on preconceived schemes of evolutionary development.

Kovalevskii devoted a number of Caucasian studies to an elaboration and enrichment of Sir Henry Maine's description of the Aryan culture area as the matrix of modern civilization. According to Maine: "Civilization is nothing more than a name for the old order of the Aryan world, dissolved but perpetually reconstituting itself under a vast variety of solvent influences."[18]

The purpose of Kovalevskii's studies of Ossetian institutions, representing, in his opinion, survivals and local variations of the old Aryan world, was to weave the findings of empirical research into the general picture of Aryan culture. "We do not intend," he wrote in the introduction to *Modern Customs and Ancient Law*, "to present a simple description of the customs of a little-known people [the Ossets]; our purpose is to rely on gathered facts depicting the life of this people for the purpose of illuminating the hidden features of the ancient laws of the Aryans." "We hope to discover," he continues, "intermediary links without which it would be impossible to reconstruct the obscure process which led to the birth of the first legal institutions."[19] As used in these studies, the comparative method called for a coalescence of the study of modern Ossetian customs in the light of ancient Aryan law, and the study of ancient Aryan law in the light of newly revealed sociocultural characteristics of Ossetian customs. Thus the purpose of the comparative method was twofold: to add to the understanding of a local culture by identifying its historical place in a civilization that was generally well developed (at least according to Kovalevskii) and to help refine and amplify the grand picture of a civilization on the basis of "empirical" data drawn from a local culture. Although the comparative method can be an approach to the study of the law of a particular society or "the natural history of human society," it is essentially a combination of the two.[20]

Kovalevskii earned an enviable reputation not because of his articulation of the comparative method but because of his presentation of a vast amount of raw empirical data that could not be ignored by modern generalizers in sociology and cultural anthropology. He contributed to a confrontation of comparative history, which stuck steadfastly to the notion of the patriarchal family as the earliest human group, and new ethnography, which considered the patriarchal family a much later development in human society. In doing this, however, he also helped accelerate the process of making comparative history a subsidiary of cultural evolutionism, which gave primacy to theory over empirical analysis. As a comparative historian, Kovalevskii showed a strong propensity to view sociocultural survivals as a key for a generalized study of the development of human society and to attach great value to the study of the origins of social institutions and cultural values (he identified the comparative history of legal customs as "the embryology of law"). This dual interest made his transition from comparative history to evolutionary sociology a very smooth process. Indeed, Kovalevskii's failure to eliminate deduction from a scientific study of human society made his comparative history a variety of sociology.

EVOLUTIONARY SOCIOLOGY

The work in comparative history took Kovalevskii directly into the domain of sociological theory. Through personal contact with a wide array of Western

European sociologists and through close association with the activities of the International Institute of Sociology, he was exposed to all the currents in modern sociological thought. At the turn of the century and during the first decade of the twentieth century, he wrote mainly on sociological themes. All his theoretical papers showed clearly that he considered himself a follower of Comtian positivism; he mainfested a conscious distaste for every metaphysics, a belief in the epistemological unity of the sciences, and an almost passionate dedication to the idea of progress as the highest law of sociology. He looked at Comte not only as the true progenitor of modern sociology but also as a vital link in the gradual crystallization of sociological thought since the time of the French Encyclopedists. He recognized Turgot as the initial articulator of the idea of progress, the purest and most significant indication of the development of humanity. However, it was Condorcet to whom he gave the main credit for laying the foundations upon which Comte built his elaborate system of sociology. The real scientific strength of Condorcet's sociology, according to Kovalevskii, was in its unequivocal stress on the sociopsychological unity of mankind (a principle without which sociology could not formulate universal laws), the structural interaction of the principal sociocultural forces, the paramount role of knowledge in opening the paths of social evolution, and the firm insistence on the possibility of sociology as a natural science (Condorcet argued cogently in favor of an application of mathematical procedures in the study of social phenomena).[21] Kovalevskii did nothing to advance Condorcet's "social mathematics," nor was he inclined to accept the notion that science is the prime mover of modern society; however, he saw in his work a synthesis of the tradition of the Encyclopedists, the Physiocrats, the school of natural law, the champions of democratic philosophy, the spirit of modern science ("science has never produced anything that was not socially useful"), and Turgot's idea of progress—the forces that created the conditions favoring the emergence of sociology as a body of theory and a source of designs for human betterment.

In *Sociology*, published in 1910, Kovalevskii noted that during the first decade of the twentieth century most sociologists still agreed with Comte's interpretation of "the nature and functions of sociology."[22] While admitting that some significant details of Comte's magnificent theoretical edifice did not pass the test of modern criticism, he contended that six structural components of the Comtian legacy had continued to form the backbone of sociology: the notion of progress as the central theme of sociological inquiry; the basic division of sociology into "social dynamics" and "social statics" (even though not under the same labels); the status of sociology as the fundamental science in the family of disciplines concerned with human society; the rejection of every teleology in the explanation of social phenomena; the irreducibility of sociology to psychology; and the identification of the philosophy of history as a component of sociology. Kovalevskii did not suggest that contemporary sociologists had accepted the entire substance of Comte's explanations of basic sociological categories; what he suggested was simply that these categories defined the legitimate scope and scientific limits of modern theoretical concerns in sociology. In his own work, Kovalevskii was not a strict follower of Comtian sociology; between Comte and him were two strong traditions—the evolutionary theory that grew under the influence of Darwin and the historical orientation inaugurated by Sir Henry Maine. Although both these traditions found a vital place in his general theory, they did not obliterate a strong substratum of ideas generated by the founder of positivist philosophy and sociology.

Kovalevskii built his theory upon the assumption that sociology is the only abstract science in the family of disciplines devoted to the study of social reality; it draws empirical material from the other social sciences, to which it gives, in return, the principles of scientific interpretation and logical organization. "Regardless to what concrete social science we may refer—to comparative linguistics, comparative history of literature, the history of plastic arts, or the study of music—we inevitably recognize that no interpretation of the evolutionary growth of the specific domains of culture could be successfully made without the help of sociology."[23] He took special care to refute Paul Barth's identification of sociology with the philosophy of history. In the first place, sociology, according to Kovalevskii, deals with both social statics and social dynamics, while the philosophy of history deals only with social dynamics. In the second place, in the treatment of social dynamics, the philosophy of history welcomes all kinds of metaphysical and mystical interpretations, whereas sociology must adhere as much as possible to the rigor of the scientific method.

Kovalevskii equated statics with the study of social order and dynamics with the study of evolution and progress. He defined social order as an integration of the structural components of culture and society into a total pattern in which no specific set of conditions acted as primary causes. He stated explicitly that sociology should avoid efforts to reduce all causal relations in society to a set of basic determinants but should instead concentrate on the reciprocal interaction of the structural components of culture and society. In his own words: "Sociology should not be concerned with one-sided influences but with the interactions of all phenomena which make up the social life; it should not search for the primary factors—economic, legal, state, scientific, etc.—of social life; it must study closely connected facts and phenomena of human coexistence."[24] In his opinion, "All aspects of social life influence each other so much that it is impossible to talk about the priority of one over others."[25] He firmly opposed Marx's economic determinism, Tarde's psychological interpretation of social change, and Paul Lilienfeld's organismic models of social structure, for all were committed to a theory of key causes in social dynamics.[26] The guiding idea of his sociology was the Comtian dictum that no social phenomenon was scientifically significant unless it was interrelated with other social phenomena.[27] In much-used, and abused, contemporary parlance, Kovalevskii, as a student of social causation, was a "pluralist" rather than a "monist." However, his pluralism was not absolute. He allowed for two types of deviations from pure pluralism.[28] First, he contended that the social structure consists of several systems of causal relationships: the growth of population determines the economy, the economy determines political institutions, and "practical life" determines law and morality. However, the determining role of single factors should not be treated as absolute, for in the course of time new causal elements may be introduced, sometimes by sheer chance. Second, Kovalevskii admitted that an entire structure may be dominated by a single factor, but he also added that every historical period is likely to be dominated by a unique factor. The epochs of Alexander the Great, the barbarian invasion of the Roman Empire, and Napoleon were dominated by politics; the ages of Brahmanism, the papacy, and the Reformation were ruled by religion; and the modern epoch is the epoch of the paramount influence of economy.

Kovalevskii's criticism of the Marxian theory of social causation is measured and dispassionate. He gave Marx credit for having stimulated a healthy interest in economic history, a field previously neglected. He admitted that if Marx had stuck strictly to economic explanations of political systems and revolutions his work would have been fully acceptable, for it would have added a special dimension to the study of the real mechanisms of social change. He argued that not Marx and Engels but their followers were responsible for the excesses of economic determinism. Marx, according to him, did not create—and did not intend to create—a general theory of history but only a specific approach to the study of social life. Engels deserves special credit for his recognition of the relative independence of the superstructure and for the claim that the "economic factor" embraces not only the production but also the distribution of goods. However, in contrast to the general tendency of the Marxists to focus on the dependence of social, political, intellectual, and aesthetic forces on the economic base, he preferred Comtian emphasis on the *interdependence* of intellectual and "material" components of society and culture.

In a detailed analysis of Kovalevskii's theory of factors, Pitirim Sorokin noted that Kovalevskii was interested much more in the functional interrelations of social and cultural forces than in the causal sequences in the course of sociocultural evolution.[29] This may apply to Kovalevskii's empirical work in comparative history and to his general historical surveys of political and economic institutions; it does not apply to his general theory of "genetic sociology," which seeks to provide causal explanations for the origin and evolution of major institutional complexes. Indeed, Kovalevskii was critical of contemporary sociologists who worked to substitute a functional or structural approach for the evolutionary approach. Even when he focused on the interaction of institutional complexes, he was interested more in detecting the sources of change than in decoding the structural principles of social integration.

Kovalevskii is credited for having brought the contemporary social theories of France, England, and the United States to the history and law faculties of Russian universities, previously dominated by German thought. He found the French, English, and American social thought freer of metaphysical admixtures and closer to his own democratic ideology. Among contemporary sociologists, he was particularly attracted to the work of Lester Ward.[30] Ward's social theory was a challenging extension and enrichment of Comte's view of sociology as an abstract science divided into social statics and social dynamics, the former dealing with social forces in the state of equilibrium, and the latter with the social forces in the state of motion.[31]

Kovalevskii felt a strong affinity for Ward's determined efforts to find a middle course between extremist orientations in sociology. During the 1890s, sociologists were divided on the issue of the role of biological models in social theory. Some scholars built abstract sociological systems by reducing human societies to biological principles; others attacked bitterly every form of biological reductionism. Ward injected the psychological factor as an intermediary link between society and living nature, a link which freed sociology of direct (but not of indirect) dependence on biological reductionism and which opened the way for a scientific study of human society as a reality sui generis. Ward, according to Kovalevskii, revised Spencer's conception of "social organism" to free it of biological excesses and combined Comte's "intellect" and Schopenhauer's "will" as the chief mechanism of social change.

Kovalevskii gave full endorsement to Ward's notion of "synergy," which he interpreted as denoting a functional coalescence of opposite forces in the work of human society. At the time, sociologists were divided into two groups: one group treating consensus (or solidarity) and the other conflict (or competition) as the prime mover of social change in general and social progress in particular. Kovalevskii, who considered Comte (the original advocate of social consensus as the supreme law of social statics) and Marx (the father of the modern conflict theory) his teachers, was intellectually predisposed to look favorably at theories searching for a middle position in the conflict-consensus continuum. He also lauded Ward's efforts to make the studies of social "causality" and social "purposiveness" complementary rather than mutually exclusive components of sociological analysis, a view championed in Russia by Populist and neo-Kantian sociologists.

Ward appealed to the Russian intelligentsia in general, and to Kovalevskii in particular, by his unequivocal dedication to the idea that sociology should be both "pure" and "applied," that its task should be not only to enrich science but also to enhance the role of voluntary human effort in social evolution. Kovalevskii was particularly impressed with Ward's emphasis on the role of man's conscious action in social progress and, by implication, on the potential power of sociology as a source of designs for social betterment. His sociology had no room for Comte's concept of *l'évolution spontanée* and Spencer's laissez-faire philosophy. The laws of social development were absolute and universal but they were not blind, for they left much room for human direction. The function of sociology, according to both Ward and Kovalevskii, was to utilize the objective laws of social development to achieve a maximum advantage for man's subjective existence. Kovalevskii shared Ward's idea that the state is gradually emerging as the most effective source and coordinator of social reforms. Both were advocates of social welfare as the primary function of the state. Kovalevskii belonged to the group of the champions of the "state theory," according to which Russian society was a product of "state policies" since the early seventeenth century. He was convinced that the Russian state could emerge as an architect of benevolent social reforms only if it first underwent extensive reforms that would make it a true expression of the general will. He viewed constitutional monarchy as the most effective political system for transforming the Russian state into an instrument of social welfare. Only constitutional monarchy, he thought, could effectively combine the *form* of the traditional government with the *content* of national experience in the democratic process. By preserving the monarchical form of government, it would save the country from the potentially dangerous disruptions and setbacks of a more radical—and revolutionary—change.

Ward, who came off so well under Kovalevskii's detailed and penetrating examination, did not fare as well under the scrutiny of the Russian censors. In 1891, for unannounced reasons, the censors prevented the sale of a Russian translation of the first volume of his monumental *Dynamic Sociology* and stopped the presses that were printing the second volume. Commenting on this ironic development, Ward acknowledged his pleasure with the generally favorable reception of his theoretical views by Russian scholars. He was most probably correct in stating that the government condemned his book "for the liberalizing doctrines taught by it," particularly for its bold emphasis on universal education.[32] Kovalevskii reasserted the Russian scholarly community's faith in Ward's dictum that an unenlightened state is the most dangerous enemy of social progress. It should be added, however, that, despite his lavish praise, Kovalevskii did not accept Ward's sociological ideas without serious reservations. He thought that Ward's personal bias in favor of "republican parliamentarianism" was too thinly veiled to be of much help in sociological theory. Kovalevskii, too, was a champion of parliamentarianism, but he did not see any reason why it could not be paired with monarchism as effectively as with republicanism. Ward, he thought, overplayed the "psychic factor" in the structure of society and was inclined to substitute "mechanism" for "organism" as a scientific model of society. Behind the broad humanism of Ward's sociology lurked a mechanistic conception of human society.

The idea of progress is the most general and unifying theme of Kovalevskii's sociological theory. By social progress, he meant a regular, predictable transition of social orders to more advanced forms. Kovalevskii criticized René Worms, who wrote in the *Philosophy of the Social Sciences* that "the idea of progress is purely subjective," that "we identify everything as progress that appears as an improvement in comparison with the previous order, even though the criteria for judging the improvement are products of our subjective judgment," and that progress is an expression of, and is judged by, personal ideals. Kovalevskii thought that Worms had succumbed to the current discussions at the meetings of the Paris Sociological Society and at the congresses of the International Institute of Sociology, at which it had become fashionable to denigrate the idea of progress by calling it a value judgment that prevented sociology from building the foundations for a scientific theory of society. "My position," Kovalevskii noted, "is diametrically opposite to that of Worms. Like Comte, I maintain that without an idea of progress there could be no sociology and that progress, as I have stated on many occasions, is expressed in the growth of solidarity within both politically united national groups and mankind."[33]

Following the dominant trend in Russian sociology, Kovalevskii measured social and cultural progress by the increasing interaction and interdependence of individuals, groups, and societies.[34] In the theories of growing social solidarity advanced by Simmel and Durkheim, he saw only a reaffirmation and elaboration of Comtian sociology. Paradoxically, he failed to note that his notion of solidarity differed in no significant detail from Lavrov's; both claimed that solidarity cannot be explained by reliance on theology and metaphysics, for it is essentially a phenomenon with deep biological roots and therefore amenable exclusively to a scientific interpretation. Kovalevskii, like Lavrov and Kropotkin, relied on the work of modern naturalists in assuming that solidarity is characteristic not of man alone but of the entire animal kingdom.[35] He did not reject Darwin's biological theory, which saw in the struggle for existence the propelling force of evolution; however, like the Populist sociologists, he reasoned that, in regard to human society, the centripetal forces of solidarity contribute to a gradual abatement of the centrifugal forces of the struggle for existence.[36] Kovalevskii fought the Marxist theory of class struggle as the main wheel of social progress, even though his argumentation was often marred by glaring inconsistencies. While to the Marxists the state is an instrument of the exploitation of one class by another (and therefore an important wheel in the institutionalization of conflict), to Kovalevskii the state is gradually becoming the chief guardian of social solidarity.

The concept of progress and the principle of the psychological unity of mankind are at the basis of Kovalevskii's endorsement of the claim of evolutionary ethnographers that basic change in every human society is effected by internal forces rather than by external influences. In this view, independent invention (possible because of mankind's psychological unity), rather than diffusion of cultural traits, is the real mechanism of social evolution. This was the primary reason for Kovalevskii's uncompromising war against Gabriel Tarde's treatment of imitation as the main source of change; on the same grounds, he attacked Ludwig Gumplowicz's theory of conquest and ethnic stratification as the major vehicles of social progress. The essence of Kovalevskii's theory of sociocultural evolution was the recognition that similarities between societies occupying the same position on the scale of social growth could be explained exclusively in terms of a universal law of development.

A good evolutionist, Kovalevskii thought that sociology should be particularly concerned with the origins of institutions and the principal forms of human groupings; for him "genetic sociology" is one of the principal branches of general sociology. Again as a good evolutionist, he thought that revolutions were pathological aberrations rather than normal phenomena and that they resulted from "unnatural" tampering by influential individuals and groups with the "natural" growth of various components of society and culture.

Essentially an eclectic with diffuse scholarly interests, Kovalevskii made no effort to find a meeting ground between abstract categories of sociology and empirical generalizations of comparative history—that is, between deduction and induction as methods of social inquiry. As a comparative historian, he knew that the "same" institutions existing in various societies must meet the criteria of both morphological and functional similarities; that is, they must not only "look alike" but must also perform identical social roles. He emphasized the need for comparative studies of societies, thoroughly investigated by competent scholars, even though he did not always meet his high standards. As an evolutionary sociologist, he felt that "uninvestigated" societies could be adequately explained in terms of "investigated" societies occupying the same position on the unilinear scale of evolutionary development. For example, he saw no reason why Lewis H. Morgan's description of Iroquoian social organization should not be applicable to other societies at the same stage of development. As a comparative historian, Kovalevskii stressed the need for a careful analysis of historical and ethnographic data to provide empirical generalizations; as an evolutionary sociologist, he did not oppose the use of selected historical and ethnographic data to illustrate the workings of preconceived laws of social development.

Kovalevskii's fame rests on his substantive work based on comparative analysis. By a twist of irony, he embraced evolutionist sociology just as it was rapidly giving ground to newer sociological orientations that were less sweeping in their theoretical claims but more exact in describing the realities of modern society. Even though he recognized the innovative power of the neopositivist theory of knowledge, which provided new support to the notion of the unity of the sciences, the widespread controversy over the epistemological foundations of modern science in general and sociology in particular escaped him completely. Though eminently successful in connecting history and ethnography with comparative history, he failed to establish a working relationship between comparative history as an empirical sociology and general sociology as a theoretical system.

In gathering the bricks for his sociological edifice, Kovalevskii made very little use of the writings of Russian sociologists, prompting N. I. Kareev to assert that he was not part of the Russian sociological tradition.[37] Kovalevskii wrote a penetrating essay on Mikhailovskii's social theory—emphasizing his contributions to social psychology more than his articulation of the subjective method in sociology—and he was instrumental in the publication of Lavrov's *Problems of Understanding History* in Russia; but in his general theoretical treatises—*Modern Sociologists* and *Sociology*—he failed to take explicit note of Russian contributions. While he did not identify himself with any of the Russian schools of social thought concerned with sociology as a discipline, with its own research procedures and systems of logical explanations, he was very close to the group of liberal professors of history, law, economics, and political science who, while not concerned with the formal identity of sociology in the family of sciences, had made extensive use of sociological analysis in their specialized areas of inquiry. The most distinguished members of this group were the historians P. G. Vinogradov and I. V. Luchitskii, the economists A. I. Chuprov and I. I. Ianzhul, the jurists S. A. Muromtsev and Iu. S. Gambarov, and the linguist V. F. Miller.[38]

If Kovalevskii chose to ignore the Russian contributions to sociology and if his theory did not transcend the limits of nineteenth-century social thought, why, then, did his learned countrymen refer to him as the dean of Russian sociologists? Why was the first national sociological association in Russia named after him and why was he the first sociologist to be elected to full membership in the prestigious St. Petersburg Academy of Sciences? Why did M. I. Tugan-Baranovskii go so far as to assert that the death of Kovalevskii in 1916 was the heaviest national loss for Russia since the death of Tolstoy in 1910?[39]

There are several answers to these questions. Russian scholars who combined a liberal political bent with an interest in social research recognized Kovalevskii's studies not only for their empirical contributions but also for their theoretical ideas clustered around the notion of social progress. Like most Russian sociologists and sociologically oriented scholars, he developed a social theory whose focus was not on the stark realities of a society in crisis and a polity in rapid decay but on the rosy promises of the future. In a way, he combined the two strongest traditions in Russian sociology: Marxist and Populist. Like the Marxists, he dealt extensively with, and placed a comparatively strong emphasis on, the internal dynamics of economic institutions; like the Populists, he argued against all efforts to view non-material culture as a derivation from the economic base of society. He gave credit to Mikhailovskii for his forceful defense of the thesis that intellectual and economic developments follow their own distinct courses and are independent.[40] His Russian peers recognized him as the first major Russian scholar to approach sociology as a complete science, one with a distinct substantive area and an integrated theoretical framework. He criticized the neo-Kantians who viewed the existing legal codes from the standpoint of "natural law" and who treated natural law as a metaphysical notion of "absolute justice," inherent in human nature rather than created by society.[41] He stated correctly that to advocate "the metaphysical doctrine of natural law" was the same as to deny the possibility of sociology as a science. In the emergence of "formal jurisprudence" he saw a specific expression of metaphysical revival and an attack on the sociology of law.[42] Moreover, his role as an ambassador of Russian scholarship in Western Europe and America added immensely to his stature in the Russian academic community. During his long years of foreign residence, his fellow emigrants regarded him as one of their most eminent representatives; indeed, after Ivan Turgenev's death he was considered the intellectual leader of Russian emigration. In Russia, Kovalevskii was an academician, a member of the State Duma and the State Council, an editor and regular contributor to the influential *Messenger of Europe*, and a highly esteemed teacher and public speaker; in these roles, he was by far the most effective link between academic sociology and society at large. Even the platform of his political party was an elaboration of the idea of progress.

Kovalevskii's gradualist sociology and propensity to identify social progress with the inexorable affirmation of democratic principles produced a political philosophy that saw the future of Russia in a gradual democratization of political institutions and processes. But the deep-seated social and political crisis in his homeland eventually convinced him that Comte's definition of sociology as a science of social order and social progress was misleading. He learned from Russia's plight that every society does not necessarily exhibit order and that every change is not necessarily synonymous with progress. For this reason he changed his earlier philosophical outlook: the sociologist, he said, must not limit his study to tracing the grand line of evolution but must look very closely into the conditions which put the stamp of historical uniqueness on the evolutionary changes in individual societies.

Kovalevskii was not without critics in Russia. He was reproved for his failure to incorporate Russian contributions into his efforts to depict the mainstream of modern sociological thought. His repeated emphasis on the paramount role of the demographic factor in the evolution of economic life was roundly criticized and rejected. P. B. Struve noted the lack of depth in Kovalevskii's scholarly work, for which he labeled him a "Cossack in science." Kovalevskii, according to Struve, was essentially a historian; and as a historian he did not have a single clear orientation. He ventured into economic history but had little familiarity with economic theory. He wrote at length about legal usages and institutions but was not a trained jurist. He thoroughly investigated modern sociological theory but did not evolve a consistent and elaborate theoretical view of his own.[43]

Most Russian scholars had only praise for Kovalevskii's contributions to social theory. When P. N. Miliukov asserted that Kovalevskii's sociological views were "strictly scientific" he acknowledged the academic community's appraisal of Kovalevskii's work as a maximum effort to keep sociology independent of ideological controls, regardless of immediate pressures.[44]

Kovalevskii's dedication to science appealed to the growing ranks of the students of society and culture who endeavored to place their scholarship on a solid scientific footing as well as to the broad segments of the intelligentsia whose ideology saw in science the only hope for a better social existence. All this, however, does not deny the fact that as a sociologist he was much more successful as a synthesizer of the social thought of his age than as a theoretical innovator. An uncontrollable compulsion to express himself in writing and an insatiable thirst for knowledge led him into all the major areas of scholarly interests related to the structure and working of human society. However, they also prevented him from giving the fundamental problems of sociological theory the attention they deserved and from constructing a comprehensive and unified system of social thought. Throughout his scholarly career, he sought to contribute not only to scholarship but also to the liberation of Russia from the yoke of an anachronistic and rapidly decaying political system. His political credo was dominated by the conviction that Russian social tradition and cultural values contained rich indigenous resources for building a more promising future for his people. In the experience of the zemstvos he saw ample proof that the democratic process had deep and vigorous roots in Russian history. A gradualist in politics, he was a champion of the middle road in sociology. His position in politics and sociology provided the psychological basis for the eclectic nature of his social thought. His eclecticism was so broad and so generous that it did not exclude the possibilities of treating Spencerian individualism and Marxian collectivism as complementary principles of a future society that would be characterized by a higher affirmation of humanity.[45]

Despite a strong inclination toward eclecticism and a skeptical attitude toward the modern currents in sociological thought—the currents set in motion by the likes of Simmel, Durkheim, and Weber—Kovalevskii was a sociologist of a high order. He added a mass of refreshingly new empirical material to the common pool of sociological wisdom. In providing a masterful synthesis of nineteenth-century sociological traditions erected upon the foundations of positivism and evolutionism, he made a comprehensive inventory of problems which twentieth-century sociology could not ignore. One such problem, the nature and mechanism of social evolution, was pushed aside by sociological innovators of his and the succeeding generation only to be "revived" and "reestablished" during the second half of the twentieth century as a most challenging and scientifically rewarding problem treated by sociology and cultural anthropology.

7. Marxist Sociology:
Orthodoxy and Revisionism

The social and intellectual fermentation during the 1860s engendered a lively study of society based on the theoretical and methodological models of the natural sciences. The philosophical spirit of the time, best expressed in the writings of Chernyshevskii, Dobroliubov, and Pisarev, favored a general science of society that combined the materialism of Vogt, Büchner, and Moleschott and the positivism of Comte. Marx's *Critique of Political Economy*, which laid the axiomatic foundations of economic materialism as a general science of social structure and social change, and which elevated Marxism to one of the leading sociological schools of the nineteenth century, found no echo in Russia during the 1860s. Russia did not have a significant industrial proletariat which, in the Marxist view, was the moving force of modern history. Moreover, the country was preoccupied with the search for an improvement in the social and economic lot of emancipated serfs. A pronounced lack of enthusiasm for *A Critique of Political Economy* in Germany, the cultural base to which Russian intellectuals looked for guidance, may easily have been an important factor accounting for the Russian silence.

The reception of *Capital* in Russia was quite different. Published in 1867, it was immediately attacked by the young sociologist Eugene de Roberty on the ground that it was too rigid in both its ontology and economic monism.[1] In 1871, one year before the publication of the first Russian translation of *Capital*, N. I. Ziber, a young Russian economist, examined, and endorsed, Marx's economic theory in his master's thesis, *Ricardo's Theory of Value and Capital in Connection with Later Additions and Explanations*. This study brought Marxism to the arena of academic debate and scrutiny.[2] In the preface to the second edition of *Capital*, Marx acknowledged Ziber's contribution and noted that "that which astonishes the Western European in the reading of [Ziber's] excellent work, is the author's consistent and firm grasp of the purely theoretical position."[3] In his subsequent work, Ziber subjected the major categories of Marxian economic theory to a detailed and generally sympathetic scrutiny. In a long essay on Engels's *Anti-Dühring*, he presented the Russian reader not only with the foundations of Marxist philosophy and economic theory but also with an analysis of the role of Hegelian dialectic in

Marxist thought.[4] In his opinion, Marx and Engels were successful in transforming dialectic from a much maligned "mode of inquiry" into a powerful tool of scientific realism. Ziber carefully avoided a discussion of the Marxist theory of revolution. He wrote extensively about primitive economic institutions, relying heavily on ethnographic illustrations and theoretical views of Marx and Lewis H. Morgan.[5]

The economic ideas ushered in by the first volume of Marx's *Capital* caused more excitement among persons who worked in the ideological arena than among persons dedicated to pure scholarship.[6] This was particularly true for the leading spokesmen of Populism, who shared with Marx a dedication to socialist ideals and an antagonistic attitude toward the dehumanizing effects of capitalist "cooperation" in the process of production.[7] Small wonder, then, that Populists were among the chief and most interested Russian correspondents of Marx and Engels and that such influential Marxist theoreticians of the 1880s and the 1890s as P. B. Aksel'rod and G. V. Plekhanov learned the fundamental principles of Marxist theory and ideology while working for the cause of Populism.[8] N. K. Mikhailovskii deserves the major credit for having inaugurated the Populist interpretation of Marx's economic and social theory as well as for having formulated the basic points of disagreement between Populist and Marxist sociologists. Primarily through their persistent criticism of Marxist theory, Mikhailovskii and other leading spokesmen of Populism built the pillars of their sociological theory. In their view, Marxist interpretation of social change as a process of natural history is neither necessary nor defensible: while natural history is objective (that is, free of human values), social history is subjective (that is, saturated with human values). They argued that the Marxist view of capitalism as a universal stage of social development has no empirical base; they contended, for example, that Russia, by the unique configuration of her social institutions and cultural values, was a living example of a society whose normal development did not require a passage through the capitalist phase. The Populist sociologists were unwilling to endorse the Marxist claim that class struggle is the main and universal catalyst of sociocultural change. Here, too, they saw in Russia the classic example of a society in which the intelligentsia, a social group transcending the limits of class affiliation, was the architect of the future, and in which the peasants, by sheer numbers, were sociologically identifiable as the "people" rather than as a "class."

In *Our Differences* (1884), Plekhanov, now a Marxist, drew a clear and detailed picture of the theoretical and ideological abyss separating Marxism from Populism. He fired the salvo that led to a major theoretical and ideological war during the 1890s—a war out of which the Marxists emerged as one of the strongest movements opposing the established order and political regime. A combination of rapid developments in politics and changing conditions in the economy contributed to the triumphs of Marxist social thought and revolutionary zeal. During the late 1880s and early 1890s the process of industrialization, proceeding at a relatively fast pace, produced rapidly growing numbers of industrial proletarians—a social class for which Populist ideology, although sympathetic to its plight, had no room.[9] Indeed, according to Populist ideologists, the industrial proletariat—a child of industrial capitalism—had no business existing in Russia in the first place. The famine of 1891-92 and recurrent cholera epidemics produced grim population losses in several regions and caused wide despair in the country. These conditions served as a tragic reminder of the inability of the established authority to cope with the elementary forces of destruction. They also deeply undermined both the government's security system and the romanticism of Populist designs for a future society. In their sudden upsurge, the Marxists benefited from the slowness of the government in comprehending the intricacies of their political tactics and the power and timeliness of their revolutionary ideology; indeed, the government was too preoccupied with incessant surveillance of the activities of the Populists to pay much attention to the Marxist threat. After all, the Populists worked hard to reach and activate the millions in the peasant masses, while the Marxists tried to reach the relatively sparse ranks of industrial workers.[10]

The pronounced concern of Russian intellectuals, representing a wide variety of professional and political interests, with economic problems was an important factor adding to the wide diffusion of Marxist views during the 1890s. Since the early 1870s, economic studies, both theoretical and descriptive, spurred by academic as well as political interests, received an inordinately strong emphasis in popular and scholarly writing. While zemstvo organizations, the Free Economic Society, and multiple branches of the Russian Geographical Society were busy collecting raw data of economic importance, particularly in reference to agriculture, the academicians worked diligently to analyze the available information with the help of scientific methods and preconceived theoretical schemes. The scholars gathered in the Moscow Juridical Society spearheaded a massive inquiry into the legal fabric of agriculture, which was made exceedingly complicated by economic laws promulgated in the wake of the emancipation of 1861.

The obshchina, as both an economic organization and a type of rural community, was the primary subject of studies concerned with the history and the structure of Russian society. Scientific preferences and ideological biases were primarily responsible for the emergence of many theories of the commune. Three of these theories were particularly popular. The Slavophile theory postulated the obshchina as a specific Russian community, built upon a combination of unique economic principles and the Orthodox notion of *sobornost'*. Boris Chicherin was the chief articulator of the theory which viewed the obshchina not as an expression of the Russian soul but as a creation of unique fiscal policies. M. M. Kovalevskii, relying on ethnographic material, the grand scheme of social evolution formulated by Lewis H. Morgan, and Sir Henry Maine's methods of comparative history, showed that the obshchina was not a unique Russian community but a typical community for a particular phase of universal social development. The comparative studies of the obshchina inaugurated a phase of realism in the assessment of the inner strength and resources of Russian society; they replaced the idealistic Slavophile conception of Russian history, the echoes of which could be sensed in Populist sociology. Regardless of their specific interests and emphases, the new theories presented the obshchina as a complex of social relations and cultural values woven into an economic matrix.

Academic economists worked busily on keeping up with modern developments in the statistical processing of economic data and on advancing comprehensive theories in political economy; but all worked also on specific current problems of national economy, particularly in the areas of expanding capitalism. Even the famous chemist Dmitrii Mendeleev took time from his scientific work to examine the problems of vital importance for the modernization of the Russian economy.

The growing interest in the national economy encouraged a serious scholarly interest in economic history, which had long been a purely descriptive discipline steeped in undigested statistics and lost in antiquarianism. In the late 1880s and early 1890s an impressive array of younger historians introduced a new kind of economic history that combined a sensitivity for documentary detail with a systematic search for regularities in the development of economic institutions and for deeper sociological meanings in economic phenomena.[11] In 1892–94, Russian economic history entered a golden age, thanks to the publication of three works whose high quality attracted the attention of international scholarship.

In 1892, in a classic study of Russian state finances in the early eighteenth century, P. N. Miliukov undertook a logically rigorous analysis of documentary information, most of which he obtained from previously ignored archival resources, that helped him to establish the structural ties between the various components of the state administration and the principal segments of the national economy. Thanks to this approach, Miliukov was able to offer a comprehensive interpretation of Peter the Great's reforms and to draw a precise line between the continuities and discontinuities in the development of the Russian political system during the first quarter of the eighteenth century. In essence, his book was a study of the "rationalist and organic matrix" of the broader "culture" of financial reforms.

In the same year, P. G. Vinogradov, a professor first at Moscow University and then at Oxford University, published in England his noted work

Villainage in England. Vinogradov identified himself with those historians who searched for laws and generalizations that described "the complexity of human culture" as effectively as the natural sciences described the phenomena of nature.[12] Vinogradov identified his treatise as a history of "social arrangements," or recurrent patterns of social life that were similar enough to warrant comparison. His statement that political economy was the only real "science" of society accurately expressed the prevalent opinion in the Russian scholarly community at the beginning of the 1890s. A reviewer of Vinogradov's book in the *Journal of the Ministry of National Education* devoted several pages to defending the thesis that "the economic approach" is the only scientific approach to history.[13]

In 1894, M. I. Tugan-Baranovskii gave a vigorous boost to economic history by publishing an incisive study of the periodicity of industrial crises in England. The book attracted considerable attention in the Russian scholarly community and among the Populist economists, and was subsequently translated into German and French. It provided a theoretical basis for a study of the social correlates and economic mechanisms of the capitalist transformation of Russia, a theme that attracted the attention of the intelligentsia far beyond academic institutions. Here, again, was an effort to approach economic history by examining regularities in the development of certain types of social behavior.

Combining historical induction with statistical and economic analysis, Tugan-Baranovskii attempted to create a reliable pool of information from which empirical generalizations and universal social laws could be drawn. The development of the English national economy, according to him, was an important source of this information. "No matter how we look at the future of Russian capitalism, we cannot deny the real existence and rapid growth of capitalist economy in Russia. For this reason, a study of the history of English economy, in which the capitalist system had reached its highest development, may be of interest to Russian economists."[14] Tugan-Baranovskii may well have been "the father of the modern theory of crisis," as Werner Sombart had called him,[15] but in Russia his primary contribution was in helping establish a new economics—the economics of capitalism—and a new sociology to deal with the "social attributes" of capitalist economy.

In addition to historians and other representatives of the scholarly community, Russian economy, economic institutions, and economic communities attracted the attention of persons who combined the skills of research with a definite ideological commitment. Prior to 1895, the Populist economists were the most typical representatives of this group. Such prolific writers on matters of economic relevance, as N. F. Daniel'son, S. N. Iuzhakov, and V. P. Vorontsov, developed an ideologically colored theory which rested on three major assumptions: the incompatibility of capitalism with the "natural" course of economic development in Russia;* the role of the obshchina as the quintessential model of the unique features of both the Russian polity and the Russian economic system; and the inapplicability of natural science methodological and epistemological models in the study of economic phenomena, which are not only "causal" but also "teleological." One of the chief characteristics of Populist sociologists and economists was a generally conciliatory attitude toward Marx's legacy. No leading Populist writer denied the paramount role of Marxist theory in the development of modern political economy. Mikhailovskii's notion of "complex cooperation" and Marx's notion of "alienation" referred to the same evils of capitalist economy. Although Populist social theorists were ready to concede that Marx was a great diagnostician of social ills in the West, they rejected all the claims that Russia could not—even if she wanted to—avoid the capitalist phase of development. In the thick of the battle against the Marxists, the Populists expanded their criticism of Marxist theory so much that soon there was little left unchallenged.

At the time of the concerted Populist offensive on Marxist thought during the early 1890s, the Russian Marxists were not a strong force either intellectually or politically. Plekhanov readily admitted that, at the time, the Social Democratic organization "left much to be desired" in terms of internal strength and operative effectiveness in the arena of antigovernment activities.[16] An early historian of the Russian Social Democratic party noted that "at the beginning of the 1890s Marxist literature [in Russia] was almost nonexistent" and that Marx's *Capital* in a Russian translation was a "bibliographical rarity worth its weight in gold."[17] Most readers who followed the Populist attacks, particularly by reading *Russian Wealth*, discovered for the first time a detailed, even though critical and often distorted, presentation of Marx's theoretical thought. The Populist attack on Marxist social theory, coming at a time when there was virtually no Russian Marxist literature, helped create widespread interest in the writings of the fathers of "scientific socialism." It also encouraged the Marxists to make their philosophy known to the Russian reading public: the Marxists felt a particularly strong need to answer Mikhailovskii's claim that Marxist

---

*This should not be interpreted to mean that the Populist economists disregarded the development of capitalism in Russia. For example, in his *Essays on Our Post-Reform Social Economy*, N. F. Daniel'son (who wrote under the pseudonym Nikolai-on) examined in detail the growth of capitalist institutions and processes in various branches of the national economy. However, like other leading Populist economists, he considered the development of Russian capitalism a historical aberration, an artificial growth without deep roots in Russian social tradition and cultural values. While Populist writers erred in underestimating the vitality of burgeoning capitalism in Russia, Marxist economists erred in underestimating the role of precapitalist institutions in the countryside as a deterrent to a more rapid development of capitalist relations. See A. Martynov, "Glavneishie momenty," p. 309.

thought was too rigid to be of much help in the analysis of concrete historical situations and that it lacked inner unity. Writing in 1894, in *Russian Wealth*, Mikhailovskii chose to compare Marx to Darwin: "What does the work of Darwin add up to? A few closely bound generalizations which crown a whole Mont Blanc of factual material. Where is the corresponding work of Marx? It does not exist ... and not only is there no such work of Marx, but there is no such work in all Marxist literature, in spite of its magnitude and wide distribution.... The axioms which make up the very foundations of economic materialism remain disconnected and untested, which is strange for a theory that in principle relies on material and tangible facts and claims to be preeminently 'scientific'."[18] Kareev wrote in the same year that, while Darwin's theory was "an integrated system of thought" in which the basic propositions could be elaborated and substantiated, economic materialism consisted of too few propositions that offered any theory of scientific import.[19]

Of the men who met the Populist challenge, four emerged as the most influential pioneers of Marxist theory in Russia: G. V. Plekhanov, M. I. Tugan-Baranovskii, P. B. Struve, and V. I. Lenin. All four operated on two fronts: the popularization of the basic postulates of Marxist social philosophy and the Marxist interpretation of the evolution of Russian society. Their unity was most graphically expressed in their uncompromising attack on the Populist claim that capitalism was incompatible with Russia's economic tradition and national interests and in their acceptance of Marx's interpretation of the inner logic of capitalist development. In a paper on the industrial development of Russia, read before the members of the Free Economic Society in 1898, Tugan-Baranovskii reiterated the Marxist rejection of Populist claims by asserting that Marx deserved full credit for having discovered the universal laws of the development of capitalist economy and that "the facts of Russian life" were in full agreement with "Marx's theoretical scheme."[20] In the *Russian Factory*, published in the same year, he made a general statement on his allegiance to Marxist theory: "Having recognized that 'it is not the consciousness of men that determines their existence, but on the contrary, their social existence determines their social consciousness,' I have treated factory legislation and dominant social views on the factory system as an expression of given relations between various social forces."[21]

Despite their agreement on the basic postulates of Marxist sociology, the four leading Russian Marxists did not belong to the same camp. Plekhanov and Lenin were concerned with clarifying and amplifying the legacy of Marx and Engels but not with modifying it. Both operated not only as Marxist theorists but also as Marxist ideologues, actively engaged in politics. Both treated the enemies of Marx and Engels as their own enemies. Struve and Tugan-Baranovskii, the most eminent "legal Marxists," did not allow their forceful and articulate—and generally orthodox—defense of Marxist sociology to prevent them from trying to synchronize Marxist thought with selected modern developments in philosophy and social theory. Moreover, their idiom lacked the belligerence typical of Marxist ideologists. In his effort to advance a systematic and comprehensive Marxist interpretation of the Russian economy and society, Struve did not hesitate to lean on the philosophical work of Alois Riehl, who combined the neopositivist view of "theoretical philosophy" as a special "science" dealing with the origin and limits of knowledge with the neo-Kantian view of "practical philosophy" as a special study of human ideals as embodiments of values and indicators of cultural progress. Struve also dipped into the rich reservoir of ideas produced by Georg Simmel, who treated sociology as a science of the universal forms of social relations, detached from historical substance. "The work of Simmel," he wrote, "shows how fruitful is the introduction of critical philosophy [a usual label for Kantian tradition] and scientific-psychological analysis in sociology."[22] He did not mention, however, that in *Die Probleme der Geschichtsphilosophie* Simmel labeled Marxist social theory a metaphysical illusion. Tugan-Baranovskii did not look at Marx and Engels as totally irreproachable masters of scientific socialism. He, for example, described Marx's attack on Proudhon (in the *Poverty of Philosophy*) as "very harsh and not quite just"; he also argued that Marx's thinking was not completely free of Proudhon's influence.[23]

Since the Populist attack was centered on Marx's economic theory, particularly on his claim of the historical universality of capitalism, the emphasis of the Russian Marxist theoretical literature during the 1890s was on the structure and dynamics of economic institutions and processes. By the end of the decade, however, all the theoretical components of Marxist sociology were fully explained in the Russian language and by Russian authors.

The Marxists were not particularly interested in sociology as a special discipline in the family of social sciences; their general social theory was developed within the framework of political economy, theory of knowledge, and social philosophy. They made much wider use of the adjective "sociological" than of the noun "sociology." Their sociological ideas form a system, even though they are presented in scattered writings which focused on specific themes.

Echoing the thought of Marx and Engels, the Russian Marxists formulated a general theory of society around six fundamental assumptions.

First: the human society is a reality sui generis; it is explicable only in terms of its own inner constitution and dynamics. Society cannot be reduced to, or be fully understood in terms of, the behavior of the individuals. Society generates its own regularities and processes which are independent of the actions of individuals. Although society represents a special "motion of matter" and a unique extension of nature, it is not reducible to the laws of physical and organic nature. The process of social development is manifested in a gradual realization of man's independence from nature. An animal adapts to the natural environment by changing its own biological nature; man changes nature, subordinating it to his own needs, and, in the process, advances as a social being. S. N. Bulgakov added another explanation: "Necessity reigns supreme in the world and in human life, but while in the world of animals this necessity is expressed in the struggle for existence, in the life of human societies it is expressed in the dependence of the entire social being on social economy."[24] Neither psychological reductionism nor biological reductionism has a place in Marxist sociology. Society has its own inner logic of development that is most concretely expressed in the dialectics of social processes and in class struggle.

Second: societies are not mere aggregates of institutions, communities, and values; they are structured entities. To understand a society, it is much more important to comprehend the socioeconomic principles of its integration than to describe its individual components without taking serious note of their place in the structure of society. To understand a society, it is necessary to understand its structure, and to understand its structure, it is necessary to be aware of profound differences between the economic *content* and the political and ideological *form*.[25] According to Plekhanov, the structure of every society reveals five spheres of integration: (1) the state of the productive forces; (2) the economic relations conditioned by these forces; (3) the sociopolitical system built upon the economic base; (4) the mentality of persons living in a given society, "a mentality which is determined in part directly by the economic conditions obtaining, and in part by the entire sociopolitical system that has arisen on that foundation;" and (5) the various ideologies reflecting that mentality. Each of these spheres has a relative autonomy, yet, in the final analysis, each is determined by the spheres below it—and ultimately by "the state of productive forces." The spheres forming the "superstructure" may also exercise a modicum of influence on the base and on the spheres closer to it.[26]

The idea of the overall unity of society—expressing a structuralist rather than a mechanical view—was not new; indeed, it was widely used by Populist sociologists and Slavophile and official philosophers of history. These writers claimed that dominant values gave an architectonic unity to human society; the Marxists, on the other hand, treated values as specific sociocultural adaptations to, and derivations from, the economic substructure. In Lenin's words, the Marxists transferred the study of social structure from the realm of metaphysics to the realm of science.

Marxist structuralism is monistic and materialistic. It is monistic because it views all the spheres of social life as components of an integrated pattern. It is materialistic because its monistic sociology is expressed in economic determinism which, in turn, is part of a broader materialistic philosophy of nature. The essence of Marxist structuralism is forthrightly defined by Lenin: "Until the present time, sociologists have found it difficult to separate what is important from what is unimportant in the complex network of social phenomena ... and have been unable to detect in production relations an objective criterion of the structure of society, and to make it possible to apply to these relations the general scientific criterion of repetitiveness whose applicability to sociology the subjectivists denied."[27]

The Russian Marxists did not claim that Marx must be considered the sole discoverer of the economic base of social structure; they did claim that Marx was the first to give this base a thorough and scientific explanation. According to Plekhanov,

> A. Thierry, Mignet, Guizot, and other historians, speaking for the middle classes, saw in property relations the most important and deepest basis of the political system and dominant values of a country. In this respect, their views differed but little from those of Marx and Engels. When Marx wrote subsequently that legal relations and forms of government could not be explained either by their own nature or by the so-called universal development of human spirit, since they were rooted in the material conditions of life, the totality of which Hegel named civil society, he only repeated the conclusions to which the historians had come much earlier under the influence of social development and class structure. The difference was merely in that, while Marx's predecessors left the origin of property relations completely unexplained, Marx made it perfectly understood.[28]

In Marxist theory, the explanation of causal "necessity" is the key to the understanding of the inner working of human society. The heavy concern with the study of cause-effect sequences in social behavior does not eliminate a concern with the role of purposiveness in social action; however, Marxist theorists consider "purposive choices" only inasmuch as they are specific ramifications of "causal necessity." According to Plekhanov, sociology can become a science only by concentrating on "social teleology"—on "purposes" in social activities that are "necessary effects of the social process."

Third: structural unity, rooted in the economic base, does not denote the historical uniqueness of a society; it depicts the principles of integration which identify a society with a specific "socioeconomic formation." Socioeconomic formations, as viewed by leading Marxists, are universal phases in the evolution of human society. As defined by a modern interpreter of Lenin's sociology, they are "historically created, qualitatively stable systems whose existence is justified only as long as they ensure social progress, or, in other words, as long as they make room for the development of productive forces."[29] Marx's major contribution, according to Lenin, was not so much in the general theory of social development as in the discovery of the specific laws regulating the capitalist socioeconomic formation. Marx "took one of the socioeconomic formations—the system of commodity production—and on the basis of a vast mass of data ... gave a most detailed analysis of the laws governing its functioning and development. His analysis deals only with production relations between members of society: without depending on explanations outside the sphere of these production relations, Marx makes it possible to show how the commodity organization of social economy develops, how it becomes transformed into capitalist organization, creating antagonistic classes ..., and how it develops the productivity of social labor, and thereby introduces an element that stands in diametrical opposition to the foundations of the capitalist organization."[30]

In Marxist literature the socioeconomic formations are sometimes called social organisms because they pass through the phases of youth, maturity, and decline: they cease to exist when they lose the capacity to resolve mounting inner contradictions.[31] The study of socioeconomic formations, according to Lenin, enables the scholar to study a society as a "living" and "constantly developing organism" and as a link in the universal chain of social development. In brief, social evolution is a "natural-historical process of the development of socioeconomic formations."[32] These formations emerge and change neither by accident nor by the whim of persons of genius but by a spontaneous, self-generated motion invested with the power of the laws of nature.

Fourth: the recognition and elaboration of socioeconomic formations as a fundamental concept elevated Marxist sociology to the level of a natural science. Why is sociology—or political economy—a natural science? The Marxists provide two complementary answers: an ontological and an epistemological one. Ontologically, nature and society are parts of or derivations from matter and motion. Marxist theorists claim that just as there can be no dualistic philosophy, there can be no dichotomy of natural and social sciences, based on ontological differences. Epistemologically, both the natural sciences and the social sciences deal with "objective" reality, that is, the reality that is independent of the thoughts, inclinations, and sentiments of individuals. In his preface to the first edition of *Capital*, Marx declared social science to be indistinguishable from natural science. He said: "My standpoint, from which the evolution of the economic formation of society is viewed as a process of natural history, can less than any other make the individual responsible for relations whose creature he socially remains, however much he may subjectively raise himself above them."[33] According to Lenin: "Marx views social change as a natural-history process, subject to the laws which are not only independent of—but, on the contrary, determine— the will, consciousness, and intentions of individual persons."[34] Marx put his philosophy of science into a nutshell when he stated: "Natural science will in time incorporate into itself the science of man, just as the science of man will incorporate into itself natural science: there will be *one* science."[35]

Although they are united ontologically and epistemologically, the two categories of science have not reached the same level of maturity: overpowering ideological interference and the complexity of their subject-matter have contributed to a relatively slow development of the social sciences and to their dependence on the natural sciences for theoretical models and methodological guidance. Moreover, the social world has certain unique characteristics which call for special conceptual and methodological adjustments. The identification of the social sciences with the natural sciences does not mean that "society" is reducible to "nature" and that the laws of the social sciences are mere extensions of and derivations from the laws of the natural sciences. It merely means that it is possible to formulate social science laws which apply to society with the same exactitude that the natural science laws apply to nature. Marx did not search for a "natural science" of society; he merely sought a method that could produce results "with the precision of natural science."[36]

L. Aksel'rod (Ortodoks), in an excursion into the sociology of science, summed up the Marxist view on the existing differences between the two categories of science:

The bourgeois ideology gives increasing support to the superstitious belief that objective inquiry and prediction are possible in the natural sciences but impossible in sociology. To give credence to this claim, it relies on the obvious fact that at the present time the natural sciences command many universally recognized laws, while the social sciences rely on laws and conclusions entangled in frightful and violent conflicts. However, this difference is strictly historical rather than fundamental. There is hardly a known law of nature, or a significant natural science truth, that at the time of its discovery did not experience violent attacks similar to those which Marx's theories of value, class struggle, and scientific socialism experience in our time. The fact that the knowledge of, and the victories over, nature are necessary and advantageous for the bourgeois classes of our time serves as a strong impetus for a free and unimpeded development of natural science. On the other hand, the fact that an objective and serious examination of social relations increasingly endangers the contemporary social system works against a free development of the social sciences. Natural science was in a similar situation during the Middle Ages, when it appeared as a powerful instrument working against the established social order.[37]

Fifth: the Marxist social scientist does not limit his study to the formulation of universal sociological categories and specific laws governing the integration and dynamics of socioeconomic formations. He also treats society as a historical phenomenon—as a product of unique successions of historical events. Indeed, Lenin argued that the general sociological theory advanced by Marx and Engels was so complete that it required no fundamental elaboration by modern students of society. He contended that modern sociologists, political economists, and historians should concentrate, first, on defending the Marxian theoretical orthodoxy from mounting attacks from ideological adversaries and revisionists, and, second, on searching for a Marxian interpretation of the development of individual societies. He looked unfavorably at the pronounced tendency of the leading schools in Western sociology to deal exclusively with human society as an abstract and universal category, only vaguely related to existing societies as products of unique historical developments. The Marxists, he said, cannot forecast the development of a capitalist society by staying strictly within the framework of a theory that treats capitalism as a pure abstraction. He supplied a model for a concrete historical study by writing a volume on the specific features of Russian capitalism, based on an extensive use of statistical data. He made it clear that while capitalism, as a socioeconomic formation, was a theoretical construction, Russian capitalism, or Japanese capitalism, or German capitalism was a historical reality requiring a minute inquiry into the depths of national history. In neo-Kantian terminology, Marxian sociology was both idiographic and nomothetic. Or, in the terminology of a modern interpreter of Lenin's theory, the full understanding of the life of a society requires not only the knowledge of general, or abstract-sociological, laws but also of the historical, or concrete-sociological, expressions of these laws.[38]

Lenin's arguments in favor of idiographic studies contained an acute weakness: they did not recognize these studies as possible sources of innovations enriching or correcting the general theory of society advanced by Marx and Engels. Lenin valued concrete historical studies of individual societies only inasmuch as their theoretical underpinnings stayed firmly within the framework of Marxian orthodoxy. While the Populists and idealistic philosophers of history sought to portray the values and institutions which separated Russia from all other societies, the Russian Marxists were mainly concerned with the attributes which identified Russia with the capitalist socioeconomic formation as a generalized sociological catagory. A true Marxist scholar, according to Lenin, conducted minute studies of superstructural diversities within the structural unity of individual socioeconomic formations. He noted that the superstructural components of a social system played an important, if not a decisive, role in determining the length of the transition period from one socioeconomic formation to another.

Sixth: the social scientist of every description must avoid objectivism—the dedication to dispassionate, detached search for facts. He must be a partisan engaged in the battle for a new society called for by Marxian blueprints. In a society divided into feuding classes there could be no neutral truth; social science is always partisan and ideological and must always reflect class interests. In class societies, a "de-ideologized," "apolitical" stance is the unmistakable adornment of the social theory of the ruling class. In his partisanship, the social scientist, according to Lenin, must be guided by the ideas that every social discipline is immersed in ideology and that "proletarian ideology" is the only system of social thought that is both thoroughly democratic and thoroughly scientific. As ingredients of science, social facts and theoretical ideas must ultimately be judged in terms of their consistency with the proletarian ideology, as defined by the fathers of Marxism. As a partisan, the social scientist must not resort to a blank negation of all non-Marxian theories and interpretations: he must absorb non-Marxian ideas consistent with Marxism, and he must display a high degree of militance in his fight against ideas alien to the interests of the proletariat. Lenin's insistence on partisanship (*partiinost'*) in social analysis was not an innovation in Russian social theory: most of the leading Russian sociologists from Lavrov, Mikhailovskii, and Danilevskii to Kareev, Kropotkin, and Bogdanov were gallant soldiers on ideological battlefields.

MARXISM AND DARWINISM

The sociological theory of Russian Marxism was considerably broader than a simple reformulation and recasting of the doctrines advanced by Marx and Engels and their adaptations to the Russian situation. Following the tradition established by Marx and Engels, the leading Russian Marxists relied heavily on the criticism of the leading modern sociological schools opposed to Marxism for a clarification and amplification of their own theoretical views. No major contemporary non-Marxian sociological school escaped critical, and biting, scrutiny by Russian Marxist theorists.

While constantly sniping at the leading proponents of biological models in sociology, the Russian Marxists were particularly eager to articulate their position vis-à-vis sociological Darwinism. Following the lead of Marx and Engels, they accepted Darwin's theory as the greatest triumph of nineteenth-century natural science. Like Engels, Lenin likened Marx to Darwin. Just as Darwin had wrought a revolution in biology so Marx had wrought a revolution in social science. In Lenin's words: "Just as Darwin put an end to the view that the species of animals and plants are ... 'created by God' and are immutable and was the first to place biology on solid scientific foundations by establishing the mutability and succession of species, so Marx put an end to the view that society is a mechanical aggregation of individuals ..., and was the first to put sociology on a scientific footing by establishing the concept of the economic formation of society as the sum total of the given relations of production and by showing that the development of these formations is a process of natural history."[39]

Thus the most important similarities of Darwin's and Marx's theories are purely formal: both have elevated their respective disciplines to a high scientific level by giving them a unifying body of theory and by subjecting them to the methodological rigors of the law of causality. The formal similarities are summed up by Plekhanov:

Darwin succeeded in solving the problem of the origin of plant and animal species in the struggle for survival. Marx succeeded in solving the problem of the emergence of different types of social organization in the struggle of men for their existence. Logically, Marx's investigation begins precisely where Darwin's ends. Animals and plants are under the influence of *physical* environment. The physical environment acts on social man through the social relations which arise on the basis of the productive forces, which at first develop at various speeds, according to the characteristics of the physical environment. Darwin explains the origin of species not by an assumed *innate* tendency of the animal organism to develop, as Lamarck claimed, but by the adaptation of the organism to external conditions.... The spirit of research is absolutely the same in both thinkers. That is why one can say that Marxism is Darwinism in its application to social science (we know that *chronologically* this is not so, but that is unimportant.)[40]

In this particular passage, Plekhanov did not try to identify the struggle for existence as the primary agent of natural and social evolution; he referred to it merely as a concrete example of Darwin's and Marx's reliance on external causation as the chief mechanism of scientific explanation. He admitted directly that to go beyond these formal similarities would mean simply to succumb to the lures of a bourgeois sociology "with a very ugly content." According to him, the sociologist should try to emulate the scientific method of Darwin's studies, but he should not try to extend Darwin's substantive conclusions to the world of human society. He stated categorically that he did not share "the social views of Darwinists like Haeckel" who by preaching "a social struggle of each against all" elevate the instincts of the beasts of prey to the level of a universal mechanism of social development.[41] He was also eager to show that Darwin himself had no inclination toward exaggerating the role of competition in human society at the expense of cooperation. As a good Marxist, Plekhanov did not minimize the role of "struggle" and "conflict" in the general development of society; however, to him "struggle" and "conflict" were structured components of a universal dialectical process rather than unstructured parts of "a war of all against all." He viewed both the Malthusian theory of population and Hobbesian sociology of conflict as sheer sophistry. The ideas propounded by Malthus and Hobbes were at first sociological carryovers in biology and then biological transplants in sociology.

There were two basic philosophical reasons for the Marxists' rejection of sociological theories built upon Darwin's conception of biological evolution.

First, Darwinian sociologists generalized "biological man"—or "human nature"—rather than "social man," disregarding the unique features of society as a phenomenon subject to its own laws of development. Biological man is the human animal in myriads of innate potentialities; social man is a cultural being created by history. Biology studies human nature—the hereditary potentialities of human development; sociology studies the development of these potentialities under the influence of external conditions. According to Plekhanov, the Marxian theory cannot replace the Darwinian theory, just as the great scientific discoveries made by Darwin and his followers cannot replace the scientific claims of the Marxists; the Darwinists can only prepare the ground for social investigations, "just as the physicist prepares the ground for the chemist without his work in any way obviating the necessity for chemical investigations as such."[42] The ontological commitment to materialistic monism does not prevent the Marxists from treating sociology as a science irreducible to biology in its methodology, conceptualization, and explanatory principles.

Second, the Darwinian sociologists were strict evolutionists: they made Darwin's dictum, *natura non facit saltum*, a universal law of sociology. The Marxists, of course, placed great emphasis on revolutionary leaps in the development of human society. They were critical of "evolutionism" which saw both natural and social change as a continuous process of infinitesimal changes. In 1908 Plekhanov welcomed the work of Hugo de Vries whose mutation theory—according to which the development of species takes place in leaps—challenged the Darwinian commitment to gradualism and recognized, in principle at least, the role of dialectics in universal change.[43] A. M. Deborin wrote that the closer the scientists came to recognizing the role of saltatory changes the closer they came, consciously or unconsciously, to the standpoint of dialectics.[44] De Vries merely provided another proof that the Marxists were correct in their claim that the theory of evolution did not give a true account of the "objective process of development in both nature and history."[45] While rejecting the evolutionists' gradualist view, the Marxists put forth a modified version of the evolutionary notion of the continuity of change: to them, revolutionary changes were not historical discontinuities but integral parts of universal change in which evolutionary processes are from time to time "accelerated" by leaps introducing qualitative changes.

Only one social thinker of the nineteenth century—in addition to Marx and Engels—received unqualified endorsement in the writings of Russian Marxists prior to the October Revolution: Lewis H. Morgan, the author of *Ancient Society* (1877) and the codifier of the theory of sociocultural evolutionism. While Marx worked primarily on capitalism as a distinct socioeconomic formation, subject to its own laws of development, Morgan's fame lies in his bold effort to show the unilinear nature of the universal history of human society. The depth of Marx's analysis of capitalism and its socioeconomic individuality, and the breadth of Morgan's interpretation of the universal course of history, became the pillars of the Marxist theory of social change.

A foremost expert on the Iroquoian tribes, Morgan hit upon the idea that all American Indians followed the same course of social development, an insight that he also extended to the initial phases of the history of classical Greek and

Roman societies, and to all other societies before the stage of civilization. By tracing the evolution of marriage, family, property, and territorial organizations, he established clearly delineated universal stages in the evolution of human society. Every society occupies a definite place on a single line of the universal evolution, divided into three main stages: savagery, barbarism, and civilization. Morgan's idea (originally formulated by Bachofen) that the matriarchal society preceded the patriarchal society became an inviolable part of Marxist sociology. According to Engels, who elaborated Morgan's ideas in *The Origin of the Family, Private Property, and the State* (1884), "the rediscovery of the mother-right gens as the stage preliminary to the father-right gens of the civilized peoples has the same significance for the history of primitive society as Darwin's theory of evolution has for biology, and Marx's theory of surplus value for political economy."[46] Engels added: "The mother-right gens has become the pivot around which [the entire history of primitive society] turns: since this discovery we know in which direction to conduct our researches, what to investigate, and how to classify the results of our investigations." On another occasion, he stated that Morgan's theory was additional proof that the full victory of the materialist conception of history was imminent.[47]

The "rediscovery" of matriarchy impressed Engels so much that he was led to liken Morgan's contributions to those of Darwin and Marx; but it was another "rediscovery" that prompted Engels to incorporate Morgan's social evolutionism into historical materialism. He stated: "It was no less a person than Karl Marx who had planned to present the results of Morgan's researches in connection with the conclusions arrived at by his own materialist investigation of history.... For Morgan rediscovered in America, in his own way, the materialist conception of history that had been discovered by Marx forty years ago, and in his comparison of barbarism and civilization was led by this conception to the same conclusions, in the main points, as Marx had arrived at."[48] Engels credited Morgan with having made an independent discovery, or a rediscovery, of the Marxist materialist conception of history. He was impressed with the idea that in *Ancient Society* Morgan showed an almost perfect consistency in emphasizing the idea that the evolution of social institutions was an expression of the evolution of technology; that the growth of the means of production is the key indicator of structural changes in social orders. This interpretation runs throughout Morgan's book but is spelled out with particular clarity and forcefulness in the discussion of the transition of primitive society to the state of civilization.

The Russian general public was introduced to Morgan's ideas through Engels's *The Origin of the Family, Private Property, and the State* which appeared in a Russian translation in 1894. Plekhanov was quick to note that the fact that Morgan had arrived independently at the basic views of economic materialism was "all the better" for the theory of Marx and Engels.[49] He noted that while Marx and Engels never doubted that class struggle underlay Greek and Roman history, Morgan deserved full credit for having explored the dynamics of the prehistory of Greece and Rome—and for having indicated the evolutionary trends that led to the emergence of class struggle as a salient factor of social change. Plekhanov thought that, upon reading Morgan's book on ancient society, Marx modified his own interpretation of the relation of the mode of production in classical antiquity to that in the Orient. According to Plekhanov, Morgan's "discovery of the clan type of social organization is evidently destined to play the same part in social science that the discovery of the cell played in biology. While Marx and Engels were unfamiliar with this type of organization, there could not but be considerable gaps in their theory of social development, as Engels himself subsequently acknowledged."[50] Morgan, according to Lenin, broadened the perspectives of the Marxian philosophy of history by showing, on the basis of a vast amount of empirical material, that "material relations," rather than "ideological relations," unveiled the mysteries of the dynamics of tribal organization.[51] He too gave credit to Morgan for having established that the social organization of the North American Indians held "the key to all the great and hitherto unfathomable riddles of ancient Greek, Roman, and German history."[52]

After the publication of Engels's *The Origin of the Family* and its unqualified endorsement of such leading Marxists as Plekhanov and Lenin, the Marxist social theory, as applied in historical research, combined two distinct methods: the dialectical and the comparative. The dialectical method, with roots in Hegelian philosophy, allowed the Marxists to view the historical process not as a mechanical accumulation of quantitative changes but as a continuous whirlwind of conflicting processes culminating in changes of qualitative nature. For example, serfdom in the Byzantine Empire was the result of a dialectical synthesis of the institutions of slavery, a hangover from the classical period, and of the democratic clan organization characteristic of the barbarian farmers arriving in the Balkans from the steppes and marshlands of Eastern Europe. The comparative method, codified by Morgan and based on the notion of the psychic unity of mankind, was the cornerstone of the theory of the unilinear evolution of human society; it called for a generalized study of structural similarities of societies that occupied the same position on the scale of universal evolution even though they might have belonged to different historical periods. For example, the Iroquois confederation and early Greek phratries belonged to different historical periods, but they occupied the same position on the evolutionary line. This method, as modern critics have pointed out, led to a gross oversimplification of social reality, for it used historical facts only as illustrative material for logically prearranged schemes. Although it was in many respects an extension of Darwinian biological evolution to the dynamics of human society, and although it was antidialectical in its inner logic, the Marxists accepted it because its philosophy of history was "materialistic" and because it filled a vacuum in Marxist social theory. In his endorsement of Morgan's evolutionary theory, Plekhanov went so far as to claim that in one important respect Morgan was ahead of Darwin: while Darwin was not very specific in spelling out the causes and mechanisms of biological evolution in concrete details, Morgan was very successful in pointing out the key causes and primary mechanisms of social change. Marxists, however, were much more willing to accept Darwin's notion of gradualism in the development of nature than Morgan's notion of gradualism in the development of human society.

The Marxists found it necessary to crystallize their views not only on the general scientific contributions of Darwin's biological theory but also on the two major evolutionary sociological orientations: Social Darwinism, which made the struggle for existence the prime mover of social history and social progress; and classical evolutionism, which translated the idea of the unity of organic nature into the idea of the unity of the sociocultural universe and made the progress of society a part of the evolution of nature. The Marxists accepted Darwin's theory as a victory for the causal interpretation of natural processes and as a categorical negation of teleological and transcendental views of nature. They modified Darwin's notion of evolution to allow for occasional revolutionary changes which expedite, rather than violate, the course of evolutionary change. In their opinion, Social Darwinists erred in treating a blind, instinctive force as the mainspring of social change, in encouraging biologistic reductionism, and in failing to see class struggle as a structured conflict with pure social causation. Marxist writers customarily considered Social Darwinism, with its basis in the principle of *bellum omnium contra omnes*, the sociological justification of capitalism. Even though Marxist sociologists accepted Morgan's general scheme of sociocultural development, they rejected "evolutionism" as a philosophy of history with metaphysical overtones. They thought that evolutionism ignored the existence of multiple variants within specific phases of social development and that it was essentially Europocentric.

MARXISM AND POPULIST SOCIOLOGY

Populist sociology treated the individual as the essential unit of human society and as the architect of history. According to Mikhailovskii, history is made by "the living individual with all his thoughts and emotions." Plekhanov, Lenin, Struve, and Tugan-Baranovskii responded by reaffirming the Marxist axiom that "the mode of production and distribution" ultimately determined the structural principles of every society; because of this, the work of society resembled the work of nature and could be subjected to scientific inquiry as rigorous as that of the natural sciences. The Populists argued that an understanding of the individual would lead to an understanding of society, and that neither the individual nor society could be fully comprehended by a complete reliance on the methodological tools of the natural sciences. To rob sociology of its subjective element, according to Lavrov and Mikhailovskii, would remove the very essence of its competence as a scientific study of society. Marxist theory, however, asserted that sociology could totally ignore the individual, for studying the individual meant studying derivative rather than fundamental social phenomena; only by ignoring these derivative phenomena could sociology hope to achieve the precision of natural science.

By viewing sociology as a science of the actions of individuals, Populist sociologists introduced the element of nonrepetitiveness and unpredictability into social dynamics. Marxist sociologists, on the other hand, thought that the theory of class struggle elevated sociology to the level of science by making it possible to subsume countless, unaccountable, and unpredictable actions of individuals under general laws and to establish repetitiveness and regularities in social processes. No social science, in the Marxist view, can undertake the task of predicting the behavior and actions of each person because these depend on a multitude of conditions, tastes, world outlooks, and educational backgrounds. However, the Marxists saw no reason why the actions of such large groups of people as social classes should not be predictable with natural science precision.

In criticizing Populist sociology, Plekhanov argued that, although individuals can influence the "fate" of a society, sometimes considerably, the nature and extent of this influence are always determined by the society's basic structure. If a single man, even an especially talented one, is to greatly influence the course of events, two conditions must exist. "First, his talent must enable him to identify himself with the social needs of a given epoch more thoroughly than others can.... Second, the existing social order must not stand in the way of a man possessing a talent that is needed."[53] In this view, the individual is not the shaper of history, but only a tool.

The Populists believed that history is moved by "critically thinking individuals," who, in their search for the realization of the ideals of humanity, act as an integrating social force. They treated social solidarity, or cooperation, as the pivot of social life and social expectations; in the intelligentsia, whose members came from all the social classes, they saw the true architects of social progress. The Populists firmly believed that the ideology and sociocultural distinctiveness of the intelligentsia are products of critical thought and moral dedication. Russia, they emphasized, provides the classic example of a country in which class struggle could not play a decisive historical role. In nineteenth-century Russia, the word "peasants" was synonymous with the word "*narod*," for the peasants constituted over eighty percent of the total population. Most contemporary interpreters of Populist theory agreed that a close adherence to a radical version of the old Slavophile view of Russia as a unique society and culture had prevented Lavrov, Mikhailovskii, and their followers from advancing a universal theory of social change.

The Marxists could not accept the Populist view of the intelligentsia as a classless formation and as the mainspring of social progress; they were equally adamant in their rejection of the Populist identification of the peasants as nonstratified "people." They regarded class struggle as the basic instrument of social change, identified classes by economic criteria, and interpreted capitalist society as an arena of the rapidly growing class polarization. To them, the class struggle in a society at any given time is the best indicator of objective economic conditions in that society. Moreover, it is not the "critically thinking individuals" or the intelligentsia that indicate the path of future social development but the proletariat, deeply steeped in class consciousness. The Marxists also argued that the Russian intelligentsia was a product of the existing economic conditions.

The Populists contended that the distinctive pattern of Russia's dominant values freed her of the need to pass through a capitalist phase of social development. The future of Russia, according to Daniel'son, depends not on the dictates of a universal theory of social evolution but on conscious efforts to develop the communal core of native institutions. Russian scholars, he said, could be of very little help to their country by merely trying to show how, at a given historical point, it fits a distinct phase of universal social evolution. He wrote: "We must abandon all doctrinaire interpretations and must admit that the truth can be discovered only by studying [concrete] phenomena—by comparing these phenomena, discovering ties between them and observing their influence on each other." A philosophy of history concerned with the universal laws of social development is of little help to a realistic study of Russian social and economic realities; what is needed most of all is a statistical analysis of data revealing the historical uniqueness of Russian society.[54] His own empirical work, grounded in statistics, made him a staunch defender of the theory that burgeoning capitalism was a disease that threatened to divest Russian society of its most resourceful weapons in the struggle for survival. To V. P. Vorontsov, another influential Populist economist, it was "obvious that the impossibility of the development of capitalist production in Russia" made it unrealistic for Russia to copy "Western political institutions."[55]

The notion of the universality of capitalism found strong supporters among Russian Marxists. Although he was a consistent critic of the social ravages of capitalism, Plekhanov readily recognized in capitalist economy a powerful instrument for elevating Russia to the higher levels of political and cultural life that he had seen in Western Europe.[56] Struve went so far as to assert that the sooner Russia absorbed the progressive spirit of capitalism the sooner she would join the family of civilized nations and place herself on the only path leading to socialism.[57] The same idea was adopted by Lenin, who also claimed that the very question of Russia's destiny to bypass the phase of capitalism was negated by the fact that Russia had already become a capitalist country. In fact, both the Populists and the Marxists acknowledged the role of the growing industrialization in the emergence of capitalist socioeconomic relations in Russia; however, while the Populists pondered the incompatibility of these relations with the native society based on the obshchina and artel principles, the Marxists lamented the extensive survivals of the "feudal" system that stood in the way of an accelerated growth of capitalism. Lenin and Mikhailovskii agreed that the growth of capitalism in Russia was hampered by unfavorable conditions, but they differed in pinpointing these conditions as well as in their views on the indispensability and desirability of Russian capitalism. The Populists saw in the obshchina a model for future safeguards against the overreaching power of the state; Engels, on the other hand, treated the obshchina as a "localized community" inviting "centralized absolutism."[58]

In their criticism of Populist sociology, the Marxists made concessions to the views of their opponents while staying within the orthodox framework of Marxist theory. The Marxists could not accept the Populist claim that a scientific study of society required a concern with the "subjective" purposiveness no less than with the "objective" causality of social action; however, they did accept the category of purposiveness as a special ramification of social causality. "Social teleology," in Plekhanov's terminology, was a legitimate concern of scientific sociology. The Marxists rejected the Populist notion of the primary role of the individual in social history; but they were willing to ascribe the history-making role to individuals capable of achieving maximum personal freedom by acting in harmony with the objective laws of social evolution. Struve gave Hegel the primary credit for having recognized that "freedom" is "the understanding of necessity"—of the inexorable power of the laws of social and material development—and that no person is "free" unless he is acquainted with these laws and acts in accordance with them.[59] In the final analysis, both the Populists and the Marxists viewed the intellectual elite as the power that turns the wheels of history.

Although the Marxists were preoccupied with the features that Russian society shared with other societies of comparable development, they recognized, under the pressure of Populist arguments, the importance of the historical individualities of separate peoples. Plekhanov acknowledged two types of concurrent changes in every society; he did not label them, but for the sake of convenience they can be identified as "structural" and "idiosyncratic."[60] Structural changes are changes in existing principles of social integration; they occur when quantitative changes in the economic base of a society become qualitative changes, and they are uniform and predictable for all societies. In its study of structural changes, sociology is a science indistinguishable from one of the natural sciences. Idiosyncratic changes are more limited: whereas structural changes unfold as part of a universal social evolution, idiosyncratic changes are confined to individual societies. Plekhanov noted: "Every society lives in its own particular historical environment, which may be, and often is in reality, very similar to the historical environment surrounding other peoples, but can never be, and never is, identical with it. . . . This introduces an extremely powerful element of diversity into the process of social development."[61] From the very beginning, Russian Marxists were ready to admit that the socioeconomic development of Russia was only analogous, not identical, to that of Western Europe.[62]

Approaching the same problem from a different angle, Lenin stated that the "Russian sociologists" must undertake an "independent" elaboration of Marx's theory, "because this theory gives only general guiding statements which are applied in England differently than in France, in France differently than in Germany, and in Germany differently than in Russia."[63] Lenin also noted that even the intensity of the concern with the various aspects of the Marxian intellectual legacy varies from society to society, depending on unique national and historical conditions. While Germany was at first concerned primarily with the philosophical aspects of Marxism and then successively with the political and economic aspects, in Russia the initial concern was with the application of Marxist theory to the study of Russian economy, which gradually gave place to political interests and then to philosophy.[64]

Because the Russian Marxists recognized that the structural and idiosyncratic characteristics of human societies were different, they combined their search for the universal aspects of social evolution with a study of the unique historical features of Russian society. Thus Plekhanov examined the history of Russian thought as a unique development of rationalist and "materialist" tradition; and Lenin undertook a detailed study of the emergent capitalist relations in Russia. A noteworthy Marxist examination of the historical individuality of Russian society was Tugan-Baranovskii's *The Russian Factory: Past and Present*, a meticulously documented study that described the evolution of Russian industry since the early eighteenth century and analyzed the economic, social, and political forces related to the emergence of Russian capitalism. The book reaffirmed the Marxian rejection of the Populist model of peasant Russia as an alternative to "Western" industrial capitalism, but it unintentionally gave wide support to the Populist notion of the historical uniqueness of Russian socioeconomic development.[65] It placed much emphasis on domestic industry and government policies as the key factors in shaping the unique development of Russian industry. Struve called this study a "scientific-sociological study of Russian industry."[66]

Mikhailovskii stated repeatedly that he did not oppose all the ramifications of Marxist social theory, and he argued that his early writings embodied many Marxist ideas. In 1895, he cited his earlier statement that "the theoretical part of *Capital* rapidly took an indisputably high position in established science."[67] In a polemic with Tugan-Baranovskii, he wrote that he was consistently on the side of "the majority of Russian writers" who recognized the vital historical role of the economic factor. Tugan-Baranovskii, he said, erred not in emphasizing the profound role of economic institutions in the evolution of Russian society but in misrepresenting them and in attributing to them metaphysical significance.[68] Mikhailovskii's attitude toward the Marxist usage of the dialectical method was much less conciliatory. He looked upon the Hegelian triad as sheer sophistry. Lenin retorted not by defending the dialectical triad but by claiming that it is not an essential component of Marxist sociological methodology—that it does not "solve all sociological problems." Making an obvious concession to Mikhailovskii, he asserted that the dialectical method, in contrast to the metaphysical, "is nothing else but the scientific method in sociology, which consists of regarding society as a living organism in a state of constant development. . ., the study of which requires an objective analysis of the production relations that constitute the given social formation and an investigation of its laws of functioning and development."[69] In support of his claim, he noted that in such classics of Marxist literature as Marx's *Capital* and *The Poverty of Philosophy* and Engels's *Socialism: Utopian and Scientific*, the Hegelian triad is not mentioned even once. Lenin's willingness to make a concession on the methodological importance of the thesis-antithesis-synthesis triad did not extend to the other three pillars of Marxist sociology: the theory of the economic foundations of social structure, the general commitment to historicism, and the antisubjectivist orientation. However, by sacrificing the triad, Lenin, at least in his dispute with Mikhailovskii, sacrificed the inner logic of the Marxist theory of revolution.

Despite the extensive, and emotionally charged, criticism of the basic propositions of Populist sociology, the leading Marxist theoreticians made it clear that they considered Populist thought an advanced and progressive stage in the history of Russian thought and that their criticism was limited to a few basic issues in social theory and ideology. Plekhanov went so far as to admit, in 1905, that the "Marxist phase" of his thinking was a logical continuation of the "Populist phase" of his intellectual evolution.[70] Lenin lauded Mikhailovskii for his consistent and irreconcilable struggle against the lingering survivals of precapitalist institutions in Russia and for his sympathies for—and occasional participation in—the underground publication activities of the revolutionary intelligentsia.[71] All this, however, does not detract from the fact that Populist subjectivism and Marxist objectivism stood at the opposite ends of the theoretical spectrum of modern sociology.

FROM MARXISM TO REVISIONISM AND ANTI-MARXISM

By 1895 the Russian champions of historical materialism had succeeded in presenting to Russian readers a comprehensive exposition of the principal postulates of Marxist sociology. If this presentation lacked in symmetry, the main reason was that its artificers were engaged in a bitter feud with the leaders of Populist social theory. Although Marxist sociology covered the entire spectrum of the theoretical legacy of Marx and Engels, it was decidedly Russian in spirit, historical documentation, and empirical support. However, the time of the consolidation of Russian Marxist theory coincided with the beginning of its fragmentation. The seeds of revisionism were sown in Russia several years before the outcries for a modernization of orthodox Marxism began to filter in from the West. Russian revisionists fall into two distinct categories: the one group included the writers who sought a union of Marxism and Kantian philosophy; the second group included persons determined to bring Marxism in tune with modern neopositivism, particularly of the variety advanced by Ernst Mach and Richard Avenarius.

The chief representatives of the first group were P. B. Struve and M. I. Tugan-Baranovskii, who published most of their work in the open (rather than the underground) press, concerned themselves only with selected components of the Marxist legacy, and thought that Marxism was not a closed theoretical system and needed further elaboration and amplification.

The phase of revisionism started actually in 1895, when Struve, in his *Critical Remarks*, announced that the philosophical elaboration of Marxism had not yet been completed and that there was a need for a critique of historical materialism on the basis of new facts. He invited a wide search for a blending of Marxism with more modern sociological and philosophical views. In his arguments against Populist individualism, for example, he did not hesitate to seek help in Georg Simmel's views on the general principles of social differentiation. He was particularly fond of, and relied heavily on, the philosophy of Alois Riehl, who had little in common with Marxism and who worked diligently to effect a synthesis of positivism and Kantianism under the guise of a modern "scientific philosophy."

Published in a Russian translation in 1897, Rudolf Stammler's *Economy and Law* spurred several leading Russian Marxists to reexamine some of the fundamental principles of historical materialism. Stammler treated law as a social category essentially independent of the economic base, but he also questioned the scientific validity of several other axioms of orthodox Marxist philosophy. He viewed social development not as a product of forces codified in natural science laws (as viewed by orthodox Marxists) but as a purposive process, that is, a realization of goals conceived by man. Under his influence, Struve reversed his earlier identification of freedom with the knowledge of historical necessity, deeply embedded in the law of social causation. He now lauded Stammler for having pointed out the weaknesses of Engels's efforts to transpose Hegel's "metaphysical" view of freedom as "absolute necessity" into a "real" and "empirical" view of freedom as "knowledge of necessity."[72] Engels's transposition, he claimed, was based on a distinct failure to differentiate between a "logical" and a "psychological" interpretation of freedom. Logically, freedom and necessity are inseparable; they are one and the same principle. Psychologically, freedom and necessity are anchored in human thought and sentiment and are distinct, but complementary, principles. In the world of metaphysics, the future can be viewed in the light of necessity; in the real, empirical world, "the idea of the future cannot be fully submerged into the world of necessity." Moreover, the interlacing of necessity and freedom is proof of the limited scope of existing scientific knowledge as well as of "the even more profound and basic fact that neither human life nor human consciousness can be fully comprehended by knowledge, experience, and science."[73] The very possibility of human consciousness is based not on an identification of freedom and necessity but on a full recognition of the two as separate human orientations. Human ideals—human visions of the future development of society—cannot be viewed as "unconditionally necessary" either on a subjective or on an objective basis. In developing his arguments, Struve depended liberally on Kant's critical philosophy. He also endorsed Georg Simmel's sociological interpretation of social life as a synchronization of individual action (expressing freedom) and social norms (expressing necessity). By separating freedom from necessity, he reestablished the individual as an essential category of sociology. He did all this in an effort not to refute Marxism but to give it new life.

In 1899, under the influence of Eduard Bernstein, Struve took another step away from Marxist orthodoxy. He now claimed that the Marxist notion of social change by "leaps" was a relic of metaphysical thinking; and he gave unqualified support to Kant's "law of continuity" in all changes.[74] Dismissing dialectics as a "logic" transformed into an "ontology," he saw hope only in evolutionary socialism—in a gradual growth of the power of the working class within the capitalist system and a steady weakening and eventual disappearance of class conflict. Struve also argued that Marxist social theory was not a science founded on empirical facts but a union of science and utopia. Again he noted that the failure to face the epistemological problems of scientific knowledge was the weakest component of Marxist philosophy. The best that he could say about Marxism was that it was a philosophical system permeated, but not governed, by empirical facts.

In his long introduction to Berdiaev's study of Mikhailovskii's social theory, published in 1901, Struve stated that from the standpoint of epistemology and metaphysics there is no difference between the vulgar materialism of Moleschott and Büchner and the dialectical materialism of Marx and Engels.[75] He thought that Marxist social theory contains valuable elements which must be pried out of the obsolete metaphysics built upon a combination of "dialectics" and "materialism." In his opinion, Eduard von Hartmann's *Dialectical Method* is a major work contributing to the bankruptcy of both dialectical materialism and historical materialism. Struve saw no fundamental differences between Marxist and Populist theories: both, he contended, belong to the general philosophy of posivitism—not the positivism of Auguste Comte but positivism as translated into empiricism by David Hume, John Stuart Mill, and Laas.[76] Although the subjective theory of Mikhailovskii and the objective theory of orthodox Marxism are in many respects totally different, they are products of the same philosophical outlook: both are dominated by the notion of "the relativity of truth and moral law."[77] The basic weakness of the two theoretical orientations is in their total disregard of "normative teleology" as an epistemological principle and of ethics as a discipline transcending the bounds of science.

While in *Critical Remarks* Struve adhered firmly to the Marxist view that ethics is not relevant to the study of social structure, now he criticized both Marxism and Populism for their failure to consider absolute ethical norms as the essence of human society. The notion of absolute or universal attributes of moral principles came to Struve's philosophy from Kant's *Critique of Practical Reason*, particularly as articulated by various contemporary neo-Kantian schools. But it also came from Nietzsche's philosophy. In one of his earlier essays, Struve endorsed Nietzsche's effort to achieve an organic synthesis of the objective universalism and subjective individualism of morality, the first expressed in the "idealism" of absolute ethical values and the latter in the empiricism (and skepticism) of individual experience.[78] However, he quickly changed his mind; a year or two later he wrote that morality was strictly a metaphysical phenomenon and that its transcendental nature made it fully independent of individual experience.[79] Morality, in brief, could be understood not in the light of scientific empiricism but in the light of metaphysical transcendentalism.

In 1909, Struve urged the intelligentsia to abandon its "irresponsible denial" of the state and to substitute contemplation for "irreligious" production of socialist designs.[80] His contention that the intelligentsia should concentrate on inward soul-searching rather than on outward aggressiveness received full support from the spokesmen for the government. The official *Journal of the Ministry of National Education* welcomed the argument of the *Vekhi* authors that a rejuvenation of Russia should be sought not in a change of the political system but in the individual's "personal, intimate work on self-improvement."[81] The *Vekhi* writers contended that, in order to be fully understood and appreciated, such cultural values as science, art, religion, and morality must be isolated from their utilitarian connotations, from their concrete, historical place in and interaction with society. Led by men like Struve, these writers argued that the intelligentsia should turn its attention from social criticism to a contemplation about "pure science," "pure religion," "pure art," and "pure morality."

Contemporary critics did not hesitate to label Struve's turn to "metaphysics" and "religion" a withdrawal into the confused world of reactionary politics: at the time it was customary to interpret all forms of "idealism" as expressions of reactionary leanings.[82] But Struve's "withdrawal" was decidedly unique and rather original: in articulating a new philosophy, he went against the dominant forms of religious revivalism and mysticism. He opposed such leading champions of religious revival as D. Merezhkovskii who, in his opinion, concentrated more on building an antiquated "church community" than on emancipating religious thought from institutional constraints.[83] In modern society, he wrote, religion can contribute to general welfare more by encouraging individual interpretation of beliefs—the search by every person for a kingdom of God within himself—and, thus, by staying in tune with the expanding role of individuality across the entire spectrum of social and cultural activities, than by dissolving itself in a rigid system of collectivized doctrine and restrictive institutional demands. Implicit in his argumentation was the idea that the democratic nature of religious individualism offered much more to the future of Russia than the autocratic and materialistic nature of the church. Apprehensive of the limitless power of government censors and preoccupied with many other interests, Struve did not undertake a more detailed elaboration of the theme of religious individualism. Nor did he stay for long with his view of the essentially democratic nature of modern religious individualism.

Struve's acceptance of metaphysics was equally unorthodox: he made it clear that he had no use for the "old" metaphysics steeped in mysticism and providentialism and opposed to scientific thought. Without acknowledging it explicitly, he came close to the orientation of Hermann Cohen of the Marburg School of neo-Kantian philosophy, who worked on a "new" metaphysics, a metaphysics that respected the rigor of logic and the precision of the mathematical method, and that promised to build its propositions upon, rather than in opposition to, science. The function of metaphysics should be not to construct systems of dogmatic precepts but to cultivate a critical mind. Struve criticized Slavophile philosophy, which he described as consisting of a "thick cover" of metaphysics over a "miniscule core" of science; instead, he advocated a philosophy that would make metaphysics a "thin cover" over a large body of science.[84] As in his views on religious individualism, Struve saw in the new metaphysics, or "critical metaphysics," a source and an expression of intellectual individualism—a disciplined challenge to the authority of every idea and every system of knowledge and beliefs—and a specific adaptation to the growing role of individuality in modern society. Presented in a most sketchy form, the idea of "critical metaphysics," like the idea of religious individualism, received no support from his contemporaries and quickly ceased to occupy Struve's mind.

The idea of religious individualism found its way into Struve's sociological thinking about the modern state. Unlike the Populists, he reasoned that the state is not an agency of society but a self-generating and self-perfecting force without which there could be no social and cultural progress. Society, according to him, is a "system," while the state is a "unity." In the difference between "unity" and "system" he saw one of the most significant categories of sociological thought. Society, as a "system," is the sphere of irrational action, a sphere dominated by heterogenous purposes. The state, as a "unity," is the sphere of rational action dominated by autogenous purposes. Society is dominated by unconscious action; the state is dominated by conscious action.[85] While society is partly a purposive phenomenon, the state is completely purposive. The crux of Struve's social theory is that the state, as the epitome of conscious and purposive action, holds the key to the full understanding of the forces of social cohesion. Although the state represents the highest level of the rationalization of social action, it retains an element of religious mysticism. A combination of growing rationalism and residual religion produces religious individualism, the true ideology of the modern state.[86] In tying the "individualism" of religious behavior to the "rationalism" of modern social existence, Struve anticipated, but did not explore, a type of sociological analysis presented by Max Weber in his classic *The Protestant Ethic*.

Much of Struve's social theory is tied to his efforts to formulate the conceptual framework of political economy as a science of modern society. This was particularly true after 1910 when he was appointed a professor of economic history at St. Petersburg Polytechnic Institute, a modern center of higher scientific and technical training. He sought to establish political economy as an idiographic discipline—a discipline that would substitute the close scrutiny of empirical economic information and the inductive method for the traditional preoccupation with a priori principles of a universalistic orientation and the deductive method.[87] He rejected the "monistic" orientations which lumped together the "natural" (causal) and "artificial" (teleological) components of the "socioeconomic process"—the former subject to natural causation independent of human volition, the latter a pure product of human volition.[88] He recognized that the dichotomy of natural and artificial components of the social process was a long-standing one in the history of social and economic thought—that it was treated seriously even by the ancient Greeks. However, while the ancient Greeks gave this dichotomy a metaphysical-ontological explanation, he viewed it as an empirical-psychological conception. While the ancient Greek explanation was "transcendental," Struve called his explanation "immanent," because he identified teleology with the purposefulness of human action rather than with a metaphysical world-spirit as the guiding force of human history. In his effort to replace Marx's concept of "value" as a "metaphysical" notion by a concept of "price" as an "empirical" notion he showed intimate familiarity with current economic theories in Western Europe. However, his contribution lay more in bringing the theoretical ideas of such modern economists as Eugen von Böhm-Bawerk, Joseph Schumpeter, and Vilfredo Pareto to Russia and in surveying the current criticism of Marx's economic theory than in building an original system of economic thought.[89]

Unlike the Marxists, Struve argued that society and economy are distinct categories, that several economic systems can coexist in the same society.[90] The economy, to be fully understood, must be studied in its pure form, in isolation from society. To speak in terms of "social categories" means to speak about different positions of individuals and groups on the ladder of social stratification—about social inequality; to speak in terms of "economic categories" it is necessary to disentangle economic activities from the matrix of social inequality.

Struve's scholarship was inseparable from a deep involvement in politics for which he had neither vision nor stamina; he traveled a long political road, interrupted by tortuous intervals of unsettled, drifting thought. He began as a critical Marxist, continued as a neo-Kantian and a champion of constitutional monarchy, and ended as a defender of the autocracy. The ambiguity and inconsistencies in his social and economic theory were a part of a compulsive search for personal political identification. Despite his protestations to the contrary, he was a classic representative of the Russian intelligentsia: his eyes were cast more toward the nebulous future than toward the concrete, living present; he wandered freely over many scholarly and literary fields with minimum competence in most of them; and he saw politics in every branch of human endeavor. All this, however, does not detract from the fact that he had a brilliant sociological mind and a profound understanding of the most puzzling structural features of modern society.

M. I. Tugan-Baranovskii, unlike Struve, did not cut all ties with the intellectual legacy of Marxism. In 1900, he wrote that Marx's sociological conceptions were not only essentially correct but also a most original contribution to modern social science. In 1902, he asserted that "the social content of Marx's surplus value must be taken as perfectly correct; however, the economic framework of this theory is obviously without foundation and cannot be defended."[91] In Marx's economic conceptions he now saw a reworking of the ideas of Adam Smith and David Ricardo; he also claimed that in economics Marx was usually wrong when he was most original.[92] However, he believed that, in order to advance modern economic theory, it is necessary to go beyond Marx not by ignoring his theoretical contributions but by building upon them.[93]

Soon after the publication of *The Russian Factory*, in 1898, Tugan-Baranovskii produced several articles critical of Marxist theory. In one of these articles he noted that Marx was eminently successful in explaining the "dark" and "evil" attributes of man's psychology but that nobility and humanity, as generously expressed by such utopians as Owen, Saint-Simon, and Fourier, were completely alien to his frame of mind.[94] These articles prepared the ground for the *Theoretical Foundations of Marxism* (1905) and *Modern Socialism*, which were widely read in Russia and were translated into several Western European languages. Although no match for his earlier studies of industrial crises in England and of the history of Russian industry, they presented an original synthesis of ideas advanced by the masters of classical English economics, Marx, and the Austrian School. In his earlier writings, he had viewed Marx's theory as a brilliant synthesis of all previous work on the subject; now he claimed that Marx had not originated the ideals of socialism but had borrowed them from utopian socialists.[95] He also contended that in some respects utopian socialism was more scientific than Marx's "scientific socialism."

Tugan-Baranovskii's sociology, like that of most revisionists, sought to reconcile Marxism with neo-Kantianism and to relax the more rigid and scientifically unsupportable claims of Marxist theory. Under the influence of neo-Kantian philosophy, Tugan-Baranovskii argued that a truly scientific study of society must go beyond the "genetic" and "explanatory" methods that approached man merely as a "tool" of history rather than as a "goal" of social evolution. Like many of his contemporaries, he viewed human society and its history as both a mechanical and a purposive process. Not "social predictions," he said, but "social ideals" should be the guiding forces in the struggle for more advanced social arrangements. When a society is caught in a conflict between scientific "predictions" and moral "ideals" it must give the latter a position of preeminence. The evolution of human society owes more to the fortitude of great men as champions of moral principles than to the mechanical work of scientific laws.[96] The social scientist must confront both the unique historical conditions of social change and the universal ethical conditions of human existence.[97] The value theory in economics, he now argued, must recognize that human desires are an important force in the economic process.[98] The study of social change and socialism, he claimed, must consider two sets of phenomena: objective, or "causal," social relations and ethical, or purposive, norms. At first, Tugan-Baranovskii thought that the neo-Kantian notion of moral purposiveness would give Marxism greater viability and more extensive practical applicability; by 1909 he was convinced that Marxism represented a categorical denial of ethics and was essentially incompatible with neo-Kantian philosophy. To save ethics, he now believed, it was necessary to "destroy" Marxism. However, he conceded that "in destroying Marxism, it is necessary to make use of valuable material contained in it." "Although the new theory of socialism must be made mainly from Marxist elements, the latter must be integrated into a completely new system."[99] For long, no leading Russian Marxist theorist subscribed to Karl Vorländer's efforts to show the possibility of a synthesis of the fundamental principles of Kantian morality and the "hidden ethics" of Marxism. In 1911, Tugan-Baranovskii asserted that any effort to effect a coalescence of Marxism and neo-Kantianism would produce a welcome "dissolution" of Marxism.[100]

Despite his arguments in favor of a "dissolution" and "reintegration" of Marxist ideas, Tugan-Baranovskii did not abandon his firm adherence to P. L. Lavrov's dictum that "the true sociology is socialism." To him, sociology as a science of social structure and social change has proved that socialism is a necessary higher stage in the development of modern society. His own theory of socialism, as evolved under the influence of neo-Kantian philosophy, is based on the premise that Marxism owes a great debt to utopian socialism and is only in part a scientific doctrine. He argued that true socialism combines the socialization of production with the freedom of the individual and could therefore develop only in countries that combine a capitalist mode of production with political democracy.

Tugan-Baranovskii rejected the Marxist theory of class struggle as a motive force in social change, and came close to accepting the Populist theory that the intelligentsia was above class distinctions. Marx, he thought, had not really been successful in identifying specific social classes in Western Europe and had generally exaggerated the role of classes and class consciousness in modern society.[101] Rejecting Engels's claim that every political struggle is a class struggle, he asserted that, while political power often appears as an end in itself, economic power always is the means for the achievement of specific ends.[102] As human societies advance, he said, they are governed less by economic factors and more by ethical factors. In this respect, Marx had erred in not distinguishing between "class consciousness" as a centrifugal social force and "moral consciousness" as a centripetal social force.[103]

In contrast to Marx's view of the state as a tool of dominant or exploiting classes, Tugan-Baranovskii defended the notion of the state as an embodiment of "ideal values" belonging to all social classes. Even "in the purely economic area, the state is not merely an organization of the dominant class, for it is also an instrument of economic progress which meets the needs of all classes." Again, in contrast to the Marxist view, he claimed that "scientific and philosophical knowledge follows its own laws of logic which have nothing in common with class interests."[104] The Marxist theory of the class nature of morality has no foundation in "the empirical content of moral consciousness." While Marx emphasized the divisive nature of class morality, Tugan-Baranovskii stressed the unifying power of Kant's categorical imperative. "There exists," he said, "a definite direction in the development of moral principles which leads us to accept the reality of a single and universally obligatory moral code, which stands above the historical limitations of space and time."[105]

To Tugan-Baranovskii, sociology is a systematic study of socialism, which he envisaged as a product of social evolution rather than of social revolution. He contended that, although the Marxist theory of economic materialism and class struggle supplies important ingredients for true socialism, it does not provide satisfactory safeguards for a precise use of scientific concepts; concerned primarily with the socialization of the material base of production, it deals with the means, rather than with the ends, of socialism.[106] The unremitting search for a modern theory of "scientific socialism" led Tugan-Baranovskii to an intensive study of the theoretical foundations of the cooperative movement.[107] He argued that the immediate goal of this movement was not to destroy capitalism but to humanize it. This, however, should not be interpreted as meaning that he was ready to attribute unlimited duration to capitalism; he thought that although capitalism, like any other socioeconomic system, was of a transitory nature, its inevitable downfall will result from the growing inner contradictions rather than from a proliferation of socialist blueprints, regardless of their scientific merit.

In his search for a general system of socialist theory (embracing Marx's legacy only as a specific component), Tugan-Baranovskii formulated a realistic theory of social change. Human society, according to this theory, is not and cannot be a monolithic structure, for it is dominated by an irreconcilable conflict between two forces equally "inherent in human social unions": the striving of the individual for total freedom and the striving of society to subordinate the individual to its interests. A perfect society is one in which there is a maximum harmonization of individuality and sociality.[108] This theory occupies a middle position between two extremes: the anarchist theory which dreamed of a society unencumbered by restraints on the life of the individual and the Marxist theory which saw the individual as a product and a mirror of society.

8. A Blend of Marxism and Neopositivism: A. A. Bogdanov

A. A. Malinovskii, who wrote under the pseudonym of A. A. Bogdanov, was associated with three major developments in the general theory of society in Russia. He made an elaborate and refreshingly original effort to weld the social theory of Marx and Engels and the "scientific philosophy" of neopositivism into a modern system of sociological theory. He adduced elaborate arguments in favor of the sociology of knowledge as a special discipline concerned with the systematic study of the genetic and functional relationship of ideology to social structure. And he had the vision and skill to lay the foundations of a general theory of organization, a forebear of cybernetics and general systems theory.

Born in 1873 to the family of a public-school teacher, Bogdanov graduated with high distinction from Tula gymnasium and immediately enrolled in Moscow University's Department of Natural Sciences.[1] In 1894, he was exiled to Tula by the police authorities because of his participation in the student movement. Deeply involved in propaganda activities among the workers of a local weapons factory, he was at first a spokesman for Populism but gradually transferred his allegiance to Marxism. His lectures delivered for various workers' circles were the basis for *A Short Course in Political Economy* (1897) which went through many editions and was translated into several Western European languages. A comprehensive and rather original survey of Marxist economics and sociology, the book reaffirmed the orthodox Marxist idea that political economy was the only social science approaching the methodological rigor of the natural sciences and that the analysis of social structure was its primary task. In a review published in 1898, Lenin praised Bogdanov's "clear and correct" presentation of political economy as a science "concerned with the historical development of social relations in production and distribution."[2] In the autumn of 1895, Bogdanov enrolled in the medical school of Khar'kov University and immediately became active in local Social-Democratic circles. Soon after graduation in 1899, he was sent to a Moscow prison for his participation in revolutionary circles and early in 1901 was exiled first to Kaluga and then to Vologda where he remained until the end of 1903. While in exile, he worked for a while as a psychiatrist in Kuvshinov, near Vologda. In 1902, he helped edit the symposium *Essays on a Realistic World View*, a critique of the *Problems of Idealism*, edited by P. I. Novgorodtsev.[3] When the Social Democrats split into the Bolsheviks and Mensheviks in 1903, Bogdanov, still in exile, joined the former.

Early in 1904, Bogdanov went to Switzerland and was immediately elected to several ranking positions in Bolshevik organizations, serving at the same time on the editorial boards of several newspapers. He returned to Russia in time to take part in the revolution of 1905 as a Bolshevik representative in the St. Petersburg Soviet of Worker's Deputies; he also edited *The New Life,* a Bolshevik journal published legally during "the days of freedom" at the end of 1905. He was arrested again, but instead of being sent to prison he was ordered to leave the country. Unknown to the police, he stayed for a while in Kuokkala, Finland, sharing a dacha with Lenin. Although selected to serve on the central committee of the Social-Democratic party in 1907, his views on both the revolutionary philosophy and current political tactics brought him into conflict with more orthodox Marxists. In 1907, he argued with his close friend Lenin: after the dissolution of the Second State Duma, Lenin thought it advisable for the Social Democrats to take part in the forthcoming elections for the Third Duma to assure themselves of contact with legal and semilegal labor organizations. Bogdanov, on the contrary, was the chief spokesman for the so-called maximalist group, which advocated a full boycott of the election and a total retreat into illegal activities.[4]

In *Materialism and Empiriocriticism*, published in 1909, Lenin portrayed Bogdanov as a marionette dancing to the tune of Machian epistemological "idealism." The enforced isolation from official Bolshevik activities led Bogdanov to broaden his participation in the work of various fringe groups of unorthodox Marxists; he was particularly close to persons, typified by Maksim Gor'kii, who contended that a political and economic revolution could be successful only if it were preceded by an ideological, or cultural, revolution. Small wonder, then, that Bogdanov dedicated his utopian novels—*Red Star* and *Engineer Menii*—as well as several essays of programmatic nature, to the tasks of cultural revolution.

After the October Revolution, Bogdanov rejected all invitations to rejoin the Bolshevik party. He was elected a regular member of the Socialist (later Communist) Academy, a new organization concerned primarily with elaborating the theoretical legacy of the fathers of Marxism and with training new cadres of social scientists in the spirit of historical materialism. He was the leading light in the early history of the *Proletkul't*, an organization dedicated to advancing "the fourth form of labor movement: the creative role of the workers' class in culture and ideology."[5] (The other "forms" covered politics, economy, and management.) He left the *Proletkul't* in 1921, when by becoming a "cultural organ" of the Bolshevik party it lost the last vestiges of autonomy. While writing essentially on the various aspects of "cultural work" among industrial labor, he found time to complete the last phase of his monumental work on a general theory of organization. His ideas exercised a strong influence on contemporary writing in the sociology of art; and his theory of "moving equilibrium" in the development of society found a way into N. I. Bukharin's widely noted work on the formal principles of Marxist sociology. He occupied a prominent position among Marxist dissidents engaged in an uphill battle to bring dialectical materialism in tune with the broad philosophical implications of Einstein's theory of relativity. His idea that "the form of economic organization" determined "the mode of production" dominated the thinking of most early Soviet historians of precapitalist societies.[6] On top of it all, he founded one of the world's first institutes to engage in an experimental study of blood transfusion. He died in 1928, at the age of fifty-five, a tragic victim of an experiment which he performed on himself.

Bogdanov's voluminous writing is part of a tireless search for a general science of society. The function of science, according to him, is to enrich the store of knowledge helping man to find his place in nature and society. Of all scientific questions, the most important is the one concerned with the main line of social development and the basic indices of social progress. A trustworthy answer to this question can come only from a scientific study of "the basic laws of social life," a study which has introduced the most daring and the most confusing chapters in the annals of scientific thought. The major deficiencies of the traditional theories of society stemmed from the personal predispositions and interests of scholars and the awesome complexity of social life. Bogdanov claimed that it was not until 1859 that the first decisive step was made in the search for a scientific study of the structure and dynamics of human society. In that year, Marx published *A Contribution to the Critique of Political Economy* in which he set down the guiding ideas for a general scientific theory of society. Bogdanov thought that in an introductory statement Marx presented the essence of scientific sociology:

> In the social production which men carry on they enter into definite relations that are indispensable and independent of their will; these relations of production correspond to a definite stage of development of their material powers of production. The sum total of these relations of production constitutes the economic structure of society—the real foundation, on which rise legal and political superstructures and to which correspond definite forms of social consciousness. The mode of production in material life determines the general character of the social, political, and spiritual processes of life. It is not the consciousness of men that determines their existence, but on the contrary, their social existence determines their consciousness. At a certain stage of their development, the material forces of production in society come in conflict with the existing relations of production, or—what is but a legal expression of the same thing—with the property relations within which they had been at work before. From forms

of development of the forces of production these relations turn into their fetters. Then comes the period of social revolution. With the change of the economic foundation the entire immense superstructure is more or less rapidly transformed.[7]

Bogdanov contended that, during the first four decades of its existence, Marx's theory had helped explain "a mass of historical developments" and had not encountered serious opposition from other theories. Many able writers enriched it by having helped it to expand its competence over new areas of sociological problems. However, history was not at a standstill. Particularly in science, many changes of revolutionary proportions, such as Darwin's theory of evolution, raised serious questions that Marxist theory could no longer ignore. "Although the theory of historical monism did not cease to be true in its basic claims, it was no longer satisfactory."[8] It was incomplete: it did not explain a wide range of social problems. For example, it did not explain why every society needs ideology and what the relationship of ideology to economy is. Also, it suffered from an imprecise definition of the "economic structure" of society. Bogdanov wondered why Marxist theory treats law as part of the superstructure when, in reality, it is the basic element in the articulation of the social organization of production. The Marxist theory of social change, according to Bogdanov, was very much in need of establishing closer relations with new scientific (particularly biological) theories of change. Marxist theory continued to be isolated from modern psychology, founded on physiology, which was well on the way to becoming an exact science; nor did it take a stand on the accelerated mathematicization of science. After forty years of existence, Marxist sociology continued to imitate the natural sciences, even though these dealt with phenomena "which are essentially homogeneous, simpler, and more general."[9]

Bogdanov devoted the main part of his writing to an effort to harmonize Marxist theory with recent developments in science and philosophy. This devotion took him a long way from some of the fundamental principles of Marxist theory; indeed, the differences between his and Marx's theories are more pronounced than the similarities. While Plekhanov was quick to label Bogdanov's theory "a categorical denial of materialism," a more sympathetic critic wrote: "Bogdanov's studies stand in sharp contrast to the usual rumination of quotations from Marx and Engels and their commentators; they represent an effort to rely on solid content rather than on cloudy metaphors used by many advocates of historical materialism as substitutes for scientific formulations, and to advance new arguments in favor of Marxist theory."[10] Soviet critics noted correctly that Bogdanov did not limit himself to a reappraisal of individual components of Marxist theory but, on the contrary, articulated a complete system of philosophical and sociological thought in opposition to Marxism. According to one Soviet critic, he differed from other revisionists in that he made his ideas in philosophy, political economy, and sociology integral parts of a substantively and logically unified system of theoretical principles.[11]

During the last few years of his life, Bogdanov was the target of bitter attacks published in the leading journals of the Bolshevik party. Numerous adversaries attacked his ambitious efforts to replace Lenin's epistemological objectivism by a theory of knowledge steeped in neopositivist subjectivism; to substitute a mechanistic interpretation of the processes of nature and society for the Marxist dialectical interpretation; and to blur the differences between the infrastructure and the superstructure of human society.

The evolution of Bogdanov's general theoretical orientation and interests can be divided into three phases. A commitment to a special brand of historicism—a general theory of social dynamics based on a synthesis of mechanical and evolutionary views of nature—gave the first phase its most distinctive feature. During the second phase, Bogdanov worked assiduously to formulate a new philosophical system—which he labeled empirio-monism—based on an original synthesis of Ernst Mach's epistemology and Marx's sociology. The work on a general theory of organization, an early version of cybernetics that he named tektology, provided the essential characteristic of the third phase.

HISTORICISM: A SYNTHESIS OF DARWIN AND OSTWALD

Although political economy was the initial path taking Bogdanov into the realm of sociology, all his subsequent concern with sociological thought was part of an intensive search for a philosophical system intended to satisfy the fundamental principles of Marxist theory and the logical and epistemological needs of twentieth-century science, both natural and social. He entered the philosophical arena in 1899 with the *Basic Principles of a Historical View of Nature*, which marked the beginning of the first phase in the evolution of his theoretical thought. In this study he elaborated a "historical view" which, in essence, blended the Newtonian static view of nature with the Darwinian dynamic view. Combining the two views into a paradigm, he regarded historical change as universal, causal, and relative.[12] Change is universal in the sense that it applies to both nature and society with the same regularity; it is causal in the sense that it has no room for teleological explanations; it is relative inasmuch as "human knowledge has no access to unconditional and absolute truths."[13] The emphasis on the relativity of historical knowledge brought Bogdanov into conflict with orthodox Marxists, who claimed that the laws of historical development are absolute. He also rejected "dialectics" as a label for the inner logic of historical change. In none of his subsequent writings did he change his opinion on this matter.[14]

Of all Bogdanov's works, *Basic Principles* was most remote from sociology: in this book he was preoccupied with the search for a modern philosophy of science that would bring together the latest scientific views and the most modern epistemological theories. However, the work set down a number of basic principles which he later applied to social theory. To Bogdanov science is one and indivisible; therefore, sociology could rise to a scientific level only by operating on the basis of natural science models. He rejected the traditional view of philosophy as a discipline standing apart from and above science; he also argued that sociology should not be submerged in philosophy but should depend on its own substantive claims and methodological tools. At one time, he argued that the improvement in the scientific standards of sociology and other disciplines would lead to the demise of philosophy as a mode of inquiry and a body of knowledge.

In *Knowledge from a Historical Point of View* (1902), Bogdanov proposed a schema of concepts and propositions treating human society as an integral part of nature, subject to self-adjusting natural processes and precise scientific measurement. He used Ostwald's theory of energy as a model for a new theory of knowledge and an interpretation of the historical succession of social systems. The theory of energy rested on two pillars: the law of the conservation of energy and the law of the full measurability of natural processes. The law of the conservation of energy was the same as the law of the uniformity and continuity of natural processes; this is also expressed in the statement that in nature everything must issue from something else, that nothing in nature is sui generis.[15] This law makes the study of the interaction and succession of the natural phenomena the basic task of science. The law of the full measurability of natural processes denotes that mathematical methods can be employed fruitfully in the entire universe of scientific inquiry, that mathematics supplies the essential tools for every science. Bogdanov conceded, however, that since all natural phenomena cannot be treated on the same level of generality, the scope and nature of the mathematical method varies from science to science. For example, the study of biological data requires a less generalizing treatment than the study of physical data.

The energy orientation contributed to a major redefinition of "causality" as the key explanatory mechanism of the work of nature. Indeed, Bogdanov thought that the fundamental transformation of the meaning of causality was the most revolutionary development in nineteenth-century science.[16] The classical law of causality considers cause and effect as discrete (and, therefore, static) phenomena set off from each other both quantitatively and qualitatively. The energy theory is concerned, not with cause and effect as distinct phenomena, but with the processes involved in causal sequences. It represents the last and decisive step in uprooting the static notion of nature. The basic contribution of the energy orientation, according to Bogdanov, is that it shifts the focus of scientific inquiry from ontological to functional aspects of nature: modern science no longer asks what nature and society are but how they work.

Based on the notion of the unity of the sciences, the energy view justifies and makes mandatory the use of natural science models in the social sciences. In the social sciences, the energy approach is the same as the historical approach: it places the primary emphasis on the interaction of social processes, particularly on the relationship between technology and ideology, the two universal categories of social processes.[17] Social processes are to human society what the transformation of energy is to nature in general: they depict the continuity and measurability of social change. Bogdanov's sociological theory, at least as formulated in *Knowledge from a Historical Point of View*, is both historical and monistic. It is historical inasmuch as it places the primary emphasis on the dynamics of social processes; it is monistic inasmuch as it interprets all phenomena of social dynamics as specific adaptations to increases and decreases in social energy and inasmuch as it operates on the assumption that human society manifests a spontaneous tendency—which it shares with organic nature—to eliminate internal contradictions and to strengthen harmonious relations.[18] In his earlier sociological theory, Bogdanov was much closer to Comte's emphasis on social consensus than to Marx's emphasis on class warfare as the key to the mysteries of organized social life.

Bogdanov was concerned primarily with applying the energy approach to the study of the evolution of knowledge as an index of the evolution of human society: he equated the study of the socialization of knowledge with the study of the inner dynamics of social relations and the main lines of social progress. Knowledge, as the moving force of history, is not an epistemological but a sociological phenomenon. "An analysis of cooperative relations between social groups provides the basis for a study of general forms of knowledge, characteristic for the entire society; an analysis of cooperation within individual groups provides the basis for the study of special ideological tendencies."[19]

Despite a heavy dependence on natural science models, Bogdanov recognized that sociology, dealing with unique problems in logic and methodology, is quite different from physics. In the first place, a sociologist cannot conduct experiments; he must rely completely on observation as a source of data. In the second place, in his observations, a sociologist faces life with infinitely complex concrete details, all products of multiple influences.[20] The problem facing sociology is how to reduce the unlimited complexity of concrete situations and divergent influences to simple conceptions capable of scientific treatment. Without a reduction of the multitude of complex observations to limited simple notions, the sociologist can *describe* the universe of his inquiry, but he cannot *explain* it. To be a scientist, he must resort to an abstract method which, in turn, has two characteristics: it is deductive, for it draws general conclusions by testing and verifying hypotheses; it is historical, for it concentrates on social processes dominated by discernible "tendencies."[21] Bogdanov noted that the basic task of the abstract method is to detect the "tendencies" of social processes that reveal regularities of scientific import.

Regularities in social change, as recorded in cognitive culture, are the central theme of Bogdanov's sociology. He considered adaptation (a concept borrowed from Darwin's biological theory) the key process revealing the regularities of social change. In his view, social selection (a transposition of Darwin's "natural selection") of the most effective techniques for the satisfaction of changing social needs is the main mechanism of adaptation. It is also the key concept in the sociology of knowledge: in the study of the selection of adaptive techniques at a specific point of history, Bogdanov saw the surest method for discovering the social criteria of truth. The function of the sociologist is to illumine the processes of selection for the purpose of unraveling the "least relative" and "most objective" criteria of truth—the criteria that reveal the regularities in the processes of history.

As presented in his earlier studies, Bogdanov's general theory of society lacks structural unity. He provided a detailed—and in places a profound—logical analysis of what he considered to have been the pivotal concepts of sociological analysis; but he did not tie these concepts to an empirical base. His theory is a pure theory, not a guide for empirical research. His main contribution lay in pointing out the vast scope and enormous usefulness of a sociological study of knowledge. The unpopularity of Ostwald's determined efforts to transform the energy theory into a comprehensive philosophical system with implicit metaphysical leanings proved to be an important factor in Bogdanov's decision to search for new theoretical models for his general theory of society. However, he showed no inclination to return to Marxist orthodoxy; paramount in the subsequent development of his sociological theory was an elaboration of the thesis that "the social being and social consciousness are one and the same thing."

EMPIRIOMONISM: A SYNTHESIS OF MARX AND MACH

Although there are recognizable differences between the various phases in the evolution of Bogdanov's philosophy, the unity and consistency in the development of his thought can not be questioned. From the very beginning, he elaborated a philosophical view that regarded knowledge as a social product, gave primacy to technology over ideology, and treated "adaptation" and "selection" as universal concepts which make human society an extension of the natural order.

In *Essays in the Psychology of Society* and *Empiriomonism* Bogdanov advanced a set of propositions giving a firmer and more comprehensive footing to the notion of human society as an integral part of nature, subject to self-adjusting processes and to mathematical measurement. While pushing Ostwald into the background (but never abandoning him), he found new inspiration and ample models in the "scientific philosophy" of Ernst Mach and Richard Avenarius, with whom he was united not by common scientific interests but by a common theory of knowledge.[22] He named his new philosophical system "empiriomonism" and defined it as a synthesis of Mach's and Avenarius's theory of knowledge and Marx's theory of social history. The strong point of empiriomonism, according to Bogdanov, is its full congruence with the ethos of modern science and technology. This ethos places the primary emphasis on knowledge that is not only practical but also economical—knowledge that avoids circuitous and imprecise philosophical and logical procedures.

Empiriomonism rejects the mechanistic orientation in science as an ideology rooted in the custom-bound organization of social labor in the seventeenth century. The ideology of the new technical intelligentsia, elaborated by the new philosophy, is a response to the historical need for rapid technological advancement; it minimizes the role of "sacred values" in industrial work and encourages continuous search for practical inventions. The new philosophy and the ideology of technical intelligentsia are similar in yet another respect: both reject the notion that scientific laws have independent existence. Instead, they regard scientific laws as transitional products of the human mind—special methods for meeting the challenge of practical social needs.[23]

Empiriomonism, like the neopositivistic philosophies of Mach and Avenarius, demands that both philosophers and scientists abandon their traditional concern with the "explanations" of mechanically intertwined phenomena and instead emphasize the "description" of pure forms of experience, which are reducible to mathematical expression. Bogdanov fully accepted Mach's and Avenarius's view of knowledge as a derivation from experience, which produces two kinds of "elements": psychical and physical. Psychical elements consist of sense data and are basically "biological-physiological." They establish a link between the individual and the outside world; but they are completely subjective, since each man's experience is unique.[24] Physical elements are derived from psychical elements by a "collective synchronization," that is, by a long distillation of generalized wisdom from personal experience. They are objective for they have a common meaning for human groups; they make up socially functional knowledge which is accepted and integrated through interpersonal communication.[25] Psychical elements, on the other hand, are "individually organized experience," that is, experience cast within the limits of personal life. In brief, psychical elements make up the experience that is dependent on the "individual subject"; physical elements make up the experience that is dependent on the "collective subject."[26] The social scientist must be guided by the axiom that the "social milieu" (as a system of communication) is the major link between man as "the individual world of experience" and the universe as a total experience.[27] The institutionalized system of social relations is the structural core of both society and personality.

Both psychical and physical elements are historical: both are products of long historical developments characterized by improvements and enrichments in the bonds which give human experience a structured form. The history of human society is the history of the growing complexity, depth, and precision of man's knowledge of the universe. The history of society is the continuous and accumulative socialization of knowledge—the gradual, but inexorable, expansion of social experience. While the objectivity of physical elements does not have an epistemological basis, for all knowledge is individual—and therefore subjective—in origin, it has a sociological basis, for its regularity and validity stem exclusively from the fact that it is a product and a reflection of social organization.[28] Ideology, as defined by Bogdanov, is a vital force in society entrusted with the task of organizing experience into structured knowledge. Although "vital," ideology is not "primary" in social causation: every change of structural significance has its origin in technology rather than in ideology. In its relationship to ideology, technology is the independent motive force of social development.[29] Or, "there is one thing that no ideology can achieve—it cannot be a prime mover of social change."[30]

Bogdanov's empiriomonistic theory of society shows several qualitative resemblances to Marx's theory. It recognizes the "socioeconomic formations" as stages in the "natural history" of social systems; it accepts in principle the Marxian view on the relationship of the infrastructure to the superstructure of major social activities; and it places strong emphasis on strain and stress in social dynamics generated by the accumulative growth of material culture. Bogdanov claimed that he considered his concept of "technical process" identical to the Marxian notion of "social relations in production." Indeed, he recognized Marx as the founder of modern sociology; he emphasized particularly the scientific usefulness of the Marxian concept of social structure and the Marxian claim that the social existence of men determines their consciousness.[31] He asserted that empiriomonism is a synthesis of Mach's and Avenarius's neopositivist epistemology and Marxian views on social structure.

Despite all this, Bogdanov claimed that Marx's sociological theory suffers from serious shortcomings, most of them stemming from Marx's failure to consider the stream of ideas unleashed by Darwin's evolutionary theory and modern scientific (that is, neopositivist) philosophy. Marxist theory does not explain the deeper meaning of social existence and the role of ideology in modern society; nor does it offer a precise explanation of "economic structure." It treats society as totally separate from the universal processes and laws of nature; for this reason, it does not take into account the heavy dependence of sociology on biology. Particularly, as represented by Lenin, it advances the erroneous theory that knowledge is absolute epistemologically (for it reflects the objectively existing external nature) and relative historically (for its depth and reliability are limited by the availability of instruments extending the power of sense organs). To Bogdanov, knowledge is relative both epistemologically (for its origin is essentially subjective) and historically. Bogdanov thought that the absolutizing of knowledge was the principal weakness of Lenin's *Materialism and Empiriocriticism*.[32] While Lenin saw no need for a psychological orientation in sociology, Bogdanov was convinced that society is essentially a psychological phenomenon. Both Lenin and Bogdanov subscribed to what each termed "philosophical monism." Lenin's monism is essentially ontological: it is based on the axiom of the material unity of the universe, both natural and cultural. Bogdanov's monism is mainly epistemological: it is based on the notion of the unity of knowledge, on the idea of "the continuity in the system of experience" and of the unity of "cognitive material" or "psychic and physical elements."[33] Despite these differences, Lenin asserted that, had Bogdanov only rid his theory of the epistemological influences of Mach and Avenarius, he would have been a true Marxist.[34] In making this statement, Lenin weighed Bogdanov's social philosophy against his practical work for the Bolshevik cause and his unwavering faith in the forthcoming supremacy of the proletariat. Lenin's criticism did not precipitate Bogdanov's abandonment of Mach's and Avenarius's philosophical influences; it did precipitate his alienation from the cause of Bolshevism.

Bogdanov defines empiriomonism as both an ideology of the productive groups of modern society and a philosophy fully congruent with natural science, the source of the most practical and socially useful knowledge. Empiriomonism, like modern technology and science, is positive and evolutionary and can be easily applied to man's ceaseless search for gradual improvements in production techniques.[35] Philosophical materialism, on the other hand, is too impractical to be of use to the ideology of the modern technical intelligentsia; it is too involved in arguments over the ontological primacy of "matter" or "spirit" to meet the intellectual and technical needs of modern society. Mach and Avenarius—and Bogdanov, too—shifted the emphasis from ontology to epistemology, and made experience, with all its practical derivations, the central topic of philosophical discussion; rather than pursuing an impractical search for the *origins* of historical and social phenomena, they sought to elucidate the social *functions* of these phenomena.

The notion of the derivation of physical elements from psychical elements led Bogdanov to identify his theory of knowledge as "historical monism" and to claim that this theory differed appreciably from both the epistemological "parallelism" of Mach and Avenarius and the materialist ontology of Marxism. He conceded that differences between psychical and physical experience had been adequately defined by Mach and Avenarius but gave himself credit for having established precise causal ties between the two. In noting that objective or physical knowledge was produced by the socialization of subjective or psychical knowledge, Bogdanov gave credit to Marx for having laid the foundations of the modern sociology of knowledge. He endorsed Marx's notion that only in social life could human experience become a reality.[36]

Socialized knowledge, that is, knowledge based on physical elements, appears, according to Bogdanov, in two basic forms: technology and ideology. These two forms apply to different areas of human activity (they are, in fact, two basic types of social processes), but both contribute to social adaptation by integrating and assessing accumulated experience and applying it to social labor.[37] Both are systems of knowledge, and knowledge is "the basic tool of human development."[38]

Placing the main emphasis on technical forms of social adaptation, Bogdanov argued that every ideology and every change in social forms ultimately derives from the technical process. The term technology, according to him, denotes not the material equipment of a society but the organization and utilization of knowledge related to external nature.[39] Techniques are reducible to knowledge, the very essence of human social existence and the primary matrix of social relations. Science is the single most powerful component of the technical process; and it, too, is responsive to accumulative technical needs. "Every scientific advance originates in the sphere of man's direct relations to nature, that is, to the sphere of 'technical experience'."[40] Ideology, "the entire sphere of social life outside the technical process," is wholly derived from technology.[41]

Technological innovations, as viewed by Bogdanov, are always progressive, for they are based on a continuous accumulation of practical experience. Ideological adaptations are not always progressive. Powerful "ideological survivals," particularly in class-structured societies, often inhibit both historically necessary ideological adjustments and timely application of new technical discoveries. Technical progress creates the dynamic conditions for social change, but ideology determines the static conditions that regulate and modify technical innovations.

Although ideological elements are secondary in origin and are determined by technical processes, they are nevertheless very important for social development: they play a vital role in organizing the "material" and the "conditions" of social development.[42] Science, the epitome of the modern age, is a bridge between technical and ideological processes, for it encompasses both practical knowledge and theoretical thought.

Bogdanov viewed the rapidly expanding institutional base of science as the most powerful force forging the theoretical (ideology) and the practical (technology) unity of scientific knowledge. Today, he observed, there are two kinds of scientists: professors who work in university laboratories (and who traditionally were the only professional group entrusted with the development of science) and technical experts working directly in industrial laboratories. Both types of laboratories are novel conceptions, for both are "scientific enterprises" with complex machinery, elaborate physical plants, and close ties with the needs of the economy. The two types of scientists do not differ in training and in social functions: they are two sides of the modern industrial equation. They are "one and the same group."[43] The unity of theoretical and practical science has laid the foundations for the unity of science and philosophy. While philosophy has become indistinguishable from science, the latter has established itself firmly as "the systematization of technical and work experience" and as "the ideology of the 'productive forces' of society."[44] "Ideology" and "technology," the wings of the modern scientific world view, are united in their unflinching adherence to positivism and evolutionism, the former based on the denial of knowledge not susceptible to verification and the latter based on the idea of inexorable progress.

Bogdanov constantly emphasized the accelerated growth of secular knowledge as the quintessence of modern civilization. The growth of productive social forces and the resultant expansion of man's control over nature find a direct expression in scientific knowledge. While beliefs in idols and fetishes express the weakness of human society in its struggle with nature, additions to scientific knowledge mark forward steps in man's search for the full control of nature. "Where man is not victorious over nature there is the birth of fetishism."[45] Bogdanov was concerned with the negative influences of fetishes and idols as much as he was with the positive contributions of science. With regard to fetishes and idols, he stated:

Our life is still steeped in fetishes, and idols are all around us. They guide our behavior and they fill the gaps in our knowledge. The entire economic existence of modern man is permeated by the fetish known as exchange value, which interprets the working relations among men as quantities of things. The entire legal and moral existence is under the influence of idols—of juridical and ethical norms which are presented to members of society not as expressions of their own real relations but as fully independent forces, exercising pressure on men and demanding strict adherence to them. Even in the field of science, the laws of nature are viewed by most people not as real relations among things but as independent realities which rule the world. Polytheism did not die: it has only been twisted and somewhat weakened; from a vivid religious form it has been transformed into a pale metaphysical form. Theoretical knowledge about the real meaning of these idols and fetishes is still limited; even those to whom this knowledge is available find it almost impossible to rid their everyday activities of a subconscious influence of fetishes.... External defeats, inflicted on it by scientific knowledge, did not destroy fetishism but merely reduced its power. But, in any case, at the present time the kingdom of fetishism is thoroughly disorganized and is experiencing accelerated disintegration. Its power over man has been shaken, and its internal links have been strained.[46]

Negative or not, fetishes and idols are social facts. Like scientific truths, they are expressions of accumulated social experience. Although they reflect both the state of technical progress and the basic principles of social bonds. they are merely substitutes for positive knowledge; they are strongest in the areas of social behavior in which science has not asserted itself. But they also find their way into science and philosophy when these serve as expressions of class ideologies. The concept of the "thing-in-itself" is the cornerstone of both the Kantian theory of knowledge and Newtonian mechanics; however in both cases it is a fetish, for it is merely an expression of the search for absolutes, a search sociologically congruent with the authoritative nature of the earlier industrial society. The modern social orientation and neopositivist philosophy have rejected both epistemological objectivism (the knowability of the Kantian "thing-in-itself") and ontological materialism (as embodied in Newtonian science) and have identified themselves with a new ideology which has substituted relativism for absolutism in epistemology, and democratic particularism for absolutist universalism in social and political relations. Not the cognitive impenetrability of the "thing-in-itself" but the dynamics of interacting forces of nature and society is the guiding idea of modern science and modern industrial society.

Bogdanov devoted much attention to functional details of the process of social integration and differentiation. In his opinion, organizational adaptations are the most important processes of integration, operating in both technological and ideological domains. They appear in many forms, three of which—direct communication, cognitive systems, and normative constraints—are of foremost significance.

The most elementary forms of organizational adaptation belong to the general category of direct communication—communication by word and facial expression—which helps coordinate and integrate elementary human activities and psychic relations connected with these activities. "Facial expressions and words represent systems of signs whereby the experiences of individuals are pooled and 'socialized'."[47] At the lowest level of social development, the entire lexicon consists of a small number of words designating technical activities and the tools of labor necessary in the struggle with the forces of nature. The forms of direct communication are the first instruments which transform the social instinct of the primeval forms of human life into a "higher form of altruism."

Cognitive forms of organizational adaptation consist of conceptions and judgments, and their complex combinations (religious doctrines, for example), which add to the adaptive power of socially useful knowledge by raising it to increasingly higher levels of abstraction. Bogdanov argued that Marx and Mach were the first to come up with a satisfactory formulation of the social role of knowledge in the struggle for existence.[48] He was particularly interested in the links between the "forms of labor" and the "forms of knowledge." "The very character of knowledge depends directly on the character of social labor. Thus, in the epochs in which the forms of labor are stable, conservative, and dominated by habit, knowledge is *static*: all concepts and ideas present the picture of *immobile* and *immutable* nature."[49] On the other hand, in societies in which the forms of labor are mobile and mutable, knowledge is dominated by historicism: the idea of progress permeates all thinking and nature appears as a "continuous series of processes."

Normative forms of organizational adaptation reduce contradictions in social life by limiting particular functions which, if left uncurbed, would create disharmony and conflict. Their origin is in primordial customs, the ancestor of customary law, morality, and positive law.[50] Bogdanov warned that normative forms—whether expressed in customs and values or in law—have a tendency to become "sacred tradition," "absolute duty," or "pure justice" by detaching themselves from the concrete needs and interests of the members of society. The more "absolute" moral precepts and values are, the more removed they are from social reality. Unbridled optimism about the future of human society led Bogdanov to believe that normative (or coercive) forms would eventually lose their raison d'être and would cease to exist. He made no effort to document his statement that the more advanced a society is, the less it depends on the normative forms of organizational adaptations.

Bogdanov argued that the more advanced a society is, the more it depends on ideology as a reigning ingredient of the various forms of organizational adaptation. This did not prevent him from comparing the three generic forms of organizational adaptation with the nervous system. The forms of direct communication are analogous to the simple transmission of excitation through nervous cells and tissues from one part of the organism to another. Cognitive forms correspond to the formation and transformation of complex connections between various psychomotor reactions. Normative forms are analogous to the inhibitory functions of the central nervous system. He admitted, however, that the analogy is imperfect for it does not compare two equally complex phenomena but a "whole" (society) with particular parts of an organism.

Social adaptation, an extension of natural adaptation, holds the key for a full understanding of the historical nature of social phenomena. Its basic operative mechanism is social selection, which produces either positive results, when it creates the forms of adaptation that add to the intensity and plasticity of social life; or negative results, when it brings forth the forms of adjustment that reduce both the quality and the intensity of social energy. While positive social selection produces social progress, negative selection produces social regress.[51] The idea of progress, a dominant theme of classical sociology, is deeply rooted in Bogdanov's system of social thought. To him social progress is an extension of natural progress: just as natural progress is measured by the expansion of living energy and by the diversification of the forms of life, so social progress is indicated by the expansion of social energy and the growing division of social labor, the former contributing to the "fullness of social life" and the latter to social harmony.[52] Again, just as social progress is an extension of natural progress, so sociology is an extension of biology.[53]

The task of the sociologist is made difficult by the existence of two different definitions of progress: one definition is objective, dynamic and scientific, the other is subjective, static, and metaphysical. The objective definition regards social evolution as a process leading to a "complete" and "fully harmonious" social existence; the subjective definition views progress in terms of the particularistic values of individual groups or classes. The objective definition views progress as infinite; the subjective definition depicts progress as a finite realization of the ideals of individual groups or classes. The objective definition sees progress as a derivation from the socioeconomic infrastructure of society: to it, morality, as a derivative force, cannot account for social progress. The subjective definition presents progress in moral terms and treats morality as a quality irreducible to the material conditions of life: it operates on the assumption that moral purity is the propelling force of social progress. The objective view of progress is causal: it recognizes no predetermined and transcendental goals and views social life as a product of causally explained activities of infrastructural forces. The subjective view of progress is teleological: it regards the course of history as a gradual realization of a final goal which determines the main lines of social change.

The function of the sociologist, according to Bogdanov, is not merely to formulate a scientific definition of progress but also to examine and combat pseudoscientific notions of progress. He recognizes, however, that, despite its unscientific qualities, the subjective definition of progress must be recognized as an important component of social reality inasmuch as it reflects the thinking and the sentiments of various segments of the population and inasmuch as it reflects elements of dissonance in the interrelations between the vital components of the social structure. The task of the sociologist is to establish the magnitude of discrepancies between the objective and subjective interpretations of progress in specific societies. The sociologist must not overlook the possibility of a congruence of objective and subjective notions of progress which takes place when group "ideals" concur with "real progress"—when the "ideal" is "an expression, even though a partial one, of historical development."[54] "The classes that are unhampered by a narrow range of vision can produce in due course a historical and objective notion of progress. They can both comprehend the historical nature of the ideals of progress and give them an abstract formulation. Such an ideal, expressed by a leading European thinker, is universal cooperation for universal development."[55]

Bogdanov devoted much attention to the processes of social differentiation, particularly to stratification. While noting that the study of society as "a living whole with a single orientation in the selection of social forms" is the most important task of sociological scholarship, he readily admitted that this approach is correct only up to a certain point.[56] To do a thorough job, a student of social structure must also investigate the components of society which enjoy relative independence. The division of labor in society inevitably leads to the formation of groups with independent criteria for selecting and incorporating social innovations. In his analysis of social differentiation, stimulated by the division of labor, Bogdanov was concerned particularly with the emergence, evolution, and sociological attributes of social classes. The division of labor in society does not by itself lead to the formation of classes: as long as differences induced by the division of labor do not threaten the fundamental unity of society, they are not social-class ingredients. In this situation, the processes of social selection lead to a harmonization of relations between social "fragments" by working out common organizing principles. But when the emphasis on differences and contradictions is so great that individual social components evolve their own organizing principles then ideologies emerge. Without ideologies, there are no true social classes. Although the base of social classes is in the technical process, they are organized by ideology.[57] The technical process is the dynamic factor of social selection and adaptation—the motive force of social evolution; the ideological process is the static factor of social selection and adaptation—it "limits, regulates, and organizes" the products of social evolution.

There are several types of class development: the extremes are classical slavery and modern capitalism. All other types are structural variations and combinations of these two types. Slavery and capitalist systems have a common characteristic: the organizing—or dominant—class in each gradually becomes detached from the technical processes of production and in time loses the real organizing functions and becomes a parasitic group.

Despite external similarities, each type of class formation has a distinct origin and unique social attributes. In the ancient type, anchored in the patriarchal natural economy, the organizing power of the masters grew gradually until it covered the total existence of slaves. The bond between the master and the slave was fixed, that is, it could not be broken by the will of the state. The dependence of the slave on the will of the master was total and irrevocable. The workingman was transformed into a tool of production. The extreme exploitation of slaves by their masters brought about the process of the irreversible decline of the social system built upon the institution of slavery. Technical progress came to an end. Slave ideology did not develop beyond an embryonic state, and class struggle was absent. Degeneration of both classes culminated in the disorganization and destruction of the entire system of social relations.

The capitalist class system originated in the petty-bourgeois organization of production. The entrepreneur controlled only a part of the worker's existence—the working day. The bond between the entrepreneur and the worker was flexible, contractual. This type of class development led to a progressive transformation of the amorphous mass of workers into a collectivity able to respond to the constantly expanding organizational role of entrepreneurs. Fast technical progress, characteristic of this type of class development, stimulated an equally fast development of antagonistic class ideologies and an irreconcilable class warfare. The real source of modern class struggle is in the differential attitudes of the two classes toward technical progress: while the bourgeoisie views technical progress as a vehicle for widening the scope of the exploitation of the working class, the latter sees in it a way to a qualitative, that is, a revolutionary, change in social structure.[58] Every revolution has a "motive force" and an "organizing force": irreconcilable contradictions in the social organization of production and class ideologies are the "motive force"; class consciousness is the "organizing force."[59] There is no "genetic continuity" and stability in the composition of individual economic collectivities or social classes, for in a capitalist system there are neither kinship nor personal bonds for a stable class organization. In capitalist society social classes are subject to faster change than in any other type of society.

Social classes, Bogdanov noted, are not only specific groups based on distinct positions in the organization of production but are also clearly demarcated subcultures. Since each class has a unique source of experience, many "common" concepts have in reality different meanings.[60] The class status affects and shapes the entire process of cognition. The meaning of such notions as "idealism," "ideal," and "progress" varies from one social class to another. "The bourgeoisie sees regress in everything in which its ideological adversaries see a high point of progress." Like orthodox Marxists, Bogdanov considered the bourgeoisie and the proletariat the two pivotal classes of modern society; however, unlike orthodox Marxists, he placed considerable emphasis on the fact that between the two class extremes there is "an infinite number of transitions, nuances, and combinations."[61]

Bogdanov was very careful in distinguishing the relations between the proletariat and the bourgeoisie from those between the proletariat and the "technical intelligentsia," the bourgeoisie's organizing arm in the process of production. The first relationship is dominated by conflict, the second by cooperation. The first relationship is primarily that of one social class to another; the second relationship is primarily that of one professional group to another. Accordingly, the proletariat's role in the production process is only partly connected with its social-class identification. While the gap separating the proletariat from the bourgeoisie as two social classes is steadily growing wider, the gap between the proletariat and the "technical intelligentsia," as two professional groups, is steadily shrinking. Marxist sociologists placed primary emphasis on the conflict between the proletariat and the bourgeoisie; Bogdanov stressed the expanding community of interests of the workers and the "technical intelligentsia." The work of manual labor is becoming increasingly organizational and intellectual, and has begun to resemble the work of the "technical intelligentsia."[62]

Bogdanov dealt extensively with the problem of the "fragmentation of personality" as a source of alienation in industrial society. He advanced a theory according to which the fragmentation of personality was more typical of the early stage of industrial civilization than of the advanced stage. The technology of early industry emphasized strict specialization in production equipment and mechanical processes. This emphasis "crippled the body and the soul of the worker" by narrowing the range of his experience, competence, intellectual endeavor, and social identification.[63] Modern industrial production emphasizes "the knowledge of general methods" rather than "the familiarity with infinite details." It replaces fragmented work assignments by participation in complex systems of the technological process, a prelude to the coming full automation of industrial production. The unity of science as a "systematization of techniques" triumphs over the diversity of rigid specialization. While the early industrial technology reflected the fragmented nature of empirical science, the modern industrial technology reflects the integrated nature of theoretical science. The acute awareness of the unifying patterns of various types of work and the advanced scientific level of production offer the worker a broader scope of experience, responsibility, and intellectual involvement and, thereby, a new and higher integration of cultural values—and of personality.[64] While Marx saw in the economic organization of modern industrial production the main source of the alienation of the worker, Bogdanov saw in modern technological advances, and in modern science, a new condition contributing to the realization of the "wholeness" of personality. Although he did not argue against Marx's thesis, he clearly implied that the technological base of personality integration is more fundamental than the economic base of personality fragmentation.

Bogdanov believed that a new society, dominated by the proletariat, would eventually arise; but he was convinced that the proletariat could emerge victorious only by absorbing the progressive traditions of the bourgeoisie and "technical intelligentsia." In fact, he regarded the gradual eradication of the differences in the acquisition, modernization, and dissemination of technical and scientific knowledge as the main factor in the dynamics of social-class relations.[65] The proletariat, according to him, is a product of the material and nonmaterial culture of the modern industrial society. He wrote: "The proletariat has learned and will learn from bourgeois classes—in this lies one of the sources of its strength. The greatest ideologue of the working class [Marx] understood this from the very beginning. The economic science of bourgeois classes, the dialectical method of Hegel's bourgeois philosophy, the realism of bourgeois materialism, and the critique of capitalist social relations presented mainly by petty-bourgeois utopians—all these Marx incorporated, in a transmuted form, into the basic material of the new [proletarian] ideology. This synthesis contained no eclecticism and no compromises with the bourgeois world view."[66] Bogdanov stood somewhere in the middle between the Populist sociologists, who treated growing cooperation (Mikhailovskii) or solidarity (Lavrov) as the real index of social progress, and orthodox Marxists, who saw in class conflict the historical force of primary significance.

Bogdanov's theory of social-class dynamics differs from the orthodox Marxist theory in yet another important respect. While he recognized the role of "contradictions" in socioeconomic formations that harbor antagonistic social classes, Bogdanov generally had very little use for dialectics. He thought that both Hegel and Marx, by offering an imprecise formulation of dialectics, invited arbitrary interpretations. Instead of dialectics, Bogdanov stressed "moving equilibrium" as the basic process in the development of nature and society. All components of a society are engaged in a constant search for an equilibrium in their interaction and their relations to the total natural and social environment. In capitalist society, Bogdanov argued, the equilibration of interacting—and contending—social forces is achieved with the help of "external norms," that is, the norms generated and enforced by the state, rather than with the help of "internal norms," that is, the norms generated by society itself and applied without the resort to institutionalized coercion.[67] The future society, the society unencumbered by "external norms," will come about as a result of the gradual but inexorable growth of technology rather than by revolutionary political action. Technology alone can create the prerequisite conditions for the growth of social cooperation and for a full elimination of social-class conflict.

The aim of the scientific study of society, according to Bogdanov, is to rise above the "subjectivism" of class ideologies and to establish "objective truths"—"to express the life experience of all mankind" rather than of particular groups.[68] Only by dedication to universal truths can scientists hope to be in a position to undertake an objective analysis of ideologically colored views of various classes and groups. The history of social science is the history of improvements in the rigor of the scientific method. And the history of the scientific method is the gradual progress in logical procedures for distilling "typical," "repetitive," and "noncontradictory" elements from the mass of human experience. In general, in its task to disentangle the previously hidden mysteries of nature and society, science must wage a continual war on class bias.

TEKTOLOGY: THE GENERAL SCIENCE OF ORGANIZATION

Just as Bogdanov's elaboration of empiriomonism was a direct continuation of his previous studies in the "historical view of nature" and in the philosophy and sociology of knowledge, so his work on a new science, labeled tektology, was the offshoot of empiriomonism. Despite a basic continuity in the evolution of his thought, it should be stressed that, while empiriomonism is concerned mainly with the philosophical foundations of a general theory of society, tektology is presented as a "general natural science." Bogdanov borrowed the term "tektology" from Ernst Haeckel, who used it to designate a branch of morphology dealing with the organism as a complex system of morphons of various orders. In Bogdanov's usage, tektology is a science dealing with processes which regulate the organization of all systems of natural and social phenomena. He contended that all the universal aspects of both society and nature can be revealed by studying the laws of organization. He noted that individual sciences deal with the particular aspects of the universal theory of organization: mathematics, for example, studies "all kinds of complexes in a state of equilibrium." Bogdanov proposed to develop a comprehensive science that would synthesize the knowledge accumulated by specialized disciplines. Tektology, he said, "combines the abstract symbolism of mathematics with the experimental character of the natural sciences."[69] It is universal because it embraces the entire world of experience; yet it is primarily a sociohistorical science, for human society is the central problem of its inquiry.

Tektology is fully congruent with Bogdanov's philosophic orientation. It is empirical inasmuch as it considers experience the only source of scientific knowledge; and it is monistic inasmuch as it assumes the operation of the same structural principles at every level of reality. (Dialectical materialism, according to Bogdanov, is a "nonmonistic" theory, for it claims that nature and society are qualitatively different realities governed by different sets of laws.)[70] Tektology assumes that the organization of human experience reflects the organization of the universe—that human thought is as tektological as the rest of nature.[71]

Bogdanov conceptualized a world in which conflict is overshadowed by a general harmony, or complementarity, of universal processes, and in which all change is essentially gradual. He viewed conflict as an indispensable step in the growth of cooperation. Social harmony, he said, is a reconcilation, rather than the nonexistence, of social contradictions. Cooperation, not less than freedom and equality, is a cultural value that can emerge only in societies which have experienced suppression and inequality.[72] In the same vein, he viewed "disorganization" as a special form of organization. Both organization and disorganization follow the same pattern; the only difference is that organization is larger than the sum total of its individual components, whereas "disorganization is smaller."[73]

As conceived tektologically, the organizational approach is both structural and dynamic. It is structural, for it relies on a holistic view of natural and social systems; it considers a natural or social system irreducible to its component parts. According to Bogdanov, the more a system differs from the sum total of its component parts, the higher is the level of its organization. The organizational approach is dynamic inasmuch as it is concerned with continuous changes of an adaptive and selective nature. Tektology studies not only the differentiation and convergence of existing forms but also the forces contributing to the maintenance of intra- and intersystem equilibria. Bogdanov stresses "moving equilibrium" as an area of inquiry in which the structural and dynamic aspects of organization are only two different sides of the same reality. His mechanism of organization is dominated by "motion" and equilibrium; while orthodox Marxists treat equilibrium as a specific state of motion, Bogdanov views motion as a specific expression of equilibrium.

Organization, as a universal attribute of nature and society, operates through regulative and formative mechanisms. The regulative mechanism accounts for the maintenance or the preservation of the stability of such systems as a society, a social class, an organism, or a planet. It also helps maintain the continuity of natural and social development, which eliminates cataclysmic changes. Selection, the most universal tool of the regulative mechanism, is subject to growing specialization in both nature and society. One of the basic tasks of tektology is to reduce the multitude of selective processes to a small number of fundamental categories. In the scheme of selection there are three components: the object of selection, the act of selection, and the criteria of selection. Nature is the primary object of selection, social labor is the primary act of selection, and the usefulness of objects which surround man is the basic criterion of selection. Selection is "conservative" when it produces "static results," which contribute to the maintenance of a "stable equilibrium"; it is "progressive" when it produces "dynamic results," which evoke changes in the existing—or bring forth new—organizational forces. It is "positive" when it leads to a larger heterogeneity of elements and an increased complexity of internal relations; it is "negative" when it leads to growing homogeneity of elements and reduced complexity of ties between them.[74]

The formative mechanism explains the emergence and development of the most general forms of organization. The term "conjugation" denotes the most universal process of the integration of various principles into specific forms of organization. It is expressed in several basic types of bonds, which attracted much of Bogdanov's attention. Ingression stands for reversible bonds: the relations between A and B are indistinguishable from the relations between B and A. Ingression is illustrated by two rings in an iron chain, two identical crystals, or two soldiers of the same rank. It is the basic law of continuity in the universe. Egression designates the dominant type of irreversible bonds. The "centralized" systems are the best examples of egression; their essential characteristic is the absence of the bonds of equivalence between constituent parts. The sun and the earth belong to the same natural system—and the monarch and his subjects to the same social system—but they have no bonds of equivalence and are not functionally reversible. Egression plays a particularly important role in the living world. Most multicellular organisms are centralized systems: in each organism the brain is the organizational center for all other organs. The neural communication is irreversible, inasmuch as the neural tissues which transmit impulses from the brain to other parts of the body are completely separate from the neural tissues which transmit excitations to the brain.[75] Many social groups among men and animals are organized along the principles of egression. In human society, egression finds its best and most common expression in authoritative organizations typified by the family, bureaucracy, despotic monarchy, and the army. However, egression is more limited than ingression because it designates systems with finite numbers of complexes. While ingression chains may have infinite numbers of components, egression chains are bound by a central system at the top and a limited number of components at the bottom.[76]

Degression, the third basic process of universal integration of natural and social phenomena, is the opposite of egression. In egression the central, or organizing part (the brain, for example) is the most complex component of the given system; in degression, the central part is the least complex component of the given system. The skeleton of an organism provides the best example of degression; it is made of organic and inorganic matter of a relatively low complexity, but without it the brain would be unable to achieve a high level of complexity.[77] Words occupy the central position in the system of human communication; yet they are much simpler than the complex psychological processes to which they give external expression. While dominated by opposite organizational principles, degression and egression may be functionally complementary. The typical example for this complementarity is the organism in which the brain is the egressive center while the skeleton is the degressive center.[78]

Degression generally designates a conservative network of bonds in natural and social systems; it emanates from the most stable components of systems which resist change. In comparison with other systems, degressive systems are characterized by rigidity of organization. They are most typically expressed in formal organizations which may last for centuries even though they may cease to meet all functional requirements. Inasmuch as it is concerned with the transmission and preservation of values as components of sacred culture, education is essentially a degressive process. The major function of degressive processes is to preserve the equilibrium in natural and social systems—to avert revolutionary leaps. Although relative stability is their characteristic, degressive systems undergo change, primarily as a result of adaptation to complex systems.

Bogdanov contended that the ultimate intent of tektology is not merely to describe the overall structure of the social world but to produce reliable information for reshaping it. However, his immediate aim was purely theoretical: the construction of models expressing "the forms of our thought about organization combinations" and revealing the basic structural principles of universal organization.[79] Bogdanov's organization theory marked a radical departure from Marxist philosophy: while in Marxist thought "dialectics" is a universal law of change in nature and society, in Bogdanov's tektological view it is only a small component of a more universal organizational process.[80] In the opinion of a Marxist critic, the tektological theory offered a revision of "all the fundamental concepts of Marxism-Leninism."[81] In one respect, however, Bogdanov remained true to the Marxist tradition: he made the theory of universal organization a specific expression of his belief in science as the only cultural force that can guide mankind to previously unscaled heights of social progress. However, he reasoned that social progress can be assured not by present-day science, fragmented into hundreds of specialized branches, but by a new general science, "combining the entire organizational experience of mankind."[82] In the past, philosophy had a monopoly on the idea of the unity of society, as a special manifestation of the unity of the universe. Since the philosophical idea of unity is too abstract and too deeply steeped in fetishism, it must be replaced by a scientific theory based on a comprehensive study of "the methods and forms of organization."

Bogdanov's tektology shows elementary similarities with cybernetics. The concept of feedback, essential to all cybernetic systems, finds a place in Bogdanov's intricate tektological system under the name of "biregulator." Like cyberneticists, he built the tektological system on the formal similarities between neurophysiological systems, the structure of language, mathematical symbolism, and formal sociology. His theory of moving equilibrium shows much similarity with Ludwig Von Bertalanffy's theory of "open systems": both extend the Le Chatelier principle to all dynamic systems. According to a modern commentator, tektology, as a general theory, covers not only cybernetic principles, that is, the principles of information systems, but also the "hierarchical orders" in the relations between systems and the principles depicting the origin and disintegration of systems.[83]

Bogdanov may be counted among the pioneers of the general systems theory. He claimed that a discipline concerned with systems must be a special kind of science, drawing its substance from several established branches of mathematics and the natural sciences. His real contribution lay in pointing out the necessity and the feasibility of such a science, rather than in developing a system of useful scientific propositions. His tektological formulations are often vague, even in the construction of basic concepts, and the entire system lacks symmetry and logical precision. However, his ideas are bold, and his search for sociologically fruitful research models is a well-planned step in the right direction. He was one of the first Russian social theorists to undertake a detailed study of the epistemological domain where the social and natural sciences meet and where mathematical symbolism can be applied profitably to the scientific study of social behavior.[84] He was the most original Russian social thinker engaged in the study of processes which subordinate human society to the universal laws of nature. Unfortunately, Bogdanov made no effort to apply his grand design to the study of actual social existence, and left it completely untested. He was among the pioneers of the modern search for a grand theory of sociology who, preoccupied with the universal aspects of the human condition, operated far above the vagaries of everyday existence, and whose theoretical constructions were irreducible to designs for empirical research. He tried to make sociology a physics of social action at the time when classical physics, staggered by an ongoing revolution of profound philosophical significance, was too unsettled to serve as a model for other sciences. His sociology incorporates an idealistic view of knowledge and a mechanistic view of nature and society.

Although he was ignored by the wide spectrum of idealistic philosophers and bitterly condemned by orthodox Marxists, including both Plekhanov and Lenin, Bogdanov was one of the most original, productive, and accomplished Russian social philosophers of his generation. Few Russian sociologists matched the depth of his analysis, the scope of his interests, and the courage of his pioneering zeal.

Conclusion

Most major Western European schools of sociology found able representatives in Russia. The Russians were not mere imitators of Western thought; consistently they reworked Western theories to fit the specific realities of their history, social dynamics, and political ideologies. In some orientations, typified by the biological school of social theory, their contributions were equal to those of English, German, or French scholars.[1] The pioneering work of M. M. Kovalevskii in comparative history as a type of empirical sociology was widely acclaimed in the West. In some other orientations Russian social theorists were ahead of Western sociological thought. The subjective sociology of Mikhailovskii and Lavrov anticipated the efforts of neo-Kantians to marshal epistemological and logical arguments in favor of ridding social theory of a heavy reliance on natural science models. Petr Kropotkin acknowledged many intellectual ancestors for his theory of anarchism; yet he was the first to make a systematic effort to translate anarchism into an integrated and comprehensive social theory and to draw clear lines separating this theory from the views of such stalwarts of nineteenth-century sociological thought as Auguste Comte, Karl Marx, and Herbert Spencer. With his work in tektology, A. A. Bogdanov must be counted one of the pioneers of the general systems theory and of various structuralist schools in sociology concerned with the cybernetic qualities of human society.

Underneath pronounced methodological, philosophical, and ideological differences that split Russian social theorists into feuding camps, there were basic similarities in the choice of topics for primary emphasis and particular explanatory principles. All social theorists were ideological warriors and their theories were designs for a better future. And exactly for the reason that sociology was dedicated to a search for a betterment of the human condition, it was not recognized as a legitimate field of inquiry and was kept out of the school curricula. For this reason, most sociologists worked outside the academic community, and most were directly identified with ideological movements demanding radical changes in the structure of Russian society. As a punishment for illicit political activities, eighty percent of the leading sociologists served prison terms, and one-half spent some time in enforced exile either in isolated provincial towns of Russia or abroad. Of all social thinkers involved in the search for a scientific theory of society, only

N. Ia. Danilevskii stood close to the key values of the sacred culture of autocratic Russia.

As in the West, Russian social theories dealt extensively with the laws and periodization of the evolutionary process. Most sociologists treated social evolution as a coalescence of two major processes: a passive and an active evolution. They viewed passive evolution as a "natural" phenomenon: a spontaneous and mechanical process, analogous to "natural selection" in biology. In active evolution, they saw an analogue to "artificial selection" in biology: a product of purposive action. These two evolutions were not separate: "passive evolution" provided the root system for "active evolution." Initially passive, evolution gradually became active. The higher the level a society reached on the scale of evolution, the more extensive purposive social action became.[2]

All theories, with the exception of N. Ia. Danilevskii's, were dominated by a general idea of social progress; social progress, in turn, was presented as a negation of the values upon which the autocratic system was erected. Even Danilevskii, who presented a highly original theory of the cyclical nature of the universal history of society and culture, did not deny that future civilizations would meet the needs of humanity more thoroughly than previous civilizations. Even when they emphasized the sociocultural uniqueness of Russia, as in the case of Populist sociologists, they drew the picture of the future in terms of the universal ideals of humanity. Regardless of whether the idea of progress was based on the Comtian positivist theory of three stages of intellectual development, cultural evolutionism inspired by Darwin's theory, the dialectics of Marxian materialism, or a broad metaphysical assumption, it was also a call to action against the champions and defenders of the social status quo.

For the leading Russian social theorists the most meaningful and powerful indices of social progress tended to be the secularization of wisdom and the emergence of the individual as a creator of society and history.

The secularization of wisdom, as a sociological category, received its first, and clearest, formulation in the writings of the intellectuals of the 1860s, who called themselves "realists" but were more popularly known as Nihilists. Inspired by the positivist intellectualism of Auguste Comte, the logic of "moral sciences" presented by John Stuart Mill, and the popular comments on the role of science in modern society advanced by Vogt and Moleschott, these writers recognized three essential attributes of progress: the irreversible victories of rationalism over mysticism, the progressive affirmation of individuality in the interpretation of values and experience, and the continuous expansion of the utilitarian principle in the social assessment of knowledge. True, many sociologists wrote about the increasing scope of social solidarity or cooperation as the real indicators of progress, but they saw solidarity or cooperation as social forces with a cognitive base. The succeeding generations of social theorists resented the excessive scientism of Nihilist philosophy, but they seldom deviated from the view that the growth of verifiable and useful knowledge was the main engine of social evolution. In the words of N. I. Kareev, social progress is measured by the achieved level of man's understanding of history as a revelation of the "meaning of life."[3] The exaltation of rational knowledge was not merely an expression of idealistic fervor; it was a profound criticism of the autocratic system and the church, which were united by an ideology that, in its heavy reliance on supernatural authority and irrationalist philosophy, stood in the way of a more efficient modernization of Russian society and politics.

In their preoccupation with rationalism as the measuring stick of progress, Russian sociologists considered it an imperative duty to fight idealistic metaphysics as a source of wisdom. To them, the attack on metaphysics was not merely an attack on what they considered to be antiquated systems of cognition; it was also an attack on anachronistic social institutions. Idealistic metaphysicists, who articulated and defended autocratic ideology, were nearly unanimous in their claim that human society, as a product of divine action, could not be comprehended by a reliance on the tools of science and empirical knowledge. Official ideologues looked at every defense of scientific social theory as an attack on the divine will embodied in autocratic institutions. All sociologists defended, or thought they were defending, political democracy; the metaphysical critics of sociology were nearly unanimous in their condemnation of democracy in any form and shape.

If knowledge is the measuring stick of social progress, then intellectuals, entrusted with the advancement and diffusion of knowledge, must be social catalysts of the first order. The idea that the members of the intelligentsia were the real human agents responsible for social progress was one of the dominant themes of Russian sociology. Sociological literature was replete with apotheoses to "new men" (Shelgunov), "thinking realists" (Pisarev), "critically thinking individuals" (Lavrov and Mikhailovskii), and individuals who were "heroes" because their activities were a "conscious and free expression" of the inevitable and unconscious course of social development (Plekhanov). As the guiding force of social progress, the intelligentsia was not merely a generator and a custodian of socially useful knowledge; its function was also to harness this knowledge for social progress. It consisted of activists engaged in accelerating social evolution. Just as the intelligentsia was the central theme of sociological inquiry, so sociology was essentially an effort to articulate and codify the ideology of the intelligentsia.

Mikhailovskii was the first to express the view that the intelligentsia should not be considered a distinct social class, but a unique amalgam of individuals hailing from all status groups. This contention was shared by a majority of sociologists, including Tugan-Baranovskii after his break with Marxist orthodoxy. The combination of the emphases on the intelligentsia as the prime mover of social evolution and as a group transcending the boundaries of individual social classes was an important factor influencing the social theorist to place relatively little emphasis on social-class stratification. The Russian Marxists dealt with the dynamics of social classes appreciably less than their Western counterparts. A typical social theorist, influenced by the power of Populist arguments and the weight of demographic statistics, dealt much more extensively with the unifying attributes of the people (*narod*) than with the disunifying attributes of social classes. To a typical social theorist, the peasants were the *narod*, not a social class.

If the secularization of wisdom is the main path of social evolution, and if the function of the intelligentsia is to translate the secular wisdom into designs for a better social existence, the question of the essence of the secularization of wisdom remains. Although few sociologists shared the scientistic excesses of Nihilist leaders, most of them saw in science the purest and most potent expression of secular wisdom, and the most reliable source of guideposts for a modernization of society. In the eighteenth century, Mikhail Lomonosov, "the Father of Russian Science," spoke on behalf of the burgeoning intelligentsia when he looked forward to the emergence of Russian Platos and Newtons; in the nineteenth century, the great chemist D. I. Mendeleev represented the new intelligentsia when he said that Russia had no need for native Platos, only for native Newtons. The future of Russia, according to him, was in the hands of physics, not of metaphysics. He was the first to admit, however, that the contribution of science to social progress was more in providing means than in defining ends.

Echoing Mendeleev, most of the leading Russian sociologists devoted considerable attention to the multiplicity of problems which subsequently became the province of the sociology of science. They dealt extensively with such problems as the relationship of science to the moral code, the role of science in the diffusion of democratic ideals, and the growing power of science as both a specific mode of inquiry and a world view. They also showed a keen interest in the differences between the laws of the development of society and the laws of the growth of science, and in the synchronization of the obligations of the scientist as a member of the scientific community and as a member of the society at large. Russian sociologists were pioneers in the study of sociologically relevant relations between the natural sciences and the social sciences, the growing adaptability of nonscientific modes of inquiry to science, and the relationship of science to the dominant values of national cultures. An astonishing characteristic of Russian sociology was that it dealt very little with religion, at least directly; but it can be safely assumed that the voluminous attacks on spiritualistic metaphysics and mysticism covered the official religion as both a system of doctrines and an ideology of the autocratic state.

The notion of social evolution as a growing realization of individuality in social action was the second conceptual pillar of the theory of progress. According to Lavrov, to study human history means to study real individuals, who are motivated by "custom, sentiment, interest, or conviction" and who "struggle for survival by tools of solidarity and the development of cognitive processes."[4] To Bogdanov, the evolution of personality is an important index of the evolution of society. During the first phase of social evolution, according to him, there was no personality to speak of, for no individual was separated from society in any basic attributes of his psychological makeup. His life was a life of habits, fully shaped by the norms of a sacred culture intolerant of change.[5] The individual was a passive member of society; cognition as an active process of interpreting the world had not yet appeared. The second phase, divided into several major substages, was characterized, first, by the emergence of the individual not merely as a product but also as a creator, of society; and, second, by a growing "fragmentation" of personality, which was a result of the growing division of labor and was a major source of alienation. The third phase, ushered in by the rapid growth of "machine production" and the intellectualization of labor, set the stage for a full integration of personality—for a full synchronization of the interests of society and the individual. Mikhailovskii, on the other hand, sought the help from certain national Russian institutions to avert the modern technological specialization, the inevitable source of the fragmentation of personality. Bogdanov treated social classes as an indispensable step in the evolution of relations between society and the individual. Mikhailovskii, on the other hand, regarded social classes as an aberration in the "struggle for individuality," the essence of social evolution.

The inordinate emphasis on the individual as a category of social theory was undoubtedly a reaction to the underemphasis on the individual in the total configuration of Russian social institutions and political values. Viktor Chernov was correct in stating that the unceasing search for "individuality" was an expression of the groping for emancipation of the individual from the rigid and total control imposed by family patriarchalism and state authoritarianism. To emphasize the growing role of the individual in social evolution was to emphasize the coming victories of the democratic process in political, social, and economic relations. The concern with the individual was not limited to the study of the processes whereby a human animal is transformed into an active link in social cooperation. The study of socialization as an internalization of social values and as a source of cultural stability and social conformism was matched by a study of the residual nonconformism of the individual as the only true source of sociocultural change. Sociologists were concerned less with the individual who represented a full internalization of dominant values (and stagnant conformism) than with the individual at odds with values standing in the way of progress. The individual was consistently viewed as both a product of society and a social catalyst.

Much of the social criticism generated by sociologists was centered on the conditions impeding a full and harmonious development of personality. This criticism reached deeply not only into the value system born in the era of feudalism but also into the potential dangers of accelerated technological progress. Russian sociologists were the first non-Marxists to take seriously and to elaborate upon Marx's forewarning about the forces of alienation operating in industrial society.

Nineteenth-century Western sociologists are often divided into two major groups, depending on whether they espoused "social solidarity" or "social conflict" as the prime mover of history. The solidarity theories received a powerful boost from Auguste Comte's grandiose elaboration of the "social consensus," the principle according to which the elements of a social system could be best understood if they were viewed in the light of solidarity as the general principle of social integration. Emile Durkheim saw in the gradual transition from "mechanical solidarity" to "organic solidarity" the very essence of universal social evolution. The conflict theories received the strongest impetus from Darwin's evolutionary theory, but they were helped also by Marx's theory of class struggle as a prime force of social evolution. The solidarity theory found a fertile soil in Russia and was endorsed and elaborated by an overwhelming majority of sociologists. In their emphasis on solidarity, the sociologists received considerable help from biologists who, while having lauded Darwin's contributions to freeing biology of metaphysical interference, considered the notion of the paramount role of the struggle for existence in biological evolution a misguided idea that required not refinement but full rejection. The Spencerian theory of the survival of the fittest as a key mechanism of social evolution did not have a single supporter among the leading Russian sociologists. Social Darwinism propounded in the West by Schäffle, Ratzenhofer, and Gumplowitz met the same fate in Russia. The sociologists, as a vanguard of a restive intelligentsia, found it more propitious and strategically advantageous to work on cementing the solidarity of the classless intelligentsia and the "people" than on waging an open and direct war on the established order. Nor should it be overlooked that the idealized version of the communalism of the obshchina was deeply ingrained in Populist theory, the strongest Russian sociological tradition. Although "solidarity" as articulated by theorists had a historical rationale, it was phrased in universalistic terms: to Lavrov it was a "cosmic" phenomenon, to Lappo-Danilevskii a deep expression of humanity, and to Bakunin and Kropotkin an inborn—and, therefore, a biological—quality of the human species. A typical theorist viewed social progress as a gradual victory of the natural drive for cooperation over socially engendered conflict. While Thomas Hobbes required an absolute state to neutralize man's instinctive propensity for reckless conflict, Petr Kropotkin required stateless anarchism to ensure man's instinctive propensity for sound cooperation.

The relationship of the state to society attracted the attention of every leading sociologist. Most theorists accepted P. N. Miliukov's thesis that the Russian pattern of this relationship ran counter to dominant Western patterns. In the West, according to Miliukov, the state appeared at a certain point of the evolution of the estate system; its basic task was to provide juridical safeguards for the protection of the established system of social stratification, a product of "spontaneous" development.[6] In brief, the state functioned as an agency of the society at large. The state derived not only its raison d'être but also its power from society. In Russia, the relationship of the state to the system of estates was exactly the reverse: the formation of the state precipitated the formation of estates which, from the very beginning, were the instruments of political authorities. While in the West the development of estates laid the groundwork for the emergence of state structures, in Russia the state laid the groundwork for the emergence of estates. In the West, society was stronger than the state; in Russia the state was stronger than society. The typical sociologist, moved by the personal experience of living under the awesome power of autocracy, viewed the state as the chief enemy of social progress and general enlightenment. The famous surgeon N. I. Pirogov stated directly that "the antagonism between the state and society" was at the bottom of Russia's political and social crisis.[7] Mikhailovskii argued that only by making control over "social activities" a function of society at large, rather than of the state, could Russia be assured of a better future.[8] Arguing in general sociological terms, Lavrov claimed that the state had evolved from a "natural" organization of authority, providing the safeguards for the preservation of social unity, to a "pathological" organization, a tool of "economic monopoly and universal competition."[9] In essence, however, the socialism advocated by Lavrov was against the state legally devised to serve as an end in itself rather than as a tool of society; it supported the notion of the state as the guardian of social equality and economic security. He endorsed Thomas Paine's dictum that even the best state is an evil, though a necessary one.[10] According to Kistiakovskii, the power of absolute monarchies, of which Russia was a classic example, "had no source in the people" and "was totally alien to the people."[11] In the subordination of the state to society—in the constitutional limitation of the power of the state—he saw the safest path to higher standards of modern existence.

Sociologists and sociologically oriented historians made a major contribution to widening the scope of Russian history as a subject of scholarly inquiry. They helped validate the idea that the history of Russian society was much broader than the history of the Russian state. Shchapov, who may be considered the founder of "social history" in Russia as an academic discipline, showed clearly the enormous scope of social determinants in the intellectual evolution of Russia—an evolution which operated independently of, and often in direct opposition to, the policies of the state. In his extensive studies of mores and legal customs, M. M. Kovalevskii "discovered" wide ranges of Russian social history unaffected by the state. Lappo-Danilevskii prepared a precisely articulated conspectus for the study of "private law" in medieval and early modern Russia as a rich source of information on vital social relations that were not regulated by "public law," that is, by legal norms promulgated and enforced by the state.[12] Kovalevskii and Lappo-Danilevskii, as well as Populist sociologists, contended that the contemporary Russian society contained scattered, but deeply rooted, residues of democracy which had survived the persistent onslaughts of the authoritarian state and which could serve as the basis for an equalitarian society of the future.

The typical sociologist identified democracy with socialism of one kind or another. Whether he was an "anarchistic communist," an "anarchistic collectivist," a Populist, a neo-Populist, a Marxist, a Machian Marxist, a "juridical socialist," or a champion of the cooperative movement, he worked for the cause of socialism. Many sociologists wavered and changed their allegiances; but usually when they abandoned socialism, they also turned against sociology as a legitimate area of scientific inquiry. A handful of academic social theorists, typified by Kovalevskii and Lappo-Danilevskii, were devoted more to the principles of political democracy than to the ideals of socialism.

In building the theoretical foundations of their discipline, Russian sociologists made extensive forays into the natural sciences in search of appropriate guides and models. In need of their own law of gravitation, they made the doctrine of progress the supreme law of social existence and reinforced it with elaborate theoretical ramifications and auxiliary concepts. They invariably and laboriously searched for guides offered by modern biology, and they examined the theoretical orientations of such kindred disciplines as psychology, political economy, ethnography, and jurisprudence, all of which were looking for theoretical models in natural science. For a wide array of sociologists from Lavrov and Mikhailovskii to Kistiakovskii and Bogdanov sociology combined causal explanations borrowed from the natural sciences with a search into the unique attributes of the purposive nature of social action; sociology was a combination of an objective, factual substratum and a subjective interpretation of social ideals. By combining the two approaches, they concentrated not on "objective reality" per se but on "objective possibilities" (a term coined by Max Weber and Kistiakovskii) as distillations of "objective" projections of social change from masses of subjective data.

Despite all these efforts, most Russian sociologists rejected the idea of making their discipline an extension of natural science; they did not accept Comte's famous classification of the sciences, which placed sociology in the same category with such fundamental sciences as astronomy, physics, chemistry, and biology. They contended that sociological knowledge was not of the same epistemological order as the knowledge advanced by the natural sciences. While natural science knowledge was exclusively objective (that is, independent of the cognizing ego), sociological knowledge was primarily (but not exclusively) subjective (that is, dependent on the cognizing ego). As Mikhailovskii put it, the sociologist was interested in both meanings of the Russian word *pravda*: objective "truth" and subjective "justice." While natural science provided causal explanations of the work of nature (and of society as a part of nature), sociology tried to enter the magic world of social ideals. Again, while the natural sciences were engaged primarily in the search for the universal laws governing the organic and inorganic universe, sociology was of maximum usefulness when it dealt with the historical and cultural uniqueness of specific societies.

The aim of the natural sciences was to produce absolute truths; sociology operated on the assumption that all truths related to social and cultural life were essentially relative. Chernov thought that Mikhailovskii defined the true nature of sociological inquiry when he stated that there were no absolute truths, or truths free of subjective admixtures, and that social usefulness was the supreme criterion of truth. The truths dealt with by sociology were the product of social consensus; they continued to be truths as long as they rendered social service. The subjectivism and relativism which deeply permeated the philosophical explanation of the nature of sociological knowledge were to no small measure expressions of the primary concern of Russian sociologists with their own society as a unique historical formation. B. A. Kistiakovskii provided extensive documentation for his claim that the Russian sociologists worked less on unraveling the intricacies of the existing social reality than on elaborating grand plans for a future society: "desirability" and not "necessity" was the guiding explanatory principle of their theoretical schemes. He admitted, however, that the passionate search for a better society did not prevent Russian sociologists from treating many basic problems of sociological theory with meticulous care and often with innovative perspicacity.

Ethical precepts, the essence and the most stable component of human society, occupied the central position in all Russian sociological theories, with the sole exception of Marxism. In his search for a plausible explanation of this phenomenon, Mikhailovskii could only say that it was an "inborn characteristic" of every Russian to "immerse his soul into questions of morality."[13] It was noted many times that the Russian religious tradition was much more a tradition fraught with moral pathos than a tradition of intellectual dedication. The great novelists from Gogol to Dostoevskii and Tolstoy dealt with the moral foundations of society. Pisarev, the eloquent spokesman for Nihilism, made it clear that the moral code anchored in autocratic institutions had entered the stage of uncheckable decay. All Marxist revisionists and renegades abandoned historical materialism because it relegated moral questions to a secondary or derivative position. In their search for new theories, they passed through a transitional phase characterized by efforts to coalesce Marx's socialist theory and Kant's ethical views into a unitary system of philosophy.

Russian social theorists gave much attention to the rapid growth of the scientific world view in modern society as a source of higher moral standards. Like Henri Poincaré, they argued that, while science does not create moral precepts, it contributes to their purification and broader humanity. Science does this, according to Chernov, by eradicating all the "external" truths of supernatural origin, by "providing equal opportunity for *all* views to be heard," and by "inviting opposition to *every* opinion."[14] The strengths of science are in the recognition of the historical relativity of all knowledge and tolerance in intellectual communication, the inevitable sources of higher standards of moral existence. The heavy concern with moral issues helps explain the nearly unanimous agreement among Russian social theorists that, in its search for a scientific status, sociology must rise above the narrow models supplied by the natural sciences.

There were good reasons for the identification of the Populist theories as "the Russian sociological school." This orientation spilled over substantially into the sociology of anarchism and into a solid wing of academic sociology. Its basic epistemological premises were shared by Russian neopositivists and neo-Kantians. As Kareev pointed out correctly, the basic principles of Kistiakovskii's theory were indistinguishable from the philosophical commitment of Populist sociology. Kistiakovskii criticized the Populist claim that in the field of several possibilities for future development a society was presented with an opportunity to select the one that was most desirable; for example, that Russia could and should opt for the line of development bypassing capitalism and "bourgeois democracy." However, Kistiakovskii's theory was to a large extent an elaboration of the principles advanced by Populist sociologists. Some of the most recondite parts of Kistiakovskii's social theory offered an elaboration of the Populist claim that "the category of necessity" (or the law of causality), the universal explanatory principle in the natural sciences, was only of limited usefulness in the social sciences.[15] When Kistiakovskii tried to combine "inner" purposiveness and "external" causality of social action into a general paradigm of sociological explanation, he found ample precedents in the work of Lavrov and Mikhailovskii.

If Populist thought was most typical of the theoretical bent of Russian sociology, Marxist thought was most atypical. Marxist theories stressed the unity of the sciences (and therefore the notion of the social sciences as an extension of the natural sciences), the paramount role of conflict in social evolution, the derivative role of the individual in history, and the nonessential position of moral norms in social structures. Although Plekhanov and Lenin did not abandon the basic principles of Marxist orthodoxy, their writing did manifest a tendency to modulate the differences between Marxism and Populism, at least in some areas of theoretical conflict. Although Marxism was essentially a "conflict theory," Russian Marxists placed relatively little emphasis on the exploration of class conflict in modern society. Lenin's *Development of Capitalism in Russia* was the least belligerent and most academic of all his works, and it concentrated more on the necessity for a capitalist development of Russian society than on class conflict. At any rate, Russian Marxists placed much more emphasis on the solidarity of the future than on the conflict of the present. In his attacks on Populist sociology Lenin was willing to admit that the Hegelian triad—the dialectic—was not a unique mechanism of social development. In his answers to Mikhailovskii's charges that Marxists tried to subject the history of human society to universal laws of causality, Lenin answered that Marx was concerned solely with the discovery of the laws of the development of the capitalist socioeconomic formation, and that each socioeconomic formation had distinct laws of development. With these admissions, Lenin made a step in the direction of the Populist view that the social sciences could not fully depend on natural science models. Lenin responded to the Populist attacks on "economic determinism" by claiming that Marxism did not exclude the notion of the relative independence of specific components of the superstructure and the "reverse" influence of the superstructure on the base. In all these concessions to Populist theory, the leading Marxist theorists made tactical retreats without abandoning the strategic core of the Marxist legacy. Although during the 1890s they provided a crushing opposition to Populism, they were not part of the mainstream of Russian sociological thought. Populism lost ground not because of Marxist attacks on it but because of the widespread disappointment of the intelligentsia in its utopian schemes, steeped in obshchina romanticism. The mounting economic crisis and social unrest during the 1890s accelerated the erosion of Populist ideals. Although Marxist sociology ran into serious problems of theoretical splintering and growing revisionism, its orthodoxy continued to flourish.

During the two decades preceding the revolution of 1917, no sociological theory occupied the position of preeminence. This was the period of diverse efforts to detach sociology from its nineteenth-century moorings and to bring its basic theoretical premises in tune with modern developments in philosophy and science. In these efforts, the studies of two men stood out by their originality and vast scope.

B. A. Kistiakovskii, whose study *Society and the Individual* was widely noted in the West (particularly in Germany), worked on a broadly conceived plan to lay the epistemological and logical foundations for a sociology that would combine the logical categories of objective causality and subjective purposiveness—or objective "explanation" and subjective "understanding."

He looked at sociology as both a unique science and a special approach. As a science, it dealt primarily with general principles of social organization. As a special approach, it was part of a complex pattern of complementary modes of inquiry in the realm of social behavior. For example, he adduced cogent arguments in support of the thesis that a thorough study of law could be achieved only by a combination of analytical, psychological, normative, and sociological approaches. The aim of the sociological approach was to explain the nature and the functioning of mechanisms responsible for the integration of particular domains of institutionalized behavior into the overall structure of society. Sociology, he thought, must develop adequate research techniques and conceptual tools to elucidate vital discrepancies between the abstract society expressed in the normative system and the real society expressed in multitudes of compromises between the ideals of the normative order and the demands of everyday existence. It was in the discrepancies between the normative expectations and the real life that Kistiakovskii saw the most fertile ground for the study of the sources of social change. Kistiakovskii's elaboration of the four-faceted approach to social reality and his penetrating analysis and critique of the preponderant role of social ideals in the theories of the leading Russian sociological schools did not resolve all the major problems of Russian sociology. But they did mark a major step toward making sociology an empirical science, free of metaphysical encumbrances.

A. A. Bogdanov's efforts to blend Marx's theory of social structure and neopositivist epistemology produced an elaborate system of sociological thought which, in turn, laid the groundwork for pioneering studies in what subsequently became known as the general systems theory. Bogdanov argued that while Marx's theory of social structure—of the interrelationship of the infrastructural and superstructural components of society—was essentially correct, the Marxists erred in underestimating the role of the individual as the functioning member of society and the psychological dimension of social action. He argued that the Marxists simplified the structure and dynamics of social classes and that they did not place sufficient emphasis on the structural foundations of social integration. Bogdanov's extensive excursions into the sociology of science were rich in detail and theoretical insight. He viewed science as both "technology" and "ideology"—as a part of both the infrastructure and the superstructure. He was the first Russian social thinker to sense the gigantic scope of current challenges to the Newtonian view of the universe coming from both philosophers and experimental scientists. However, he did not take an anti-Newtonian stand; indeed, he thought that the time had come not for a rejection of the classical mechanistic model but for the creation of a new model in which Newtonian mechanicism would share the spotlight with Darwinian evolutionism and Ostwaldian energeticism. In its application to sociology, the new model preserved the principle of causality as the basic instrument of scientific explanation, but it also translated Darwinian evolution into a principle of historical relativity, and Ostwald's energetics into a principle of epistemological subjectivism and the psychological foundations of human society.

Although deeply embedded in ideology, Russian sociological theory had a realistic dimension: the ideals propounded by the sociologists represented an outright negation of the moral fabric and structural principles of the existing society. The "ideals" were not merely dreams about a better future; they were, above everything else, guides in a systematic criticism of existing reality. Sociology did not acquire the rigor and the predictive power of natural science; its strength was primarily in articulating the social consciousness and the social conscience of the intelligentsia. It was one of the stronger pillars of Russia's rationalist tradition.

Notes

Introduction

1. Bulgakov, "Osnovnye problemy," p. 16. See also Berdiaev, *Sub specie aeternitatis*, pp. 119-21, 131.
2. See, for example, Lavrov, *Zadachi istorii mysli: podgotovlenie cheloveka*, p. 75; Kareev, "Sotsiologiia," *Entsiklopedicheskii slovar*, ed. Brokhauz and Efron, 31:82-83.

Chapter 1

1. Shelgunov, *Vospominaniia*, p. 191.
2. Kizevetter, *Istoricheskie otkliki*, p. 192.
3. Ibid., p. 193. For the views of other Slavophiles, see Sh. M. Levin, *Ocherki*, pp. 293-311. See also Kornilov, *Obshchestvennoe dvizhenie*, p. 12.
4. Saltykov [Shchedrin], *Poshekhonskaia starina*, p. 5. See also Dzhanshiev, *Epokha*, p. 577.
5. The literary emphasis on the "men of action" was a specific reflection of a general exaltation of work as the main index of human dignity. E. A. Solov'ev [Andreevich], *Ocherki po istorii*, pp. 199-200.
6. Kotliarevskii, "Ocherki," no. 11 (1912), p. 275. See also Modzalevskii, "Iz istorii," pp. 137-39; and Skabichevskii, *Sochineniia*, 1:37-39.
7. Chernov, "Gde kliuch?" p. 114.
8. Masaryk, *The Spirit*, 2:51.
9. Kotliarevskii, "Ocherki," no. 11 (1912), pp. 275-76. Similar views are expressed by Demidova, "D. I. Pisarev," pp. 55-59; Plotkin, *Pisarev*, p. 223; Svatikov, *Obshchestvennoe dvizhenie*, 2:4-5.
10. For a discussion of the meaning of the term "Nihilism," see Koz'min, *Literatura*, pp. 225-42.
11. Skabichevskii, *Istoriia*, pp. 103-4. Herzen gave the following definition of Nihilism: "Nihilism ... is a logic without structure, a science without dogma, an unconditional submission to experience and an unquestioning acceptance of all consequences, regardless of what they might be, which come from observation and are demanded by reason" (Herzen, *Polnoe sobranie sochinenii*, 20 (pt. 1: 349).
12. E. A. Solov'ev [Andreevich], *Ocherki po istorii*, p. 244. See also Lampert, *Sons*, pp. 304-5.
13. Shchapov, *Sochineniia*, 2:158-59.
14. As cited in Sidorov, "Melkoburzhuaznaia teoriia," p. 333.
15. E. A. Solov'ev, *Opyt*, p. 260.
16. Pisarev, *Polnoe sobranie sochinenii*, 4:5, 17, 141. See also Mikhailovskii, *Polnoe sobranie sochinenii*, 2:635-40.
17. Nozhin, "Nasha nauka," no. 1, p. 20.
18. E. A. Solov'ev, *D. I. Pisarev*, p. 219.
19. Pisarev, *Polnoe sobranie sochinenii*, 4:138.
20. As cited by Mikhailovskii, "Literatura i zhizn'," no. 1 (1895), p. 145.
21. Chernov, "Gde kliuch?" p. 114; Viner, *Bibliograficheskii zhurnal*, pp. 155-58.
22. Koz'min, *Iz istorii*, p. 42.

23. Pisarev, *Polnoe sobranie sochinenii*, 2:238.
24. Pavlov, *Polnoe sobranie sochinenii*, 4:441; Coquart, *Dmitri Pisarev*, p. 431.
25. Lesevich, *Polnoe sobranie sochinenii*, 1:11-12.
26. V. K., "Pozitivizm," no. 3, pp. 9-10.
27. Pisarev, *Polnoe sobranie sochinenii*, 4:146.
28. Koz'min, *Literatura*, p. 304.
29. Tolstoi, *Polnoe sobranie sochinenii*, 8:232.
30. Wortman, *The Crisis*, p. 2.
31. Kareev, "Iz vospominanii o P. L. Lavrove," p. 20.
32. Stadlin, "Istoricheskaia shkola," pp. 257-90; Vatson, *Etiudy*, pp. 388-89; Mechnikov, *Sorok let*, pp. 199-200; Koialovich, *Istoriia*, p. 576; Timiriazev, *Sochineniia*, 8:175; M. G. Fedorov, *Russkaia progressivnaia mysl'*, pp. 108-10.
33. Shchapov's sociological ideas are presented in several essays. See particularly his "Obshchii vzgliad na istoriiu intellektual'nogo razvitiia v Rossii" (1867), "Istoricheskie usloviia intellecktual'nogo razvitiia v Rossii" (1908), "Estestvenno-psikhologicheskie usloviia umstven-nogo and sotsial'nogo razvitiia russkogo naroda" (1870), and *Sotsial'no-pedagogicheskie usloviia razvitiia russkogo naroda* (1870). (All these are available in Shchapov, *Sochineniia*.) For an analysis of Shchapov's sociological ideas, see Serbov, "Shchapov," pp. 8-10; Luchinskii, "Afanasii P. Shchapov," pp. xcvi-cix; Aleksinskii, "Istorik-publitsist," pp. 64-75; Seliverstova, "O filosofskikh i sotsiologicheskikh vozzreniiakh," pp. 131-41; Pokrovskii, *Izbrannye proiz-vedeniia*, 3:243-46. For a negative attitude toward Shchapov's search for a scientific study of social history, see Aristov, "Zhizn'," no. 12, pp. 609-11.
34. Uevell, *Istoriia*, 2:xli.
35. Lewes, *Comte's Philosophy*, pp. 8-9.
36. Timiriazev, *Sochineniia*, 8:174-75.
37. Leffler, *Sonia Kovalewsky*, p. 11.
38. Serno-Solov'evich, "Ne trebuet' li nyneshnee sostoianie znanii novoi nauki?" pp. 496-505.
39. Ibid., p. 499.

Chapter 2

1. Rusanov, "Nikolai Konstantinovich Mikhailovskii," p. 128; idem, "Petr Lavrovich Lavrov," p. 105.
2. Lavrov, *Filosofiia i sotsiologiia*, 2:631-32.
3. Firsov [Ruskin], "Vospominaniia," no. 1, p. 106.
4. For details, see Dobrovol'skii, "Pervyi kurs," pp. 47-49. See also Bogatov, "P. L. Lavrov i estestvoznanie," pp. 118-29; Noetzel, *Petr L. Lavrovs Vorstellungen*, pp. 194-96.
5. Chernyshevskii, *Selected Philosophical Essays*, pp. 54-55. See also Bogatov, "Istoriia odnoi filosofskoi polemiki," pp. 68-72; Pomper, *Peter Lavrov*, pp. 48-49. Antonovich, one of the early critics of Lavrov's epistemological views, noted many years later that after the early 1860s Lavrov abandoned eclecticism and made an effort to advance an integrated, homogeneous, and scientifically grounded philosophy (Antonovich, "Vospominaniia," p. 241).
6. Rusanov, "Petr Lavrovich Lavrov," p. 106.
7. Lavrov, *Tri besedy*, pp. 16-25. For a brief analysis of Lavrov's philosophical views, see Ossip Lourié, *La philosophie russe*, pp. 167-73. Vyrubov, a follower of Auguste Comte, formulated the epistemological view that dominated Lavrov's philosophical and sociological thought: "The truth is neither something abstract nor something that can exist independently of the human mind; on the contrary, the truth is a relative and conditional conception, a result of observation and experience, produced by the methods of special sciences. Without man, or, more correctly, without science—without a complex system of research methods—the truth is impossible" (G. Wyrouboff, "Le certain et le probable," p. 171).
8. Lavrov, "Mekhanicheskaia teoriia mira," p. 492.

9. For a summary of Lavrov's earlier philosophical ideas and their reception, see Bogatov, "Istoriia odnoi filosofskoi polemiki," pp. 65-76. For a particularly critical contemporary assessment, see Antonovich, *Izbrannye stat'i*, pp. 7-90. A perceptive modern analysis is presented in Pomper, *Peter Lavrov*, chap. 2.

10. As cited in A. Vasil'ev, "P. L. Lavrov," p. 375.

11. Lavrov was arrested three weeks after Karakozov's unsuccessful attempt on the life of Alexander II. The authorities did not charge Lavrov with implication in the "Karakozov affair." He was dismissed from his teaching position and exiled to Vologda on charges that he was in close contact with such dangerous persons as Chernyshevskii and Mikhailov, that he published articles injurious to the best interests of the state, and that he wrote "poems disrespectful of the emperor" (Firsov [Ruskin], "Vospominaniia," no. 2, p. 496).

12. Lavrov, *Zadachi pozitivizma*, p. 61.

13. Lavrov, *Filosofiia i sotsiologiia*, 1:591.

14. Ibid., 1:592.

15. Rusanov, "Petr L. Lavrov," pp. 103-4.

16. Aptekman, "Flerovskii-Bervi," p. 129.

17. Firsov [Ruskin], "Vospominaniia," no. 2, p. 503.

18. For more details on the relationship of Lavrov to Marx and Engels, see Pomper, *Peter Lavrov*, pp. 126-27.

19. According to Walicki, while the Bakuninists were rightly called "the rebels" because of their tendency to exaggerate the readiness of the Russian peasant to rise in rebellion, the Lavrovists were known as "propagandists" because of their involvement in the peaceful spreading of socialist ideas (Walicki, *The Controversy*, p. 91). According to Karpovich, the disagreement between Bakunin and Lavrov "was over tactics, not over principles" (Karpovich, "P. L. Lavrov," pp. 35-37). See also Meijer, *Knowledge*, pp. 158-63.

20. *K. Marks, F. Engels i revoliutsionnaia Rossiia*, pp. 457-58, 745.

21. Sh. M. Levin, *Ocherki*, p. 185.

22. Rudnitskaia, "Nikolai Nozhin," p. 461.

23. For a comparative analysis of Mikhailovskii's and Nozhin's orientations, see Chernov, "Gde kliuch?" p. 101; Rafailov, "Sistema pravdy," pp. 207-15. See also Gaisinovich, "Biolog-shestidesiatnik," pp. 391-92; and Safronov, *M. M. Kovalevskii*, pp. 183-87.

24. Rusanov, "N. K. Mikhailovskii i obshchestvennaia zhizn'," pp. 15-16; and Kovarskii, *N. K. Mikhailovskii*, pp. 12-14.

25. Mikhailovskii, *Revoliutsionnye stat'i*, pp. 5-10. See also Sedov, "K voprosu ob obshchestvenno-politicheskikh vzgliadov," pp. 205-6.

26. Mikhailovskii, *Revoliutsionnye stat'i*, pp. 11-33; Gorev, *N. K. Mikhailovskii*, pp. 45-46.

27. Rusanov, "N. K. Mikhailovskii i obshchestvennaia zhizn'," pp. 16-17.

28. Rusanov, "Nikolai K. Mikhailovskii," p. 117. According to V. Lunkevich: "There is an organic—I would call it intimate—unity in all Mikhailovskii's studies: all embody the same principles, sentiments, and ideals" (Lunkevich, *N. K. Mikhailovskii*, p. 54).

29. Mikhailovskii articulated his critique of the use of biological models in sociology in "Analogicheskii metod v obshchestvennoi nauke" (*Sochineniia*, 1:333-90). The main target of his critique was *Istoriia i metod* by A. Stronin, an ambitious effort to make sociology an extension of biology.

30. Mikhailovskii, *Sochineniia*, 1:65; Lavrov, *Stat'i po filosofii*, 6:13.

31. Chernov, *Filosofskie i sotsiologicheskie etiudy*, p. 199.

32. This problem is treated in Krasnosel'skii, *Mirovozzrenie*, chap. 11.

33. Struve, *Kriticheskie zametki*, pp. 54-63.

34. Kistiakovskii, *Sotsial'nye nauki*, pp. 80-82.

35. Occupying a middle position, S. N. Iuzhakov argued cogently against the thesis that the concern with purposiveness makes sociology automatically subjective; he wanted to expand the

scientific methodology to embrace both "efficient causes" and "final causes" of social processes. His basic argument was that, while there are differences between various scientific subject-matters, there should be only one scientific methodology (Iuzhakov, *Sotsiologicheskie etiudy*, pp. 256-58).

36. Mikhailovskii, *Sochineniia*, 3:381-82.

37. Chernov, *Filosofskie i sotsiologicheskie etiudy*, p. 220.

38. Lavrov, *Formula progressa*, pp. 43-44.

39. Lavrov, *Filosofiia i sotsiologiia*, 2:43.

40. Mikhailovskii, *Polnoe sobranie sochinenii*, 10:178.

41. Kamkov, "Istoriko-filosofskie vozzreniia," no. 7, p. 128.

42. Mikhailovskii, *Polnoe sobranie sochinenii*, 2:12-13; Lunkevich, *N. K. Mikhailovskii*, pp. 7-10.

43. Krasnosel'skii, *Mirovozzrenie*, p. 71.

44. Mikhailovskii, *Sochineniia*, 1:777. "It is true," wrote N. I. Kareev, "that N. K. Mikhailovskii, as a sociologist-realist, recognized a natural course in the development of society, that is, the tendency of society to develop as an organism, the vital role of the struggle for existence in social development, and the great importance of the economic factor. However, he did not reduce the natural course of social development to one specific set of phenomena; he never lost sight of the role of consciously acting human will; and he dealt not only with theoretical questions but also with ethical orientations" (Kareev, "N. K. Mikhailovskii kak sotsiolog," p. 4).

45. Lavrov, *Zadachi pozitivizma*, p. 44. See also Sorokin, "Osnovnye problemy," pp. 251-52.

46. Mikhailovskii, *Polnoe sobranie sochinenii*, 8:43.

47. Lavrov, *Izbrannye sochineniia*, 4:75.

48. Lavrov, *Zadachi istorii mysli*, pp. 75-76.

49. Lavrov, *Formula progressa*, p. 143.

50. Mikhailovskii, *Sochineniia*, 6:113-14.

51. Lavrov, *Izbrannye sochineniia*, 2:182.

52. Lavrov, *Gosudarstvennyi element*, p. 43.

53. Mikhailovskii, *Literaturnye vospominaniia*, 2:425.

54. For a detailed discussion of the relationship of the individual to society, see Mikhailovskii, *Sochineniia*, 1:421-594; Lavrov, *Filosofiia i sotsiologiia*, 2:110-19; Chernov, *Filosofskie i sotsiologicheskie etiudy*, pp. 13-14; Kareev, "Novyi istoriko-filosofskii trud," pp. 400-401.

55. Relevant details on Mikhailovskii's theory of progress are presented in Kazakov, *Teoriia progressa*, pp. 64-97; and Ranskii, *Sotsiologiia*, pp. 49-55.

56. Mikhailovskii, *Sochineniia*, 1:151. The reaction of Russian social analysts to Darwin's biological theory of evolution is discussed in J. A. Rogers, "Russia."

57. Mikhailovskii, *Sochineniia*, 1:150.

58. Chernov, "Gde kliuch?" p. 111.

59. Ibid.

60. For an excellent discussion of Mikhailovskii's formulation of simple and complex cooperation, see Kolosov, *Ocherki*, pp. 43-53.

61. Rusanov, "N. K. Mikhailovskii i obshchestvennaia zhizn'," p. 27.

62. Lavrov, *Zadachi istorii mysli*, pp. 75-76. See also Kazakov, *Teoriia progressa*, pp. 20-59; and Sorokin, "Osnovnye problemy," pp. 255-60.

63. Lavrov, *Formula progressa*, p. 6; Chernov, *Filosofskie i sotsiologicheskie etiudy*, p. 238; Kareev, "P. L. Lavrov kak sotsiolog," pp. 239-40.

64. Lavrov, *Izbrannye sochineniia*, 1:400.

65. Lavrov [Arnol'di], *Zadachi ponimaniia istorii*, pp. 32-36. See also Sorokin, "Osnovnye problemy," pp. 279-91.

66. Lavrov [Arnol'di], *Zadachi ponimaniia istorii*, pp. 32-33.

67. Lavrov, *Filosofiia i sotsiologiia*, 2:415.

68. Lavrov, *Formula progressa*, p. 137.

69. Mikhailovskii, *Sochineniia*, 5:539. See also Otto Müller, *Untersuchungen*, pp. 297–307. For a general characterization of the intelligentsia, see Pollard, "The Russian Intelligentsia," pp. 27–28; and Berdiaev, *Sub specie aeternitatis*, p. 130.

70. Mikhailovskii, *Sochineniia*, 5:539; A. P. Mendel, "N. K. Mikhailovskii," p. 341.

71. For a similar view, see Tugan-Baranovskii, "Intelligentsiia," pp. 239–40. See also Karpovich, "P. L. Lavrov," p. 33.

72. Lavrov, *Historical Letters*, pp. 150–51.

73. Gizetti, "Individualizm," p. 34.

74. For example, while Krasnosel'skii (*Mirovozzrenie*) emphasized the theory of personality development, Kolosov (*Ocherki*) and Kovarskii (*N. K. Mikhailovskii*) dealt primarily with the Populist theory of socialism.

75. Mikhailovskii, *Sochineniia*, 6:894.

76. Lavrov, *Formula progressa*, p. 136.

77. Mikhailovskii, *Sochineniia*, 6:894–95.

78. Berdiaev, *Sub'ektivizm*, p. 28; idem, *Sub specie aeternitatis*, p. 201.

79. Lavrov, *Historical Letters*, p. 122.

80. Mikhailovskii's social-psychological views are discussed in Parygin and Rudakov, "N. K. Mikhailovskii," pp. 277–95; Kovalevskii, "N. K. Mikhailovskii," pp. 192–212; and Krasnosel'skii, *Mirovozzrenie*, pp. 7–14.

81. See particularly Mikhailovskii, *Polnoe sobranie sochinenii*, 2:95–365. For sympathetic comments on this work, see Iuzhakov, "Sotsiologicheskaia doktrina," pp. 363–65.

82. Lavrov, *Stat'i po filosofii*, 6:15.

83. Briullova-Shakol'skaia, "Lavrov i Mikhailovskii," p. 405.

84. Lavrov, *Formula progressa*, pp. 40–41.

85. Gorev, *N. K. Mikhailovskii*, pp. 33–34.

86. Lavrov, *Formula progressa*, p. 42.

87. For a broader analysis of Lavrov's brand of socialism, see A. Kimball, "The Russian Past," pp. 32–44.

88. Ivanov-Razumnik, *Istoriia*, 2:127.

89. Rusanov, "Nikolai K. Mikhailovskii," p. 118.

90. Walicki, *The Controversy*, p. 131. The relevance of Populist social theory to "the modern ideological currents in the Third World" is discussed in Khoros, "Problema 'Narodnichestva' " and "Narodnichestvo."

91. Mikhailovskii, *Sochineniia*, 4:390.

92. Lange, *The History of Materialism*, 2:246–47; Mikhailovskii, *Sochineniia*, 4:387–88.

93. Buckle, *History*, 1:659–61.

94. Ibid., p. 662.

95. Mikhailovskii, *Sochineniia*, 3:284; 1:904.

96. Ibid., 1:904.

97. Ibid., 1:905–6.

98. Ibid., 3:293.

99. Ibid., 3:285–86.

100. Ibid., 3:773–74.

101. Ibid., 1:908.

102. Lavrov, *Izbrannye sochineniia*, 1:157.

103. Ibid., p. 160.

104. Mikhailovskii, *Sochineniia*, 3:424.

105. Mikhailovskii, *Polnoe sobranie sochinenii*, 8:602.

106. Lavrov discusses the relationship of religion to science and morality in *Formula progressa*, pp. 130–31.

107. Chernov, *Filosofskie i sotsiologicheskie etiudy*, p. 6. For a similar view see Gorev, *N. K.*

Mikhailovskii, pp. 88–89; Kudrin, "Chem russkaia obshchestvennaia zhizn' obiazana N. K. Mikhailovskomu?" pp. 7–8. For a detailed scrutiny of "subjective analysis," see Kablits, *Osnovy*, 2:156. See also Nevedomskii, "N. K. Mikhailovskii," p. 25.

108. Berdiaev, *Sub'ektivizm*, p. 267.

109. Struve, "Predislovie," pp. xxiv–xxv.

110. Berdiaev, "Narodnicheskoe i natsional'noe soznanie," pp. 90–91.

111. Novgorodtsev, "Nravstvennyi idealizm," p. 265.

112. Filippov, "Teoriia kriticheski-mysliashchei lichnosti," p. 757.

113. Ibid., pp. 773–75. For a similar view by a Soviet writer, see Bogatov, *Filosofiia*, p. 115. For a criticism of Mikhailovskii's "utopianism," see Evg. Solov'ev, "Semidesiatye gody," pp. 302–16.

114. Mikhailovskii, *Polnoe sobranie sochinenii*, 8:624. For a comparison of Mikhailovskii's and Durkheim's sociological views, see Walicki, *The Controversy*, pp. 74–75.

115. Durkheim, *The Division of Labor*, p. 41. For a comparison of Durkheim's and Mikhailovskii's theories, see Rozhkov, "Review of E. Durkheim."

116. Mikhailovskii, *Polnoe sobranie sochinenii*, 8:605–6; Durkheim, *The Division*, p. 354.

117. Mikhailovskii, *Polnoe sobranie sochinenii*, 8:629–30.

118. Plekhanov, "O sotsial'noi demokratii," pp. 252–56; Tun, *Istoriia*, p. xix.

119. Lavrov, *Iz istorii sotsial'nykh uchenii*, p. 5.

120. Lavrov [Arnol'di], *Zadachi ponimaniia istorii*, pp. 354–55.

121. Chernov, "Gde kliuch?" p. 85.

122. Kovalevskii, "N. K. Mikhailovskii," p. 192.

123. Iuzhakov, "Sotsiologicheskaia doktrina," pp. 356–57.

124. Kareev, *Vvedenie*, p. 222.

125. See particularly his *Istoriko-filosofskie i sotsiologicheskie etiudy*, pp. 114–34.

126. Ibid., p. 132; and idem, *Vvedenie*, pp. 103–4.

127. Kareev, *Vvedenie*, pp. 98–100.

128. Kareev, *Istoriko-filosofskie i sotsiologicheskie etiudy*, p. 161.

129. Kareev, *Vvedenie*, p. 359.

130. Sociology, according to Kareev, combines the "objective" notion of "evolution" and the "subjective" notion of "progress" (*Istoriko-filosofskie i sotsiologicheskie etiudy*, pp. 295–97). See also, idem, *Vvedenie*, pp. 309–10.

131. Kareev, *Vvedenie*, pp. 309–10, 326.

132. Ibid., p. 332.

133. Ibid., pp. 271–75.

134. Kareev, *Osnovnye voprosy*, p. 108. See also his *Teoriia istoricheskogo znaniia*, pp. 286–88. For a contemporary criticism, see Miliukov, "Istoriosofiia."

135. Khoros, *Narodnicheskaia ideologiia*, p. 149. Neo-Populism, as the ideology of the Socialist Revolutionary party, is discussed in Radkey, "Chernov," pp. 65–80.

136. Chernov, *Krest'ianin*, pp. 13–44.

137. Chernov, *K teorii klassovoi bor'by*, pp. 38–39.

138. Radkey, *The Agrarian Foes*, p. 45.

139. Ivanov-Razumnik, *Chto takoe intelligentsiia?*, p. 17.

140. Ibid., p. 25.

141. Ibid., p. 22. For a critical discussion of Ivanov-Razumnik's notion of *meshchanstvo* from a Marxist point of view, see Lunacharskii, "Meshchanstvo."

142. Rusanov, *Sotsialisty Zapada i Rossii*, p. 388.

143. Sukhanov, "Po voprosakh nashikh raznoglasii," no. 6, p. 3.

144. As cited in Radkey, *The Agrarian Foes*, p. 45.

145. Chernov, "K voprosu o 'polozhitel'nykh' i 'otritsatel'nykh' storonakh kapitalizma," pp. 228–43.

146. Chernov, "Etika i politika," no. 2, p. 73.
147. Chernov, "Tipy," pp. 60-69.
148. Chernov, "Etika i politika," no. 2, p. 75.
149. Chernov, Zapiski, 1:21.
150. Chernov, Konstruktivnyi sotsializm, 1:12-17.
151. Chernov, Marks, p. 115.
152. Radkey, "Chernov," pp. 66-67.
153. Chernov, The Great Russian Revolution, p. 398.
154. Radkey, The Agrarian Foes, p. 461.
155. Kacharovskii, "Narodnichestvo," no. 3, p. 74.
156. Chernov, Filosofskie i sotsiologicheskie etiudy, pp. 224-25. For a similar interpretation, see N. K., "Istoriko-teoreticheskie vzgliady," pp. 118-19. For a detailed study of similarities and differences between the theories of Rickert and Lavrov, see Kamkov, "Istoriko-filosofskie vozzreniia," no. 7, pp. 112-39.
157. Rickert, Science and History, p. 22.
158. Chernov, "Nauchnoe postroenie," pp. 145, 182.
159. Chernov, "Ekonomicheskii materializm," p. 643.
160. Chernov, "Ratsionalizm," p. 48.
161. Chernov, "Politika i etika," no. 7, p. 86.
162. Chernov, "Sub'ektivnyi metod," no. 7, pp. 236-56, and Filosofskie i sotsiologicheskie etiudy, p. 13.
163. Chernov, "Sentimental'naia etika," p. 120.
164. Chernov, Filosofskie i sotsiologicheskie etiudy, p. 238.
165. Chernov, "Tipy," p. 64.
166. Ivanov-Razumnik, Istoriia, 2:117.
167. According to Walicki, Lavrov, like Chernyshevskii, appreciated not so much the existing forms of communal life (including obshchina) as the abstract social principles attributed to them (Walicki, The Controversy, p. 91). For Lavrov's views on the role of the obshchina in a socialist society of the future, see Lavrov, Stat'i sotsial'no-politicheskie, 7:125, 127.
168. Rusanov, "N. K. Mikhailovskii i obshchestvennaia zhizn'," pp. 15-17.
169. Kacharovskii, "Narodnichestvo," no. 6, p. 79.
170. Ibid., no. 3, p. 74.
171. Labry, Herzen et Proudhon, pp. 157-58; Koz'min, Iz istorii, p. 376.
172. Mikhailovskii, Sochineniia, 3:643; 1:894. See also Rogers, "Proudhon," pp. 514-23.
173. Mikhailovskii, Sochineniia, 4:97.

Chapter 3

1. Bakunin's early initiation into philosophy and intellectual interaction with Belinskii and Herzen are discussed in Scheibert, Von Bakunin, pp. 133-51.
2. Carr, Michael Bakunin, pp. 10-11.
3. Richard Wagner, Sämtliche Schriften, Vol. 11, p. 225.
4. Archives Bakounine, 1 (pt. 2): 346.
5. Polonskii, M. A. Bakunin, p. 5.
6. Steklov, Mikhail Aleksandrovich Bakunin, 3:141.
7. Bakunin, The Political Philosophy, p. 13.
8. Venturi, Roots, p. 429.
9. Hoffman, Revolutionary Justice, p. 85.
10. In Steklov, Mikhail A. Bakunin, 1:197.
11. Kaminski, Bakounine, pp. 240-41.
12. Bakunin, Izbrannye sochineniia, 3:158.
13. Ibid., p. 154.

14. Ibid., p. 155.
15. Ibid., p. 153.
16. Ibid., p. 154.
17. As cited in Sh. M. Levin, *Obshchestvennoe dvizhenie*, pp. 260–61.
18. Bakunin, *The Political Philosophy*, p. 82.
19. Masaryk, *The Spirit*, 1:431.
20. Bakunin, *Izbrannye sochineniia*, 2:148.
21. Stepniak, *Underground Russia*, p. 15.
22. Steklov, *Mikhail A. Bakunin*, 3:164.
23. Ibid.
24. Bakounine, *Ouevres*, 1:134.
25. Lavrov, *Gosudarstvennyi element*, p. 47.
26. Cole, *Socialist Thought: Marxism and Anarchism*, p. 222.
27. Bakunin, *Izbrannye sochineniia*, 2:243. For a modern Soviet appraisal, see Zil'berman, *Politicheskaia teoriia*, pp. 57–71.
28. Bakunin, *Izbrannye sochineniia*, 3:185–86.
29. Bakunin, *Bakunin on Anarchy*, p. 257.
30. Bakounine, *Ouevres*, 1:53.
31. Bakunin, *Archines Bakounine*, 3:6.
32. Lampert, *Studies*, p. 139. For interesting comments on Bakunin's social-class theory and its affinity with the Bolshevik theory, see Pyziur, *The Doctrine*, pp. 80–81.
33. Bakunin, *Archives Bakounine*, 3:175.
34. Bakunin, *Izbrannye sochineniia*, 2:155.
35. Lebedev, ed., *Perepiska*, p. 125.
36. Kropotkin, *Dnevnik P. A. Kropotkina*, pp. 262–63.
37. For details on Kropotkin's contributions to geography, see Obruchev, "Petr Alekseevich Kropotkin," pp. 497–507.
38. The full text of the manifesto is presented in Kropotkin, *Selected Writings*, pp. 46–117. See also M. A. Miller, "Manifestoes," pp. 13–18.
39. Kropotkin, *Rechi*, pp. 339–40.
40. Kropotkin, "Unsuspected Radiations," pp. 384–85.
41. For a detailed analysis of Kropotkin's interpretation of the social dynamics of the French Revolution, see Kareev, "P. A. Kropotkin," pp. 108–38.
42. Chernov, *The Great Russian Revolution*, p. 439.
43. For details on Kropotkin's biography, see Woodcock and Avakumović, *The Anarchist Prince*; M. Miller, "Introduction"; Lebedev, "P. A. Kropotkin: chelovek"; and Pirumova, *Petr Alekseevich Kropotkin.*
44. Kropotkin, "Ideal v revoliutsii," p. 41.
45. Kropotkin, *Revolutionary Pamphlets*, p. 192.
46. Kropotkin, *Modern Science*, pp. 62–63.
47. Kropotkin, *Revolutionary Pamphlets*, p. 150.
48. Kropotkin, *Modern Science*, p. 23.
49. Ibid., p. 26.
50. Ibid.
51. Ibid., p. 27.
52. Kropotkin, *Ethics*, pp. 12–15; Darwin, *The Descent*, 2:132.
53. Huxley, *Evolution*, p. 81.
54. Kropotkin, *Mutual Aid*, pp. 3–5.
55. Ibid., p. 8; Banina, *K. F. Kessler*, pp. 126–27.
56. Lebedev, "P. A. Kropotkin kak teoretik," pp. 98–99.
57. Kropotkin, *Modern Science*, pp. 20–21.
58. Kropotkin, *Ethics*, pp. 325–26.

59. Ibid., p. 327.
60. Bakunin, *The Political Philosophy*, p. 85.
61. Lebedev, "P. A. Kropotkin kak teoretik," p. 98.
62. Kropotkin, *Sovremennaia nauka*, pp. 166-67.
63. Ibid., p. 168.
64. Kropotkin, *Revolutionary Pamphlets*, p. 62.
65. Kropotkin, *Fields*, pp. v, 5.
66. For differences between Marx and Bakunin, see Kropotkin, *Memoirs*, p. 267; Iakovlev, *Aktivnoe narodnichestvo*, pp. 72-73; Kaminski, *Bakounine*, pp. 237-41; Leser, *Die Odyssee*, pp. 231-72.
67. Kropotkin, *Revolutionary Pamphlets*, p. 152.
68. Ibid., pp. 146-47.
69. Kropotkin, *Ethics*, p. 9.
70. Kropotkin, *Revolutionary Pamphlets*, pp. 118-19.
71. Tugan-Baranovskii, *Modern Socialism*, pp. 180-81.

Chapter 4

1. Danilevskii, *Rossiia*, p. 150.
2. Ibid., pp. 163-64.
3. Ibid., p. 141.
4. Ibid., p. 146.
5. Ibid., pp. 170-71.
6. Kareev, "Teoriia kul'turno-istoricheskikh tipov," pp. 19-28.
7. Borozdin, "N. Ia. Danilevskii," pp. 68-69.
8. Danilevskii, *Darvinizm*, 1 (pt. 2): 504-5.
9. Strakhov, "Zhizn' i trudy," p. xiii.
10. Bestuzhev-Riumin, "Teoriia," p. 562.
11. Dostoevskii, *Pis'ma*, 2:181.
12. V. Solov'ev, "Rossiia," no. 2, pp. 745-46. P. G. Vinogradov noted that the question of Slavic sociocultural unity played a very modest role in the philosophy of Slavophilism and that the eyes of leading Slavophiles were turned not toward the pending formation of an original Slavic cultural type but toward a revitalization of the pre-Petrine system of cultural values and social institutions. According to I. V. Kireevskii, as interpreted by Vinogradov, the Russian cultural life is distinguished by "the organic wholeness of its spiritual principles" and "the harmonious unity of the intellect, the heart, and the will." The philosophy of Eastern Orthodoxy is the underlying force of the unity of Russian culture (P. G. Vinogradov, "I. V. Kireevskii," pp. 102-3, 115).
13. Miliukov, "Razlozhenie," p. 63.
14. For a critical analysis of the sociological characteristics of the Slavic cultural-historical type, see Miliukov, "Razlozhenie," p. 63.
15. Ibid., pp. 51-64.
16. Miliukov, *Ocherki*, 2:7.
17. Miliukov, "Razlozhenie," p. 55.
18. V. Solov'ev, "Mnimaia bor'ba," p. 3; Strakhov, "Istoricheskie vzgliady," pp. 154-83. Pokrovskii noted that, while Danilevskii had not read Rückert, Heinrich Rickert had not read Danilevskii. Yet in *Die Grenzen*, Rickert elaborated the thesis, previously held by Danilevskii, that only national history could aspire to become scientific (Pokrovskii, *Izbrannye proizvedeniia*, 4:258-59).
19. Sorokin, *Modern Historical and Social Philosophies*, p. 327.
20. For interesting and pertinent details on Danilevskii's philosophy of history, see Sorokin, *Historical and Social Philosophies*, pp. 49-71; Thaden, *Conservative Nationalism*, pp. 102-15; Petrovich, *The Emergence*, pp. 72-77; V. Solov'ev, "Rossiia i Evropa," no. 2 (1888): 742-61;

no. 4 (1888): 725-67, and idem, "Mnimaia bor'ba," pp. 1-20; Borozdin, "N. Ia. Danilevskii," pp. 67-72; Mikhailovskii, *Sochineniia*, 3:854-87. For Soviet appraisals, see Evgrafov et al., eds., *Istoriia filosofii v SSSR*, 3:332-38; Mordovskii, "K kritike 'filosofii istorii'," pp. 261-99; Chesnokov, *Sovremennaia burzhuaznaia filosofiia istorii*, pp. 16-24.

21. Troeltsch, *Der Historismus*, p. 120.

22. Rickert, *Die Grenzen*, p. 224; P. Pertsov, "Gnoseologicheskie nedorazumeniia," pp. 32-36.

23. Chernov, *Filosofskie i sotsiologicheskie etiudy*, p. 225.

24. Ibid., p. 230.

25. Ibid., pp. 197-99 and idem, "Ekonomicheskii materializm," pp. 609-44.

26. For detailed comments on Stammler's theory, see Gaidarov, "Rudol'f Shtammler," pp. 30-57; N. Alekseev, "Sotsial'naia filosofiia," pp. 1-26.

27. See, for example, Bulgakov, "O zakonomernosti," pp. 575-611; Struve, *Na raznye temy*, pp. 120-39. For details on the influence of neo-Kantian philosophy on Berdiaev, Struve, and Tugan-Baranovskii, see Vorländer, *Kant und Marx*, pp. 109-208.

28. Novgorodtsev, *Kant i Gegel'*, pp. 93-94.

29. For biographical data on Lappo-Danilevskii, see D'iakonov, "Aleksandr Sergeevich Lappo-Danilevskii," pp. 359-66; Presniakov, *Aleksandr Sergeevich Lappo-Danilevskii*; "Lappo-Danilevskii, Aleksandr Sergeevich," autobiography, pp. 405-13; Grevs, "Aleksandr Sergeevich Lappo-Danilevskii," pp. 44-81; Ol'denburg, "Rabota," pp. 164-80.

30. E. Fedorov, "Poteri nauki," pp. 924-28.

31. Presniakov, *Aleksandr Sergeevich Lappo-Danilevskii*, p. 18.

32. Grevs, "Aleksandr Sergeevich Lappo-Danilevskii," p. 61.

33. Miliukov hailed the publication of this study as "the most important event in the development of modern Russian historical literature" (Miliukov, review of Lappo-Danilevskii, *Organizatsiia priamogo oblozheniia*, pp. 412-13).

34. Presniakov, *Aleksandr Sergeevich Lappo-Danilevskii*, p. 84.

35. For a discussion of private law as a source of sociological knowledge, see his *Ocherk istorii diplomatiki chastnykh aktov*, chap. 1.

36. Rainov, "O filosofskikh vzgliadakh," pp. 53-54.

37. Lappo-Danilevskii, *Metodologiia istorii*, 2 vols., St. Petersburg, 1910-1913. The third edition of volume 1, cited in this study, appeared in 1923.

38. Grevs, "Aleksandr Sergeevich Lappo-Danilevskii," p. 79.

39. Lappo-Danilevskii, *Metodologiia*, 1:3.

40. Ibid., pp. 8-9.

41. Lappo-Danilevskii, "Osnovnye printsipi," p. 473.

42. Ibid., pp. 474-75.

43. Ibid., p. 487.

44. Ibid.

45. Lappo-Danilevskii, *Metodologiia*, 1:192.

46. Ibid., p. 192.

47. Ibid., pp. 193-94.

48. Ibid., p. 195.

49. Ibid., pp. 246-61.

50. Ibid., p. 247.

51. Ibid., p. 255.

52. Ibid., p. 257.

53. Ibid., pp. 50-53.

54. Ibid., pp. 264-65. For a critique of Lappo-Danilevskii's theory from a Marxist point of view, see Pokrovskii, *Izbrannye sochineniia*, 4:369-70; Cherepnin, "A. S. Lappo-Danilevskii," pp. 30-51; Shapiro, *Russkaia istoriografiia*, pp. 34-37.

55. Lappo-Danilevskii, *Metodologiia*, 2:321.

56. For a brief discussion of Lappo-Danilevskii's views on the interrelationship of idiographic and nomothetic approaches, see Kareev, "Istoriko-teoreticheskie trudy A. S. Lappo-Danilevskogo," pp. 124-25.

57. Lappo-Danilevskii, "Ideia gosudarstva," p. 27.

58. Ibid., p. 27.

59. As cited in Presniakov, *Aleksandr Sergeevich Lappo-Danilevskii*, pp. 86-87; Shapiro, *Russkaia istoriografiia*, pp. 35-36.

60. Lappo-Danilevskii, "The Development of Science," p. 223.

61. Ibid., p. 229.

62. Lappo-Danilevskii, *Metodologiia*, 2:318.

63. Ibid., p. 223. For pertinent observations on Lappo-Danilevskii's harmonization of "individualizing" and "generalizing" approaches in history, see Kareev, review of Lappo-Danilevskii, *Metodologiia istorii*, pp. 64-69.

64. Presniakov, "A. S. Lappo-Danilevskii kak uchenyi i myslitel'," p. 87.

Chapter 5

1. Published biographical data on Kistiakovskii are very limited. With the exception of a short biography in *Filosofskaia entsiklopediia*, 2:513, he has been completely overlooked by modern Soviet writers. Among the earlier sources, the best is Nik. Vasilenko, "Akademik Bogdan Oleksandrovich Kistiakovs'kii."

2. *Kantstudien* 5 (1900): 252-55; Vierkandt's review in *Zeitschrift für Socialwissenschaft*, no. 10 (1900): 748-49; Karl Diehl's review in *Jahrbücher für Nationalökonomie und Statistik* 22 (1901): 878-80.

3. Kelsen, *Der soziologische und der juristische Staatsbegriff*, pp. 106-13.

4. Pipes, *Struve*, pp. 333-34.

5. A. A. Chuprov, *Ocherki*, pp. 31-33.

6. Kistiakovskii, review of A. A. Chuprov, *Ocherki*, pp. 183-200.

7. Kistiakovskii, "Russkaia sotsiologicheskaia shkola," pp. 297-393.

8. Gerth and C. Wright Mills, "Introduction," p. 37. See particularly Max Weber, "Zur Lage der bürgerlichen Demokratie in Russland," *Archiv für Sozialwissenschaft und Sozialpolitik* 22 (1906): 234-53.

9. Kistiakovskii, "V zashchitu prava," p. 155.

10. For additional comments on the ideological split among the *Vekhi* contributors, see Brooks, "*Vekhi*," pp. 44-50.

11. Kistiakovskii, *Sotsial'nye nauki*, pp. 8-9.

12. Ibid., pp. 5-6.

13. Ibid., p. 6.

14. Ibid., p. 10.

15. Ibid., pp. 21-22.

16. Ibid., p. 254.

17. Ibid., p. 288.

18. Kistiakowski, *Gesellschaft*, pp. 19-42.

19. Kistiakovskii, *Sotsial'nye nauki*, pp. 15-16.

20. Ibid., p. 163.

21. Ibid., pp. 135-39.

22. Ibid., p. 142.

23. Ibid., p. 81.

24. Ibid., p. 64.

25. Ibid., p. 52.

26. Ibid., p. 78.

27. Ibid., p. 172.

28. Max Weber, *Gesammelte Aufsätze*, pp. 230, 269, 288-90. For relations between Kistiakovskii and Weber, see Marianne Weber, *Max Weber*, p. 373; Mommsen, *Max Weber*, pp. 64-65.

29. Kistiakowski, *Gesellschaft*, p. 73.

30. For comments on Kistiakovskii's two-faceted theory, see Kelsen, *Der soziologische und der juristische Staatsbegriff*, pp. 106-13.

31. Kistiakowski, *Gesellschaft*, p. 73.

32. Kistiakovskii, *Sotsial'nye nauki*, p. 251.

33. Kareev, review of Kistiakovskii, *Sotsial'nye nauki*, pp. 348-49. For a comparison of Lavrov's and Rickert's epistemological interpretations of differences between the natural and social sciences, see N. K., "Istoriko-teoreticheskie vzgliady," pp. 118-20.

34. Kistiakovskii, *Sotsial'nye nauki*, p. 321.

35. Ibid., pp. 338-39. For pertinent biographical data on Muromtsev, see Miliukov, "Sergei Andreevich Muromtsev"; Kokoshkin, "S. A. Muromtsev"; Gredeskul, "Pervaia Duma"; and Lednitskii, "S. A. Muromtsev."

36. Kablukov, "V Iuridicheskom obshchestve," p. 132.

37. Miliukov, "Sergei Andreevich Muromtsev," p. 37; Kizevetter, *Na rubezhe*, pp. 25-26.

38. Muromtsev, "Pravo i spravedlivost'," pp. 1-12; Kistiakovskii, *Sotsial'nye nauki*, p. 354.

39. Shershenevich, "S. A. Muromtsev," pp. 88-89.

40. Kistiakovskii, *Sotsial'nye nauki*, pp. 353-54.

41. Muromtsev, "Odinochnaia bor'ba," pp. 19-21.

42. Kareev, *Istoriko-filosofskie i sotsiologicheskie etiudy*, p. 132.

43. For pertinent comments on Muromtsev's sociology of law, see Chernov, "Tipy," p. 50; Kareev, *Vvedenie*, pp. 150-52.

44. Kistiakovskii, *Sotsial'nye nauki*, 353-54.

45. Ibid., p. 355.

46. Sh. M. Levin, *Obshchestvennoe dvizhenie*, p. 499.

47. Pospelov, "Iz zhizny," p. 109; Svatikov, "Opal'naia professura," pp. 22-23.

48. When in 1912 Kistiakovskii was appointed the editor of the *Juridical Messenger* he wrote to his mother that he considered himself particularly honored to have been chosen to fill the position once occupied by Muromtsev (Vasilenko, "Akademik Bogdan O. Kistiakovs'kii, p. xxix).

49. For details on Petrazhitskii's contributions to the theory of law, see Timasheff, "Petrazhitsky's Philosophy of Law" and "Introduction"; Gintsberg, "Uchenie"; Babb, "Petrazhitsky: Theory of Law" and idem, "Petrazhitsky: Science and Legal Policy"; Gurvitch, *Le temps présent*, pp. 279-95, and idem, *L'expérience juridique*, pp. 153-69; Langrod and Vaughan, "The Polish Psychological Theory." See particularly Kistiakovskii, *Sotsial'nye nauki*; and Reisner, "Sovremennaia iurisprudentsiia" and "The Theory of Petrazhitskii."

50. For Petrazhitskii's views on the leading theories of law, see his *Teoriia prava*, vol. 1, chap. 3.

51. For details on the general principles of Petrazhitskii's legal philosophy, see his *Vvedenie*, part 2.

52. Trubetskoi, "Filosofiia prava," pp. 30-32.

53. Kistiakovskii, *Sotsial'nye nauki*, pp. 265-66.

54. Petrazhitskii, *Vvedenie*, p. 305, and idem, *Teoriia prava*, vol. 1, pp. 49-59.

55. For comments on "the politics of law," see V. Gessen, "Vozrozhdenie," pp. 476-77.

56. When, after the October Revolution, he migrated to Poland and served as a professor on the Faculty of Law of Warsaw University, he concerned himself with the sociology of law. He shifted the emphasis of his research from "the methodological problems of legal theory" to "legal policy" as a means for "planned and rational modifications of social order" (Langrod and

Vaughan, "The Polish Psychological Theory," p. 329). However, his sociological theories were not published and are preserved only in the notebooks and memories of students.

57. Petrazhitskii, "Obychnoe pravo i narodnyi dukh," no. 7, p. 328.

58. Ibid., p. 329.

59. Petrazhitskii, "Po povodu voprosa o tsennosti obychnogo prava," no. 5, p. 220, and idem, "Obychnoe pravo i narodnyi dukh," no. 7, p. 323.

60. Petrazhitskii, Vvedenie, p. viii.

61. Reisner, "Sovremennaia iurisprudentsiia," no. 2, p. 46.

62. Petrazycki, Law and Morality, pp. 225-26.

63. Petrazhitskii, Teoriia, vol. 1, pp. 135-42. For a summary of Petrazhitskii's views on these differences, see Sorokin, Society, pp. 83-85. For an effort to make Petrazhitskii's ideas on the nature of legal and moral norms tools of empirical research, see Podgorecki, "Normy," pp. 31-51.

64. Kistiakovskii, Sotsial'nye nauki, p. 285.

65. Langrod and Vaughan do not share Kistiakovskii's generally negative attitude toward Petrazhitskii's studies of the social attributes of law. They state: "The psychological doctrine contains elements which allow a better understanding of the social essence and function of law.... The key to this problem is provided by Petrazycki's differentiation, unchallenged by other authors, between two social functions of law: the organizational and the attributive.... Both correspond to ... 'tendencies of legal mentality and of the development of that mentality ... to produce a stable and coordinated system of social conduct evoked by law—a firm and precisely defined order—with which individuals and masses can and should conform, and upon which there can be reliance and calculation as regards economic and other plans and enterprises and in the organization of life in general'" (Langrod and Vaughan, "The Polish Psychological Theory," p. 360). These authors, however, do not challenge Kistiakovskii's claim that Petrazhitskii's "sociology" did not provide an analytical methodology for a concrete study of the social functions of law. See also Sorokin, Contemporary Sociological Theories, pp. 701-5.

66. Kistiakovskii, Sotsial'nye nauki, p. 296. According to W. Seagle: "However admirable his [i.e., Petrazhitskii's] theory may be as a description of the formal aspects of law, it is quite useless as a historical and sociological tool, for it explains not a single legal phenomenon. It has value, however, as a demonstration of futility of all disputes as to the nature of law, and it has obviously reenforced the prevailing political pluralism. Petrazhitskii himself must have recognized the trend of his theory for he evolved a 'politics of law' in addition to a philosophy of law to take care of the practical problems of jurisprudence" (Seagle, "Trends," p. 679). In his Sociology of Law, G. Gurvitch, while giving credit to Petrazhitskii for having "discovered" the imperative-attributive structure of law, noted that he had limited his studies to a "purely psychological analysis" (Gurvitch, Sociology of Law, p. 51). According to F. S. C. Northrop: "In Petrazycki's psychological jurisprudence, even when its reaction to sociological jurisprudence is clarified, one is left normatively with a merely formal system, the content of which is a cultural, historical or psychological accident" (Northrop, The Complexity, p. 91). At the other extreme, M. Clifford-Vaughan and M. Scotford-Norton, with no documentation, claimed that Petrazhitskii's "sociology" rose above Durkheim's "sociologism" and Pareto's "cybernetics" (Clifford-Vaughan and Scotford-Norton, "Legal Norms," p. 276).

67. Kistiakovskii, Sotsial'nye nauki, p. 323.

68. "Novgorodtsev, Pavel Ivanovich," p. 282.

69. Novgorodtsev, "Pravo estestvennoe," p. 889.

70. Novgorodtsev, "Nravstvennyi idealizm," pp. 250-55.

71. Novgorodtsev, Kant i Gegel', p. 183.

72. Novgorodtsev, "Znachenie filosofii," p. 109.

73. Novgorodtsev, Istoricheskaia shkola, pp. 7-8.

74. Ibid., pp. 1-22. See also his "O zadachakh," pp. 1747-48.

75. For an interesting comparison of Novgorodtsev's views with those of Mikhailovskii and Lavrov, see Kareev, "Estestvennoe pravo," pp. 9-17. See also Kareev, "Nuzhno li vozrozhdenie," pp. 9-15.

76. For a comparative analysis of the theories of Stammler and Kistiakovskii, see N. Alekseev, "Sotsial'naia filosofiia," pp. 6-15.

77. Novgorodtsev, "Kant kak moralist," pp. 29-35.

78. The antimechanistic arguments were subsequently brought together and analyzed in two excellent studies: Spektorskii, *Problemy sotsial'noi fiziki* and N. Alekseev, *Nauki.*

79. Novgorodtsev, "Nravstvennyi idealizm," pp. 255, 296.

80. Novgorodtsev, "Znachenie filosofii," pp. 108-15.

81. Novgorodtsev, "Ideia prava," p. 113.

82. Kistiakovskii overlooked some of the leading Russian theorists of law who carefully avoided exaggerated emphasis on specific attributes of legal action and behavior. N. M. Korkunov, for example, provided elaborate analyses of the interlacing of "political" and "social" attributes of law. See Yaney, "Bureaucracy," pp. 473-86.

83. Kistiakovskii, *Sotsial'nye nauki,* p. 346.

84. Ibid., pp. 346-47.

85. Kistiakovskii, *Stranitsy proshlogo,* p. 116.

86. Trainin, "The Relationship," p. 438.

87. Kistiakovskii, "Gosudarstvo," pp. 506-7.

88. For an excellent summary of Kistiakovskii's theoretical views, see Kelsen, *Der soziologische und der juristische Staatsbegriff,* pp. 106-13. See also von Beyme, *Politische Soziologie,* pp. 42-46, 96-98.

Chapter 6

1. Miliukov, "M. M. Kovalevskii," p. 143.

2. Worms, "Maxime Kovalewsky," p. 262.

3. Kareev, "M. M. Kovalevskii," pp. 171-72.

4. Kovalevskii, "Moe nauchnoe i literaturnoe skital'chestvo," pp. 64-65.

5. Ibid., p. 65; "Kovalevskii, Maksim Maksimovich," p. 315.

6. Fateev, *Maksim Kovalevskii,* p. 46.

7. Ibid., p. 52.

8. For pertinent comments on his dismissal, see Timiriazev, *Nauka,* p. 368.

9. "Russkaia shkola v Parizhe," pp. 3-4; Safronov, *M. M. Kovalevskii,* p. 28.

10. Verrier, *Roberty,* p. 160.

11. Ibid., p. 162.

12. Kovalevskii, *Obshchinnoe zemlevladenie,* vol. 1, p. 1. For details on Kovalevskii's interpretation of the obshchina as a type of rural community, see Laptin, *Obshchina,* pp. 193-213.

13. This book was soon translated into Russian and Spanish.

14. The latter book was translated into German and published in seven volumes as *Die ökonomische Entwicklung.*

15. A critic suggested that Kovalevskii's introduction to *The Economic Growth* had little connection with the material and interpretations presented in the book. See L. S. Z., "Novyi trud," p. 119.

16. Kovalewsky, *Régime économique* and "The Origin and Growth of Village Communities."

17. Kovalevskii, "Dimitrii Andreevich Dril'," pp. 427-28; M. G., "Parizhskii sotsiologicheskii kongress," p. 84.

18. Maine, *Village-Communities,* p. 230.

19. Kovalevskii, *Sovremennyi obychai,* l:vi. See also A. Filippov, "M. M. Kovalevskii," p. 223.

20. Kovalevskii, "Istoriko-sravnitel'nyi metod," p. 69. (Cited by Safronov, *M. M. Kovalevskii,* p. 251.)

21. Kovalevskii, "Kondorse," no. 3, pp. 140-44; idem, no. 4, pp. 494-507.
22. Kovalevskii, *Sotsiologiia*, 1:6.
23. Ibid., p. 30.
24. Rubakin, *Sredi knig*, 2:903.
25. Kovalevskii, *Sotsiologiia*, 1:115.
26. Ibid., pp. 115, 262. See also Kovalevskii, *Sovremennye sotsiologi*, pp. 53-54 and "Psychologie et sociologie."
27. Kovalevskii, *Sotsiologiia*, 1:197.
28. Kazakov, *Teoriia progressa*, pp. 121-22.
29. Sorokin, "Teoriia faktorov," pp. 180-95. See also Kondrat'ev, "Rost' naseleniia," pp. 211-17.
30. Kovalevskii, *Sotsiologiia*, 1:264-300.
31. Ibid., p. 286.
32. Ward, *Dynamic Sociology*, l:xvii.
33. Kovalevskii, "Sovremennye frantsuzskie sotsiologi," pp. 351-52.
34. Kovalevskii, "Progress," p. 258 and "N. K. Mikhailovskii," pp. 206-7.
35. Kovalevskii, *Sotsiologiia*, 2:30.
36. Kazakov, *Teoriia progressa*, p. 107.
37. Kareev, "M. M. Kovalevskii," p. 178.
38. Safronov, *M. M. Kovalevskii*, p. 22.
39. Tugan-Baranovskii, "M. M. Kovalevskii," p. 51.
40. Kovalevskii, "N. K. Mikhailovskii," p. 210.
41. Kovalevskii, "Sotsiologiia i sravnitel'naia istoriia," p. 13.
42. K. Sokolov, "M. M. Kovalevskii," p. 240.
43. Struve, "M. M. Kovalevskii," pp. 98-100.
44. Miliukov, "M. M. Kovalevskii," p. 139.
45. Kovalevskii, "Dve zhizni," no. 7, p. 22.

Chapter 7

1. Resis, "Das Kapital," p. 226.
2. Filippov, "Sovremennye russkie ekonomisti," pp. 1541-42. For details on various Russian translations of *Capital*, see Tikhomirov, "Iz istorii," pp. 7-43. For details on the first translation of *Capital* into Russian and its reception, see Resis, "Das Kapital." According to Resis, when the Russian translation of *Capital* appeared in 1872, the belief of its publishers that it would be much in demand proved correct. "Three points were frequently made in reviews. Most of the reviewers found Marx's description of the horrors of capitalism inflicted on the proletariat in the West of the greatest interest. . . . A second group, mostly academics, concerned themselves with Marx's method. A third group, however, manifested a new interest, a concern with Marx's 'laws' and stages of economic development as they applied to Russia" (Resis, "Das Kapital," p. 228). See also Sh. M. Levin, *Obshchestvennoe dvizhenie*, pp. 338-48.
3. Marx, *Capital*, p. 21; K. *Marks, F. Engels i revoliutsionnaia Rossiia*, p. 42.
4. For interesting comments, see Mikhailovskii, "Literatura i zhizn'," no. 1, 1895, pp. 140-41.
5. For more details on Ziber's research interests and contributions, see Reuel', *Russkaia ekonomicheskaia mysl'*, chap. 6.
6. P. B. Struve noted that the Russian academic community—as represented by political economists—turned against the "abstract method" in political economy and "economic liberalism" built upon Adam Smith's theoretical legacy under the direct influence not of Marx but of German "academic socialists" (Struve, *Istoricheskoe vvedenie*, pp. 5-6). For interesting comments, see Wortman, *The Crisis*, pp. 146-47.
7. Martov, "Obshchestvennye i umstvennye techeniia," p. 49.
8. Baron, "Plekhanov," pp. 59-60.

9. Kondrat'ev, *Mikhail Ivanovich Tugan-Baranovskii*, p. 35. For a detailed analysis of the economic, social, and political background of Russian Marxism during the 1890s, see Keep, *The Rise*, chap. 2.

10. For additional details, see Baron, "The First Decade," pp. 323-30.

11. Kareev, *Istoriko-filosofskie i sotsiologicheskie etiudy*, p. 236.

12. Vinogradoff, *Villainage*, pp. vi-vii.

13. Nine years earlier, I. V. Luchitskii, the well-known Russian expert on French economic history, stated that economic history is the only history that has scientific foundations and that its future was not merely in tracing the main lines of economic growth but in analyzing the relations of economy to all major categories of institutions. Kareev, *Istoriko-filosofskie i sotsiologicheskie etiudy*, pp. 178-79.

14. Tugan-Baranovskii, *Promyshlennye krizisy*, p. i.

15. Kindersley, *The First Russian Revisionists*, p. 58. Tugan-Baranovskii's influence on Western economic theory is discussed in Moisseev, "L'évolution d'une doctrine." See also Kondrat'ev, *Mikhail Ivanovich Tugan-Baranovskii*, pp. 81-82; Tschebotareff, *Untersuchungen*, pp. 39-54; and Timoshenko, "M. I. Tuhan-Baranovsky," pp. 813-22.

16. Plekhanov, "O sotsial'noi demokratii," p. 275.

17. Liadov, *Istoriia*, pp. 145-46.

18. Mikhailovskii, "Literatura i zhizn'," no. 1 (1894), pp. 105-6. See also Plekhanov, *Izbrannye filosofskie proizvedeniia*, 1:677.

19. Kareev, *Istoriko-filosofskie i sotsiologicheskie etiudy*, pp. 191-92.

20. Tugan-Baranovskii, *Statisticheskie itogi*, pp. 40-41.

21. Tugan-Baranovskii, *Russkaia fabrika*, p. iv.

22. Struve, *Kriticheskie zametki*, p. 35.

23. Kindersley, *The First Russian Revisionists*, p. 56. In a later study, Tugan-Baranovskii claimed that "without Proudhon's *Système des contradictions économique ou Philosophie de la misère* (1846) Marx would have found it impossible to write *Capital*. Both the general plan and many specific features of Proudhon's *Système* exercised a powerful influence on the author of *Capital*, who attributed no value to the work to which he was so much indebted" (Tugan-Baranovskii, "Ocherki," no. 2 [1902]: 84, 90).

24. Bulgakov, "O zakonomernosti," p. 611. For additional comments, see A. P. Mendel, *Dilemmas*, pp. 133-34.

25. Lenin, *Polnoe sobranie sochinenii*, 1:429.

26. Plekhanov, *Fundamental Problems of Marxism*, pp. 80-81.

27. Lenin, *Polnoe sobranie sochinenii*, 1:137.

28. Plekhanov, *Izbrannye filosofskie proizvedeniia*, 2:483-84. See also Krivtsov, "Plekhanov kak sotsiolog," p. 51.

29. Aref'eva and Lysmankin, "Razvitie," p. 278.

30. Lenin, *Polnoe sobranie sochinenii*, 1:138.

31. Ibid., 1:167, 429.

32. Ibid., p. 166.

33. Marx, *Capital*, p. 15.

34. Lenin, *Polnoe sobranie sochinenii*, 1:166.

35. Marx and Engels, *The Economic and Philosophic Manuscripts*, p. 143.

36. Marx and Engels, *Selected Works*, p. 183.

37. Aksel'rod (Ortodoks), *O 'Problemakh idealizma'*, pp. 41-42. The scientific nature of Marx's political economy was analyzed in Filippov, "Sotsiologicheskoe uchenie," no. 2, pp. 41-44. Filippov likened Marx's study of English capitalism to the work of a chemist who studied a substance in its pure (or classic) form. Marx, he thought, combined Ricardo's "geometric precision" with Adam Smith's catholicity of interests.

38. Rumiantsev, Osipov, and Burlatskii, "Lenin," p. 268.

39. Lenin, *Polnoe sobranie sochinenii*, 1:139.
40. Plekhanov, *Izbrannye filosofskie proizvedeniia*, 1:690-91.
41. Plekhanov, *Unaddressed Letters*, p. 19.
42. Ibid., pp. 18-19.
43. Plekhanov, *Fundamental Problems of Marxism*, pp. 46-47.
44. Deborin, *Filosofiia i politika*, p. 65.
45. Ibid., pp. 65-66.
46. Marx and Engels, *Selected Works in Three Volumes*, 3:201.
47. Marx and Engels, *Selected Correspondence*, p. 518.
48. Marx and Engels, *Selected Works in Three Volumes*, 3:191.
49. Plekhanov, *Izbrannye filosofskie proizvedeniia*, 1:686.
50. Plekhanov, *Fundamental Problems of Marxism*, pp. 63-64.
51. Lenin, *Polnoe sobranie sochinenii*, 1:149.
52. Ibid., p. 146.
53. Plekhanov, *Sochineniia*, 8:299. See also Tugan-Baranovskii, "Znachenie ekonomicheskogo faktora," p. 111.
54. Daniel'son [Nikolai-on], "Apologiia," no. 2, pp. 23, 34.
55. Vorontsov [V. V.], *Sud'by kapitalizma*, p. 5.
56. Baron, "Legal Marxism," p. 123.
57. Struve, *Kriticheskie zametki*, 1:288.
58. Marx and Engels, *Selected Works in Three Volumes*, 3:157. For a detailed Marxist critique of the economic premises of the Populist theory of *obshchina* as a model rural community, see Plekhanov [A. Volgin], *Obosnovanie narodnichestva*, pp. 82-175, idem, *Nashi raznoglasiia*, chap. 3, and Laptin, *Obshchina*, pp. 100-118.
59. Struve, *Kriticheskie zametki*, pp. 63-64.
60. Plekhanov, *Sochineniia*, 7:211.
61. Ibid.
62. Dan, *The Origins*, p. 174.
63. Lenin, *Polnoe sobranie sochinenii*, 4:184.
64. Ibid., 20:128.
65. For Tugan-Baranovskii's views on Populist economic theory see his *Russkaia fabrika*, pp. 542-60.
66. Struve, *Na raznye temy*, pp. 462-64. See also Filippov, "Sub'ektivizm." For a critical survey of Marxist views on the "capitalist" transformation of Russian agriculture, see Martynov, "Glavneishie momenty," pp. 307-13. The substantive and theoretical richness of *Russkaia fabrika* had led V. P. Timoshenko to assert that Tugan-Baranovskii's work was "in close relation to the theoretical and historical work in Western Europe" and that Tugan-Baranovskii not only gave a masterful analysis of the evolution of Russian economy but also contributed to "the creation of a theory of capitalist development, both in Russia and in general" (Timoshenko, "M. I. Tuhan-Baranovsky," pp. 814-15).
67. Mikhailovskii, "Literatura i zhizn'," no. 1 (1895): 151. For a survey of the anti-Marxist campaign of Mikhailovskii and other *Russian Wealth* writers, see Kareev, *Starye i novye etiudy*, pp. 230-67.
68. Mikhailovskii, "Literatura i zhizn'," no. 1 (1896): 40-66; Gorev, *N. K. Mikhailovskii*, p. 66; Khoros, *Narodnicheskaia ideologiia*, pp. 121-22. According to Lunkevich: "While having recognized the gigantic role of the economic factor, Mikhailovskii refused to treat it as an exclusive and universal force behind historical events" (Lunkevich, *N. K. Mikhailovskii*, p. 84). If anything, Kareev argued, the Populist critics were inclined to exaggerate the importance of the economic factor in history (Kareev, *Starye i novye etiudy*, p. 267).
69. Lenin, *Polnoe sobranie sochinenii*, 1:165.
70. Polianskii, *Plekhanov*, p. 71.

71. Kazakov, *Teoriia progressa*, p. 63. See also Khoros, "V. I. Lenin"; Sh. M. Levin, "V. I. Lenin i problema revoliutsionnogo narodnichestva," pp. 139–230; Sh. M. Levin, "V. I. Lenin i russkaia obshchestvenno-politicheskaia mysl'," pp. 286–306.

72. Struve, *Na raznye temy*, pp. 499–500.

73. Ibid., p. 504.

74. Struve, "Die Marxsche Theorie," p. 680. See also Potresov, "Evoliutsiia," pp. 588–89. The metamorphosis of Marxian social theory in the 1890s is described in Struve, "Na raznye temy," *Mir bozhii*, no. 6 (1901): 17–20; Martynov, "Glavneishie momenty," pp. 318–20.

75. Struve, "Predislovie," p. vi.

76. Ibid., p. vii.

77. Ibid., p. xxiii.

78. Struve, *Na raznye temy*, p. 520.

79. Struve, "Predislovie," pp. liii–liv.

80. Struve, "Intelligentsiia i revoliutsiia," pp. 169–74.

81. Miloradovich, Review of *Vekhi*, p. 432.

82. For Struve's defense of his new orientation, see his "Na raznye temy," *Russkaia mysl'*, no. 5 (1909): 123. He was particularly critical of D. I. Shakhovskoi's claim that his "social reaction" was more portentous than "government reaction."

83. Struve, "Na raznye temy," *Russkaia mysl'*, no. 1 (1909): 209–10; and idem, "Religiia i sotsializm," p. 159.

84. Struve, "Na raznye temy," *Russkaia mysl'*, no. 12 (1909): 191.

85. Struve, *Khoziaistvo i tsena*, 1:39.

86. Struve, "Otryvki," pp. 192–93.

87. Struve, "Khoziaistvo i tsena," pp. 134–35.

88. Struve, *Khoziaistvo i tsena*, 1:60–61. See also Struve, "Sovremennyi krizis," pp. 138–42.

89. For a critical appraisal, see Ratner, "Uchenyi podkhod," pp. 60–61.

90. Struve, *Khoziaistvo i tsena*, 1:7. For a critical review, see Tugan-Baranovskii, "Novyi trud," pp. 374–76.

91. Tugan-Baranovskii, "Ocherki," no. 9 (1902): 134.

92. Kindersley, *The First Russian Revisionists*, p. 163.

93. Tugan-Baranovskii, "Osnovnaia oshibka," p. 974.

94. Tugan-Baranovskii, "Ocherki," no. 7 (1902): 162.

95. Tugan-Baranovskii, *Modern Socialism*, p. 9.

96. Tugan-Baranovskii, "Ocherki," no. 10 (1902): 302.

97. Tugan-Baranovskii, *Modern Socialism*, pp. 11–14.

98. Tugan-Baranovskii, "Subjektivismus," p. 564.

99. Tugan-Baranovskii, "Predislovie," pp. iv–viii. See also L. Slonimskii, "Spory," pp. 734–36.

100. Tugan-Baranovskii, "Kant und Marx," pp. 187–88.

101. Tugan-Baranovskii, "Chto takoe obshchestvennyi klass?" pp. 64–72.

102. Tugan-Baranovskii, "Bor'ba klassov," p. 243.

103. Tugan-Baranovskii offered detailed criticisms of Marxian sociology in "Bor'ba klassov," "Chto takoe obshchestvennyi klass?" and "Intelligentsiia i sotsializm." See also Vorländer, *Kant und Marx*, pp. 200–206; and Bernstein, "Tugan-Baranowsky als Sozialist."

104. Tugan-Baranovskii, "Bor'ba klassov," p. 249.

105. Ibid., p. 252.

106. Tugan-Baranovskii, *Obshchestvenno-ekonomicheskie idealy*, p. 4.

107. Tugan-Baranovskii, *Sotsial'nye osnovy kooperatsii*, chap. 1.

108. Tugan-Baranovskii, *Modern Socialism*, pp. 180–81.

Chapter 8

1. For biographical data on Bogdanov, see Grille, *Lenins Rivale*, pp. 39–72; Shcheglov, *Bor'ba*

Lenina, pp. 72-74; Pokrovskii, "A. A. Bogdanov," pp. v-x; Krivtsov, "Pamiati A. A. Bogdanova," pp. 179-86. For an autobiographical note, see "Bogdanov (Malinovskii), Aleksandr Aleksandrovich," pp. 29-33. See also Utechin, "Philosophy and Society," pp. 117-25; and Yassour, "Bogdanov et sa oeuvre," pp. 446-49.

2. Lenin, *Polnoe sobranie sochinenii*, 4:35.

3. *Leninskii sbornik*, 11:333; Grille, *Lenins Rivale*, p. 50.

4. Krivtsov, "Pamiati A. A. Bogdanova," p. 182.

5. Ibid., p. 185. See also Denisova, "V. I. Lenin," pp. 52-59.

6. Danilova, "Stanovlenie marksistskogo napravleniia," pp. 75-76.

7. Marx, *A Contribution*, pp. 11-12.

8. Bogdanov, *Iz psikhologii obshchestva*, p. 40.

9. Ibid., p. 42.

10. *Leninskii sbornik*, 11:332; M. Vol'skii, "Ekonomicheskii materializm," no. 8, pp. 1-2.

11. Gonikman, "Teoriia obshchestva," p. 27.

12. Bogdanov, *Osnovnye elementy*, p. 206.

13. Ibid., p. 9.

14. Ibid., p. 18. See also his *Filosofiia zhivogo opyta*, p. 208.

15. Bogdanov, *Poznanie*, p. 3.

16. Ibid., p. v.

17. Ibid., p. 186.

18. Ibid., p. 160.

19. Ibid., pp. 193-94.

20. Ibid., p. 168.

21. Ibid., p. 171.

22. For a summary discussion of the epistemological foundations of empiriomonism, see Bogdanov, *Filosofiia zhivogo opyta*, pp. 208-43. For orthodox Marxist criticism, see Lenin, *Polnoe sobranie sochinenii*, 18:133-40, 237-44, 342-51; Deborin, *Filosofiia i politika*, pp. 53-61; Plekhanov, *Izbrannye filosofskie proizvedeniia*, 3:202-301; N. Karev, "Tektologiia." For a critique from a neopositivist position, see N. V. Vol'skii [Valentionov], *Filosofskie postroeniia*, pp. 252-307.

23. Bogdanov, "Filosofiia sovremennogo estestvoispytatelia," p. 46.

24. Bogdanov, *Empiriomonizm*, 1:38.

25. Ibid., 1:250.

26. Bogdanov, *Prikliucheniia*, p. 46.

27. Bogdanov, *Novyi mir*, p. 12. The cited chapter, "Sobiranie cheloveka," was originally published in *Pravda* in 1904.

28. Bogdanov, *Padenie*, pp. 179-80.

29. Bogdanov, *Empiriomonizm*, 3:88.

30. Ibid., p. 66.

31. Bogdanov, *Iz psikhologii obshchestva*, pp. 38-39; Marx, *A Contribution*, pp. 11-12.

32. Bogdanov, *Padenie*, pp. 141, 155-57.

33. Bogdanov, "Filosofiia sovremennogo estestvoispytatelia," p. 73.

34. Lenin, *Polnoe sobranie sochinenii*, 18:344.

35. Bogdanov, "Filosofiia sovremennogo estestvoispytatelia," pp. 43-44.

36. Bogdanov [Verner], "Nauka i filosofiia," p. 29.

37. Bogdanov, *Iz psikhologii obshchestva*, p. 77.

38. Bogdanov, *Novyi mir*, p. 16.

39. Bogdanov, *Empiriomonizm*, 3:59.

40. Ibid., 3:66.

41. Ibid., 3:48, 55.

42. Ibid., 3:83-84; Bogdanov, *Padenie*, p. 180.

43. Bogdanov, "Filosofiia sovremennogo estestvoispytatelia," p. 39.

44. Ibid., p. 43.
45. Bogdanov [Bogdanov, E.], "Strana idolov," p. 217.
46. Ibid., pp. 215-16.
47. Bogdanov, *Iz psikhologii obshchestva*, p. 69.
48. Bogdanov, *Empiriomonizm*, 3:42.
49. Bogdanov, *Iz psikhologii obshchestva*, p. 76.
50. Ibid., p. 80.
51. Ibid., p. 51.
52. Ibid., p. 16.
53. Ibid., p. 42.
54. Ibid., p. 28.
55. Ibid., p. 29.
56. Bogdanov, *Empiriomonizm*, 3:85.
57. Ibid., p. 89. For an analysis of the evolution of the workers' class, see his *Elementy proletarskoi kul'tury*, chaps. 1-3.
58. Ibid., p. 137.
59. Bogdanov, *Iz psikhologii obshchestva*, pp. 270-71.
60. Ibid., p. 11.
61. Ibid., p. 12.
62. Bogdanov, "Filosofiia sovremennogo estestvoispytatelia," p. 98.
63. Bogdanov, *Elementy proletarskoi kul'tury*, p. 29.
64. Bogdanov, *Novyi mir*, pp. 41-49. For interesting comments and the historical setting of Bogdanov's theory of personality and alienation, see J. D. White, "The First *Pravda*," pp. 195-96.
65. Bogdanov, *Kul'turnye zadachi*, p. 55.
66. Bogdanov, "Filosofiia sovremennogo estestvoispytatelia," p. 96.
67. Bogdanov, *Novyi mir*, pp. 105-7.
68. Bogdanov, *Iz psikhologii obshchestva*, p. 12.
69. Bogdanov, *Vseobshchaia organizatsionnaia nauka*, 1:38.
70. Shcheglov, *Bor'ba*, p. 126.
71. Bogdanov, *Vseobshchaia organizatsionnaia nauka*, 1:217.
72. Bogdanov, *Novyi mir*, p. 15.
73. Bogdanov, *Vseobshchaia organizatsionnaia nauka*, 1:3, 11.
74. Ibid., p. 108.
75. Ibid., p. 190.
76. Ibid., p. 229.
77. Ibid., p. 193.
78. Ibid., p. 231.
79. Bogdanov, *Sotsializm nauki*, pp. 102-4.
80. Bogdanov, *Filosofiia zhivogo opyta*, pp. 207-8.
81. Narskii and Suvorov, *Pozitivizm*, p. 36.
82. Bogdanov, *Sotsializm nauki*, pp. 92-94.
83. Setrov, "Printsip sistemnosti," p. 63. See also Setrov, "Ob obshchikh elementakh," pp. 56-60.
84. For additional details on the basic principles of tektology, see Takhtadzhian, "Tektologiia," pp. 205-29; Karev, "Tektologiia," and Grille, *Lenins Rivale*, pp. 190-200. For a general critique of tektology from a Marxist point of view, see Vainshtein, *Organizatsionnaia teoriia*.

Conclusion

1. In *Gedanken*, Paul Lilienfeld elaborated the notion of human society as a living organism, not in a figurative but in a real sense. Jacques Novicow, a Russian who spent most of his life in

France, wrote a number of studies united by a search for a humanistic interpretation of the role of Darwinism in sociological theory (Barnes, "The Sociological Doctrines," pp. 419-40).

2. For an elaboration of this theme within the context of Populist sociology, see Kacharovskii, "Narodnichestvo," no. 4, p. 89; idem, no. 5, p. 44.

3. Kareev, *Istoriko-filosofskie i sotsiologicheskie etiudy*, p. 103.

4. As cited in Chernov, "Sub'ektivnyi metod," p. 112.

5. Bogdanov, *Novyi mir*, pp. 13-14.

6. Miliukov, *Ocherki*, 1:116.

7. Pirogov, *Sochineniia*, 1:355.

8. Mikhailovskii, *Revoliutsionnye stat'i*, pp. 9-10.

9. Lavrov, *Gosudarstvennyi element*, pp. 44-45.

10. Ibid., chaps. 4, 7.

11. Kistiakovskii, "Gosudarstvo," p. 481.

12. Lappo-Danilevskii, *Ocherk russkoi diplomatiki*.

13. As cited in Chernov, "N. K. Mikhailovskii kak eticheskii myslitel'," p. 1.

14. Chernov, "Etika i politika," no. 7, p. 85.

15. Kistiakovskii, *Sotsial'nye nauki*, p. 34.

Bibliography

Agafonov, V. "Ob individual'nosti i individualizme." *Mir bozhii*, no. 2 (1904), section 1, pp. 282-97.

Aksel'rod [Ortodoks], L. *O'Problemakh idealizma'*. Odessa, 1905.

Alekseev, N. N. *Nauki obshchestvennye i estestvennye v istoricheskom vzaimootnoshenii ikh metodov.* Moscow, 1912.

———. "Sotsial'naia filosofiia Rudol'fa Shtammlera." *Voprosy filosofii i psikhologii*, no. 96 (1909), section 2, pp. 1-26.

Aleksinskii, Grigorii. "Istorik-publitsist Afanasii Prokof'evich Shchapov." *Russkaia mysl'*, no. 7 (1901), section 2, pp. 28-75.

Antonovich, M. A. *Izbrannye stat'i.* Leningrad, 1938.

———. "Vospominaniia." In *Shestidesiatye gody*, edited by V. Evgen'eva-Maksimova and G. F. Tizengauzen, pp. 15-246. Leningrad, 1933.

Aptekman, O. V. "Flerovskii-Bervi i chaikovtsy." *Byloe*, no. 19 (1922): 119-34.

Aref'eva, G. S., and Lysmankin, E. N. "Razvitie V. I. Leninym ucheniia ob obshchestvenno-ekonomicheskoi formatsii." In *Lenin kak filosof*, edited by M. M. Rozental, pp. 273-93. Moscow, 1969.

Aristov, N. Ia. "Zhizn' Afanasiia Prokof'evicha Shchapova." *Istoricheskii vestnik*, no. 10 (1882): 5-44; no. 11 (1882): 295-336; no. 12 (1882): 575-618.

Arsen'ev, K., et al. *Intelligentsiia v Rossii: sbornik statei.* St. Petersburg, 1910.

———. *M. M. Kovalevskii: uchenyi, gosudarstvennyi i obshchestvennyi deiatel' i grazhdanin.* Petrograd, 1917.

B., A. "Kriticheskie zametki." *Mir bozhii*, no. 2 (1903), section 2, pp. 1-12.

Babb, H. "Petrazhitsky: Theory of Law." *Boston University Law Review*, no. 18 (1938): 511-78.

———. "Petrazhitsky: Science and Legal Policy." *Boston University Law Review*, no. 17 (1937): 793-829.

Bakounine, Michele. *Oeuvres.* Vol. 1 (5th edition), vols. 2-4 (1st edition). Paris, 1907-13.

Bakunin, M. A. *Archives Bakounine.* Arthur Lehning, ed. 5 vols. Leiden, 1961-74.

———. *Bakunin on Anarchy: Selected Works by the Activist-Founder of World Anarchism.* Edited by S. Dolgoff. New York: Vintage Books, 1971.

———. *Izbrannye sochineniia.* Vols. 1-2, 2d ed.; vols. 3-5, 1st ed. Petrograd-Moscow, 1921-22.

———. *Neizdannye materialy i stat'i.* Moscow, 1926.

———. *The Political Philosophy of Bakunin: Scientific Anarchism.* Compiled and edited by G. P. Maximoff. Glencoe, Ill.: The Free Press, 1953.

———. *Selected Writings.* Edited by A. Lehning. New York: Grove, 1973.

Banina, N. N. *K. F. Kessler i ego rol' v razvitii biologii v Rossii.* Moscow, 1962.

———. "O nauchnom mirovozzrenii K. F. Kesslera." *Trudy Instituta Istorii estestvoznaniia i tekhniki* 31 (1960): 254-67.

Barnes, H. E. "The Sociological Doctrines of Jacques Novicow: A Sociological Criticism of War and Militarism." in *An Introduction to the History of Sociology*, edited by H. E. Barnes, pp. 419-40. Chicago: The University of Chicago Press, 1948.

Barnes, H. E., ed., *An Introduction to the History of Sociology.* Chicago: The University of Chicago Press, 1948.

Baron, Samuel H. "The First Decade of Russian Marxism." *The American Slavic and East European Review* 14, no. 3 (1955): 315–30.

——. "Legal Marxism and the 'Fate of Capitalism' in Russia." *The American Slavic and East European Review* 16, no. 2 (1957): 113–26.

——. "Plekhanov and the Origin of Russian Marxism." In *Soviet Sociology*, edited by A. Simirenko, pp. 56–68. Chicago: Quadrangle Books, 1966.

Barth, Paul. *Die Philosophie der Geschichte als Soziologie.* 2d ed., Leipzig, 1915.

Bazarov, V. et al. *Ocherki po filosofii marksizma: filosofskii sbornik.* St. Petersburg, 1908.

Berdiaev, N. A. "Narodnicheskoe i natsional'noe soznanie." *Russkaia mysl'*, no. 7–8 (1917), section 2, pp. 90–97.

——. *Sub'ektivizm i individualizm v obshchestvennoi filosofii: kriticheskii etiud o N. K. Mikhailovskom.* St. Petersburg, 1901.

——. *Sub specie aeternitatis.* St. Petersburg, 1907.

——, et al. *Vekhi: sbornik statei o russkoi intelligentsii.* 2d ed. Moscow, 1909.

Bernstein, Eduard. *Evolutionary Socialism.* Tr. by E. C. Harvey. New York: Schocken, 1961.

——. "Tugan-Baranowsky als Sozialist." *Archiv für Sozialwissenschaft und Sozialpolitik* 28 (1909): 786–96.

Bestuzhev-Riumin, K. N. "Teoriia kul'turno-istoricheskikh tipov." In *Rossiia i Evropa* by N. Ia. Danilevskii, 4th ed., pp. 559–610. St. Petersburg, 1889.

Beyme, Klaus von. *Politische Soziologie in zaristischen Russland.* Wiesbaden, 1965.

Blauberg, I. V., et al., eds. *Problemy metodologii sistemnogo issledovaniia.* Moscow, 1970.

Bogatov, V. V. *Filosofiia P. L. Lavrova.* Moscow, 1972.

——. "Istoriia odnoi filosofskoi polemiki. (K voprosu formirovaniia filosofskikh vzgliadov P. L. Lavrova." *Vestnik Moskovskogo universiteta (Filosofiia)*, no. 5 (1971): 65–76.

——. "P. L. Lavrov i estestvoznanie (k 150-letiiu so dnia rozhdeniia P. L. Lavrova)." *Filosofskie nauki*, no. 5 (1973): 118–29.

Bogdanov, A. A. See Malinovskii, A. A.

Borovoi, A. A., and Lebedev, N., eds. *Sbornik statei posviashchennyi pamiati P. A. Kropotkina.* Petrograd-Moscow, 1922.

Borovoi, Aleksei. "Problema lichnosti v uchenii P. A. Kropotkina." In *Sbornik statei posviashchennyi pamiati P. A. Kropotkina,* edited by A. A. Borovoi and N. Lebedev, pp. 30–51. Petrograd-Moscow, 1922.

Borozdin, A. "Danilevskii, Nikolai Iakovlevich." *Russkii biograficheskii slovar'* 6 (1905): 67–72.

Briullova-Shaskol'skaia, N. V. "Lavrov i Mikhailovskii." in *P. L. Lavrov: stat'i, vospominaniia, materialy* by E. Radlov et al., pp. 404–19. Petrograd, 1922.

Brooks, Jeffrey. "*Vekhi* and the *Vekhi* Dispute," *Survey*, no. 86 (1973): 21–50.

Buckle, Thomas Henry. *History of Civilization in England.* 2 vols. New York: Hearst's International Library, 1913.

Bulgakov, S. N. "Osnovnnye problemy teorii progressa." In *Problemy idealizma,* edited by P. I. Novgorodtsev, pp. 1–47. St. Petersburg, 1902.

——. "O zakonomernosti sotsial'nykh iavlenii." *Voprosy filosofii i psikhologii*, no. 35 (1896), section 2, pp. 575–611.

Carr, E. H. *Michael Bakunin.* London: Macmillan, 1937.

Cherepnin, L. "A. S. Lappo-Danilevskii—burzhuaznyi istorik i istochnikoved." *Voprosy istorii,* no. 8 (1949): 30–51.

Cherkezov, V. "Znachenie Bakunina v internatsional'nom revoliutsionnom dvizhenii." In *Izbrannye sochineniia* by M. Bakunin, vol. 1, pp. 3–43. Petrograd-Moscow, 1922.

Chernov, V. M. "Ekonomicheskii materializm i kriticheskaia filosofiia." *Voprosy filosofii i psikhologii,* no. 39 (1897): 609–44.

——. "Etika i politika." *Zavety,* no. 2 (1912), section 2, pp. 55–86; no. 3 (1912), section 2, pp. 90–120; no. 7 (1912), section 2, pp. 77–97.

————. *Filosofskie i sotsiologicheskie etiudy*. Moscow, 1907.

————. "Gde kliuch k ponimaniiu N. K. Mikhailovskogo?" *Zavety*, no. 3 (1913), section 2, pp. 82–132.

————. *The Great Russian Revolution*. Tr. and abridged by Philip E. Moseley. New Haven: Yale University Press, 1936.

————. *Konstruktivnyi sotsializm*. Vol. 1. Prague, 1925.

————. *Krest'ianin i rabochii kak ekonomicheskaia kategoriia*. Moscow, 1906.

————. *K teorii klassovoi bor'by*. Moscow, 1906.

————. "K voprosu o 'polozhitel'nykh' i 'otritsatel'nykh' storonakh kapitalizma." *Russkoe bogatstvo*, no. 4 (1901), section 1, pp. 222–54.

————. *Marks i Engels o krest'ianstve*. Moscow, 1906.

————. "Nauchnoe postroenie idealov i chistoe poznanie." *Zavety*, no. 12 (1913), section 2, pp. 142–83.

————. "N. K. Mikhailovskii kak eticheskii myslitel'." *Zavety*, no. 1 (1914), section 2, pp. 1–32.

————. "Ratsionalizm v etike." *Zavety*, no. 9 (1913), section 2, pp. 23–57.

————. "Sentimental'naia etika i nauchnaia etika." *Zavety*, no. 6 (1916), section 2, pp. 84–121.

————. "Sub'ektivnyi metod v sotsiologii i ego filosofskie predposylki." *Russkoe bogatstvo*, 1901, section 1: no. 7, 231–56; no. 8, 219–62; no. 10, 107–56; no. 11, 115–62; no. 12, 123–75.

————. "Tipy psikhologicheskogo i sotsiologicheskogo monizma." *Russkoe bogatstvo*, no. 1 (1899), section 1, pp. 33–69.

————. *Zapiski sotsialista-revoliutsionera*. Vol. 1. Berlin-Petrograd-Moscow, 1922.

Chernyshevsky, N. G. *Selected Philosophical Essays*. Moscow, 1953.

Chesnokov, D. I. "Lenin i marksistskaia sotsiologiia." In *Lenin kak filosof*, edited by M. M. Rozental, pp. 255–72. Moscow, 1969.

Chesnokov, G. D. *Sovremennaia burzhuaznaia filosofiia istorii*. Gorky, 1972.

Chuprov, A. A. *Ocherki po teorii statistiki*. Moscow, 1959.

Clifford-Vaughan, M., and Scotford-Norton, M. "Legal Norms and Social Order: Petrazycki, Pareto, Durkheim." *The British Journal of Sociology* 18, no. 3 (1967): 269–77.

Cole, G. D. H. *Socialist Thought: Marxism and Anarchism—1850-1890*. London: Macmillan, 1957.

Coquart, Armand. *Dmitri Pisarev (1840-1868) et l'idéologie du nihilisme russe*. Paris, 1946.

Dan, Theodore. *The Origins of Bolshevism*. Translated from the Russian by J. Carmichael. New York: Harper, 1964.

Daniel'son, N. F. [Nikolai-on]. "Apologiia vlasti deneg kak priznak vremeni." *Russkoe bogatstvo*, no. 1 (1895), section 2, pp. 155–85; no. 2 (1895), section 2, pp. 1–34.

Danilevskii, N. Ia. *Rossiia i Evropa*. 4th ed. St. Petersburg, 1889.

————. *Darvinizm: kriticheskoe issledovanie*. 2 vols. St. Petersburg, 1885–89.

Danilova, L. V. "Stanovlenie marksistskogo napravleniia v sovetskoi istoriografii epokhi feodalizma." *Istoricheskie zapiski* 76 (1965): 62–119.

Darwin, Charles. *The Descent of Man*. 2 vols. New York: Fowle, 1874.

Deborin, A. M. *Filosofiia i politika*. Moscow, 1961.

Demidova, V. V. "D. I. Pisarev i nigilizm 60-kh godov." *Vestnik Leningradskogo universiteta*, no. 5 (1965): 54–65.

Denisova, L. F. "V. I. Lenin i Proletkul't." *Voprosy filosofii*, no. 4 (1964): 49–59.

D'iakonov, M. A. "Aleksandr Sergeevich Lappo-Danilevskii." *Izvestiia Rossiiskoi Akademii nauk* 3 (1919), series 6, pp. 359–66.

Dobrovol'skii, V. A. "Pervyi kurs po istorii fiziko-matematicheskikh nauk v Rossii P. L. Lavrova." *Voprosy istorii estestvoznaniia i tekhniki* 34 (1971): 47–49.

Dostoevskii, F. M. *Pis'ma*. Edited by M. S. Dolinin. 4 vols. Moscow-Leningrad, 1928–59.

Duff, J. D., ed. *Russian Realities and Problems*. Cambridge: Cambridge University Press, 1917.

Durkheim, Emile. *The Division of Labor in Society.* 3d ed. Tr. from the French by G. Simpson. Glencoe, Ill.: The Free Press, 1947.

Dzhanshiev, G. A. *Epokha Velikikh Reform.* 9th ed. St. Petersburg, 1905.

Evgrafov, V. E., et al., eds. *Istoriia filosofii v SSSR.* Vol. 3. Moscow, 1968.

Fateev, A. *Maksim Kovalevskii.* (*K godovshchine smerti*). Moscow, 1917.

Fedorov, L. "Poteri nauki: pamiati I. A. Lappo-Davilevskogo." *Priroda,* no. 9 (1931): 924-28.

Fedorov, M. G. *Russkaia progressivnaia mysl' XIX v. ot geograficheskogo determinizma k istoricheskomu materializmu.* Novosibrisk, 1972.

Filippov, Aleksandr. "M. M. Kovalevskii kak issledovatel' obychnogo prava." In *M. M. Kovalevskii: uchenyi, gosudarstvennyi i obshchestvennyi deiatel' i grazhdanin,* by K. Arsen'ev et al., pp. 218-32. Petrograd, 1917.

Filippov, M. "Sovremennye russkie ekonomisty." *Nauchnoe obozrenie,* no. 8 (1899): 1540-63.

————. "Sotsiologicheskoe uchenie Karla Marksa." *Nauchnoe obozrenie,* no. 1 (1897): 64-80; no. 2 (1897): 40-67; no. 3 (1897): 72-100; no. 4 (1897): 16-35.

————. "Sub'ektivizm i narodnichestvo." *Nauchnoe obozrenie,* no. 12 (1897): 114-30.

————. "Teoriia kriticheski-mysliashchei lichnosti." *Nauchnoe obozrenie,* no. 4 (1900): 755-75.

Firsov, N. N. [L. Ruskin]. "Vospominaniia o P. L. Lavrove." *Istoricheskii vestnik,* no. 1 (1907): 95-119; no. 2 (1907): 494-510.

Gaidarov, N. "Rudol'f Shtammler i ego teoriia sotsial'nogo monizma." *Russkoe bogatstvo,* no. 10 (1902), section 1, pp. 30-57.

Gaisinovich, A. E. "Biolog-shestidesiatnik N. D. Nozhin i ego rol' v razvitii embriologii i darvinizma." *Zhurnal obshchei biologii* 13, no. 5 (1952): 373-92.

Galaktionov, A. A., and Nikandronov, P. F. *Ideologi russkogo narodnichestva.* Leningrad, 1966.

Gerth, H. H., and Mills, C. Wright. Introduction to *Essays in Sociology* by Max Weber. Translated by H. H. Gerth and C. Wright Mills, pp. 3-74. New York: Oxford University Press, 1946.

Gessen, V. "Vozrozhdenie estestvennogo prava." *Pravo,* no. 10 (1902): 475-84.

Gintsberg, V. Ia. "Uchenie L. I. Petrazhitskogo o prave i ego predposylki." *Voprosy filosofii i psikhologii,* no. 97 (1909), section 1, pp. 204-60.

Gizetti, A. "Individualizm i obshchestvennost' v mirovozzrenii N. K. Mikhailovskogo." *Zavety,* no. 1 (1914), section 2, pp. 33-46.

G., M. "Parizhskii sotsiologicheskii kongress." *Russkoe bogatstvo,* no. 3 (1895), section 2, pp. 82-91.

Gonikman, S. "Teoriia obshchestva i teoriia klassov Bogdanova." *Pod znamenem marksizma,* no. 12 (1929): 27-62.

Gorev, B. I. *N. K. Mikhailovskii.* Moscow, 1925.

Gredeskul, N. A. "Pervaia Duma i eia predsedatel'." In *Sergei Andreevich Muromtsev,* edited by D. I. Shakhovskoi, pp. 309-32. Moscow, 1911.

Grevs, I. M. "Aleksandr Sergeevich Lappo-Danilevskii. (Opyt istolkovaniia dushi)." *Russkii istoricheskii zhurnal,* no. 6 (1920): 44-81.

Grille, Dietrich. *Lenins Rivale.* Köln, 1966.

Gurevich. A. "Sovremennoe sostoianie sotsiologii." *Voprosy filosofii i psikhologii,* no. 67 (1903) section 2, pp. 159-67.

Gurvitch, Georges. *Sociology of Law.* New York: Philosophical Library, 1942.

————. *Le temps présent et l'idée du droit social.* Paris, 1932.

————. *L'expérience juridique et la philosophie pluraliste du droit.* Paris, 1935.

Hecker, Julius F. *Russian Sociology.* New York: Columbia University Press, 1915.

Herzen, A. I. *Polnoe sobranie sochinenii.* Vol. 20, part 1. Moscow, 1960.

Hoffman, Robert L. *Revolutionary Justice: The Social and Political Theory of P.-J. Proudhon* Urbana: University of Illinois Press, 1972.

Hoselitz, Bert F. Publisher's Preface. In *The Political Philosophy of Bakunin*, edited by G. P. Maximoff, pp. 9-16. Glencoe, Ill.: The Free Press, 1953.

Huxley, Thomas H. *Evolution and Ethics, and Other Essays*. New York: Appleton, 1896.

Iakovlev, V. Ia. [V. Bogucharskii]. *Aktivnoe narodnichestvo semidesiatykh godov*. Moscow, 1912.

Itenberg, B. S. *Dvizhenie revoliutsionnogo narodnichestva*. Moscow, 1965.

Iuzhakov, S. N. "Sotsiologicheskaia doktrina N. K. Mikhailovskogo." In *Na slavnom postu, 1860-1900: literaturnyi sbornik posviashchennyi N. K. Mikhailovskomu*, by D. Mamin-Sibiriak et al. 2d ed., pp. 352-69. St. Petersburg, 1906.

―――. *Sotsiologicheskie etiudy*. St. Petersburg, 1891.

Ivanov-Razumnik, R. V. *Istoriia russkoi obshchestvennoi mysli*. 2 vols. 3d ed. St. Petersburg, 1911.

―――. *Chto takoe intelligentsiia?* Berlin, 1920.

Kablits, I. [I. Iuzov]. *Osnovy narodnichestva*. 2d ed. 2 vols. St. Petersburg, 1888-93.

Kablukov, N. A. "V Moskovskom Iuridicheskom obshchestve." In *Sergei Andreevich Muromtsev*, edited by D. I. Shakhovskoi, pp. 116-40. Moscow, 1911.

Kacharovskii, K. "Narodnichestvo kak sotsiologicheskoe napravlenie." *Zavety* (1913): no. 3, section 2, pp. 68-81; no. 4, section 2, 72-89; no. 5, section 2, pp. 1-44; no. 6, section 2, pp. 75-83.

Kaminski, H. E. *Bakounine: La vie d'un révolutionnaire*. Paris, 1938.

Kamkov, Boris. "Istoriko-filosofskie vozzreniia P. L. Lavrova." *Zavety* (1913): no. 6, section 2, pp. 1-22; no. 7, section 2, pp. 112-39.

Kareev, N. I. "Estestvennoe pravo i sub'ektivnaia sotsiologiia (po povodu odnoi novoi knigi)." *Russkoe bogatstvo*, no. 10 (1902), section 2, pp. 1-17.

―――. *Istoriko-filosofskie i sotsiologicheskie etiudy*. St. Petersburg, 1895.

―――. "Istoriko-teoreticheskie trudy A. S. Lappo-Danilevskogo." *Russkii istoricheskii zhurnal*, no. 6 (1920): 112-31.

―――. "Iz vospominanii o P. L. Lavrove." *Byloe*, no. 9 (1918): 11-23.

―――. "P. L. Lavrov kak sotsiolog." In *P. L. Lavrov: stat'i, vospominaniia, materialy*, by E. L. Radlov et al., pp. 193-248. Petrograd, 1922.

―――. "M. M. Kovalevskii kak istorik i sotsiolog." In *M. M. Kovalevskii: uchenyi, gosudarstvennyi deiatel' i grazhdanin*, by K. Arsen'ev et al., pp. 169-79. Petrograd, 1917.

―――. "N. K. Mikhailovskii kak sotsiolog." *Russkie vedomosti*, no. 318 (November 15, 1900): 3-4.

―――. "Novyi istoriko-filosofskii trud." *Voprosy filosofii i psikhologii*, no. 45 (1898): 388-415.

―――. "Nuzhno li vozrozhdenie estestvennogo prava?" *Russkoe bogatstvo*, no. 4 (1902), section 2, pp. 1-15.

―――. *Osnovnye voprosy filosofii istorii*. 3d ed. St. Petersburg, 1897.

―――. "P. A. Kropotkin o Velikoi Frantsuzskoi Revoliutsii." In *Sbornik statei posviashchennyi pamiati P. A. Kropotkina*, edited by A. Borovoi and N. Lebedev, pp. 108-38. Petrograd-Moscow, 1922.

―――. Review of A. S. Lappo-Danilevskii, *Metodologiia istorii*. *Nauchnyi istoricheskii zhurnal*, no. 1 (1913): 64-69.

―――. Review of B. A. Kistiakovskii, *Sotsial'nye nauki i pravo*. *Golos minuvshego*, no. 11-12 (1917): 345-51.

―――. "Sotsiologiia." *Entsiklopedicheskii slovar'*. Vol. 31, pp. 77-83. St. Petersburg: Brokgauz and Efron, 1901.

―――. *Starye i novye etiudy ob ekonomicheskom materializme*. St. Petersburg, 1896.

―――. *Teoriia istoricheskogo znaniia*. St. Petersburg, 1913.

―――. "Teoriia kul'turno-istoricheskikh tipov." *Russkaia mysl'*, no. 9 (1889), section 2, pp. 1-32.

―――. *Vvedenie v izuchenie sotsiologii*. St. Petersburg, 1897.

Karev, N. "Tektologiia i dialektika." *Pod znamenem marksizma*, no. 1–2 (1926): 90–114; no. 3 (1926): 29–52.

Karpovich, Michael M. "P. L. Lavrov and Russian Socialism." *California Slavic Studies* 2 (1963): 21–38.

Kazakov, A. P. *Teoriia progressa v russkoi sotsiologii kontsa XIX veka.* (*P. L. Lavrov, N. K. Mikhailovskii, M. M. Kovalevskii.*) Leningrad, 1969.

Keep, J. L. H. *The Rise of Social Democracy in Russia.* Oxford: Clarendon, 1963.

Keldysh, M. V., ed. *Lenin i sovremennaia nauka.* 2 vols. Moscow, 1970.

Kelsen, Hans. *Der soziologische und der juristische Staatsbegriff.* 2d ed. Tübingen, 1962.

Khoros, V. G. *Narodnicheskaia ideologiia i marksizm.* Moscow, 1972.

————. " 'Narodnichestvo' na sovremennom etape natsional'no-osvoboditel'nogo dvizheniia." *Narody Azii i Afriki*, no. 3 (1973): 4–16.

————. "Problema 'Narodnichestva' kak internatsional'noi modeli ideologii razvivaiushchikhsia stran." *Narody Azii i Afriki*, no. 2 (1973): 46–57.

————. "V. I. Lenin i problema genezisa sub'ektivnoi sotsiologii v Rossii." *Voprosy filosofii*, no. 3 (1970): 40–49.

Kimball, Alan. "The Russian Past and the Socialist Future in the Thought of Peter Lavrov." *Slavic Review* 30, no. 1 (1971): 28–44.

Kindersley, Richard. *The First Russian Revisionists: A Study of "Legal Marxism" in Russia.* Oxford: Clarendon, 1962.

Kistiakovskii, B. A. "Ideia ravenstva s sotsiologicheskoi tochki zreniia." *Mir bozhii*, no. 4 (1900), section 1, pp. 160–69.

————. "Gosudarstvo pravovoe i sotsialisticheskoe." *Voprosy filosofii i psikhologii*, no. 85 (1906): 469–507.

————. Review of A. A. Chuprov, *Ocherki po teorii statistiki. Voprosy prava*, no. 1 (1910): 183–200.

————. "Russkaia sotsiologicheskaia shkola i kategoriia vozmozhnosti pri reshenii sotsial'no-eticheskikh problem." In *Problemy idealizma*, edited by P. I. Novgorodtsev, pp. 297–393. Moscow, 1902.

————. *Sotsial'nye nauki i pravo.* Moscow, 1916.

————. *Stranitsy proshlogo: k istorii konstitutsionnogo dvizheniia v Rossii.* Moscow, 1912.

————. "V zashchitu prava." In *Vekhi*, by N. A. Berdiaev et al., 2d ed., pp. 125–55. Moscow, 1909.

Kistiakowski, T. *Gesellschaft und Einzelwesen.* Berlin, 1899.

Kizevetter, A. A. *Na rubezhe dvukh stoletii.* Prague, 1929.

————. *Istoricheskie otkliki.* Moscow, 1915.

K., N. "Istoriko-teoreticheskie vzgliady Chernyshevskogo, Lavrova i Mikhailovskogo." *Nauchnyi istoricheskii zhurnal*, no. 1 (1913): 113–24.

Koialovich, M. O. *Istoriia russkogo samosoznaniia po istoricheskim pamiatnikam i nauchnym sochineniiam.* 3d ed. St. Petersburg, 1901.

Kokoshkin, F. F. "S. A. Muromtsev i zemskie s'ezdy." In *Sergei Andreevich Muromtsev*, edited by D. I. Shakhovskoi, pp. 205–50. Moscow, 1911.

Kolosov, E. E. *Ocherki mirovozzreniia N. K. Mikhailovskogo.* St. Petersburg, 1912.

Kondrat'ev, N. D. *Mikhail Ivanovich Tugan-Baranovskii.* Petrograd, 1923.

————. "'Rost' naseleniia kak faktor sotsial'no-ekonomicheskogo razvitiia v uchenii M. M. Kovalevskogo." In *M. M. Kovalevskii: uchenyi, gosudarstvennyi deiatel' i grazhdanin*, by K. Arsen'ev et al., pp. 196–217. Petrograd, 1917.

————. "Teoriia istorii A. S. Lappo-Danilevskogo." *Istoricheskoe obozrenie* 20 (1915): 105–24.

Kornilov, A. A. *Obshchestvennoe dvizhenie pri Aleksandre II (1855–1881).* Paris, 1905.

Kotliarevskii, Nestor. "Ocherki iz istorii obshchestvennogo nastroeniia shestidesiatykh godov." *Vestnik Evropy*, no. 11 (1912): 268–94; no. 12 (1912): 229–56.

Kovalevskii, M. M. "Dimitrii Andreevich Dril'." *Vestnik Evropy*, no. 12 (1910): 427-36.
———. "Dve zhizni." *Vestnik Evropy*, no. 6 (1909): 495-522; no. 7 (1909): 5-23.
———. "E. V. De Roberti." *Vestnik Evropy*, no. 5 (1915): 421-23.
———. "Kondorse." *Vestnik Evropy*, no. 3 (1894): 99-144; no. 4 (1894): 469-507.
———. "Moe nauchnoe i literaturnoe skital'chestvo." *Russkaia mysl'*, no. 1 (1895), section 2, pp. 61-80.
———. "N. K. Mikhailovskii kak sotsiolog." *Vestnik Evropy*, no. 4 (1913): 192-212.
———. "Novoe izdanie knigi Maurera." *Russkaia mysl'*, no. 7 (1896), section 2, pp. 37-43.
———. *Obshchinnoe zemlevladenie: prichiny, khod i posledstviia ego razlozheniia*. Vol. 1. Moscow, 1879.
———. "The Origin and Growth of Village Communities in Russia." *Archaeological Review* 1 (1888): 266-73.
———. "Progress." *Vestnik Evropy*, no. 2 (1912): 225-60.
———. *Sotsiologiia*. 2 vols. St. Petersburg, 1910.
———. "Sotsiologiia i sravnitel'naia istoriia prava." *Vestnik vospitaniia*, no. 2 (1902): 1-35.
———. "Sovremennye frantsuzskie sotsiologi." *Vestnik Evropy*, no. 7 (1913): 339-69.
———. *Sovremennye sotsiologi*. St. Petersburg, 1905.
———. *Sovremennyi obychai i drevnii zakon: obychnoe pravo osetin v istoriko-sravnitel'nom osveshchenii*. 2 vols. Moscow, 1886.
———. "Sravnitel'naia istoriia religii kak predmet prepodavaniia." *Vestnik Evropy*, no. 8 (1909): 843-51.
———. *Tableau des origines et de l'évolution de la famille et de la propriété*. Stockholm, 1890.
"Kovalevskii, Maksim Maksimovich." In *Materialy dlia biograficheskogo slovaria deistvitel'-nykh chlenov Imperatorskoi Akademii nauk*. Vol. 2, pp. 311-22. Petrograd, 1916. An autobiography.
Kovalevskii, M. M., and de Roberti, E. V., eds. *Novye idei v sotsiologii*. Vol. 2. St. Petersburg, 1914.
Kovalewsky, M. "Psychologie et sociologie." *Annales de l'Institut intenational de sociologie* 10 (1904): 247-64.
———. *Régime économique de la Russie*. Paris, 1898.
Kovarskii, B. N. K. *Mikhailovskii i obshchestvennoe dvizhenie 70-kh godov*. St. Petersburg, 1909.
Kozlov, A. "Pozitivizm Konta." *Voprosy filosofii i psikhologii*, no. 15 (1892), section 1, pp. 53-70; no. 16 (1893), section 1, pp. 41-70.
Koz'min, B. P. *Iz istorii revoliutsionnoi mysli v Rossii*. Moscow, 1961.
———. *Literatura i istoriia*. Moscow, 1969.
Krasnosel'skii, A. I. *Mirovozzrenie gumanista nashego vremeni: osnovy ucheniia N. K. Mikhailovskogo*. St. Petersburg, 1900.
Krivtsov, St. "Pamiati A. A. Bogdanova." *Pod znamenem marksizma*, no. 4 (1928): 179-86.
———. "Plekhanov kak sotsiolog." *Pod znamenem marksizma*, no. 6-7 (1923): 45-58.
[Kropotkin, P. A.] *Dnevnik P. A. Kropotkina*. Petrograd, 1923.
Kropotkin, P. A. *Ethics: Origin and Development*. New York: MacVeagh, 1924.
———. *Fields, Factories and Workshops*. New York: Greenwood, 1968.
———. *The Great French Revolution: 1789-1793*. Tr. from the French by N. F. Dryhurst. 2 vols. New York: Vanguard Press, 1927.
———. "Ideal v revoliutsii." *Byloe*, no. 17 (1921): 39-41.
———. *Ideals and Realities in Russian Literature*. New York: A. A. Knopf, 1919.
———. *Memoirs of a Revolutionist*. London: Swan, 1908.
———. *Modern Science and Anarchism*. 2d ed. London: Freedom Press, 1923.
———. *Mutual Aid*. Boston: Extending Horizons, n.d.

————. *Rechi buntovshchika.* Tr. from the French under the editorship of the author. Petrograd-Moscow, 1921.

————. *Revolutionary Pamphlets.* New York: Vanguard Press, 1927.

————. *Selected Writings on Anarchism and Revolution.* Edited by Martin A. Miller. Cambridge, Mass.: M.I.T. Press, 1970.

————. *Sovremennaia nauka i anarkhiia.* Petrograd-Moscow, 1921.

————. "Unsuspected Radiations." *Annual Report of the Board of Regents of the Smithsonian Institution for the Year Ending June 30, 1900.* Washington, D.C., 1901, pp. 371–85.

Kudrin, N. "Chem russkaia obshchestvennaia zhizn' obiazana N. K. Mikhailovskomu." In *Na slavnom postu (1860–1900): literaturnyi sbornik posviashchennyi N. K. Mikhailovskomu.* 2d ed. Vol. 2, pp. 1–44. St. Petersburg, 1905.

K., V., "Pozitivizm v russkoi literature." *Russkoe bogatstvo,* no. 3 (1889), section 2, pp. 3–41; no. 4 (1889), section 2, pp. 116–40.

Labedz, Leopold, ed. *Revisionism: Essays on the History of Marxist Ideas.* New York: Praeger, 1962.

Labry, Raoul. *Herzen et Proudhon.* Paris, 1928.

Lampert, E. *Sons against Fathers: Studies in Russian Radicalism and Revolution.* Oxford: Clarendon, 1965.

————. *Studies in Rebellion.* London: Routledge and Kegan Paul, 1957.

Lange, Frederick Albert. *The History of Materialism and Criticism of Its Present Importance.* Tr. by E. C. Thomas. 3d ed. London: Routledge, 1925.

Langrod, Georges S., and Vaughan, Michalina. "The Polish Psychological Theory of Law." In *Polish Law throughout the Ages,* edited by W. J. Wagner, pp. 299–362. Stanford, Calif.: Hoover Institution Press, 1970.

"Lappo-Danilevskii, Aleksandr Sergeevich." In *Materialy dlia biograficheskogo slovaria deistvitel'nykh chlenov Imperatorskoi Akademii nauk.* Vol. 1, pp. 405–13. Petrograd, 1915. An autobiography.

Lappo-Danilevskii, A. S. "The Development of Science and Learning in Russia." In *Russian Realities and Problems,* edited by J. D. Duff, pp. 153–229. Cambridge: Cambridge University Press, 1917.

————. "Ideia gosudarstva i glavneishie momenty eia razvitiia v Rossii so vremeny smuty i do epokhi preobrazovanii." *Golos minuvshego,* no. 12 (1914): 5–38.

————. *Metodologiia istorii.* Vol. 1, 3d ed., Petrograd, 1923; vol. 2, 1st ed., St. Petersburg, 1913.

————. *Ocherk russkoi diplomatiki chastnykh aktov.* Petrograd, 1920.

————. "Osnovnye printsipi sotsiologicheskoi doktriny O. Konta." In *Problemy idealizma,* edited by P. I. Novgorodtsev, pp. 394–490. Moscow, 1902.

Laptin, P. F. *Obshchina v russkoi istoriografii poslednei treti XIX–nachala XX v.* Kiev, 1971.

Lavrov, P. L. *Gosudarstvennyi element v budushchem obshchestve.* London: Vpered! 1876.

————. *Filosofiia i sotsiologiia.* 2 vols. Moscow, 1965.

————. *Formula progressa N. K. Mikhailovskogo. Protivniki istorii. Nauchnye osnovy istorii tsivilizatsii.* St. Petersburg, 1906.

————. *Historical Letters.* Translated by James P. Scanlan. Berkeley: The University of California Press, 1967.

————. *Izbrannye sochineniia na sotsial'no-politicheskie temy.* 4 vols. Moscow, 1934–35.

————. *Iz istorii sotsial'nykh uchenii.* Petrograd, 1919.

————. "Mekhanicheskaia teoriia mira." *Otechestvennye zapiski* 123 (1859), section 1, pp. 451–92.

————. *Stat'i sotsial'no-politicheskie.* Vol. 7. Petrograd, 1920.

————. *Stat'i po filosofii.* Vol. 6. Petrograd, 1918.

————. *Tri besedy o sovremennom znachenii filosofii.* St. Petersburg, 1861.

————. *Zadachi istorii mysli: podgotovlenie cheloveka.* Geneva, 1894.

————. *Zadachi pozitivizma i ikh reshenie.* 2d ed. St. Petersburg, 1906.

————. [Arnol'di, S. S.] *Zadachi ponimaniia istorii.* Moscow, 1898.

Lebedev, N. "P. A. Kropotkin: chelovek, myslitel', revoliutsionner." In *Sbornik statei posviashchennyi pamiati P. A. Kropotkina,* edited by A. Borovoi and N. Lebedev, pp. 3–12. Petrograd-Moscow, 1922.

————. "P. A. Kropotkin kak teoretik bio-sotsiologicheskogo zakona vzaimo-pomoshchi." *Byloe,* no. 17 (1921): 95–99.

————, ed. *Perepiska Petra i Aleksandra Kropotkinykh.* Vol. 2. Moscow-Leningrad, 1933.

Lednitskii, A. R. "S. A. Muromtsev v tiurme." In *Sergei Andreevich Muromtsev,* edited by D. I. Shakhovskoi, pp. 350–72. Moscow, 1911.

Leffler, A. C. *Sonia Kovalewsky: Biography and Autobiography.* Tr. by L. von Cossel. New York: Macmillan, 1895.

Lelevich, G. "Bogdanov, A." *Literaturnaia Entsiklopediia* 1 (1929): 526–30.

Lemke, Mikh. *Ocherki osvoboditel'nogo dvizheniia shestidesiatykh godov.* St. Petersburg. 1908.

Lenin, V. I. *Polnoe sobranie sochinenii.* 5th ed. 55 vols. Moscow, 1958–65.

————et al. *Soviet Legal Philosophy.* Tr. from the Russian by H. W. Babb. Cambridge, Mass.: Harvard University Press, 1951.

Leser, Norbert. *Die Odyssee des Marxismus.* Vienna, 1971.

Leninskii sbornik. Vol. 11. 2d ed. Moscow-Leningrad, 1931.

Lesevich, V. V. *Sobranie sochinenii.* 3 vols. Moscow, 1915–17.

Levin, Sh. M. *Obshchestvennoe dvizhenie v Rossii v 60-70-e gody XIX veka.* Moscow, 1958.

————. *Ocherki po istorii russkoi obshchestvennoi mysli: vtoraia polovina XIX-nachalo XX v.* Leningrad, 1974.

————. "V. I. Lenin i problema revoliutsionnogo narodnichestva 70-kh godov." In *V. I. Lenin i russkaia obshchestvenno-politicheskaia mysl' XIX-nachala XX v.,* edited by Sh. M. Levin, S. N. Valk, and V. S. Diakin, pp. 139–230. Leningrad, 1969.

————. "V. I. Lenin i russkaia obshchestvenno-politicheskaia mysl' 80-kh-nachala 900-kh godov." In *V. I. Lenin i russkaia obshchestvenno-politicheskaia mysl' XIX-nachala XX v.,* edited by Sh. M. Levin, S. N. Valk, and V. S. Diakin, pp. 231–390. Leningrad, 1969.

————, Valk, S. N., and Diakin, V. S., eds. *V. I. Lenin i russkaia obshchestvenno-politicheskaia mysl' XIX-nachala XX v.* Leningrad, 1969.

Lewes, G. H. *Comte's Philosophy of the Sciences.* London: Bohm, 1853.

Liadov, M. *Istoriia Rossiiskoi Sotsialisticheskoi rabochei partii.* Vol. 1. St. Petersburg, 1906.

Lilienfeld, Paul. *Gedanken über die Socialwissenschaft der Zukunft.* 5 vols. Mitau, 1873–81.

Lourié, Ossip. *La philosophie russe contemporaine.* 2d ed. Paris, 1905.

Luchinskii, G. A. Introduction to A. P. Shchapov, *Sochineniia.* Vol. 3, pp. xcvi–cix. St. Petersburg, 1909.

Lunacharskii, A. "Meshchanstvo i idealizm." In *Ocherki filosofii kollektivizma: sbornik statei.* Vol. 1, by N. Verner [A. A. Malinovskii] et al., pp. 219–349. St. Petersburg, 1909.

Lunkevich, V. *N. K. Mikhailovskii: kharakteristika-eskiz.* Moscow, 1906.

Maine, Henry S. *Village-Communities in the East and West.* New York: Holt, 1889.

Malato, Sh. "Kropotkin i Bakunin." In *Sbornik statei posviashchennyi pamiati P. A. Kropotkina,* edited by A. Borovoi and N. Lebedev, pp. 67–70. Petrograd-Moscow, 1922.

Malinin, V. V. *Filosofiia revoliutsionnogo narodnichestva.* Moscow, 1972.

Malinovskii, A. A. [Bogdanov, A.]. *Die Kunst und das Proletariat.* Tr. from the Russian by Gr. Jarcho. Leipzig, 1919.

————. [Bogdanov, A. A.] "Bogdanov (Malinovskii), Aleksandr Aleksandrovich." In *Deiateli Soiuza Sovetskikh Sotsialisticheskikh Respublik i Oktiabr'skoi Revoliutsii: avtobiografii i biografii.* Vol. 1, pp. 29–33. Moscow, n.d. An autobiography.

————. *Elementy proletarskoi kul'tury v razvitii rabochego klassa.* Moscow, 1920.

————. *Empiriomonizm.* 3 vols. St. Petersburg, 1904–1906.

————. "Filosofiia sovremennogo estestvoispytatelia." In *Ocherki filosofii kollektivizma.* Vol. 1, by A. A. Malinovskii [N. Verner] et al., pp. 37–142. St. Petersburg, 1909.

————. *Filosofiia zhivogo opyta.* Moscow, 1920.

————. *Iz psikhologii obshchestva.* 2d ed. St. Petersburg, 1906.

————. *Kul'turnye zadachi nashego vremeni.* Moscow, 1911.

————. *Nauka ob obshchestvennom soznanii.* Moscow, 1914.

————. *Novyi mir.* (*Stat'i 1904–1905*). Moscow, 1905.

————. *Osnovnye elementy istoricheskogo vzgliada na prirodu.* St. Petersburg, 1899.

————. *Padenie velikogo fetishizma: vera i nauka.* St. Petersburg, 1910.

————. *Poznanie s istoricheskoi tochki zreniia.* St. Petersburg, 1902.

————. *Prikliucheniia odnoi filosofskoi shkoly.* St. Petersburg, 1908.

————. *Sotsializm nauki.* (*Nauchnye zadachi proletariata*). Moscow, 1918.

————. *Tektologiia. Vseobshchaia organizatsionnaia nauka.* 3 vols. Berlin-Petrograd-Moscow, 1922.

————. *Vseobshchaia organizatsionnaia nauka* (*tektologiia*). 2 vols. St. Petersburg, 1913–17.

————. [Bogdanov, E.] "Strana idolov i filosofiia marksizma." In *Ocherki po filosofii marksizma: filosofskii sbornik,* by V. Bazarov et al., pp. 215–42. St. Petersburg, 1908.

————. [Verner, N.] et al. *Ocherki filosofii kollektivizma.* Vol. 1. St. Petersburg, 1909.

————. [Verner, N.] "Nauka i filosofiia." In *Ocherki filosofii kollektivizma.* Vol. 1, by A. A. Malinovskii [N. Verner], et al., pp. 9–33. St. Petersburg, 1909.

Mamin-Sibiriak, D., et al. *Na slavnom postu* (*1860–1900*)*: literaturnyi sbornik posviashchennyi N. K. Mikhailovskomu.* 2 vols. 2d ed. St. Petersburg, 1906.

Martov, L. "Obshchestvennye i umstvennye techeniia 70-kh godov." In *Istoriia russkoi literatury XIX veka.* Vol. 4, edited by D. N. Ovsianiko-Kulikovskii, pp. 1–52. Moscow, 1910.

———— et al., eds. *Obshchestvennoe dvizhenie v Rossii v nachale XX-go veka.* Vol. 2 (part 2). St. Petersburg, 1910.

Martynov, A. "Glavneishie momenty v istorii russkog marksizma." In *Obshchestvennoe dvizhenie v Rossii v nachale XX-go veka.* Vol. 2 (part 2), edited by L. Martov et al., pp. 285–339. St. Petersburg, 1910.

Marx, Karl. *Capital: A Critique of Political Economy.* Tr. from the German by E. Moore and E. Aveling. New York: The Modern Library, 1906.

————. *A Contribution to the Critique of Political Economy.* Tr. from the second German edition by N. J. Stone. New York: International Library, 1904.

Marx, Karl, and Engels, Friedrich. *The Economic and Philosophic Manuscripts of 1844.* New York: International Publishers, 1964.

————. *Selected Correspondence.* Moscow, Date?

————. *Selected Works.* Moscow, 1968.

————. *Selected Works in Three Volumes.* Moscow, 1969–70.

[Marx, K.] *K. Marks, F. Engels i revoliutsionnaia Rossiia.* Moscow, 1967.

Masaryk, Thomas G. *The Spirit of Russia.* 2d ed. Tr. From the German by E. and C. Paul. London: Allen and Unwin, 1955.

Maslin, A. N. "D. I. Pisarev v bor'be za materializm i sotsial'nyi progress." *Voprosy filosofii,* no. 8 (1968): 107–14.

Materialy dlia biograficheskogo slovaria deistvitel'nykh chlenov Imperatorskoi Akademii nauk. 2 vols. Petrograd, 1916–17.

Maximoff, G. P. ed. *The Political Philosophy of Bakunin.* Glencoe, Ill.: The Free Press, 1953.

Mechnikov, I. I. *Sorok let iskaniia ratsional'nogo mirovozzreniia.* Moscow, 1913.

Meijer, J. M. *Knowledge and Revolution: The Russian Colony in Zurich.* Assen, Holland, n.d.

Mendel, Arthur P. *Dilemmas of Progress in Tsarist Russia.* Cambridge, Mass.: Harvard University Press, 1961.

————. "N. K. Mikhailovskii and His Criticism of Russian Marxism." *The American Slavic and East European Review* 14, no. 3 (1955): 331-45.

Miakotin, V. A. *Iz istorii russkogo obshchestva.* St. Petersburg, 1906.

Mikhailovskii, N. K. "Literatura i zhizn'." *Russkoe bogatstvo,* no. 1 (1894), section 2, pp. 88-123; no. 1 (1895), section 2, pp. 124-54; no. 1 (1896), pp. 40-66.

————. *Literaturnye vospominaniia i sovremennaia smuta.* Vol. 2, St. Petersburg, 1900.

————. *Polnoe sobranie sochinenii.* 4th ed. 10 vols. St. Petersburg, 1906-14.

————. *Revoliutsionnye stat'i.* Berlin, 1906.

————. *Sochineniia.* 6 vols. St. Petersburg, 1896-97.

Miliukov, P. N. "Intelligentsiia i istoricheskaia traditsiia." In *Intelligentsiia v Rossii: sbornik statei* by K. Arsen'ev et al, pp. 89-191. St. Petersburg, 1910.

————. "Istoriosofiia g. Kareeva." *Russkaia mysl',* no. 11 (1887), section 2, pp. 90-101.

————. "Iuridicheskaia shkola v russkoi istoriografii." *Russkaia mysl',* no. 6 (1886), section 2, pp. 80-92.

————. "M. Kovalevskii kak sotsiolog i kak grazhdanin." In *M. M. Kovalevskii: uchenyi, gosudarstvennyi i obshchestvennyi deiatel' i grazhdanin* by K. Arsen'ev et al., pp. 136-43. Petrograd, 1917.

————. "Novaia kniga po sotsiologii." *Mir bozhii,* no. 12 (1899), section 1, pp. 196-215.

————. *Ocherki po istorii russkoi kul'tury.* Vol. 1, St. Petersburg, 1896; vol. 2, 4th ed., St. Petersburg, 1905.

————. "P. L. Lavrov (nekrolog)." *Mir bozhii,* no. 3 (1900), section 2, pp. 32-34.

————. "Razlozhenie slavianofil'stva (Danilevskii, Leont'ev, Vl. Solov'ev)." *Voprosy filosofii i psikhologii,* no. 18 (1893), section 1, pp. 46-96.

————. Review of Lappo-Danilevskii. *Organizatsiia priamogo oblozheniia v Moskovskom gosudarstve. Russkaia mysl',* no. 9 (1890), section 2, pp. 412-14.

————. "Sergei Andreevich Muromtsev: Biograficheskii ocherk." In *Sergei Andreevich Muromtsev,* edited by D. I. Shakhovskoi, pp. 1-52. Moscow, 1911.

————. "V. O. Kliuchevskii." In *V. O. Kliuchevskii: kharakteristiki i vospominaniia,* pp. 181-217. Moscow, 1915.

Miller, Martin A. Introduction to *Selected Writings on Anarchism and Revolution* by P. A. Kropotkin, edited by M. A. Miller, pp. 1-44. Cambridge, Mass.: M.I.T. Press, 1970.

————. "Manifestoes of the Chaikovsky Circle." *The Slavic Review* 29 (1970): pp. 1-21.

Miloradovich, K. M. Review of *Vekhi: sbornik statei o russkoi intelligentsii. Zhurnal Ministerstva narodnogo prosveshcheniia* 27 (1909), new series, section 3, pp. 423-34.

Modzalevskii, B. A. "Iz istorii Petersburgskogo universiteta, 1857-59 gg." *Golos minuvshego,* no. 1 (1917): 135-70.

Moisseev, M. "L'évolution d'une doctrine. La théorie des crises de Tougan-Baranovsky et la conception moderne des crises économiques." *Revue d'histoire économique et sociale* 20 (1932): 1-43.

Mommsen, Wolfgang J. *Max Weber und die deutsche Politik, 1890-1920.* Tübingen, 1959.

Müller, Otto W. *Untersuchungen zur Geschichte eines politischen Schlagwortes.* Frankfurt, 1971.

Muromtsev, S. A. "Odinochnaia bor'ba i sotrudnichestvo." *Voprosy prava,* no. 3 (1910): 3-20.

————. "Pravo i spravedlivost'." *Sbornik pravovedeniia i obshchestvennykh znanii* 2 (1893): 1-12.

————. *Stat'i i rechi.* 5 vols. Moscow, 1910.

Narskii, I. S., and Suvorov, L. N. *Pozitivizm i mekhanicheskaia reviziia marksizma.* Moscow, 1962.

Na slavnom postu (1860-1900): literaturnyi sbornik posviashchennyi N. K. Mikhailovskomu. 2 vols. 2d ed. St. Petersburg, 1906.

Nechkina, M. V. ed. *Revoliutsionnaia situatsiia v Rossii v 1859-1861 gg.* Moscow, 1962.

278   **Bibliography**

—————. *Russkaia istoriia v osveshchenii ekonomicheskogo materializma.* Kazan, 1922.
—————. et al., eds. *Ocherki istorii istoricheskoi nauki v SSSR.* Vol. 2. Moscow, 1960.
Nevedomskii, M. "N. K. Mikhailovskii. (Opyt psikhologicheskoi kharakteristiki)." *Mir bozhii,* no. 4 (1904), section 2, pp. 1-32.
Nikolai-on. *See* Daniel'son, N. F.
Noetzel, Hermann-Gerd. *Petr L. Lavrovs Vorstellungen vom Fortschritt für Russland aus den Jahren vor seiner Emigration.* Köln, 1968.
Northrop, F. S. C. *The Complexity of Legal and Ethical Experience.* Boston: Little, Brown and Co., 1959.
"Novgorodtsev, Pavel Ivanovich." *Granat Entsiklopedicheskii slovar',* 7th ed. Vol. 30, pp. 282-84.
Novgorodtsev, P. I. "Ideia prava v filosofii Vl. S. Solov'eva." *Voprosy filosofii i psikhologii,* no. 1 (1901), section 1, pp. 112-29.
—————. *Istoricheskaia shkola iuristov: ee proiskhozhdenie i sud'ba.* Moscow, 1896.
—————. *Kant i Gegel' v ikh ucheniiakh o prave i gosudarstve.* Moscow, 1901.
—————. "Kant kak moralist." *Voprosy filosofii i psikhologii,* no. 76 (1905), section 1, pp. 19-36.
—————. "Moral i poznanie." *Voprosy filosofii i psikhologii,* no. 64 (1902), section 1, pp. 824-38.
—————. "Nravstvennyi idealizm v filosofii prava." In *Problemy idealizma,* edited by P. I. Novgorodtsev, pp. 236-96. Moscow, 1902.
—————. "O zadachakh sovremennoi filosofii prava." *Pravo,* no. 40 (1902): 1745-51.
—————. "Pravo estestvennoe." *Entsiklopedicheskii slovar',* Brokgauz and Efron, vol. 24, pp. 885-90. St. Petersburg, 1898.
—————, ed. *Problemy idealizma.* Moscow, 1902.
—————. "Znachenie filosofii." *Nauchnoe slovo,* no. 4 (1903): 108-15.
Nozhin, N. D. "Nasha nauka i uchenye: uchenye knigi i izdaniia." *Knizhnyi vestnik,* nos. 1, 2, 3, and 7 (1866).
Obruchev, V. A. "Petr Alekseevich Kropotkin." In *Liudi russkoi nauki: geologiia i geografiia,* ed. by I. V. Kuznetsov, pp. 497-507. Moscow, 1962.
Ol'denburg, S. "Rabota Aleksandra Sergeevicha Lappo-Danilevskogo v Akademii nauk." *Russkii istoricheskii zhurnal,* no. 6 (1920): 164-80.
Ovsianiko-Kulikovskii, D. N., ed. *Istoriia russkoi literatury XIX v.* Vol. 4. Moscow, 1910.
Parygin, B. D., and Rudakov, L. I. "N. K. Mikhailovskii o psikhologicheskom faktore v istoricheskom protsesse." In *Istoriia i psikhologiia,* edited by B. F. Porshnev and L. I. Antsyferova, pp. 277-95. Moscow, 1971.
Pavlov, I. P. *Polnoe sobranie sochinenii.* Vol. 6. Moscow, 1952.
Pavlov, L. "Bogdanov (nast. familiia—Malinovskii), Aleksandr Aleksandrovich," *Filosofskaia entsiklopediia* 1 (1960): 177-78.
Pertsov, P. "Gnoseologicheskie nedorazumeniia. (Po povodu klassifikatsii nauk Genrika Rikkerta)." *Voprosy filosofii i psikhologii,* no. 96 (1909), section 2, pp. 27-72.
Petrazhitskii, L. I. "Obychnoe pravo i narodnyi dukh." *Pravo,* no. 7 (1899): 319-32; no. 8 (1899): 377-83.
—————. "Po povodu voprosa o tsennosti obychnogo prava i ego izucheniia." *Pravo,* no. 2 (1899): 65-72; no. 5 (1899): 209-21.
—————. *Teoriia prava i gosudarstva v sviazi s teoriei nravstvennosti.* 2d ed. 2 vols. St. Petersburg, 1909.
—————. *Vvedenie v izuchenie prava i nravstvennosti.* 2d ed. St. Petersburg, 1907.
Petrazycki, Leon. *Law and Morality.* Tr. by H. W. Babb. Cambridge, Mass.: Harvard University Press, 1955.
Petrovich, Michael B. *The Emergence of Russian Panslavism: 1859-1870.* New York: Columbia University Press, 1955.

Pipes, Richard. *Struve: Liberal on the Left, 1870-1905.* Cambridge, Mass.: Harvard University Press, 1970.

Pirogov, N. I. *Sochineniia.* Vol. 3. Kiev, 1910.

Pirumova, N. M. *Petr Alekseevich Kropotkin.* Moscow, 1972.

Pisarev, D. I. *Polnoe sobranie sochinenii v shesti tomakh.* 6 vols. St. Petersburg, 1891-1909.

Plekhanov, G. V. *The Development of the Monist View of History.* Moscow, 1956.

————. *Fundamental Problems of Marxism.* New York: International Publishers, 1969.

————. *Izbrannye filosofskie proizvedeniia.* 5 vols. Moscow, 1956-58.

————. *Nashi raznoglasiia.* Moscow, 1906.

————. "O sotsial'noi demokratii v Rossii." In *Istoriia revoliutsionnykh dvizhenii v Rossii,* by A. Tun, pp. 251-75. Geneva, 1903.

————. *Sochineniia.* 24 vols. Moscow, 1920-27.

————. *Unaddressed Letters and Art and Social Life.* Moscow, 1957.

————. [Volgin, A.] *Obosnovanie narodnichestva v trudakh g-na Vorontsova.* St. Petersburg, 1896.

Plotkin, L. A. *Pisarev i literaturno-obshchestvennoe dvizhenie shestidesiatykh godov.* Leningrad-Moscow, 1945.

Podgorecki, Adam. "Normy prawne a normy moralne." In *Poglady spoleczenstwa polskiego na moralnosc i prawo,* by A. Podgorecki et al., pp. 31-51. Warsaw, 1971.

Pokrovskii, M. N. "A. A. Bogdanov (Malinovskii)." *Vestnik Kommunisticheskoi akademii* 26 (1929): v-x.

————. "A. P. Shchapov. (K 50-letiiu so dnia ego konchiny)." *Istorik-Marksist,* no. 3 (1927): 5-13.

————. *Izbrannye proizvedeniia.* 4 vols. Moscow, 1965-67.

————, ed. *Russkaia istoricheskaia literatura v klassovom osveshchenii.* Vol. 1. Moscow, 1927.

Polianskii, F. Ia. *Plekhanov i russkaia ekonomicheskaia mysl'.* Moscow, 1965.

Pollard, Allan P. "The Russian Intelligentsia: The Mind of Russia." *California Slavic Studies* 3 (1964): 1-32.

Polonskii, V. P. *Mikhail Aleksandrovich Bakunin.* Moscow, 1920.

————. "Mikhail Aleksandrovich Bakunin: opyt kharakteristiki." In Mikhail Bakunin, *Neizdannye materialy i stat'i,* pp. 170-78. Moscow, 1926.

Pomper, Philip. *Peter Lavrov and the Russian Revolutionary Movement.* Chicago: The University of Chicago Press, 1972.

Porshnev, B. F. and Antsyferova, L. I., eds. *Istoriia i psikhologiia.* Moscow, 1971.

Pospelov, I. "Iz zhizni nashei shkoly." *Vestnik vospitaniia,* no. 4-6 (1914): 98-114.

Potresov, A. "Evoliutsiia obshchestvenno-politicheskoi mysli v predrevoliutsionnuiu epokhu." In *Obshchestvennoe dvizhenie v Rossii v nachale XX-go veka.* Vol. 2 (part 2), pp. 538-640. St. Petersburg, 1910.

Presniakov, A. E. *Aleksandr Sergeevich Lappo-Danilevskii.* Petrograd, 1922.

————. "A. S. Lappo-Danilevskii kak uchenyi i myslitel'." *Russkii istoricheskii zhurnal,* no. 6 (1920): 82-96.

Pyziur, Eugene. *The Doctrine of Anarchism of Michael A. Bakunin.* Milwaukee, Wisc.: The Marquette University Press, 1955.

Radkey, Oliver H. "Chernov and Agrarian Socialism before 1918." In *Continuity and Change in Russian and Soviet Thought,* edited by E. J. Simmons, pp. 63-80. Cambridge, Mass.: Harvard University Press, 1955.

————. *The Agrarian Foes of Bolshevism.* New York: Columbia University Press, 1958.

Radlov, E., et al. *P. L. Lavrov: stat'i, vospominaniia, materialy.* Petrograd, 1922.

Rafailov, M. "Sistema pravdy i nashi obshchestvennye otnosheniia." In *Na slavnom postu (1860-1890): literaturnyi sbornik posviashchennyi N. K. Mikhailovskomu.* 2d ed. Vol. 2, pp. 198-230.

Rainov, T. I. "O filosofskikh vzgliadakh i pedagogicheskikh priemakh A. S. Lappo-

Danilevskogo (k 25-letiiu uchenoi deiatel'nosti)." *Zhurnal Ministerstva narodnogo pros-veshcheniia* 56 (1915), new series, section 4, pp. 43-57.

Ranskii, S. P. *Sotsiologiia N. K. Mikhailovskogo.* St. Petersburg, 1901.

Ratner, M. B. "Problemy idealizma v russkoi literature." *Russkoe bogatstvo,* no. 10 (1903), section 2, pp. 1-29.

―――. "Uchenyi podkhod protiv Marksa." *Zavety,* no. 1 (1914), section 2, pp. 60-86.

Reisner, M. A. "The Theory of Petrazhitskii: Marxism and Social Ideology." In *Soviet Legal Philosophy,* by V. I. Lenin et al., pp. 71-109. Tr. from the Russian by H. W. Babb. Cambridge, Mass.: Harvard University Press, 1951.

―――. "Sovremennaia iurisprudentsiia i uchenie L. I. Petrazhitskogo." *Russkoe bogatstvo,* no. 1 (1908), section 2, pp. 27-55; no 2 (1908), section 2, pp. 26-59.

Resis, Albert. "*Das Kapital* Comes to Russia." *Slavic Review* 29 (1970): 219-37.

Reuel', A. L. *Russkaia ekonomicheskaia mysl' 60-70kh godov XIX veka i marksizm.* Moscow, 1956.

―――. *Kapital Karla Marksa v Rossii 1870-kh godov.* Moscow, 1939.

Rickert, Heinrich. *Die Grenzen der naturwissenschaftlichen Begriffsbildung.* 2d ed. Tübingen, 1913.

―――. *Science and History: A Critique of Positivist Epistemology.* Tr. from the German by G. Reisman. New York: Van Nostrand, 1962.

Rogers, James A. "Proudhon and the Transformation of Russian Nihilism." *Cahiers du monde russe et soviétique* 13 (1972): 514-23.

―――. "Russia: Social Sciences." In *The Comparative Reception of Darwinism,* edited by T. F. Glick, pp. 256-68. Austin: University of Texas Press, 1974.

Rozental, M. M., ed. *Lenin kak filosof.* Moscow, 1969.

Rozhkov, N. *Istoricheskie i sotsiologicheskie etiudy: sbornik statei.* Vol. 1. Moscow, 1906.

―――. Review of E. Durkheim, *O razdelenii obshchestvennogo truda. Zhizn',* no. 11 (1910): 341-43.

Rubakin, N. A. *Sredi knig.* 2d ed. Vol. 2. Moscow, 1913.

Rubinshtein, N. L. *Russkaia istoriografiia.* Moscow, 1941.

Rudnitskaia, E. L. "Nikolai Nozhin." In *Revoliutsionnaia situatsiia v Rossii,* edited by M. V. Nechkina, pp. 444-62. Moscow, 1962.

Rumiantsev, A. M., Osipov, G. V., and Burlatskii, F. M. "V. I. Lenin i sotsiologiia." In *Lenin i sovremennaia nauka.* Vol. 1, edited by M. V. Keldysh, pp. 275-93. Moscow, 1970.

Rusanov, N. S. "Nikolai Konstantinovich Mikhailovskii." In *Istoriia russkoi literatury XIX v.* Vol. 4, edited by D. N. Ovsianiko-Kulikovskii, pp. 118-28. Moscow, 1910.

―――. "N. K. Mikhhailovskii i obshchestvennaia zhizn' Rossii." *Golos minuvshego,* no. 2 (1914): 5-27.

―――. "Petr Lavrovich Lavrov." In *Istoriia russkoi literatury XIX veka.* Vol. 4, edited by D. N. Ovsianiko-Kulikovskii, pp. 104-16. Moscow, 1910.

―――. *Sotsialisty Zapada i Rossii.* St. Petersburg, 1908.

"Russkaia shkola v Parizhe." *Russkie vedomosti,* no. 326 (1904): 3-4.

Safronov, B. G. *M. M. Kovalevskii kak sotsiolog.* Moscow, 1960.

Saltykov, M. E. [Shchedrin, N.] *Poshekhonskaia starina.* Moscow, 1950.

Saval'skii, V. "Kritika poniatiia solidarnosti v sotsiologii O. Konta." *Zhurnal Ministerstva narodnogo prosveshcheniia* 361 (1905), section 2, pp. 94-106.

―――. *Osnovy filosofii prava v nauchnom idealizme.* Moscow, 1908.

Sayre, Paul, ed. *Interpretations of Modern Legal Philosophies.* New York: Oxford University Press, 1947.

Scheibert, Peter. *Von Bakunin zu Lenin: Geschichte der russischen revolutionären Ideologien, 1840-95.* Vol. 1. Leiden, 1956.

Seagle, William. "Trends in Modern Jurisprudence." In *Contemporary Social Theory,* edited by H. E. Barnes, H. Becker, and F. H. Becker, pp. 669-87. New York: Appleton-Century, 1940.

Sedov, M. G. "K voprosu ob obshchestvenno-politicheskikh vzgliadakh N. K. Mikhailovskogo." In *Obshchestvennoe dvizhenie v poreformennoi Rossii: sbornik statei k 80-letiiu so dnia rozhdeniia B. P. Koz'mina*, edited by E. S. Vilenskaia et al., pp. 179-210. Moscow, 1965.

Seliverstova, N. P. "O filosofskikh i sotsiologicheskikh vozzreniiakh A. P. Shchapova." In *Filosofskie i sotsiologicheskie issledovaniia*, pp. 130-41. Leningrad, 1969.

Serbov, N. "Shchapov, Afanasii Prokof'evich." *Russkii biograficheskii slovar'* 24 (1912): 1-11.

Serno-Solov'evich, N. A. "Ne trebuet' li nyneshnee sostoianie znanii novoi nauki?" In *Ocherki osvoboditel'nogo dvizheniia shestidesiatykh godov*, by Mikh. Lemke, pp. 496-505. St. Petersburg, 1908.

Setrov, M. I. "Ob obshchikh elementakh tektologii A. Bogdanova, kibernetiki i teorii sistem." *Uchenye zapiski kafedr obshchestvennykh nauk vuzov g. Leningrada: filosofskie i sotsiologicheskie issledovaniia* 8 (1967): 49-60.

―――. "Printsip sistemnosti i ego osnovnye poniatiia." In *Problemy metodologii sistemnogo issledovaniia*, edited by I. V. Blauber et al., pp. 49-63. Moscow, 1970.

Shakhovskoi, D. I., ed. *Sergei Andreevich Muromtsev*. Moscow, 1911.

Shapiro, A. L. *Russkaia istoriografiia v period imperializma*. Leningrad, 1962.

Shchapov, A. P. *Sochineniia*. 3 vols. St. Petersburg, 1906-8.

Shcheglov, A. V. *Bor'ba Lenina protiv bogdanovskoi revizii marksizma*. Moscow, 1937.

Shelgunov, N. V. *Vospominaniia*. Moscow, 1967.

Shershenevich, G. F. "S. A. Muromtsev kak uchenyi." In *Sergei Alekseevich Muromtsev*, edited by D. I. Shakhovskoi, pp. 80-90. Moscow, 1911.

Shteinberg, I. Z. "Mesto anarkhizma v levom narodnichestve." In *Sbornik statei posviashchennyi pamiati P. A. Kropotkina*, edited by A. Borovoi and N. Lebedev, pp. 139-49. Petrograd-Moscow, 1922.

Sidorov, A. "Melkoburzhuaznaia teoriia russkogo istoricheskogo protsessa: A. P. Shchapov." In *Russkaia istoricheskaia literatura v klassovom osveshchenii*, edited by M. N. Pokrovskii. Vol. 1, pp. 277-350. Moscow, 1927.

Simirenko, Alex, ed. *Soviet Sociology*. Chicago: Quadrangle Books, 1966.

Skabichevskii, A. M. *Istoriia noveishei russkoi literatury, 1848-1909 gg*. St. Petersburg, 1909.

―――. *Sochineniia*. Vol. 1. St. Petersburg, 1890.

Slonimskii, L. "Spory o sushchnosti marksizma." *Vestnik Evropy*, no. 8 (1909): 731-45.

Sokolov, K. "M. M. Kovalevskii kak uchitel' konstitutsionnogo prava." In *M. M. Kovalevskii: uchenyi, gosudarstvennyi i obshchestvennyi deiatel' i grazhdanin*, by K. Arsen'ev et al., pp. 233-44. Petrograd, 1917.

Solov'ev, E. A. *D. I. Pisarev*. Berlin-Petrograd-Moscow, 1922.

―――. "Semidesiatye gody." *Zhizn'*, no. 8 (1899): 303-33.

―――― [Andreevich]. *Ocherki po istorii russkoi literatury XIX veka*. St. Petersburg, 1907.

―――― [――――]. *Opyt filosofii russkoi literatury*. St. Petersburg, 1905.

Solov'ev, V. S. *Sobranie sochinenii*. 9 vols. St. Petersburg, 1902-7.

―――. "Mnimaia bor'ba s Zapadom." *Russkaia mysl'*, no. 8 (1890), section 2, pp. 1-20.

―――. "Rossiia i Evropa." *Vestnik Evropy*, no. 2 (1888): 742-61; no. 4 (1888): 725-67.

Sorokin, Pitirim. *Contemporary Sociological Theories*. New York: Harper, 1928.

―――. *Modern Historical and Social Philosophy*. New York: Dover, 1963.

―――. "Osnovnye problemy sotsiologii Lavrova." In *P. L. Lavrov: stat'i, vospominaniia, materialy*, by E. Radlov et al., pp. 249-91. Petrograd, 1922.

―――. *Society, Culture, and Personality*. New York: Harper, 1947.

―――. "Teoriia faktorov M. M. Kovalevskogo." In *M. M. Kovalevskii: uchenyi, gosudarstvennyi i obshchestvennyi deiatel' i grazhdanin*, by K. Arsen'ev et al., pp. 180-95. Petrograd, 1917.

Spektorskii, E. *Problema sotsial'noi fiziki v XVIII stoletii*. Vol. 1. Warsaw, 1910.

Stadlin, A. "Istoricheskaia teoriia Boklia." *Russkii vestnik*, no. 7 (1874): 257–90.

Steklov, Iu. *Mikhail Aleksandrovich Bakunin: ego zhizn' i deiatel'nost'*. 4 vols. Moscow-Leningrad, 1926–27.

Stepniak [Kravchinskii, S. M.] *Underground Russia*. Tr. from the Italian. London: Lowell, 1883.

Strakhov, N. N. "Istoricheskie vzgliady G. Riukerta i N. Ia. Danilevskogo." *Russkii vestnik*, no. 10 (1894): 154–83.

———. "Zhizn' i trudy N. Ia. Danilevskogo." In *Rossiia i Evropa*, by N. Ia. Danilevskii, 4th ed., pp. ix–xxxv. St. Petersburg, 1889.

Stronin, A. *Istoriia i metod*. St. Petersburg, 1869.

Struve, P. B. *Collected Works in Fifteen Volumes*. Edited by Richard Pipes. Ann Arbor: University Microfilms, 1970.

———. "Intelligentsiia i revoliutsiia." In *Vekhi*, by N. A. Berdiaev et al. 2d ed., pp. 156–74. Moscow, 1909.

———. *Istoricheskoe vvedenie v politicheskuiu ekonomiiu*. Petrograd, 1916.

———. *Khoziaistvo i tsena*. Vol. 1. St. Petersburg-Moscow, 1913.

———. "Khoziaistvo i tsena." *Russkaia mysl'*, no. 3–4 (1917), section 2, pp. 130–36.

———. *Kriticheskie zametki k voprosu ob ekonomicheskom razvitii Rossii*. Vol. 1. St. Petersburg, 1894.

———. "Die Marxsche Theorie der sozialen Entwicklung: ein kritischer Versuch." *Archiv für soziale Gesetzgebung und Statistik* 14 (1899): 658–704.

———. "M. M. Kovalevskii." *Russkaia mysl'*, no. 5 (1916), section 2, pp. 98–100.

———. *Na raznye temy (1893–1901 gg.): sbornik statei*. St. Petersburg, 1902.

———. "Na raznye temy." *Mir bozhii*, no. 6 (1901), section 2, pp. 12–27.

———. "Na raznye temy." *Russkaia mysl'*, no. 1 (1909), section 2, pp. 194–210; no. 5 (1909), section 2, pp. 113–26; no. 12 (1909), section 2, pp. 181–91.

———. "Otryvki o gosudarstve i natsii." *Russkaia mysl'*, no. 5 (1908), section 2, pp. 187–93.

———. "Predislovie." In *Sub'ektivizm i individualizm v obshchestvennoi filosofii: kriticheskii etiud o N. K. Mikhailovskom*, by N. A. Berdiaev, pp. i–lxxxi. St. Petersburg, 1901.

———. "Religiia i sotsializm." *Russkaia mysl'*, no. 8 (1909), section 2, pp. 148–56.

———. "Sovremennyi krizis v politicheskoi ekonomii." *Logos*, no. 1 (1911): 123–44.

———. "Svoboda i istoricheskaia neobkhodimost'." *Voprosy filosofii i psikhologii*, no. 36 (1897), section 2, pp. 120–39.

Sukhanov, Nik. "Po voprosakh nashikh raznoglasii." *Zavety*, no. 6 (1912), section 2, pp. 1–23; no. 7 (1912), section 2, pp. 1–45.

Svatikov, S. G. *Obshchestvennoe dvizhenie v Rossii (1700–1895)*. Vol. 2. Rostov, 1905.

———. "Opal'naia professura 80-ykh gg." *Golos minuvshego*, no. 2 (1917): 5–78.

Takhtadzhian, A. L. "Tektologiia: istoriia i problemy." *Sistemnye issledovaniia* 3 (1971): 200–277.

Takhtarev, K. "Glavneishie napravleniia v razvitii sotsiologii." *Sovremennyi mir*, 1910, section 1: no. 8, pp. 170–202; no. 10, pp. 164–79; no. 12, pp. 153–84.

———. *Sotsiologiia kak nauka o zakonomernostiakh obshchestvennoi zhizni*. Petrograd, 1916.

Thaden, Edward C. *Conservative Nationalism in Nineteenth-Century Russia*. Seattle: University of Washington Press, 1964.

Tikhomirov, G. S. "Iz istorii izdaniia i rasprostraneniia 'Kapitala' Marksa v Rossii." In *Sbornik statei i materialov po knigovedeniiu*. Vol. 2, pp. 7–43, Leningrad, 1970.

Timasheff, N. S. "Petrazhitsky's Philosophy of Law." In *Interpretations of Modern Legal Philosophies*, edited by Paul Sayre, pp. 736–50. New York: Oxford University Press, 1947.

———. "The Sociological Theories of Maksim M. Kovalevsky." In *Soviet Sociology*, edited by Alex Simirenko, pp. 83–99. Chicago: Quadrangle Books, 1966.

———. Introduction to *Law and Morality*, by Leon Petrazycki, pp. iii–xlvi. Cambridge, Mass.: Harvard University Press, 1955.

Timiriazev, K. A. *Sochineniia.* 10 vols. Moscow, 1937-40.

------. *Nauka i demokratiia.* Moscow, 1963.

Timoshenko, V. P. "M. I. Tugan-Baranovsky and Western European Economic Thought." *The Annals of the Ukrainian Academy of Arts and Sciences in the U.S.* 3 (1954): 803-23.

Tolstoi, L. N. *Polnoe sobranie sochinenii.* Vol. 8. Moscow, 1936.

Trainin, I. P. "The Relationship Between State and Law." In *Soviet Legal Philosophy,* by V. I. Lenin et al., pp. 433-56. Cambridge, Mass.: Harvard University Press, 1951.

Troeltsch, Ernst. *Der Historismus und seine Probleme.* Vol. 1. Tübingen, 1922.

Trubetskoi, Evgenii. "Filosofiia prava professora L. I. Petrazhitskogo." *Voprosy filosofii i psikhologii,* no. 2 (1901), section 2, pp. 9-32.

------. "Panmetodizm v etike. (K kharakteristike ucheniia Kogena)." *Voprosy filosofii i psikhologii,* no. 97 (1909), section 1, pp. 121-64.

Tschebotareff, Valentine. *Untersuchungen über die Krisentheorie von Michael von Tugan-Baranowsky.* Würzburg, 1936.

Tugan-Baranovskii, M. I. "Bor'ba klassov kak glavneishee soderzhanie istorii." *Mir bozhii,* no. 9 (1904), section 1, pp. 242-59.

------. "Chto takoe obshchestvennyi klass?" *Mir bozhii,* no. 1 (1904), section 1, pp. 64-72.

------. "Intelligentsiia i sotsializm." In *Intelligentsiia v Rossii: sbornik statei,* by K. Arsen'ev et al., pp. 235-58. St. Petersburg, 1910.

------. "Kant und Marx." *Archiv für Sozialwissenschaft und Sozialpolitik* 33 (1911): 180-88.

------. "M. M. Kovalevskii kak chelovek." In *M. M. Kovalevskii: uchenyi, gosudarstvennyi i obshchestvennyi deiatel' i grazhdanin,* by K. Arsen'ev et al., pp. 51-53. Petrograd, 1917.

------. *Modern Socialism in Its Historical Development.* Tr. from the Russian by M. I. Redmount. London: Sonnenschein, 1910.

------. "Novyi trud po ekonomicheskoi teorii." *Russkoe bogatstvo,* no. 10 (1913): 37-82.

------. *Obshchestvenno-ekonomicheskie idealy nashego vremeni.* St. Petersburg, 1913.

------. "Ocherki po istorii politicheskoi ekonomii." *Mir bozhii,* no. 2 (1902), section 1, pp. 77-100; no. 8, section 1, pp. 239-76; no. 9, section 1, pp. 98-134; no. 10, section 1, pp. 272-303.

------. "Osnovnaia oshibka abstraktnoi teorii kapitalizma Marksa." *Nauchnoe obozrenie,* no. 5 (1899): 973-85.

------. "Predislovie." In *Kant i Marks,* by Karl Forlender, pp. iv-viii. St. Petersburg, 1909.

------. *Promyshlennye krizisi v sovremennoi Anglii, ikh prichiny i vlianie na narodnuiu zhizn'.* St. Petersburg, 1894.

------. *Russkaia fabrika.* Vol. 1. 2d ed. St. Petersburg, 1900.

------. *Sotsial'nye osnovy kooperatsii.* Berlin, 1921.

------. *Statisticheskie itogi promyshlennogo razvitiia Rossii.* St. Petersburg, 1898.

------. *Theoretische Grundlagen des Marxismus.* Leipzig, 1905.

------. "Subjektivismus und Objektivismus in der Wertlehre." *Archiv für Sozialwissenschaft und Sozialpolitik* 22 (1906): 557-64.

------. "Znachenie ekonomicheskogo faktora v istorii." *Mir bozhii,* no. 12 (1895), section 1, pp. 101-18.

Tun, A. *Istoriia revoliutsionnykh dvizhenii v Rossii.* Geneva, 1903.

Uevell, Vil'iam. *Istoriia induktivnykh nauk.* 3 vols. Tr. from the English by M. A. Antonovich and A. N. Pypin. St. Petersburg, 1867.

Utechin, S. V. "Philosophy and Society: Alexander Bogdanov." In *Revisionism: Essays on the History of Marxist Ideas,* edited by Leopold Labedz, pp. 117-25. New York: Praeger, 1962.

Vagner, Vladimir. "Iz istorii darvinizma v sotsiologii. (Pamiati Mikhailovskogo)." *Russkaia mysl',* no. 8 (1904), section 2, pp. 1-29.

Vainshtein, I. *Organizatsionnaia teoriia i dialekticheskii materializm. Sistematicheskaia kritika A. Bogdanova.* Moscow-Leningrad, 1927.

Vasilenko, Nik. "Akademik Bogdan Oleksandrovich Kistiakovs'kii." *Zapiski Sotsial'no-*

ekonomicheskogo viddilu (*Ukrainskaia Akademiia nauk*) 1 (1923): pp. viii–xl.

Vasil'ev, A. "P. L. Lavrov—istorik i filosof matematiki." In *P. L. Lavrov: stat'i, vospominaniia, materialy*, by E. Radlov et al., pp. 373–84. Petrograd, 1922.

Vatson, E. K. *Etiudy i ocherki po obshchestvennym voprosam*. St. Petersburg, 1892.

Veber, B. G. "Kareev, Nikolai Ivanovich." *Sovetskaia istoricheskaia entsiklopediia* 7 (1965): 27–30.

Venturi, Franco. *Roots of Revolution*. Tr. from the Italian by F. Haskell. New York: Grosset & Dunlap, 1966.

Verrier, René. *Roberty: le positivisme russe et la foundation de la sociologie*. Paris, 1934.

Vilenskaia, E. S. et al., eds. *Obshchestvennoe dvizhenie v poreformennoi Rossii: sbornik statei k 80-letiiu so dnia rozhdeniia B. P. Koz'mina*. Moscow, 1965.

Viner, E. N. *Bibliograficheskii zhurnal "Knizhnyi vestnik"* (*1860–1867*). Leningrad, 1950.

Vinogradoff, Paul. *Villainage in England*. Oxford: Clarendon, 1892.

Vinogradov, P. G. "I. V. Kireevskii i nachalo moskovskogo slavianofilstva." *Voprosy filosofii i psikhologii*, no. 11 (1892), section 1, pp. 98–126.

V. O. Kliuchevskii: kharakteristiki i vospominaniia. Moscow, 1912.

Vol'skii, M. "Ekonomicheskii materializm v ponimanii A. Bogdanova." *Zavety*, no. 8 (1913), section 2, pp. 1–23; no. 9 (1913), section 2, pp. 1–22.

Vol'skii, N. V. [Valentinov, N.] *Filosofskie postroeniia marksizma*. Moscow, 1908.

Vorländer, Karl. *Kant und Marx*. 2d ed. Tübingen, 1926.

Vorontsov, V. P. [V.V.] *Sud'by kapitalizma v Rossii*. St. Petersburg, 1882.

Wagner, Richard. *Sämtliche Schriften*. Vol. 14. Leipzig, 1911.

Wagner, Wenceslas, ed. *Polish Law throughout the Ages*. Stanford, Calif.: Hoover Institution Press, 1970.

Walicki, A. *The Controversy over Capitalism: Studies in the Social Philosophy of the Russian Populists*. Oxford: Clarendon, 1969.

Ward, Lester F. *Dynamic Sociology*. 2d ed. New York: Greenwood, 1968.

Weber, Marianne. *Max Weber: Ein Lebensbild*. Heidelberg, 1950.

Weber, Max. *Gesammelte Aufsätze zur Wissenschaftslehre*. 2d ed. Tubingen, 1951.

———. *Essays in Sociology*. Tr. by H. H. Gerth and C. Wright Mills. New York: Oxford University Press, 1946.

———. *The Theory of Social and Economic Organization*. Tr. by A. Henderson and T. Parsons. New York: Oxford University Press, 1947.

White, James D. "The First *Pravda* and the Russian Marxist Tradition." *Soviet Studies* 26 (1974): 181–204.

Woodcock, George and Avakumović, Ivan. *The Anarchist Prince: A Biographical Study of Peter Kropotkin*. London: Boardman, 1950.

Worms, René. "Maxime Kovalewsky." *Revue internationale de sociologie* 24 (1916): 257–63.

Wortman, Richard. *The Crisis of Russian Populism*. Cambridge: Cambridge University Press, 1967.

Wyrouboff, G. "Le certain et le probable." *La philosophie positive* 1 (1867): 165–82.

Yaney, George L. "Bureaucracy and Freedom: N. M. Korkunov's Theory of the State." *American Historical Review* 71 (1966): 468–86.

Yassour, A. "Bogdanov et sa oeuvre." *Cahiers du monde russe et soviétique* 10 (1969): 546–84.

Z., L. S. "Novyi trud prof. M. M. Kovalevskogo." *Russkoe bogatstvo*, no. 11 (1898), section 2, pp. 110–19.

Zak, L. "Sud'by krest'ianskoi obshchiny v Germanii." *Russkoe bogatstvo* (1895), section 1: no. 9, pp. 81–113; no. 10, pp. 137–73; no. 11, pp. 183–212.

Zil'berman, I. B. *Politicheskaia teoriia anarkhizma M. A. Bakunina*. Leningrad, 1960.

Index